CYBERSEMIOTICS:
WHY INFORMATION IS NOT ENOUGH!

A growing field of inquiry, biosemiotics is a theory of cognition and communication that unites the living and the cultural world. What is missing from this theory, however, is the unification of the information and computational realms of the non-living natural and technical world. *Cybersemiotics* provides such a framework.

By integrating cybernetic information theory into the unique semiotic framework of C.S. Peirce, Søren Brier attempts to find a unified conceptual framework that encompasses the complex area of information, cognition, and communication science. This integration is performed through Niklas Luhmann's autopoietic systems theory of social communication. The link between cybernetics and semiotics is, further, an ethological and evolutionary theory of embodiment combined with Lakoff and Johnson's 'philosophy in the flesh.' This demands the development of a transdisciplinary philosophy of knowledge as much common sense as it is cultured in the humanities and the sciences. Such an epistemological and ontological framework is also developed in this volume.

Cybersemiotics not only builds a bridge between science and culture, it provides a framework that encompasses them both. The cybersemiotic framework offers a platform for a new level of global dialogue between knowledge systems, including a view of science that does not compete with religion but offers the possibility for mutual and fruitful exchange.

(Toronto Studies in Semiotics and Communications)

SØREN BRIER is a professor in semiotics in the Department of International Culture and Communication Studies at the Centre for Language, Cognition, and Mentality, Copenhagen Business School.

A Transdiciplinary Approach to Information, Cognition, and Communication Studies, through an Integration of Niklas Luhmann's Communication Theory with C.S. Peirce's Semiotics.

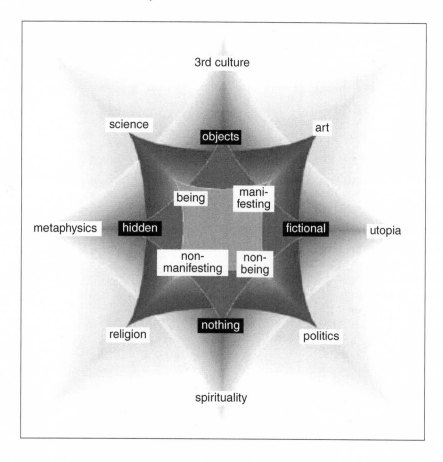

SØREN BRIER

Cybersemiotics

Why Information Is Not Enough!

UNIVERSITY OF TORONTO PRESS
Toronto Buffalo London

© University of Toronto Press 2008
Toronto Buffalo London
www.utppublishing.com
Printed in the U.S.A.

Reprinted in paperback 2013, 2014

ISBN 978-0-8020-9220-5 (cloth)
ISBN 978-1-4426-2636-2 (paper)

Printed on acid-free paper

Toronto Studies in Semiotics and Communication
Editors: Marcel Danesi, Umberto Eco, Paul Perron, Roland Posner,
Peter Schulz

Library and Archives Canada Cataloguing in Publication

Brier, Søren
    Cybersemiotics : why information is not enough! / Søren Brier

(Toronto studies in semiotics and communication)
Includes bibliographical references and index.
ISBN 978-0-8020-9220-5 (bound)   ISBN 978-1-4426-2636-2 (pbk.)

1. Information theory.   2. Science – Philosophy.   3. Information science.
4. Semiotics.   I. Title.   II. Series: Toronto studies in semiotics and communication.

P99.B74 2008   003'.54   C2007-906956-8

The University of Toronto Press acknowledges the financial assistance to its
publishing program of the Canada Council for the Arts and the Ontario Arts
Council.

  Canada Council   Conseil des Arts
                      for the Arts   du Canada

University of Toronto Press acknowledges the financial support for its
publishing activities of the Government of Canada through the
Book Publishing Industry Development Program (BPIDP).

The publication of this book was supported by the Danish Research Council
for the Humanities.

In honour of my father, Knud Harald Stig Nielsen, who spent eighteen months in Nazi concentration camps during the Second World War for being part of the Danish resistance against Nazism and who suffered for it the rest of his life; and to my mother Dorte Brier and my father's four sisters Kamma, Ebba, Eva, and Inger, who stood by him and later in so many ways helped me during this academic project.

My gratitude also goes to my parents-in-law Else and Gunner Frøssing, and to my uncle Bent Brier, all also part of the Danish resistance, and to Bent's wife Ulla and my aunt Bodil Skotte, for their loving and supportive presence during my childhood and youth.

But most of all I am indebted to my wife Kirsten and our children Anders and Signe for their enduring love and support.

Contents

List of Figures

Foreword: From Cybernetics to Cybersemiotics

MARCEL DANESI

Why do we communicate? Is it for survival? Are there any other reasons? How does communication unfold? These are questions that have intrigued human beings since their origins. Because communication involves the exchange of signs, messages, and meanings, it is of obvious interest to semioticians. This was certainly the opinion of the late Thomas A. Sebeok (1920–2001), one of leading semioticians and linguists of the twentieth century, who was instrumental in expanding the boundaries of semiotics proper to include the study of communication among all species. Inaugurating the *biosemiotic* movement, Sebeok showed that by studying communication across species, we can get a better idea of what makes human communication unique. Biosemiotics seeks to understand how animals are naturally endowed with the capacity to use specific types of signals and signs for survival (*zoosemiosis*), and thus how human semiosis (*anthroposemiosis*) is both linked to and different from animal semiosis. The objective of this new branch of semiotics is to distill the elements of semiosis common to its manifestations across species, integrating them into a taxonomy of notions, principles, and procedures for understanding the phenomenon of communication in its totality.

The goal of this brilliant book by Danish semiotician Søren Brier is to bring biosemiotics, in its 'cybersemiotic' version, to a general public of scholars, students, and interested people. Brier himself has been instrumental in the development of biosemiotics. A member of the American Society for Cybernetics for more than two decades, he founded the journal *Cybernetics and Human Knowing* in collaboration with renowned cyberneticians and biosemioticians. This is a timely book, since it is my belief that the biosemiotic or cybersemiotic agenda is fast becoming the 'only' agenda for serious work on signs and their exchange in communicative settings.

The initial agenda of the science of *cybernetics* was to study communication and control in living organisms, machines, and organizations. It was conceived by the great mathematician and computer scientist Norbert Wiener (1894–1964), who coined the term in 1948. The early cyberneticians viewed communication and control in all self-contained complex systems as comparable. Their approach differed from that of the physical sciences (physics, biology, etc.) in seeing the material form of communication as irrelevant in itself, focusing instead on its organization. Because of the increasing sophistication of computers and the efforts to make them behave in humanlike ways, cybernetics today is closely allied with artificial intelligence and robotics, drawing heavily on ideas developed in information theory.

In many ways, the late Marshall McLuhan (1911–1981) could be characterized as a cybernetician *avant la lettre*, since he shared many of the same interests of the early cyberneticians. For example, McLuhan believed that the type of technology developed to record and transmit messages determines how people process and remember them. Moreover, any major change in how information is represented and transmitted brings about a concomitant paradigm shift in cultural systems. Ancient cuneiform writing, impressed indelibly on clay tablets, allowed the Sumerians to develop a great civilization; papyrus and hieroglyphics transformed Egyptian society into an advanced culture; the alphabet spurred the ancient Greeks on to extraordinary advances in science, technology, and the arts; the alphabet also made it possible for the Romans to develop an effective system of government; the printing press facilitated the dissemination of knowledge broadly and widely, paving the way for the European Renaissance, the Protestant Reformation, and the Enlightenment; radio, movies, and television brought about the rise of a global pop culture in the twentieth century; and the Internet and the World Wide Web ushered in a veritable 'global village' as the twentieth century came to a close.

The term 'information' invariably comes up in any cybernetic discussion of communication. As Brier argues, however, this is problematic term, requiring in-depth commentary, which the reader will get throughout this book. Information can be defined simply as data that can be received by humans or machines. In the modern theory of information, it is considered as something mathematically probabilistic – an alarm that is ringing conveys more information than one that is silent, because the latter is the 'expected state' of the alarm system and the former its 'alerting state.' The one who developed the mathematical aspects of information theory was the American telecommunications engineer Claude Shannon (1916–2001). He showed, essentially, that the information contained in a signal is inversely proportional to its probability. The more probable a signal, the less information 'load' it conveys; the less likely a signal, the more information.

Shannon devised his mathematical model in order to improve the efficiency of telecommunication systems. The model essentially depicts information transfer as a unidirectional process dependent on probability factors, that is, on the degree to which a message is expected or not in a given situation. It is called the 'bullseye model' because a sender of information is defined as someone or something aiming a message at a receiver of the information as if he, she, or it were in a bullseye target range. Shannon also introduced several key terms into the general study of communication: channel, noise, redundancy, and feedback. Shannon's model has been useful, over the years, in providing a terminology for describing aspects of communication systems, but it tells us nothing about how messages and meanings shape and ultimately determine the nature of human communication events. The main objective of Brier's book is, in fact, to investigate precisely how such events unfold in semiotic terms. It shows, in effect, why 'cybernetics' must necessarily be refashioned as 'cybersemiotics.' As such, it can be considered a branch of biosemiotics. The objective in biosemiotics is to document which properties or features of semiosis cut cross species and systems (including mechanical ones), and which ones are specific to one or several species or systems. Determining the universality or specificity of particular properties is one of the primary objectives of Brier's book.

Biosemiotics takes its impetus from the work of the biologist Jakob von Uexküll (1864–1944), who provided empirical evidence to show that an organism does not perceive an object in itself, but according to its own particular kind of mental modelling system. This allows the organism to interpret the world of objects and events in a biologically unique way and, subsequently, to respond to these objects and events in semiotically specific ways. The modelling system of a species routinely converts its external world experiences into internal states of knowing and remembering that are unique to the species. Access to those states without possessing the same mental modelling system will always be partial. Thus, we will never really be able to understand what an animal feels, what it thinks about, and more importantly how it thinks about something.

Brier's book is particularly timely for explaining the evolution of communication in the 'digital galaxy,' as our wired world of instant communications can be called. In this galaxy, it is no longer correct to talk about 'competing' modes of communication. The convergence of the computer with all other media technologies is the defining characteristic of mass communications today. But this has its drawbacks. Over-reliance on computers and digital media has produced a mindset that sees digitization as an intrinsic, almost mythical, component of the human condition. This became apparent on the threshold of the year 2000 when the 'millennium bug' was thought to be a harbinger of doom. So reliant had people become on the computer that a mere technological problem – making sure that computers could read the new '00' date as '2000,' and not '1900' or some other '—00' date – was interpreted in moral and apocalyptic terms. This was striking evidence that computers had acquired social meaning that far exceeded their original function as 'computing machines.' Constant exposure to cyberspace, moreover, is leading surreptitiously and gradually to an entrenchment of a bizarre modern form of Cartesian dualism, the view that the body and the mind are separate entities. Incidentally, the term *cyberspace* was coined by American writer William Gibson in his 1984 science fiction novel *Neuromancer*, in which he described cyberspace as a place of 'unthinkable complexity.' As Brier's treatment suggests, digital media have put people in the position of having to rebuild modern cultures from the residue of signs that belonged to a different galaxy – the Gutenberg one, as McLuhan called it. But, as it turns out, the new signs are not that much different from the old ones, as people begin to realize that their bodies are as much involved in creating signs as are their minds. Paradoxically, therefore, the digital galaxy is engendering a desire to communicate with the voice. Brier's trek through cybersemiotics emphasizes this very point by implication.

The cybersemiotic agenda is shaped by a search for the biological, psychic, and social roots of the human need for meaning. Brier's book shows that this agenda is leading to the development of a dynamic, vibrant, ever-changing science of signs. The reader will, no doubt, come away from this book convinced of the singular verity, expressed so well by Charles Peirce, that as a species we are programmed to 'think only in signs.'

CYBERSEMIOTICS:
WHY INFORMATION IS NOT ENOUGH!

Introduction:
The Quest of Cybersemiotics

I.1 Subject Matter and Aims

What information, cognition, communication, intelligence, and meaning are is a very old philosophical problem. Later it reappeared during various attempts to create psychological and communicative sciences. But today, since Shannon's information theory and Wiener's cybernetics, these questions are being formulated in the transdisciplinary context of computers, information systems, and ultimately the Internet.

Understanding Computers and Cognition (1986) is a famous book by Terry Winograd and Fernando Flores that illustrates the complexity of these areas as it deals with the technological design of computers and information systems in light of theories of animal and human cognition and communication, including the autopoiesis theory of Maturana and Varela as well as speech act theory and pragmatic linguistics. Their book was an inspiration for my dissertation *Information Is Silver ...* (published in Danish in 1994).

The present book goes further: it is an inter- and trans-disciplinary project in the philosophy of science that analyses modern efforts to arrive at a unified conceptual framework, one that encompasses the complex fields of information, cognition and communication science, and semiotic scholarly studies – fields that together are often referred to as information science.

This book offers an interpretation of those 'information science' research programs of the sort which unified information science can offer; it also discusses what is needed to supplement present approaches. As such, it is part of the Foundation of Information Science (FIS) research program, in that it asks whether there can be a transdisciplinary information science that encompasses the technical,

natural, and social sciences, as well as the humanities, in its understanding of understanding and communication, a vision that originally
came from Norbert Wiener in his book *Cybernetics; or, Control and Communication in the Animal and the Machine* (1961). But it also stems from
an interest in Konrad Lorenz and Niko Tinbergen's efforts to develop
ethology into a science that is neither mechanistic nor vitalistic.
Wiener's book and cybernetics are said to deal with the 'scientific explanation of the relationship between animal thought processes and artificial learning devices.' This is one reason why ethology and its debate
with comparative psychology (not least Skinner's behaviourism) is relevant here. Another reason is that these discussions – among other
factors – led Miller, Gallanter, and Pribram to formulate a theory of the
foundations of cognitive science in *Plans and the Structure of Behavior*
(1960). Yet it is well known that cognitive science's information processing paradigm – which in many ways is a modern version of Wiener's
cybernetic dream – encounters severe problems with the role of embodiment in cognition, understanding, and communication. Hayles, for
example, points this out in her profound book *How We Became Posthuman: Virtual Bodies in Cybernetics, Literature, and Informatics* (1999).
Within pragmatic linguistics, I have found Lakoff and Johnson's embodied cognitive semantics and Wittgenstein's language game theory especially useful to connect bodyhood, culture, and signification. But since
both ethology and biology in general – as well as cybernetics/computer
science, in my view – encounter problems with the concepts of
meaning, subject, and consciousness, I want to reformulate certain
aspects of them into a biosemiotics based on Peirce, Sebeok, Hoffmeyer,
Kull, and Emmeche's work, my goal being to understand the role of
embodied mind in cognition and communication.

This book aims to formulate a new transdisciplinary framework based
on Peirce's semiotics, second-order cybernetics, Luhmann's systems
theory, cognitive semantics, and language game theory. I apply concepts
found in second-order cybernetics and the semiotics of Charles Sanders
Peirce to solve various transdisciplinary conceptual problems at the
heart of cognitive science, since cybernetics was among the original
contributors to modern information and communication science. I will
refer to this transdisciplinary framework as 'Cybersemiotics.'

In the first part of this book, I analyse a number of present-day mainstream approaches and theories. My intention is not to criticize specific
researchers or theories, but rather to describe the results of various
research programs and paradigms and point out their limitations and

outstanding problems. In the second part, I discuss these problems in depth, and offer solutions.

I am presenting a new theory; clearly, then, I am not fully satisfied with earlier ones. Yet each of these older theories provides useful concepts that have helped me in my search for a framework broad enough to encompass our present experience and knowledge. I do not want to slide over this earlier work in my efforts to arrive at a new conception of our present situation. Indeed, I acknowledge that each of these theories has offered progress. I will be using them as well as I can, incorporating them into a new framework that can take us yet another step forward. Reviewing these approaches will indicate where too-radical solutions did not accomplish their tasks. These analyses will then serve as arguments for other possible solutions. When I finally describe my theory, I will be taking these useful components, placing them in a new framework, and renaming them to evoke new meanings emerging from the totality of the new framework.

This process I will be following amounts to an acknowledgment that science grows through collaborative processes and suggests how different paradigms can help us develop a transdisciplinary framework. I will describe the practical consequences of this framework for two subject areas.

The first deals with the problem of how to conceptualize cognition and communication in a way that is compatible with the conceptual framework of both the sciences and the phenomenological aspects of psychology and the social science theories of meaning and communication once considered specific to humans. Here, finally, both biology and previous efforts to connect life and cognition with the ethological paradigm (as an example) become central.

Second, I want to describe some practical consequences for library and information science (LIS), with a focus on the problems of indexing electronic scientific documents for subject searching based on the semantic interpretation of texts for (again as an example) the Internet and management information systems (MISs). In the past twenty years it has become increasingly clear how important this area is for all computerized exchange, storage, and retrieval of human knowledge. It has also become increasingly obvious that in order to function optimally, LIS must be based on a theory of cognition, information, and communication that bridges technical science, cognitive science, communication science, and linguistics, including the phenomenological, social, and cultural aspects of signs.

I admit that this is not an unambitious book. I am discussing some of the grand theories underlying our world view and culture, and throughout this project I have always felt myself to be a mountain of papers and books behind, and needing to write a hundred more pages to complete my argument. My only excuse for this imperfect attempt to achieve a grander synthesis is my strong feeling of how necessary it is, for the survival of our culture, to make the climb. I hope to make a small contribution and that my efforts will inspire others to continue the work.

I apologize to all those who have done significant work in this huge field and whom I could not include or simply did not encounter. The limitation is mine. In transdisciplinary work, it is best to dig into subject areas only to the depth that is necessary to build one's transdisciplinary framework or else you will drown in the details. I am looking forward to constructive feedback and criticism.

This book amounts to a first primitive overview of a new transdisciplinary and even trans-scientific theory. The first steps are always the most difficult, as they lay the foundations and in so doing provide conceptual groundwork for the future. It has taken me twenty-five years to come this far – or rather, near!

Many of my colleagues in the social sciences and the humanities fear trans-scientific frameworks because past ones have been so reductionistic in the mechanical, functional, or ideological sense. Most of these frameworks lack self-reflection and modesty regarding their own truth, value, and comprehensiveness. I hope not to fall into any of these traps when I bring signification, qualia, and the importance of our bodyness into the framework of cybersemiotics. We anyway make these frameworks more or less implicit, and we use them as tacit knowledge that creates conflicts between paradigms. So it is better for discussion, cooperation, and the development of knowledge if we conceptualize them explicitly.

It is important to note that when researchers in the humanities and the social sciences do the philosophy and sociology of 'science,' it is within their subject area of society and culture. That is why they often provide, as ultimate explanations, sociological and historical descriptions of the formation processes of institutions and institutional practices of producing knowledge – generally, however, without any interest in concepts of truth as these relate to some form of independent reality, as in the natural and technical sciences as well as in much of philosophy.

The scientist who has become a philosopher of science does not feel tempted to explain the theories and methods of science solely from the perspective of social-cultural history. He wants to know if – or rather how – we have moved forward or backward in our pursuit of truth (and goodness) as science has developed, be it slowly or through occasional revolutions. Crucial to him is the relationship between our knowledge and some sort of stable reality, be it external or internal to us as individuals.

To ensure that the whole idea of science is not consumed by relativism, and by radical or social constructivism, he is therefore forced to look for a metascientific framework that is also meta to the humanities and the social sciences. Having been educated first as a biologist specializing in neurophysiology and ethology, I find myself compelled to carry out a philosophical and metaphysical analysis of the frameworks underlying the present conceptions of science, in a way that closely reflects the way and spirit in which the problem is stated by Michael Luntley in *Reason, Truth and Self*:

> We need to legitimize a use of the concepts of truth, rationality and self against the postmodernist critique. To achieve such legitimation it is not sufficient to criticize the theories on the basis of which the postmodernist claims are made. What is required, therefore, is a description of how, given the opacity of all experience, the concepts of truth, rationality and self can still have a legitimate role to play in the business of making sense of our lives. This book is, if you like, an essay in descriptive metaphysics. It is an essay which describes the structure of and connections between the key concepts of truth, rationality and self. It is an attempt to provide the metaphysics or model that shows how truth, rationality and the self work; it is a model to replace the defunct model inherited from the Enlightenment. (1995, 21–2)

I share that spirit, although Luntley and I take somewhat different approaches in practice. Having worked in applied philosophy and theory of science for many years, I find it necessary at this point to make some preliminary statements about how I view the nature of science. These are introductory remarks; discussing them with references and citations would take up too much space and lead the book in a direction other than the one I want. As the argument in the book unfolds, it will use and develop the criteria roughly stated here. Philosophers will remark that although this book is about philosophical matters, it is not written like professional philosophy with its standard references. The discourse is situated at a transdisciplinary level and is not subject-specific.

The main and broadly accepted result of the past fifty years of investigation, analysis, and discussion of the philosophy, theory, and sociology of science is that no absolute criteria for scientific knowledge can be constructed. We can, however, propose some pragmatic criteria for deeming a theory to be scientific. As Popper points out, a theory may for some time be both wrong and controversial (it may even be offensive) without necessarily being unscientific. This does not mean that we have to know the truth about the subject matter of the theory in order to say whether or not it is scientific. We are never in that situation, as science is one of our primary methods for seeking the truth and evaluating whether its findings are true. Yet it must be possible to determine whether a theory or theorist is seriously interested in the truth, and to do so independently of whether the theory is in fact true. The essence of the criteria I want to propose as the baseline for my analysis here is that the 'scientificity' of a theory relies on its relationship with the truth – a truth that goes beyond the truth concept in formal theories of logic and mathematics, as it must also say something about empirical findings. Here is how far I have come towards a consensus view of science and scholarly investigations that is the point of departure for the present work:

1. Scientific theories – not necessarily every piece of empirical or theoretical investigation – should predict some aspect of observable reality. Predictive power, however, does not in itself prove or verify truth. At most, it indicates a correspondence with empirical observations. It strengthens our belief in our theories.
2. Only negative proofs of theories are possible – that is, a theory can be said to have withstood falsification, not to have undergone verification. Since all observations are laden with theory, however, neither can a clear logical inference be drawn from falsification. While one of the important criteria for a theory being scientific is that it strives for the possibility of falsification, that falsification must be interpreted too.
3. Theories are never entirely consistent (in a logical sense) regarding every aspect of the subject. Yet all scientific theories should strive to be as consistent as possible. It should ideally be possible to deduce their empirical consequences with the highest obtainable reliability and objectivity.
4. No facts are absolutely free of context. The important thing is to discuss them, to compare them, to calibrate them according to

standards determined by our dealings with other facts, while consciously reflecting on the significance of the context.

5. All scientific observations (empirical studies) are theory laden. Since scientific objects are theory laden, you need to supplement your discussion of methods and what you belive they measure with an explicit analysis of your metaphysical ideas of the nature of the subject area and the kind of knowledge you expect to obtain.

6. Observation is always carried out on the basis of a problem. Observations are never truly disinterested and objective in themselves. Objectivity requires us to clearly state the interests and assumptions that frame the problem at hand.

7. Theories make presumptions about the nature of reality, cognition, and knowledge; from these, we derive methods, scientific objects, and subject areas. When formulating projects, we should state these presumptions as openly and clearly as possible. Objectivity demands that we reflect on these presumptions and on how they relate to other theories.

8. A scientific theory should define a subject area that covers all central aspects of the problem being investigated. The sense one gives to 'central' here determines the character and territory of the subject area, and constitutes the basis of methodology. Relativity and quantum mechanics have changed our view of the subject area of Newton's laws, for instance. Delimiting the subject area for a theory is an ongoing interpretative work.

9. In our experience so far, all fundamental, universal theories and models have in part been falsified (that is, have been proved false in some particulars or areas). They should be kept only if good reasons exist to believe that the problems can be solved with the present strategy of their new (most of them limited) subject areas. Much here depends on interpretation, and objectivity depends on being open about one's interpretations.

10. Good scientific theories should fit into a network of other well-tested theories. Some of these may be false, but all theories should not be discarded in their entirety. Theories should aim at being compatible with what we already know as far as possible without distorting the basic picture.

11. The general aim of the sciences and humanities is to produce as much consistency and coherence in our thinking about ourselves and the world as possible.

12. How useful a scientific theory is depends on how well it fits with part of the intended subject area and with a social comprehension of the ideas involved. A pragmatic criterion of truth cannot on its own guarantee universal truth, but in combination with other criteria, it is useful in general evaluations that rely on human judgment.

13. The scientific theories accepted at present are not the final truth about the world or reality; nevertheless, they contain a great deal of knowledge about parts of the regularities of the world, and no matter how different they are they may still turn out to show us complementary aspects of reality.

14. Our knowledge is growing, but we cannot prove that our theories are getting closer to some kind of universal truth or basic model of the laws of the universe. We do not know the overall direction of the growth. Truth can be in all directions and aspects, which supplement one another. What seems a Multiverse (Maturana) may still be aspects of a Universe, but perhaps a hypercomplex one.

15. Theories should be open about their metaphysical commitments. These should be made clear for others to evaluate. Scientific world views, methods, epistemologies and methodologies are constantly evolving, as is everything else in culture and nature. They interact with one another, and their development should be discussed. Science cannot *prove* that nature is at bottom truly mathematical, mechanical, or something else; nor can it *prove* the truth of any particular 'world view' or 'ontology' that is the philosophical foundation for theories and methods (Kuhn's disciplinary matrix). Yet at the same time, we cannot say that 'everything goes.' Reality does present constraints.

16. The differences between the types of knowledge gained through quantitative and qualitative methods, and the differences between the knowledge types produced by nomothetic and ideographic goals, make it questionable whether the entire scientific–scholarly endeavour as such will ever be able to produce one single true and coherent theory of reality. On their own, notions of unification that have arisen from classical science (and later positivism) are at cross-purposes with the ideographic endeavour and its project to uncover the deeper meaning of historical events and the actions of specific individuals. The nomothetic and hermenutic approaches, which work with universal laws and with cultural

and personal meaning respectively, seem to defy a common framework. This is so, unless we accept a world view of irreversibility and hypercomplexity that is open to a level of nature that allows for mind and meaningful interpretation to develop in the course of evolution, and that at the same time is open to the view that it may be that none of the grand theories can be expected to reduce the complexity of reality to a single final form of knowledge. Complexity will always leave room open for further interpretation. Nevertheless we have to strive for compatibility between the various forms of reason.

17. Scientists should recognize and discuss the limits to their paradigms. They should be willing to discuss their world views and methods. Methodology will never take the complete load off observation (there will never be pure observations; they are always to some degree theory impregnated). There is no final 'scientific method,' so scientists should always be discussing their methods and instruments. But it is difficult to establish final criteria capable of telling us what should count as a legitimate argument. Scientists want to deal with facts, and they ask themselves what sorts of observations generate empirical 'scientific' facts. The answer for that is based on human judgment.

18. It cannot be proved that scientific methods are capable of covering all aspects of reality. It may well be that personal knowledge (one's inner life), tacit knowledge, social-personal practices, and the meaning of life generally are all areas that scientific methods can only partly penetrate and for which more ideographic methods are needed. There are still large areas of experience that science has so far failed to make sense of – at least, to the satisfaction of those who have the first person experiences. In the functional differentiated society (cf. Luhmann) it is important not to consider such experiences less real because of this. The realm of consciousness, will, and meaning is still one of the greatest problems of our culture's quest for scientific knowledge as a basis for democratic civilization.

19. In some ways, science can be demarcated from other knowledges, meanings, and power concerns, so it seems fair to say that it cannot cover everything. Precisely *because* science is not theology, politics, or art, the specific tasks that 'scientists' or 'scholars' undertake (as scientists and scholars) become interesting to talk about. But of course science, money, love, power, art, and religion

influence one another all the time, partly because metaphysics – though necessary – cannot be proven.

20. Now if science is essentially an approach to facts that involves (but does not depend solely upon) methodology, objectivity, good reasons for belief, and so on, and if all of these terms are open to interpretation, then 'What is science?' and 'What is science not?' are permanently open questions. Science is an important part of the collective art of arriving at good reasons to believe strongly in something (Peirce), (that is, it is a procedure for producing socially reliable knowledge). The tougher we make our criteria, the closer to the surface rise the imperfections of humans and knowledge institutions.

Summing up, we can say that inquiry is never disinterested. As Popper and Peirce point out, it is usually an answer to questions or problems. Truth is not merely socially determined, so it seems that questions of what, how, and why are always intertwined. Nor is it simply a matter of what works (pragmatism) – for instance, to satisfy desire or relieve pain – or of maximizing happiness (utilitarism). Furthermore, what counts as true is not a simple given essence, be it abstract ideas (Plato), mathematical laws (scientism), or phenomenological noumenial structures (Husserl). The problem is that knowledge of facts presupposes knowledge of theories, which form concepts and categorizations, but knowledge also presupposes values. Conversely, knowledge of theories and values presupposes knowledge of facts. The hermeneutic circles evolve into a spiral movement in understanding. Thus truth is a normative term as well as a descriptive one (Peirce). Simple correspondence between word and object – or sentence and state of affairs – provides very little explanatory force and value alone (correspondence theories of truth). Inquiry is never disinterested, so while facts in the world are of course a necessary feature of what it means to talk about truth, there are always underlying ontological, epistemological, and axiological commitments in holding a term or sentence to be true. This is why Kuhn's paradigm concept (rather, his disciplinary matrix) is a useful analytical tool in the philosophy and sociology of the sciences. But in my view (Brier 2005) it is not to be used to discourage the search for compatibility among the various ways of striving for publicly accessible and controllable meaning and knowledge.

So it is a fair question when scholars ask why I have been working for so many years to construct the cybersemiotic framework. The answer is that though I am aware of the cultural and social context of all our thinking, I believe in the need to consciously construct and discuss basic philosophical perspectives, and to contemplate the limits and possibilities of human knowing and the place and nature of the sciences in it, as a means to develop and attempt to optimize the common good in civilizations. I will be developing this perspective alongside my analysis of the limits and inconsistencies of the prevailing scientific paradigms. This kind of work cannot be done without an ongoing dialogue between metatheory *and* specific theory, especially in the information, cognition, and communication sciences. When there is an ongoing dialogue with the aims and forces of technology, development is unavoidable.

In establishing a new framework, I also hope to create a third culture, one that transcends the incommensurability between C.P. Snow's two cultures: science-technology, and the humanities and social sciences. I am trying to draw a map onto which a multitude of viewpoints can be plotted and their subject areas characterized and compared with other approaches. By erecting this framework I hope to expand the dialogue between sciences, the humanities, the social sciences, philosophy, and the existential quest to broaden our concept of reason in accordance with my stance towards making common frames for the open and systematic pursuits of knowledge and meaning.

It is my view that the problems we face as a global(izing) culture make this necessary for our survival. In many respects, we stand at the threshold of a new Enlightenment. The earlier Enlightenment's definition of rationality and science has carried our civilization far, but it is now showing signs that it is based on foundations too narrow to meet the needs of a new global knowledge society. In order to survive the future that awaits us, we need to make the leap to a new *level* of knowledge and *understanding* of knowledge. Here I have been especially inspired by Luhmann's and Peirce's work with new transdisciplinary conceptual frameworks.

In future publications I hope to elaborate more on these topics. This book aims to present the main argument for the necessity of a new framework, and to outline it in an economical way. It is an attempt to present the general idea.

This book provides visual models as an approach to synthesizing theories. I use these figures to represent my ideas, despite criticisms from colleagues in the humanities and social sciences, who often remind me that they reduce the complexity of the subject area. I use them partly because of my background in the sciences (in which models are a language), and partly based on my belief in Herman Hesse's ideas in *Magister Ludi*[1] and Brockmann's idea (1995) of a 'third culture' between art and science, in which scientists serve as productive philosophers and designers of knowledge. As the amount of knowledge continues to grow exponentially and the subject areas we deal with become exceedingly complex, more concentrated ways of conveying knowledge must be applied. Visual models are one way, but of course I always complement them with natural and scholarly language.

I.2 Approach to Writing and Developing the Argument

I have long realized that it is not really possible to prove my point of view through a linear argument, because of the complexity of my ideas and their ongoing reflective interactions with the background assumptions briefly sketched here. In writing even this much, I can already see the challenges the idea of cybersemiotics will be setting for me, and has been setting for me over the past twenty years. What I will do, then, is sketch out where I stand fairly briefly in the beginning; and then, spiralling through what amounts to a series of open concentric circles, analyse specific areas of my argument. When I judge it necessary, I will return to my arguments in the previous chapter and integrate the new results to make my interpretation clear and to build the cybersemiotic framework still higher, even though I know these iterations will sometimes be somewhat redundant.

I will be describing and analysing many grand theories. My analytical method, shaped as it is by my interest in the philosophical framework underlying the theories, is to go immediately to the bones and structure of the theory at hand. This means, for instance, that I am not very interested in Wiener's ethics or specific technological contribution, in Bateson's anthropological work, learning theory, and double-bind model, in Luhmann's detailed analysis of various functionally differentiated social systems, or in the logical and mathematical developments of Peirce's philosophy. I focus instead on what the theory can contribute to a general framework for information, cognition, signification, meaning, and communication both in nature and in living psychological, sociological, and technical systems. When I work in this manner, scholars who prefer more specific and applied approaches are often dissatisfied, though at the same time the philosophical inconsistencies in the theory's framework do not trouble them much. But my interest lies elsewhere. I am interested in how concepts derive their meaning from the philosophical framework – or what Thomas Kuhn calls the disciplinary matrix – and in what kind of subject area can be covered in a consistent way when a theory's ontology, epistemology, values, and concepts are constructed in this manner (rather than in what problems the paradigm or research program claims to be able to solve). Furthermore, I do not have the space here to discuss in detail all the various theories in a way that would allow readers to follow the argument easily without any prior knowledge of them. I will be presuming that my readers have a general acquaintance with the theories; on that basis, I will be pointing out the most conspicuous aspects of each theory and its framework for analysis and discussion. Often I will do so during the discussion of a different theory as a new aspect of the problem emerges. As the book develops, the discussion will shift levels as more theories are introduced. In any case, it would be boring to go through every theory systematically and afterwards compare them.

I.3 Technical Points

A technical note: Many of the extracts from Peirce's work are cited as, for example, (CP, 5.345). This refers to the *Collected Papers of Charles Sanders Peirce, 1931–58* (book and section), and here I am following the accepted convention. In this book I am using the electronic version of those papers (1994 [1866–1913]).

The book is an extended synthesis of many of my past articles, and thus replaces the following:

1992. 'Information and Consciousness: A Critique of the Mechanistic Concept of Information.' *Cybernetics and Human Knowing* 1, nos. 2/3: 71–94.
1993. 'A Cybernetic and Semiotic view on a Galilean Theory of Psychology.' *Cybernetics and Human Knowing* 2, no. 2: 31–45.
1993. 'Cyber-Semiotics: Second-Order Cybernetics and the Semiotics of C.S. Peirce.' In *Proceedings from the Second European Congress on Systemic Science*, vol. 2: 427–36.
1995. 'Cyber-Semiotics: On Autopoiesis, Code-Duality and Sign Games in Bio-Semiotics.' *Cybernetics and Human Knowing* 3, no. 1: 3–14.
1996. 'Cybersemiotics: A New Interdisciplinary Development Applied to the Problems of Knowledge Organization and Document

Retrieval in Information Science.' *Journal of Documentation* 52, no. 3 (September): 296–344.

1996. 'The Necessity of a Theory of Signification and Meaning in Cybernetics and Systems Science.' In *Proceedings of the Third European Congress on Systems Science*, 693–7. Rome, 1–4 October 1996. Rome: Edizioni Kappa.

1996. 'From Second-Order Cybernetics to Cybersemiotics: A Semiotic Reentry into the Second-Order Cybernetics of Heinz von Foerster.' *Systems Research* 13, no. 3: 229–44 (A Festschrift for Heinz von Foerster).

1996. 'The Usefulness of Cybersemiotics in Dealing with Problems of Knowledge Organization and Document-Mediating Systems.' *Cybernetica: Quarterly Review of the International Association for Cybernetics* 34, no. 4: 273–99.

1997. 'The Self-Organization of Knowledge: Paradigms of Knowledge and their Role in the Decision of What Counts as Legitimate Medical Practice.' In S.G. Oleson, B. Eikard, P. Gad, and E. Høg, eds. *Studies in Alternative Therapy 4: Lifestyle and Medical Paradigms*, 112–35. Odense, Denmark: INRAT, Odense University Press.

1997. 'What Is a Possible Ontological and Epistemological Framework for a True Universal "Information Science": The Suggestion of Cybersemiotics.' *World Futures* 49: 287–308.

1998. 'Cybersemiotics: A Transdisciplinary Framework for Information Studies.' *BioSystems* 46: 185–91.

1998. 'The Cybersemiotic Explanation of the Emergence of Cognition: The Explanation of Cognition, Signification and Communication in a Non-Cartesian Cognitive Biology.' *Evolution and Cognition* 4, no.1: 90–102.

1998. 'Cybersemiotics: A Suggestion for a Transdisciplinary Framework for Description of Observing, Anticipatory, and Meaning Producing Systems.' In D. Dubois, ed., *Computing Anticipatory Systems; CASYS-First International Conference, Liege, Belgium, 1997*, 182–93. American Institute of Physics Conference Proceedings 437.

1999. 'C.S. Peirce's Holistic, Triadic, and Pragmaticistic View of Evolution and Signification.' *Proceedings of the Fifteenth International Congress on Cybernetics, Namur, Belgium, 24–28 August 1998*, 776–81. Association Internationale de Cybernetique.

1999. 'Biosemiotics and the Foundation of Cybersemiotics. Reconceptualizing the Insights of Ethology, Second-Order Cybernetics and

Peirce's Semiotics in Biosemiotics to Create a Non-Cartesian Information Science.' *Semiotica* 127, nos. 1/4: 169–98. Special issue on biosemiotics.

1999. 'On the Conflict between the Informational and the Semiotic Communicational Paradigm.' In *Proceedings from the ISSS99 Conference, 28 June–2 July, Asilomar, CA.* CD-ROM, Article no. 99169.

1999. 'The Self-Organization of Knowledge in a World of Complexity: The Interplay of Paradigms of Knowledge in the Non-Cartesian Transdisciplinary Epistemological Framework of Cybersemiotics.' In *Proceedings from the ISSS99 Conference, 28 June–2 July, Asilomar, CA.* CD-ROM, Article no. 99122.

2000. 'Konstruktion und Information. Ein semiotisches re-entry in Heinz von Foerster's metaphysische Konstruktion der Kybernetik zweiter Ordnung.' In *Beobachtungen des Unbeobachtbaren*, 254–95. Weilerswist: Velbrück Wissenschaft.

2000. 'Trans-Scientific Frameworks of Knowing: Complementarity Views of the Different Types of Human Knowledge.' *Yearbook Edition of Systems Research and Behavioral Science* 17, no. 5: 433–58.

2001. 'Cybersemiotics and Umweltslehre.' *Semiotica* 134, nos. 1/4: 779–814.

2001. 'Cybersemiotics, Biosemiotics and Ecosemiotics.' In ISI Congress Papers, Part IV. Nordic Baltic Summer Institute for Semiotic and Structural Studies, Imatra, Finland. 12–21 June 2000. *Ecosemiotics: Studies in the Environmental Semiosis, Semiotics of the Biocybernetic Bodies, Human/Too Human/Post-Human*, ed. Eero Tarasti, 7–26.

2001. 'Cybersemiotics: A Reconceptualization of the Foundation for Information Science.' *Systems Research and Behavioral Science* 18: 421–7.

2001. 'Ecosemiotics and Cybersemiotic.' *Sign Systems Studies* 29, no. 1: 107–20.

2002. 'Intrasemiotics and Cybersemiotics.' *Sign System Studies* 30, no. 1: 113–27.

2002. 'Varela's Contribution to the Creation of Cybersemiotics: The Calculus of Self-Reference.' ASC-column, *Cybernetics and Human Knowing* 9, no. 2: 77–82.

2002. 'The Five-Leveled Cybersemiotic Model of FIS.' In R. Trappl, ed. *Cybernetics and Systems*, vol. 1: 197–202. (Best Paper Award in its session.)

2002. Team 3: Foundation of Information Science. Søren Brier (coordinator), Gerhard Chroust, John Collier, Allan Combs, Magdalena Kalaidjieva, Len Troncale, *The Eleventh Fuschl Conversation (April 7 to 12, 2002)*, Austrian Society for Cybernetic Studies, Reports, ISB 3 85206 166 0.

2003. 'The Cybersemiotic Model of Communication: An Evolutionary View on the Threshold between Semiosis and Informational Exchange.' *TripleC* 1, no. 1: 71–94.

2004. 'Cybersemiotics and the Problem of the Information-Processing Paradigm as a Candidate for a Unified Science of Information behind Library and Information Science.' *Library Trends* 52, no. 3: 629–57

Thellefsen, T.L., S. Brier, and M.L. Thellefsen. 2003. 'Problems Concerning the Process of Subject Analysis and the Practice of Indexing: A Peircian Semiotic and Semantic Approach toward User-Oriented Needs in Document Searching.' *Semiotica* 144, nos. 1/4: 177–218.

All of these papers have been steps on the way towards the current state of the theory of the cybersemiotic framework. As such, they have been revised according to that theory's development. *This means that as of early 2006, this book represents the current state of the theory and supercedes the papers published before this point.*

I.4 Acknowledgments

I could not have completed this work without help from colleagues in many fields. So I thank all of those experts who have so generously provided insight from their respective fields of knowledge, which they have cultivated for most of their working life and on which I was only trespassing during my transdisciplinary quest. I hope that the new perspective this cybersemiotic framework gives to their work will pay back a little of my debt.

I would especially like to thank the following people (in alphabetical order), who contributed to the creation of the arguments in this book by discussing earlier manuscripts or simply discussing ideas with me: Peter Bøgh Andersen, Dirk Baecker, Lucia Santaella Braga, Bela Antal Banathy, Jeanette Bopry, Michael Buchland, Pille Bunnell, Peder Voetmann Christiansen, John Collier, Allan Combs, Marcel Danesi, John

in all this is to explain qualia, life, and consciousness as emergent phenomena resulting from the evolution of material, energetic, and informational systems. Employed to this purpose are analytical tools such as non-equilibrium thermodynamics, non-linear systems dynamics, deterministic chaos theory, complexity theory, and fractal mathematics. This development has helped mechanistic and functionalistic science create better models of the cognition and communication of living systems, yet these systems are still viewed from an unembodied informational perspective that does not really acknowledge the connotative and emotional aspects of cognition and communication.

But for its followers this cognitive information paradigm presents great and unexpected difficulties when it comes to modelling both the semantic dimensions of language, perception, and intelligence and the influence of these on cognition, communication, and action. According to many scholars and scientists, this is an indication that the research program is inherently limited and that we must establish a broader basis for information science if we hope to encompass the phenomenological[3] and social aspects of cognition, language, and communication, as well as the biological nature and behaviour of living systems.

Many scholars posit that the great problem of the cognitive sciences is that ever since Descartes, it has completely separated subject from object in the cognitive process. In contrast, Konrad Lorenz and Niko Tinbergen's science of ethology created a biological theory of innate cognition and communication based on an evolutionary theory of instinctive motivation, perception, and action. Thus analysing this line of inquiry may shed new light on the nature of cognitive systems.

Lorenz was inspired by Jacob von Uexküll, who noted hat somehow the cognition of a living system partly creates the 'reality' in which it is living. He talked about the animal's *Umwelt* – an idea not far from Husserl's concept of 'life world' in human phenomenology. Like Lorenz and Tinbergen, the Danish biopsychologist Iven Reventlow sought new foundations for an extended ethological theory of cognition. He did his work in Denmark during and after the Second World War, when Lorenz's ethology was entering its mature phase as an accepted science. We will follow the progress that Reventlow made in this field, as well as the paradox of the creative power of cognition that he unearthed with his concept of the 'rependium.'

But Reventlow, too, realized the limits of his approach, and at the end of his research he started to look for new interdisciplinary concepts to bridge the inner and the outer realities of living systems. As one of his pupils, I turned to the new cybernetics of Bateson, to Maturana and Varela's theory of 'autopoiesis,' and to von Foerster's 'second-order cybernetics' in search of broader foundations.

Gregory Bateson's cybernetic concept of the mind as a system of differences travelling in cybernetic loops, together with his definition of information as 'a difference that makes a difference,' was to some a strong departure from Wiener's objective first-order cybernetic foundation of the cognitive and information sciences. It also served as an impetus for the development of what Heinz von Foerster came to call 'second-order cybernetics.' Second-order cybernetics defines information as something that an observer notes as internally created in an autopoietic system and that has formed structural couplings in reaction to perturbations from the environment. Clearly, this account steps away from the objectivistic, denotative, and logical theories of information and language. It moves towards more constructivist theories; it goes beyond social constructivism by moving into biology, or even beginning with biology and moving from there towards sociology.

Second-order cybernetics and autopoiesis focus on the individuality of an observing system. Von Foerster considered the nervous system a closed functional system; like Bateson, he grasped that the real evolutionary and thinking system is the organism *plus* its cognitive domain. The conceptual forerunner for biosemiotics, Jacob von Uexküll, called these *Innerwelt* and *Umwelt*. With their theory of autopoiesis, Maturana and Varela have expressed the same phenomenon. According to them, a living system's connection to its environment, and the mutual communicative connections between the two systems, can be conceptualized as a 'structural coupling.' Such structural couplings organize the cognitive apparatus established through evolution. It follows that the 'cognitive domain' is the world of cognitive processes of a living system and includes the totality of structural couplings. Maturana and Varela contend that everything in the organism is structurally dependent. Unfortunately, partly because they do not want to use the objectivist category of information, they continue to use cybernetic explanatory terms even when they talk about a living system's cognitive domain. But their idea of dependence is a non-deterministic mechanicism. This is well explained by von Foerster when he says that even if we view the organism as a machine, it is not a trivial machine. A non-trivial machine is mathematically unpredictable because every time it runs a function it changes the state from which the function will run the next time. In this way the next run becomes unpredictable.

Like Jakob von Uexküll, both Maturana and Varela and von Foerster find it difficult to establish a common universe because their theories are so bioconstructivist in their point of departure. They start with the organization and cognition of living systems and, from there, reflect on science. When Maturana and Varela speak of reality, they see a multiverse, not a universe. When speaking about communication, they develop a theory of reciprocal and mutual structural couplings they call 'languaging' – that is, the coordination of coordinations of behaviour. Von Foerster refers to language as constituting a double closure. In his view, every system is closed in relation to other systems, and communication only works through mutual structural couplings. (Here he has been inspired by his exchange of ideas with the systemic sociologist Niklas Luhmann.) Socio-communication establishes its own socially shared *Umwelt*. Consciousness, according to von Foerster, is 'conscience' that establishes mutual knowledge through the co-constructing of a world. When faced with the problem of solipsism in constructivism, von Foerster contends that there is no logical solution. One has to choose whether to consider other phenomena in one's *Umwelt* as part of one's own conception, or as independent systems.

But the basis of second-order cybernetics is still logical discrimination and the computation of differences. Luhmann (1995) has developed a systems-theoretical model of social communication by incorporating parts of the biocognitive second-order cybernetics with parts of the autopoiesis theory of cognition. He extends the concept of autopoiesis in order to encompass the psyche and the social communicative system. He then reformulates the basic problem of psychology by asserting that cognitions and communications must be studied as phenomena based on three independent systems of inquiry – the biological, the psychological, and the socio-communicational – and their mutual interpenetrations. These are of qualitatively different natures. Luhmann (1990) argues that they are closed to one another and can only communicate through interpenetration. The biological and psychological autopoietic systems are silent. Only communication communicates! He develops the socio-communicative aspect and criticizes the idea of a transcendental self. But he does not really develop a phenomenological theory of cognition, meaning, and signification within a reflective phenomenological theory of the embodied self and its existentiality, will, and emotions. He is inspired by Husserl, but not much by Merleau-Ponty. He focuses on the sociological aspects, to some degree ignoring the importance of the biological and psychological systems in generating signification and meaning.

Luhmann's systems theory is based on Spencer-Brown's dualistic philosophy of differences. This seems to make it incompatible with the triadic semiotics of the American pragmatic semiotician Charles Sanders Peirce, which seems to offer a transdisciplinary theory of meaning and signification that the cybernetic–functionalistic informational approaches are missing. But in his seminal work *A Calculus of Self-Reference*, Varela notes that the need for a third element in autopoiesis theory and second-order cybernetics has been overlooked. He adds it to the system in a way that renders it compatible with Peirce's semiotics while maintaining the connection to cybernetics and autopoiesis. Later, Varela also worked with theories of embodied cognition, until his too early death.

Galilean science has dominated us for more than three hundred years. It has shown us that some aspects of reality are amenable to precise mathematical analysis. This has been an enormously productive insight. We must admit that even mind has its 'sluggish' sides, especially in a primitive nervous system that may be partially describable by functional laws. This does not mean, however, that the content of all behaviour and language can be transferred to computers, as some eliminative materialists (Churchland 2004) and functionalists believe. There is a 'background problem.' In both physics and psychology (especially the latter), that which can be described formally is rooted in that which is not formally describable: hypercomplex phenomena, which besides the predictable and regular are also comprised of the spontaneous, unpredictable (chaotic), intentional, and unconscious.

Since we cannot avoid discussing the nature of reality as a prerequisite for various scientific paradigms, I suggest it would be more useful to regard it not simply as complex, but as hypercomplex. In its entirety as well as in its specific manifestations, reality cannot be reduced to something simple, deterministic, random, material, or spiritual. It is not something that can be contained completely in a linguistic or mathematical formulation. The spontaneous, intentional, anticipatory mind is inescapably part of that same reality.[4] We will probably never be able to completely separate subject and object,[5] neither for our natural sciences nor for the intentional systems we study in humanities and social sciences. Because reality is hypercomplex, there will always be 'noise' in all measurements that will affect our results unpredictably. We always draw an arbitrary distinction between the observed system and ourselves (Bohr 1954), and between the observed system and its 'environment' as we define it through our own experiences and our attempts to explain the 'reactions' of the observed system(s).

In evolutionary philosophy – which does not deny that reality can possess 'deep' but formally indescribable absolute features – we may see the development of even more complex and selectively unstable 'far from equilibrium' individual–environment systems. Maturana and Varela's autopoietic systems are one example of nature's capacity to reflect, in ever increasing degrees, the spontaneous, unpredictable, and intentional sides of reality. This capacity allows these systems to be centres of their own and to draw a line between themselves as systems and their environment. Through the use of language in society, systems can finally represent themselves socially, and by this means establish an individual, inquiring point of view from which to reflect on knowledge, existence, and meaning. But Maturana's theory leaves unexplained first-person experience, qualias, and emotions – not to speak of free will.

In Peirce's, pragmatic, and evolutionary semiotics, phenomenology is integrated with the triadic theory of semiosis. Peirce operates with a triad composed of a sign vehicle (the Representamen), an Object (a certain aspect of reality), and an Interpretant, which is a more developed sign in the mind of the perceiver/observer/communicator. Each of these three is a kind of sign and is necessary to create cognition, information, and communication. Each belongs to one of Peirce's three basic categories. In Peirce's view, Kant's twelve categories (see *Critique of Pure Reason* [Kant 1990]) were too many. Peirce's three categories are universal connections between the inner and the outer worlds; they are ontological and epistemological at the same time. He considered his three categories so basic that he called them Firstness, Secondness, and Thirdness.

Let me offer some examples of how Peirce approached the fundamental relationships of cognition, evolution, and signification through his triadic philosophy. In the sign process, Representamen is first, Object is second, and Interpretant is third. In cosmogony, mind is first, matter is second, and evolution is third. In cognitive psychology, perception is first, experience is second, and understanding is third. Ontologically, chance is first, mechanical law is second, and the tendency to make or take habits is third. Peirce defines his Firstness as a chaos of living feeling with the tendency to assume habits. He also assigns qualia and 'pure feeling' to the category of Firstness. In Peirce's triadic scheme, feelings, qualia, habit formation, and signification are basic ontological constituents. He is therefore rejecting the mechanical view that matter is 'dead' and deterministically governed by mathematical, non-probabilistic laws. For him, matter has an inner aspect of living feeling – a hylozoistic view, and one that he shares with Aristotle.

Peirce considers the whole developmental process of signs through history as well as in living beings through evolution. Through the biosemiotic approach taken by Thomas Sebeok, Peirce's semiotics can be extended to animals, in that motivation makes it possible for something to stand for something else for somebody in a certain way. Here we encounter an obvious connection with Lakoff and Johnson's work. In their embodied cognitive semantics metaphor theory, they work with 'idealized cognitive models' (ICMs) as the sources of the meaning in messages. ICMs are based on lived social expectations. Similarly, Wittgenstein pointed out that signification is created in language games set in systems by specific life forms. For Wittgenstein, language is functional or pragmatic in that it is what it *does*. There is no essence to language. It is a system of conventional signs. But language has a social foundation in the 'forms of life,' which are what undergird his language theory.[6] The centre of language meaning is the constantly shifting and dynamic 'forms of life.'

The 'forms of life' concept, which Wittgenstein mentioned only five times in his *Philosophical Investigations* (PI), has given rise to interpretative disputes and contradictory readings. Forms of life can be understood as changing and contingent and as dependent on culture, context, and history. This encourages us to interpret forms of life as grounding a relativistic reading of Wittgenstein. However, we can also approach the concept in terms of the forms of life common to humankind. He explains them to be 'the system of reference by means of which we interpret an unknown language' – clearly a universalistic turn. He recognizes that the use of language is made possible by the human form of life as opposed to, for instance, the life form of a lion (which he used in another example). This is the thread that I, as a biosemiotician, want to follow. I see no problem in interpreting forms of life at the level of species, of cultures, and of subcultures (this is in line with Bourdieu's habitus concept, which is the silent subconscious background for interpreting concepts, metaphors, and life conduct). From there, the next jump is to specific life situations such as finding a mating partner; competing for status and territory; hunting; fighting for one's own life and the life of the family; fleeing; and caring for the young. As we shall see, these rather universal situations are the basis for the various specific motivations with which ethologists work, and which are connected to what we usually call 'conceptual schemes'; and for Lakoff's idealized cognitive models (ICMs), which we shall consider more closely in chapter 7. I see a pattern repeating itself at various levels, starting at the semiotic level, where Peirce talks of 'ground,' which is also valid for the biosemiotic levels, where Lorenz talks about innate response release mechanisms (IRRMs) with specific motivations (which are the 'grounds' at this level). Since animals do not have language in the narrower sense, I have extended the concept of language games into the world of living systems as the pragmatic basis of meaning by creating the new concept of *sign games*. These are related to specific motivations and innate response mechanisms. In this way I am advancing the pragmatic criteria of meaning from humans into all living systems through ethology and biosemiotics. We can see that the forms of life are the a priori, the given, which differ depending on time and place. Consequently, language games reflect this changing nature, and interact and redefine it in an ongoing process.

To date, two non-mechanistic transdisciplinary frameworks have attempted to start a useful dialogue between Snow's two possible cultures. These are the second-order cybernetics and autopoiesis theories of von Foerster, Maturana, Varela, and Luhmann, on the one side; and Peirce's triadic semiotics in the form of biosemiotics, especially as developed by Sebeok, Hoffmeyer, Emmeche and Kull, combined with pragmatic language theories such as that of Wittgenstein, on the other.

The theory of autopoiesis solves some of Bateson's problems about for whom the difference makes a difference, even though the relationship between mind and matter is still unclear. Maturana and Varela's concepts of autopoiesis and multiverse are invoked. But where deriving information from the concept of neg-entropy is too physicalistic,[7] Maturana's idea of a multiverse is too close to constructivistic idealism. Our project is to develop a more useful non-reductionist world view, a more pragmatic understanding of physics – such as Prigogine and Stengers's, where thermodynamics is understood as the basic discipline and mechanics as an idealization – opens the way for a non-reductionist conceptualization of chaos. However, this is not fully developed by Prigogine and Stengers. My attention is therefore caught by Peirce's conception of pure chance as living spontaneity with a tendency to make habits. I see this as a realistic but non-reductionist theory that comprises a solution to the world view problems of Bateson, Maturana, Prigogine and Stengers, and the ethologists. A useful link between second-order cybernetics and semiotics will then be possible through the new biosemiotics. Kull explains why in the following quote:

> Biosemiotics can be defined as the science of signs in living systems. A principal and distinctive characteristic of semiotic biology lays in the understanding that in living, entities do not interact like mechanical bodies, but rather as messages, the pieces of text. This means that the whole determinism is of another type ... The phenomena of recognition, memory, categorization, mimicry, learning, communication are thus among those of interest for biosemiotic research, together with the analysis of the application of the tools and notions of semiotics (text, translation, interpretation, semiosis, types of sign, meaning) in the biological realm. (Kull 1999, 386)

Thus biosemiotics can serve as a bridge between the technical-scientific and the humanistic-social aspects of cybernetics, and can be used to develop a cybersemiotics.

The cybersemiotic paradigm attempts to unite the two paradigms of cybernetics and semiotics by utilizing sign concepts as well as information concepts and by combining these with science on the one hand and the humanities on the other. I agree that when we combine semiotics with second-order cybernetics, we can see that reality is full of countless differences that can become information for certain systems, and that signification is created inside autopoietic systems at the moment when a biologically, psychologically, or culturally meaningful interpretant is established. Differences in reality can become meaningful only when they are based on choices made against the background of a field of meaning. Thus the framework seems compatible with *critical realism*,[8] but has not been related to it in any systematical way so far.

In Peircean semiotics, information is not perceived to be transmitted through communication. Only representamens are transferred. Information is partly (re)created through the reinterpretation of signs by the receiver of intentional communication. It follows that utterance, meaning, and information are connected; however, they are different aspects of communication – as Luhmann also points out in his system theory of communication, which includes second-order cybernetics and autopoiesis theory in a larger framework.

One of the major challenges facing any attempt to create a transdisciplinary information science is that a way must be found to unite the phenomenological aspects of signification and communication with their biological, sociological, logical, and physical aspects without reducing them to either the phenomenological or the mechanical. See Figure I.1 for an illustration of this idea.

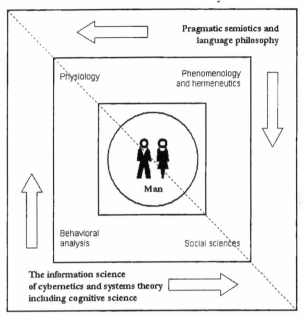

I.1 A view of cybersemiotics. The middle square shows the four qualitatively different approaches to the study of information, cognition, communication, and signification in humans and animals. They are complementary and cannot be integrated into a single science of psychology or cognitive science. This model illustrates with the outer square how two major transdisciplinary research programs have supplementary approaches to the subjects of information, cognition, signification, and communication. One is cybernetics and systems science's information processing paradigm, which has been developed into the linguistic area. The other is the pragmatic semiotics of Peirce, which is connected to pragmatic language philosophies such as Wittgenstein's language games theory and to embodied cognitive semantics such as Lakoff and Johnson's experientalistic cognitive semantics. The first is a functionalistic approach based on an objective information concept, the other is based on a pragmatic concept of meaning. Thus cybersemiotics attempts to create a metaframework that unites phenomenology and functionalism in a pragmatic, evolutionary non-reductionist triadic view of the self-organization of signs and signification processes.

The cybersemiotic paradigm combines a non-mechanistic universal evolutionary semiotic approach to epistemology, ontology, and signification with a systemic and cybernetic approach to self-organization, drawing on Luhmann's theories of social communication.[9] This combines a semiotics of nature with pragmatic linguistics in a second-order approach, one that reflects the role of the observer as the producer of meaningful contexts that make processes and differences informational. Bateson contended that information is a difference that makes a difference; Maturana and Varela, clarified that structurally coupled autopoiesis is necessary for any cognition to take place. Like Peirce, I will be claiming that an interpretant, and therefore a sign process, must be established to create signification, which differs from objective information because of its meaning content.

A short version of how integration between the different approaches can be made could be the following: Individual interpreters see differences in their world that make a difference to them as information. Thus 'the world' is the world of Heidegger (1973), in which the observer is thrown among things 'ready at hand,' through which a 'breakdown' of the original unconscious unity become 'present at hand.' This situation is possible only when signs are assigned to differences and interpreted against a general non-reducible context. Living autopoietic systems do this by producing signs as parts of life forms. Thus signs can be said to obtain meanings through sign games. In the human social sphere forms of life give rise to language games. This part of social autopoiesis is what Luhmann calls socio-communication, and it employs what Peirce calls genuine triadic signs. Thus cognition and communication are self-organizing phenomena at all three levels: biological, psychological, and sociological/cultural. They produce meaningful information by bringing forth an *Umwelt* – which in cybersemiotics is called a signification sphere – connected to specific life practices such as mating, hunting, tending the young, and defending. These characteristics distinguish cognition and communication in living systems from the simulations of these processes by computers. The forces and regularities of nature influence and constrain our perceptions and spark evolution. This process can be explained scientifically to some degree, but probably never in any absolute or classical scientific conception of the word, as Laplace posited. Meaning is created only when a difference makes such a difference to the living system that it must make signs, join a group of communicating observers, and produce a meaningful world.

The semantic capacity of living systems (the ability to assign meaning to differences perturbing the system's self-organization) seems to be a prerequisite for the phenomena of cognition, communication, language, and consciousness. The capacity of living systems to anticipate seems intricately connected with their ability to observe and perceive meanings by reducing complexity through signification. The phenomenon of imprinting in ducks is the standard example of programmed anticipation; so also are some of the complicated mechanisms behind the way birds learn to sing. These anticipations are expectations of meaning and order related to the signification sphere that an organism constructs as its individual world. On this basis, events that perpetuate the living (autopoietic) system are reduced to meaning – that is, as related to the survival and procreation of the individual living system.

Thus it is no mystery that the electronic manipulation of human language has been the most complicated task of all and has crushed the dreams of classical hard AI. It has therefore become essential to discover the most important differences between the ways in which computers and living systems process signs. Recently, research in ethology and biological information systems has been united through the founding of biosemiotics as a field of study. Both biosemiotics and Lakoff and Johnson's cognitive semantics demonstrate the essential role in signification and categorization played by the body and its perceptual motivation. Computers do not – yet? – possess inner and outer sensations. When we place a computer in a robot that has sensors, we are making the first move in this direction, but those robots are still far from autopoietic.

Cybersemiotics is a transdisciplinary map for cognition and communication science. It is a metaframe that encompasses the research programs of information theory, information science, Luhmann's cybernetics system science, cognitive science (the information processing paradigm as well as cognitive semantics), Peircean biosemiotics, pragmatic linguistics, and language game theory.

My basic method in this book will be to heed the wishes, dreams, and ideologies of these programs, in the hope of achieving their common goal of a unified information science. I will connect these programs within the new cybersemiotic framework and thereby provide new inter- and transdisciplinary connections in a way that does not reduce all cognitive and informational processes to information processes without meaning.

I will be analysing the benefits and shortcomings of each theory as well as synthesizing their most useful materials. I will then broaden the resulting synthesis to develop a more comprehensive philosophical framework – constructed on the basis of Peirce's semiotic philosophy – having adapted and reconstructed the relevant philosophical background.

To bridge the physicochemical, the biological, the psychological, and the social levels, I will be developing new semiotic concepts. 'Intrasemiotics' will refer to the process of interpenetration between the biological and the psychological autopoiesis. 'Phenosemiotics' will refer to the non-conceptualized psychological processes. 'Thought semiotics' will refer to the conceptualized self-aware psychological process generated when the silent psyche and the conceptual and symbolic language system of socio-communication interpenetrate. 'Signification sphere' will refer to the world of meaningful semiotic relations for living systems (a semiotic version of Uexküll's *Umwelt* concept). 'Information' will refer to what Peirce would have called protosemiotic processes that have not yet achieved the full-fledged triadic state of genuine signs. Regarding computers, information will be referred to as 'quasi-semiotic' to the extent that it is created by semiotic beings.

Next, I suggest a new, five-level ontological perspective that combines Peirce with modern science, information science, and the humanities:

1. The first level is that of quantum vacuum fields and their entangled causality. But the fields are not considered physically dead, as is usually the case in physicalistic physics. Cybersemiotics conceives this first level as a part of Firstness, which also holds qualia and pure feeling.
2. The second level of efficient causation is clearly what Peirce describes as Secondness. This realm is ontologically dominated by physics as classical kinematics and thermodynamics. But for Peirce it is also the willpower of mind.
3. The third level of information is where the formal causation manifests itself clearly and where regularities and Thirdness become crucial for interactions through stable patterns. In ontological terms, this level is dominated by the chemical sciences.
4. At the fourth level, life has organized itself, and the actual semiotic interactions emerge, at first internally in multicellular organisms as 'endosemiotics' and between organisms as 'sign games.'
5. Finally, at the fifth level of syntactic language games, human self-consciousness emerges, and with that rationality, logical thinking, and creative inferences (intelligence). Intelligence is closely connected to abduction and conscious finality. Abduction is crucial to signification. It is the ability to see something as a sign for something else.

This book is based on the papers listed earlier. It represents the current state of my theory as I have developed it over the years. The material has been revised and rearranged, and no chapter is linkable to any specific article. I end here my overview of the problem to be dealt with and the direction the analysis and synthesis will take. The following chapters will develop the analysis and argument in more detail.

1 The Problems of the Information-Processing Paradigm as a Candidate for a Unified Science of Information

1.1 The Conflict between Informational and Semiotic Paradigms

Two key strategies for gaining a systematic transdisciplinary under-standing of the 'laws' of information, cognition, signification and com-munication are the informational and the semiotic. Each is transdisci-plinary and universal in scope, but they approach the basic ideas of information, cognition, and communication from different angles. Nöth (1995, 34) writes about the relationship between the common sense and the mechanical uses of the information concept: 'Informa-tion in its everyday sense is a qualitative concept associated with mean-ing and news. However, in the theory of information, it is a technical term, which describes only quantifiable aspects of messages. Informa-tion theory and semiotics have goals of similar analytic universality: Both study messages of any kind, but because of its strictly quantitative approach, information theory is much more restrictive in its scope.'

In this book I deal with the technical-theoretic concepts, because my focus is on scientific and theoretical developments and their ability to produce comprehensive and consistent knowledge. In this chapter I describe the conflict between informational and semiotic approaches to cognition and communication. I point to crucial differences between the metaphysical frameworks underlying the pan-informational and the pan-semiotic paradigms. These differences impede the work of building a transdisciplinary framework in the search for a theoretical apparatus able to encompass the concepts of law and meaning, the quantitative and the qualitative, science and the humanities. I will then apply this discussion to some basic practical problems of subject searching in library and information science (LIS). This – and the discussion that has been going on within LIS for decades – will constitute my first effort to highlight the practical consequences, limits, and problems of the universal theory of objective information as the foundation for cognition and communication science and the basis for LIS practises and information technologies.

This universal theory is often referred to as the 'information processing paradigm.' It is built on an objective information concept combined with an approach to computation that is generally algorithmic. The information processing paradigm prevailing in cognitive science is mechanistic and rationalistic. It is also the predominate approach in this transdisciplinary area, which is dominated by computer science and informatics and thus is very important for the development of technology. In the analysis that follows, I demonstrate that the logical and mechanistic approach cannot by itself offer an understanding of human signification and its roots in biological, psychological, and social relationships. I then confront the ontological and epistemological problems of the idea of 'information science' by discussing information concepts and paradigms that are based on other basic epistemological and ontological theories.

In discussing the possibility of a universal information science (which must include a universal science of communication and cognition), it is important to analyse the nature of subject areas that a universal information science must combine, such as physics, biology, social science, the humanities, library and information science, computer science, cybernetics, communication, and linguistics. The strategy for developing an information science was then to extract various aspects of information, knowledge, perception, and intelligence from the earlier philosophical traditions and their ruminations on phenomenology, qualia, consciousness, meaning and signification, epistemology, and ontology, and from there develop an 'efficient' objective science called cognitive science.[1] Such an approach is an attempt to release us from more than two thousand years of philosophical discussions on cognition, signification, and meaning, by turning the subject into an empirical science.

Many information 'scientists' would contend that it is precisely the restrictions imposed by the scientific approach that make it possible to construct a universal theory of information and cognition. In their view, the qualitative phenomenological and pragmatic approach of semiotics seems to make it unsuitable for the sciences, which at present are grounded in either mechanistic atomistic determinism or in some type of Gibbs probabilistic complexity theory (see Hayles's analysis [1999,

88–90] of Wiener's theoretical foundation; see also Prigogine and Stengers 1984).

I will be treating these differences as general philosophical and methodological problems for the study of information, cognition, signification, and communication as a transdisciplinary field. These problems are fundamental to the entire field. A basic question raised in this book is whether the functionalistic and cybernetic research program of information and cognitive sciences must be viewed as complementary to a phenomenological-hermeneutical-semiotic line of theorizing on signification and meaning that ignores ontological questions outside culture, or whether these might be united within one paradigmatic framework through a revision of the ontological and epistemological foundations of both classical and modern science, as Peirce attempts.

1.2 Wienerian: Pan-Information

Pan-information philosophy is based on a functional-quantitative information concept that amounts to an advance on the work of Shannon, who conceives of information as entropy (Shannon and Weaver 1969). Shannon posits that functional communication is based on a pre-established code with a limited number of possible outcomes of signs. However, this combinatorial freedom imposes no limits on interpretation – for instance, the Morse alphabet's interpretations of the Latin alphabet can be combined into innumerable words and sentences. Shannon defined information as a probability function without any dimension. Thus the most surprising information I could send over a telegraph using the Morse code would be a random sequence of letters. Information increases as the probability of the event occurring becomes smaller, because the greater is the uncertainty it reduces in the mind. Put simply, information is a choice that reduces uncertainty.

Essentially, the mathematical theory of information defines information as merely the statistical property of a message, irrespective of its meaning. Information is seen as a selection among signals. In information theory, a signal contains information when it excludes the occurrence of other signals that could have occurred instead. The quantification of information depends on the number of excluded alternatives and the probability with which a signal can be expected to occur. The informational value of a signal is calculated as the probability that it will occur in a message. What counts is the statistical rarity of signs – or rather, codes. Shannon's information theory, when applied in a broader scientific sense, presumes that signals are meaningful codes established in a system of signs, such as the Morse code for the alphabet, that makes sense to humans. Here we can relate this information concept to the quantitative side of meaningful communication without addressing the presupposed meaning that makes the calculation worth doing.

In the Wienerian approach followed by Schrödinger, and later by Bateson and Stonier, information is not viewed as entropy, but rather as neg-entropy. Entropy is viewed as disorder; it follows that it makes much more sense to understand information as negative entropy, which can then be seen as order or organization. Accordingly, information is a pattern in an otherwise random and complex world view. This information theory is structurally based and is connected to thermodynamics through the concept of neg-entropy, which Schrödinger advocated strongly in *What Is Life?* ([1944] 1967). Schrödinger introduced the idea that information was necessary to explain heredity and life as a physical phenomen. The belief that 'information is information, not matter nor energy,' which Wiener ([1948] 1961, 132) expounded in his foundational book on cybernetics, as well as the analogy between information and thermodynamic neg-entropy, supports the contention that the links between matter and mind are informational. The presumed mind-like aspect of information is fused here with the matter-like aspect of thermodynamics. And this is accomplished through a kind of neutral monistic philosophy of the matter–mind relation. This may also provide support for the possibility of real artificial intelligence (AI). Chalmers (1996) develops this notion, but contrary to most, Chalmers takes the phenomenological aspect of consciousness seriously. The question of why and how first-person experience exists in nature Chalmers calls 'the hard question.' I agree with Chalmers' analysis that we have to accept consciousness as an irreducible aspect of nature – and culture as well. The ability to have sense experiences and to be able to distinguish between qualitatively different ones (qualia) – sweet and sour, hot and cold, red and green – is basic to knowledge, understanding, communication, and intelligent reasoning. In his influential book Chalmers, through his use of the information concept beyond functionalism and computationalism, allows for a kind of panpsychism. I will argue that he needs to add Peirce's semiotic philosophy to his theory in order to do that. Wiener, however, and the cyberneticians after him up to Bateson, does not even recognize this problem.

In Stonier's further development of Wiener's theory (1997), neg-entropy becomes the organizational power of creating structures and systems in nature. It is a kind of organizing power that starts with the elementary 'infon particle' – the existence of which he postulates – and that finally emerges as the human brain with its powers of meaningful cognition and communication. Stonier does not discuss at length the place of mind in his informational philosophy; mind, however, is visible in his discussion of how new qualities evolve as a series of emergences. He describes emergence in a systemic view as the 'wholeness' quality of new systems, a quality that supersedes the qualities of individual elements. The integration of these elements into a new system creates new entities, the qualities of which are more than the sum of their parts. It is a supervenience principle, but it does not say anything specific about how the system can suddenly experience qualia.

Many researchers today use von Bertalanffy's ([1968] 1976) general systems theory without reflecting on its origins in organismic ontology. When we analyse systematic theories for ontological presumptions, we can see implicit physicalistic concepts (Walter et al. 2003) such as Stonier's, or organismic views such as Sally Goerner's (1993), which are quite distinct. But one can at least argue that the modern systems' vision of an all-embracing information science seems to be based on an approach to evolutionary systems that combines matter, energy, and information as objective ontological components in an emergent dynamics scientifically based on (among other things) non-equilibrium thermodynamics as described for instance in Prigogine's work. But many researchers on systems and cybernetics then go much further in an effort to explain qualia, life, and consciousness as emergent phenomena in the evolutionary process undergone by material, energetic, and informational systems. My view is that much theory in systems research, cybernetics, and information science rests on cloudy metaphysics and for that reason often results in some vague type of functionalism that does not take a clear stand on first-person experience, the qualia of perception and emotions, and the problem of free will. Most likely this is because these subjects are outside what is usually taken seriously in the scientific enterprise. Many researchers with a scientific-technical background deny the reality of Chalmers' 'hard problem.'

Modern versions of the pan-informational paradigm often combine functionalism with non-equilibrium thermodynamics, non-linear systems dynamics, deterministic chaos theory, and fractal mathematics as descriptive tools. But again, we seldom encounter systematic reflec-

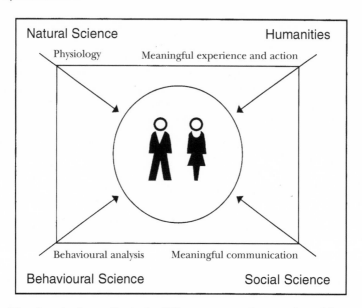

1.1. The four basic qualitatively different approaches to the subject areas of human cognition and communication, often collected under the broad concept of 'psychology.'

tions on how these versions differ from mechanistic views (except on the reality of randomness) or on the nature of a concept of meaning and how signification arises in minds. This is a general philosophical problem in psychology and cognitive science. At least two of the methodologies in the fields of human behaviour, thinking and communication presume that humans are meaning-producing systems (see Figure 1.1). These two are the phenomenological and hermeneutical qualitative approaches in the humanities and the social sciences – approaches in which one can also place hermeneutics as the socially reflected study of text interpretation.[2]

In Figure 1.1 the sharp differences between the scientific approaches on the left side and the phenomenological–hermeneutical approaches on the right continue to fuel the debate over whether psychology can ever establish itself as one science. Cognitive science and the information processing paradigm are two attempts that ignore the problems of meaning addressed by phenomenology, hermeneutics, and semiotics.

1.3 Peircean-Based Pan-Semiotics

The past twenty years have seen the development of a semiotic and communicational paradigm largely based on Peirce's 'semiotics, that is, the
doctrine of the essential nature and fundamental varieties of possible
semiosis' (CP, 5.448). Semiotics develops a general theory of all possible
kinds of signs, their modes of signification and information, and whole
behaviour and properties. It studies the existence of meaningful communication in living and social systems, and it looks to cultural historical dynamics and evolutionary ecology for explanations of the dynamics
of signification and communication. Peirce founded semiotics as a
logical and scientific study of dynamic sign action in humans – in their
language, science, religion, and other cultural products – as well as
signs in non-human nature. In the form of biosemiotics (Sebeok 1976,
1989), this view is now penetrating biology as an alternative to both
mechanistic and purely system-dynamical explanations. Work has been
undertaken in biology (Hoffmeyer and Emmeche 1991), organic chemistry, and pure physics (Christiansen 1995).

From Peirce's semiotic philosophy, we can construct a pan-semiotic
philosophy by extracting a few key quotations. The first pertains to
the ontological question of the basic elements of reality: 'The entire
universe is perfused with signs, if it is not composed exclusively of
signs' (CP, 5.448n). In other words, when we think, we never have
access to the thing in itself, but only to the way it appears to us
through signs. Since we are living in a 'semiosphere' (Hoffmeyer
1997) in our individual and collective 'signification spheres,'[3] we
never get 'behind' the signs to 'reality.' So why not admit that signs
are the only reality we will ever know? Even humans are only signs. As
Peirce writes: 'For, as the fact that every thought is a sign, taken in
conjunction with the fact that life is a train of thought, proves that
man is a sign; so, that every thought is an external sign, proves that
man is an external sign. That is to say, the man and the external sign
are identical, in the same sense in which the words homo and man
are identical. Thus my language is the sum total of myself; for the
man is the thought' (CP, 5.318).

Accordingly, semiotics becomes the fundamental doctrine and philosophy to grasp knowing and reality. Yet for signs to work as cognitive
tools, there must be a basic precoupling between the organism and the
environment. One has to know where to look and what to look for in
order to obtain further information from a sign: 'The sign can only rep-

resent the object and tell about it. It cannot furnish acquaintance with a recognition of that object ... It presupposes an acquaintance in order to convey some further information concerning it' (CP, 2.231).

The problem is whether this acquaintance presupposes certain pre-semiotic experiences, as does much of hermeneutic philosophy. Regardless, in semiotics, meaning and signification do not have much to do with informational bits. The phenomenological theory established in Peirce's semiotics underscores the fact that qualia are at least as important as the quantitative selection and measuring of bits.

In Peirce's triadic philosophy,[4] feelings, qualia, habit formation, and signification are basic ontological constituents of reality. This suggests that the semiotic paradigm should be able to penetrate beyond chemistry and physics to 'the bottom of nature.' This amounts to a clash with basic beliefs in sizable parts of information science, which seems to want to construct meaning as a bottom-up procedure from a thermodynamically based information science.

We seem to have two very distinct points of departure for these theories, both of which aim to be universal. The difference between the two paradigms is fundamental. The information paradigm is based on an objective, quantitative information concept and works with algorithmic models of perception, cognition, and communication. Semiotics, in contrast, is based in human language's meaningful communication and is phenomenological as well as dependent on a theory of meaning.

One way to approach the problem is to view the pan-informational paradigm as a 'bottom-up' explanation and the pan-semiotic paradigm as a 'top-down' explanation. One could further combine this with an epistemological perspective, which suggests that no final reductive scientific explanations can be given to anything in this world, including the behaviours of organisms. All we have are complementary explanations that work well in different situations. We can never attain a full view. Accordingly, it may be impossible to unite the two paradigms by manipulating basic definitions into unifying compromises (see Figure 1.2).

One of the consequences of this is that concepts of meaning and the objective statistical information concept are defined within two distinct paradigms. This makes the informational aspect of communication as an objective and quantifiable entity completely independent of any meaningful interpretation by the recipient and any intent on the part of the sender. In linguistics this opposition is seen from the perspective of ana-

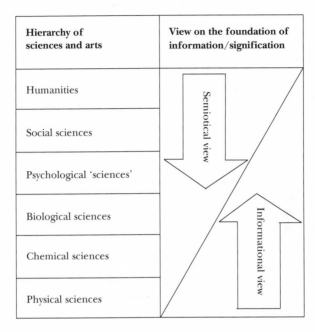

Hierarchy of sciences and arts	View on the foundation of information/signification
Humanities	
Social sciences	
Psychological 'sciences'	
Biological sciences	
Chemical sciences	
Physical sciences	

1.2.   The relevance of the bottom-up informational view and the top-down semiotic view in the area of the foundation of information science. On the left is a hierarchy of sciences and their objects, from physics to the humanities. On the right is an illustration of the two most common 'scientific' schemas for understanding and predicting communicative and organizational behaviour: (1) the semiotic top-down paradigm of signification, cognition, and communication, and (2) the informational bottom-up functionalistic view of organization, signal transmission, and AI. The width of the two paradigms in correlation with the various subject areas serves as an estimate of how the relevance of the paradigm is generally considered, although both claim to encompass the entire spectrum.

lytical philosophy, which perceives semantics as a question of the representational truth function of a token, whereas pragmatic linguistics posits that meaning arises from the use of signs and words in real-life situations. For instance, Wittgenstein (1958) showed the intricate dynamic connection that must exist between the life form (as a kind of practice) and language games in order to establish meaningful relationships. Thus it seems fair to say that both for humans and for animals, context, motivation, and anticipation are crucial elements in the cognition of something as meaningful. Some kind of 'Eigenvalue'[5] must establish itself and connect with a habit of living. For anything to appear as a relatively stable object, there must be a complex interplay between biological evolutionary dynamics and social-historical processes of meaning. It is a delicate process to establish a perceptual object or category, as Lakoff (1987) demonstrates in a perspective he calls 'experiential cognitive semantics,' which he bases on the internal realism described by Hilary Putnam (1992). I will analyse this perspective more thoroughly later.

The opposition between the two paradigms has another important aspect. It amounts to a confrontation between the scientific and objectivistic realistic views of knowledge and science and the phenomenological–hermeneutic–humanistic approach to meaning, signification, and communication. We shall explore this problem and a possible solution in later chapters. As I shall discuss later, it is also debatable whether Peirce himself was actually a pan-semiotician in the way defined above.

Having provided a theoretical sketch of the problem to be analysed in detail below, let us turn to the concrete example of the problems involved in developing a unified information science. I will now analyse the difficulties faced by library and information science (LIS) when it comes to constructing a user-friendly system for mediating electronic documents – especially for information retrieval (IR) – by applying the cognitive information processing paradigm. The main problem with this paradigm is that its concept of information and language does not systematically address how social and cultural dynamics determine the meaning of those signs and words, which are LIS's basic tools for organizing and retrieving documents. Furthermore, the paradigm does not distinguish clearly between how computers manipulate signs and how meaning is generated in autopoietic systems.

1.4 The Document-Mediating System

The past three decades have seen the extremely rapid development of technologies for information and document retrieval. This has spurred developments in the field of librarianship for constructing formal theories of document retrieval (often called information retrieval)[6] to take advantage of these new technologies. Huge international databases – largely in the sciences – have been developed. These are oriented towards documentation specialists and include FX, Chemical Abstracts, BIOSIS, Medline, and Compendex. For a variety of reasons – among them the economic interest in attracting more users and the growing exposure to non-specialists through the Internet – the next phase has been to make these highly technical and specialized systems accessible to users with no special training in either librarianship or the sciences. User interfaces with the retrieval systems are having to be changed if the original ones presuppose user knowledge of classification and indexing principles and of the scientific organization of the subject areas. So the goal recently has been to establish general principles to guide cognition and retrieval of information by the human mind through natural language. The idea is to organize the retrieval process in a natural way so as to make the enormous number of documents produced internationally widely available.

The main expertise of librarians, archivists, and documentalists has always been the storage, indexing, retrieval, and mediation of materials carrying data, knowledge, meaning, and experience. First and foremost, the objective of information science is to promote communication. This can include recorded measurements and observations, theoretical knowledge, and meanings and visions or experiences, through media such as documents, books, records, tapes, programs,[7] floppy disks, hypertext, compact discs, pictures, films, and videograms. These mediating forms (and future ones) can be summarized under the general LIS concept of a 'document' (see, for example, Vickery and Vickery 1987; Buckland 1991). Following Buckland's discussion, I will define a document as a human work with communicative intent directed towards other human beings and that is recorded in a material way.

For librarians and documentalists, information science is primarily concerned with finding the most suitable rules for the design of systems and procedures for collecting, organizing, classifying, indexing, storing, retrieving, and mediating those materials which support data, knowledge, meaning, and experience. Librarians, documentalists, and archivists have done this for thousands of years.

As an offshoot of both indexing and communication to users with different requirements, one must study the origins of the various document types, how they are produced, for which users, and under what economic constraints. It is recognized that producers of documents generally have specific consumers in mind, and these consumers can often be manufacturers themselves. In this way the system closes in

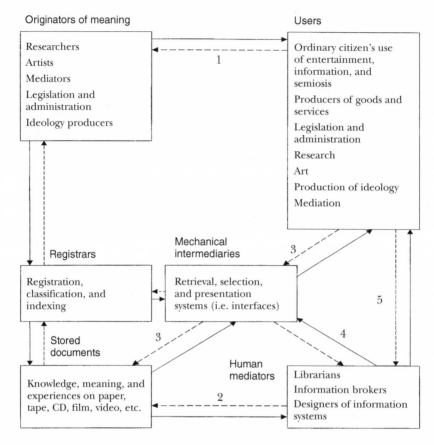

1.3. The document-mediating information system as a self-organizing cybersemiotic system with semantic feedback. The unbroken arrows are document transport. The broken arrows are feedback in the form of approval or critique of the contents of documents or of system performance. 1. The direct circulation of documents between producer and user is often seen in the sciences with preprints. 2. The direct access of librarians to a collection. 3. End user's access directly through online systems. 4. The librarian as mediator of the collection through mechanical (electronic) intermediaries. 5. An information broker's mediation of documents to a user.

upon itself, as Luhmann (1995) underlines for communication systems in general, and then cannot see its surrounding society and culture directly. But it does react to perturbations and changes in the production and use of document types through internal adjustment. This is shown in Figure 1.3, in which the broken arrows represent a structure or result-changing feedback that is vital for the system's self-organizing ability and its ability to survive through self-adjustment.

This is one of the developments – along with the development of cognitive science – that promoted the idea of a unified information science for humans, machines, and animals (see for instance Vickery and Vickery 1988). As mentioned earlier, the hope of cognitive science is that information processing will follow certain 'universal syntactic, logical and mathematical laws' (Fodor 1987).

One should reflect on the fact that nearly everything, aside from computer programs found on the Internet and in all management information systems, is a document. Therefore this problem is very general and has massive proportions. It is no wonder that Google has outgrown Microsoft! The first goal is to make intelligent user interfaces. The second is to reorganize databases. The latter does not seem practical or economically feasible for most of the huge international scientific bibliographic databases, since each is built with a rigid scientific classification or thesaurus that controls its indexing practices. Furthermore, they house millions of documents that are already indexed.

1.5 The Technological Impetus for the Development of Information Science

Information science did not really take off until the development of computer technology in the 1960s and its increasing use as information technology in the LIS domain. From society's point of view, the primary problem has been how to handle cheaply and constructively the burgeoning production of documents from science, industry, and culture. In industrial terms, the aim has been to develop a technology for increasing access to knowledge (that is, the buying and selling of it); information is becoming a strategic resource on a level with capital, technology, and labour.

The information retrieval industry has become a large-scale industry in the so-called information society. The computer and communication industry has exploded since the Second World War and is now entering a synthetic phase. The computer's various technologies – including telecommunication, language, and calculation technology – and more recently its sound and image technologies, are beginning to merge into a multimedia interaction technology.

It seems clear that document retrieval – which includes registration, indexing, and classification technologies – is playing a growing and inescapable role in academe; in design, development, and construction (CAD, CAM); in landscape planning (GIS); in management information systems (MISs); and in all kinds of knowledge-sharing systems. The larger these systems become, the more central the document-mediating component will become and the more serious the problem of indexing and intellectual access.

As Blair (1990) has pointed out, there is a qualitative shift in the problem of document retrieval once databases exceed 100,000 documents. First, the sheer number of retrieved documents becomes a problem: there are too many documents to sort for relevance. Second, the level of 'noise' becomes intolerable, especially for full-text documents indexed automatically in natural language. Third, it becomes nearly impossible to know what degree of relevance really exists in a base with 15 million documents, such as BIOSIS.

On the one hand, the user is buried in too many documents of different levels of relevance and knowledge quality. On the other, the user may miss the most relevant documents – the ones especially suited to the user's problems, interests, knowledge background, focus, knowledge level, and time for reading. Anyone who has made a subject search on the Internet understands what I am referring to.

The Internet is improving physical access to information in electronic documents for growing numbers of people; it is also increasing intellectual access for many first-time and occasional users of document systems. But access to high-quality documents is becoming a growing problem for those who rely on it in their daily work: researchers, teachers, journalists, and managers. Overload, noise, lack of precision, and ignorance of recall are modern problems of document retrieval. The crucial document is either not found or is buried in the noise of too many hits.

One way to improve intellectual access is to create interfaces for users who have domain knowledge but who lack LIS-technical skills. Menu-driven systems are a big help here, but they are seldom as quick and sophisticated as the command-driven systems that utilize classification and indexing. These difficult cognitive and communicative problems are connected to providing access to users who lack knowledge in the pertinent field and who therefore do not know the specialized meanings of the terms being employed, some of which are the same as those used in everyday language.

There is no question that technological developments are transforming traditional LIS areas of document retrieval and knowledge mediation. So constructive ways must be found to respond to the challenge. This will require an approach rooted in science that encompasses the technical, sociological, psychological, and linguistic aspects of the problem of how to translate people's information needs into system-functional queries. This is a serious problem for the traditional, system-driven approach to IR, which is based on the Cranfield experiments using fixed queries. Ingwersen (1996, 22) writes: 'The classical main-stream research setting has constantly been geared to make available and test isolated techniques for the retrieval of *simulated* static and well-defined information needs, founded on an assumption of total cogni-tive stability regarding knowledge state, problem, work task and domains.' The earliest research on electronic bibliographic bases involved testing the ability of various precisely formulated queries to retrieve documents in the test databases that were known to be relevant. As explained above, these conditions no longer reflect reality: they are far from the current social reality of information seeking.

In the same paper, Ingwersen describes several types of searchers and the differences in their search behaviours and responses to different types of feedback. More than ever, it is becoming necessary to work with real users and their behaviours with regard to judging relevance. It is now widely recognized within IR that tests must be performed with real users on larger databases (Blair 1990).[8] Warner (1990, 18) summarizes: 'The experimental simulation, under artificially isolated conditions, of such activities as information retrieval rests on an unproven, and ques-tionable, assumption that there will be a direct correspondence be-tween the performance of information retrieval systems under experi-mental, and under operational, conditions. Such scientific models for investigation have not yielded convincing explanations, with predictive value, of information behavior. 'Information man' remains a shadowy and unreal figure.'

Like 'economic man,' 'information man' is a fiction used for simpli-fying for a computer's sake the social-communicative characteristics of humans. What we need is an interdisciplinary conceptualization of the problem area; from, this we will then have to develop conceptualization methods to ensure that all important aspects of the design of document-mediating systems and other types of information systems have been addressed.

Judging from the past twenty years of computer systems development, it is clear that the manipulation of natural language by machines in a social-communicative setting with humans poses major theoretical and practical problems. Language is at the very core of human existence. When a traditional mechanistic perspective is taken, it is practically impossible to understand how the meanings of signs and words become fixed within a social and cultural practice. Attempts to build interdisciplinary information sciences on the basis of the entropic conceptions of information in information theory and thermodynamics have in both theory and practice been unable to solve the problem of how humans communicate meaning. The functionalist (or information processing) paradigm in cognitive science faces this additional difficulty: how to provide a theoretical background for approaching the problems that IR has with words and sentences that have multiple meanings. Because documents are complex semantic sign and language systems, they are some of the most difficult items to handle in computer systems designed for a broad public's retrieval needs. As Blair (1990) argues, users are the only reliable sources when it comes to judging relevance, and only users can turn information into knowledge.

No doubt, the development of interactive and graphic interfaces could improve search quality for occasional users. But something more fundamental to our scientific understanding of document-mediating systems is at stake: the qualitative difference in the way computers and humans deal with the complexity of information. As Luhmann (1995) points out, humans reduce complexity through meaning. If it is to improve the design of document-mediating systems, LIS must move away from a mechanistic, information-processing understanding of document retrieval based on only cognitive science's information processing paradigm, towards true integration with a more pragmatically semiotic, cybernetic, and socio-linguistic theory of understanding. The theoretical foundations of LIS in the field of IR must be replaced by a broader foundation that incorporates the semantic production of meaning.

To summarize, LIS faces four major problems:

1. The lack of a theory on how to design the best possible document-mediating system for one or more well-known user groups.
2. The lack of a theory on how to design interfaces for non-specialists for huge document bases originally created for documentalists within certain subject areas or domains, most often scientific and technical such as chemistry, biology, and medicine.
3. The lack of full recognition from computer and software designers, and from the arts and sciences, of the interdisciplinary complexity and scientific depth of the problems of document mediation.

4. The lack of a full theoretical scientific foundation for the practice of librarianship in the age of the computer. The lack of a fully developed theoretical and scientific self-awareness is a problem for LIS, as it hinders recognition by other scientific subjects and research groups of the seriousness of the problems it addresses and the depth of the knowledge it has already acquired through centuries of practice.

1.6 The Development of the Information Processing Paradigm in Cognitive Science

At present, much effort is being spent on information systems research, based on a desire to acquire the general user's money. I am thinking here of the organization and design of databases and database hosts. It is precisely this attempt to gain the broadest end-user group that has led information science to work on AI and cognitive science. Unfortunately, the intensive development of the 'user-friendly' computer has diverted attention from users' needs and requirements. This resembles the early days of flight, when passengers were pleased to be able to fly at all and pilots were heroes: LIS developers of information technology have become standard bearers.

For a long time, this meant that in IR there was typically a computer-based systematic research tradition that was unconnected to the user-oriented social research tradition. These traditions had great difficulty in uniting, because they defined their research objects and ideals of science very differently.

Cognitive science's theory of general mechanisms or programs in nervous systems and computers that control the manipulation of symbols and meanings in rational communication was an interdisciplinary attempt to bridge this gap (see, for example, Ingwersen 1992). A common theory of information processing in humans, machines, and nature was sought. Such a theory would have implications for the theoretical formulation that information science could achieve. LIS is an interdisciplinary, complex, and somewhat fragmented domain, and one that is striving to build a common identity and a functional paradigm to compete with other areas of information science.

Figure 1.4 depicts the complexity of cognitive and informational processes from the perspective of LIS. When Ingwersen places epistemology on an equal footing with other sciences, we encounter a number of researchers' ambitions to solve some of the fundamental philosophical questions in the LIS domain. Also, it is worth noting that information science can be understood as a subset of cognitive science, in Ingwersen's view. Thus it is assumed that it falls within this research program, with its information processing paradigm, and that the central questions are formulated in this context. But researchers from biology, chemistry, and physics also contend that their subjects contribute to and are part of information science.

Cognitive science as a research program found its calling in the 1970s, but even before then, in the postwar years, it was an element in the scientific dissemination of the humanities. 'Cognitive science' means the 'science of cognition' – that is, the science of epistemological processes. The very name reflects the hope that the sciences can wrest parts of epistemology away from philosophy, as has been the case in other areas – such as psychology – that over time have been diverted from philosophy.

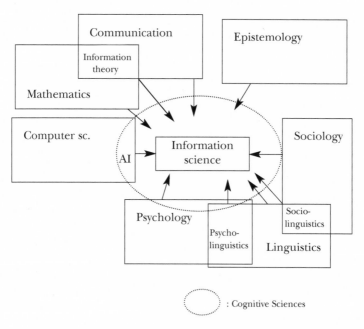

1.4. Information science seen as a part of cognitive science (Ingwersen 1992, 7)

Originally, cognitive science was a logical, natural-science-oriented, interdisciplinary research program. It included philosophy of language, formal language, linguistics, artificial intelligence, information and communication sciences, brain research, parts of anthropology, and the natural science areas of psychology such as the neurosciences. The computer was both its tool and its research model.

Cognitive science thus refers to a research program that attempts to reveal the laws of cognition, thought, and conduct in the human individual, with the computer as its paradigm. It is based on concepts established in the first-order cybernetics of Norbert Wiener and the von Neumann computer that led to AI and expert systems. It is founded on statistical information theory and on Wiener's version of the statistical information concept, which fuses information theory with thermodynamics to arrive at a general concept of objective information (Stonier 1990). The fusion of Wiener's objective information theory with the algorithmic thinking of AI is the conceptual foundation of the 'information processing paradigm' that currently dominates cognitive science. Now that behaviourism has fallen from grace, cognitive science is scientific rationality's newest and most powerful attempt to achieve a firm footing for a science of knowledge. Gardner (1985, 6, 8) writes:

> I define cognitive science as a contemporary based effort to answer long-standing epistemological questions – particularly those concerned with the nature of knowledge, its components, its sources, its development, and its deployment.
>
> Approaching these fields from a methodological point of view, I raise the questions whether philosophy will eventually come to be supplanted by an empirically based cognitive science and whether anthropology can (or even should) ever transcend the individual case study.

A fairly recently published textbook of library and information science (Vickery and Vickery 1989, 43) states, like Stonier, that information is as fundamental to reality as matter and energy. The authors see nature as full of information. There is no doubt that here, Vickery and Vickery are promoting a world view in which information is more fundamental than the observer because energy, matter, and information are the basic elements of reality. Visions of the world as a giant computer are also becoming more common.

In this information 'metaphysics,' energy, matter, and information are mutually joined concepts that explain the emergence, formation, structure, and dynamics of mind and knowledge. Accordingly, natural objective information must have been present before living beings and human minds arose from the expanding universe. Information is much more fundamental than the observer or interpreter.

From the mechanistic scientific perspective, knowledge is eternal and universal mathematical laws control all movement. Furthermore, the sciences have and will grant us access to the fundamental natural laws underlying all matter, information, and intelligence. This theory posits that life, consciousness, humans, and language are by-products, whose creation and function science will be able to explain 'in the long run' through the study of evolution, genes, cognition, and intelligence. Adding the Wienerian cybernetic information theory to the mechanical scientific ideology[9] would thus seem to promote a scientific totalitarianism in which philosophy, cosmology, and epistemology are wrested from philosophy – as Gardner hints at in the above quotation – and then become a total science formulated in 'nature's own language': mathematics.

Information is viewed as an objective and universal law-determined thing that both humans and machines absorb into their minds from nature, change by thinking, and bring into society through language. So it must be possible to establish a unifying science of information. To do so, however, one would need to explain human mind, intelligence, and meaningful communication in terms of information or consciousness and meaning as real or as the reality of first-person consciousness. Information science would then also include cognitive science, and all epistemological problems could be solved empirically. It is this development – along with the development of the cognitive science(s) – that promoted the idea of a unified information science for humans, machines, and animals (the Vickerys and Stonier also include all other natural systems and thereby declare themselves true pan-informationalists).

The basic idea of cognitive science is that information processing follows certain universal syntactic, logical, and mathematical laws. This is the foundation for cognitive science as originally developed by Leibniz. Gardner aptly summarizes the basic goals and beliefs of cognitive science:

> First of all, there is the belief that, in talking about human cognitive activities, it is necessary to speak about mental representations and to posit a level of analysis wholly separate from the biological or neurological, on the one hand, and the sociological or cultural, on the other.

Second, there is the faith that central to any understanding of the human mind is the electronic computer. Not only are computers indispensable for carrying out studies of various sorts, but, more crucially, the computer also serves as the most viable model of how the human mind functions ...

The third feature of cognitive science is the deliberate decision to de-emphasize certain factors, which may be important for cognitive functioning but whose inclusion at this point would unnecessarily complicate the cognitive-scientific enterprise. These factors include the influence of affective factors or emotions, the contribution of historical and cultural factors, and the role of the background context in which particular actions or thoughts occur.

As a fourth feature, cognitive scientists harbor the faith that much is to be gained from interdisciplinary studies ...

A fifth and somewhat more controversial feature is the claim that a key ingredient in contemporary cognitive science is the agenda of issues, and the set of concerns, which have long exercised epistemologists in the Western philosophical tradition.

Feelings and cultural context are not essential, the model for cognition is the algorithmic machine, and the goal is for epistemology and cognition to be understood as aspects of 'human information processing.' This is the title of Lindsay and Norman's widely used textbook on psychology, which is supportive of cognitive science. In their view (1977, 579), 'nevertheless, the principles of information processing are highly relevant to all systems that make use of information, including the human mind. The general principles of information processing must apply to all systems that manipulate, transform, compare, and remember information.' This will eventually become a new super-science: information science, which will restructure the whole field of knowledge. It will be a true science of sciences! And clearly, mechanical physics is its ideal of science. Stonier (1990, 112–13) writes about the need to develop a general theory of information based on a physicalistic paradigm (see, for instance, Walter and Heckmann 2003 for a description of the physicalist paradigm):

To create such a theory, we need to start with the most fundamental aspect of information. And the most fundamental aspect of information is not a construct of the human mind but a basic property of the universe. Any general theory of information must begin by studying the physical properties of information as they manifest themselves in the universe. This must be done before attempting to understand the various and much more complex forms of human information. The next step must involve an examination of the evolution of information systems beyond physical systems – first in biological, then in the human, cultural sphere.

In short, one can summarize the main epistemological and ontological assumption in the cognitive 'information processing paradigms' as follows (based on Fodor 1987; Gardner 1985; Lindsay and Norman 1977; Lakoff 1987;[10] Winograd and Flores 1986; Searle 1989; Warner 1994):

1. Different information systems such as humans, machines, animals, and organizations process information in the same way. What is crucial is not the hardware but the software. What is essential are the algorithms in the program that process information. This is the central idea in the information processing paradigm. It is often called *functionalism*, because it is the function, not the structure, that is crucial.
2. Conscious, logical thinking is generally taken as a model for cognitive processes. It does not consider intuitive and emotionally based sources for cognition.
3. Understanding is viewed as classical-categorical. The analytical-categorical of classical set theory is emphasized.
4. Cognitive processes can be broken down into component parts and finally into a series of linear choices. Perception is primarily categorical and denotative (concrete description) and organized as classical sets.
5. Learning happens according to rules and principles and primarily according to the construction of structures of knowledge.
6. A language system is primarily a formal mechanism for transferring information via symbol manipulation among humans, machines, and the human–machine.
7. The subject is primarily a cognitive subject, for which embodiment and emotions play a minor role.
8. The cognitive subject is analogous to the computer.
9. The mechanism behind memory, the growth of meaning, and the handling and understanding of symbols together constitute a so-called 'semantic network.' When one attempts to define the meaning of symbols and ideas lexically, this occurs with reference

to other symbols and conceptions in a logical way. Meaning thus hangs within a network of mutually defined conceptions: a so-called 'knowledge structure.' The cognitive perspective is in this way highly structural. This network is an effect of the aforementioned approaches and has a denotative and atomic character. It represents a formal entry into semantics. Put in another way, words are primarily context-free lexically described symbols.[11]

10. The emphasis on the syntactic-structural aspect in cognition, thought, and communication leads to a decreased interest in the cultural–societal and historical dimensions of the meaning of human cognition and communication. This clearly renders the social sciences, humanities, and arts much less important in finding the processes of the construction of meaning than most researchers in these domains themselves believe.

11. The meaning of language is primarily seen as the logical truth conditions of the mapping of the concepts of the contents of sentences upon the 'natural things or kinds' of the world. This approach stresses logical analysis and the idea that meaning is captured by so-called truth conditions. Determinations of truth tend to be based on a transcendental 'God's eye' view of knowledge.

The information processing paradigm thus attempts to integrate the development of intelligent computers with the psychological–societal understanding of the user's needs and know-how through a transdisciplinary framework. It follows that this integration occurs on the basis of a structural–syntactical understanding of language and knowledge as cognitive information structures. These structures are believed to be common to all cognitive systems, including those of computers. In the following, the functionalist Fodor (1987, 18–19) offers the essence of this theory, which he at this time[12] advocates:

> Here, in barest outline, is how the new story is supposed to go: You connect the causal properties of a symbol with its semantic properties *via its syntax*. The syntax of a symbol is one of its higher-order physical properties. To a metaphorical first approximation, we can think of the syntactic structure of a symbol as an abstract feature of its shape. Because, to all intents and purposes, syntax reduces to shape, and because the shape of a symbol is a potential determinant of its causal role, it is fairly easy to see how there could be environments in which the causal role of a symbol correlates with its syntax. It's easy, that is to say, to imagine symbol tokens interacting

causally *in virtue of* their syntactic structures. The syntax of a symbol might determine the causes and effects of its tokenings in much the way that the geometry of a key determines which locks it will open.

But, now, we know from modern logic that certain of the semantic relations among symbols can be, as it were, 'mimicked' by their syntactic relations; that, when seen from a very great distance, is what proof-theory is about. So, within certain famous limits, the semantic relation that holds between two symbols when the proposition expressed by the one is entailed by the proposition expressed by the other can be mimicked by syntactic relations in virtue of which one of the symbols is derivable from the other. We can therefore build machines which have, again within famous limits, the following property:

The operations of the machine consist entirely of transformations of symbols; in the course of performing these operations, the machine is sensitive solely to syntactic properties of the symbols; and the operations that the machine performs on the symbols are entirely confined to altering their shapes.

Yet the machine is so devised that it will transform one symbol into another if and only if the propositions expressed by the symbols that are so transformed stand in certain *semantic* relations – e.g., the relation that the premises bear to the conclusion in a valid argument.

This is a concentrated and clear expression of the basic beliefs of the information processing paradigm in the research program of cognitive science. It expresses what is also called 'the language of thought' theory. Fodor was at one time one of its most prominent supporters but he has softened his views lately (Fodor 2001). This is one of the most important theories behind the paradigm of strong AI, which is attempting to produce computers that can accomplish intelligence. To the extent that these projects succeed, a belief grows that the knowledge one builds to put this project into effect is a general and true theory that will make it possible to synthesize cognition and intelligence in a scientific manner. Computers will become conscious.

This is connected to the basic idea of computing established through Turing's theoretical computer (the Turing machine). Through the concept of the bit, it is connected to the information theory of Shannon. Through Wiener's cybernetic formulation, information theory is connected to classical thermodynamics based on the statistical ensemble atomistic theory of Boltzmann. From this view of cybernetics, an information theory of mind and intelligence was developed. The pan-informational theory promotes a purely functionalistic concept of mind. In this view even emotions are seen as computations – namely, computations of relationship. Regarding how the mystery of mind is resolved through the relation between the concept 'information' and the concept 'negative entropy,' Ruesch and Bateson (1987, 177) write: 'Wiener argued that these two concepts are synonymous; and this statement, in the opinion of the writers, marks the greatest single shift in human thinking since the days of Plato and Aristotle, because it unites the natural and the social sciences and finally resolves the problems of teleology and the body–mind dichotomy which Occidental thought has inherited from classical Athens.'

This statement characterizes the views of many researchers who are using this framework within systems, cybernetics, and informatics. This research program and paradigm has had a strong influence as a background ideology for LIS and on the way the computer industry considers the problems of building document-mediating electronic systems.

1.7 Critique of the Objective Concept of Information in the Information Processing Paradigm

The information processing paradigm has never been able to describe the central problems of mediating the semantic content of documents from producer to user that documentalists and librarians deal with. It fails in this regard because it does not address the social and phenomenological aspects of cognition ('becoming informed,' in Buckland's 1991 terminology), which is the bottom line of document mediation. This leads to serious doubts as to whether the scientific object exists in its postulated form of 'objective information processing.'

In his well-known analysis of the concept of information, Machlup (1983, 657) concludes that information should take as its starting point the human communicative situation. From this, he thereby develops a critique of the objective concept of information on which cognitive science is based, from a position within the humanities. This critique takes as its point of departure precisely that aspect of information most weakly represented in the information processing paradigm – namely, the sociophenomenological aspect of signification in human communication. Let me hasten to say that I do not agree entirely with Machlup's critique (as Stonier 1997 seems to believe); I will be referring to it here because it is a well-formulated critique from the humanities, even though in some ways it is as limited as the information processing paradigm.

Machlup points out that lexically, 'information' is tightly linked to the verb 'to inform': to give form to something, especially mind, consciousness, or character, through learning or instruction, and to pass on knowledge about facts or events. Thus the essential historical meanings of the concept 'information' are 'to tell something to someone,' and 'that which one is told.'

Note that this is a definition with a starting point in communication between individuals in a cultural and social context. It begins with linguistics-semiotics. This semiotic aspect will be discussed below, but I point out here that this offers an important opening towards the socio-hermeneutic aspect.

This is the broad general definition of information used by Machlup. But science is often developed through efforts to define the meaning of everyday conceptions in certain connections; thus, various restrictions have been formulated in different domains and paradigms with regard to the general concept of information:

1. Information should be about something previously unknown.
2. Information should be about something barely known.
3. Information should affect the scope of, or the structure of, the receiver's knowledge.
4. Information must only consist of un-interpreted 'raw' data.
5. Information should be useful.
6. Information can be used in decision-making.
7. Information should affect the receiver's possible actions.
8. Information should reduce the receiver's uncertainty.
9. Information should help identify the contextual meaning of words.
10. Information should change the receiver's acceptances/assumptions, especially as to the disposition of possibilities (for actions).

Yet none of these criteria capture the full meaning of the cognitive phenomena. On the contrary, these demands often restrict our understanding of information in relation to our present epistemology and scientific knowledge.

Regarding the relationship between knowledge and information, Machlup raises a number of important points, which are often missing in the cognitive sciences' understanding of information, but which I will develop here:

1. Neither knowledge nor information needs to be correct or universally true.
2. New knowledge can be achieved without the addition of new data through thought/insight/making sense.
3. Empirically based cognition is not the reception of information.[13]
4. Data are given to the receiver or the researcher to extract information from. They are not necessarily numbers. For any given instance, data are not different from information, except in computer language, where they constitute the information (input) that is to be treated in the system. Used generally in this way, 'data' is a relative concept. What data are for one person, information is for another.
5. From Machlup's traditional humanistic perspective, only people can send and receive information.
6. From his point of view, the use of the information concept in neurophysiology, brain research, and genetics must therefore be considered an analogy.

But Machlup also wants to limit the use of the genuine information concept at the level of the social sciences; thus, it would be considered a metaphorical usage if one were to claim that institutions or society as such receive or give information. It is, in his view, always individual humans who induce meaning among themselves, even though this always happens against a social-historical background.

Regarding the use of the information concept in connection with Shannon and Weaver's technical statistical theory, Machlup is very clear that this is taking the analogy too far. Here the theory is about impulses and activities, and the transmission of signals, but not about any form of meaning. One should always attach a prefix such as technical, statistical, or similar, if one uses the concept in these contexts.

All of these negatives point towards the conclusion that the creation and communication of information demands some basic characteristics associated with mind. Thus to me it seems that neither the information processing paradigm nor a pure phenomenological paradigm based solely on the language communication of human individuals is able to establish a unifying principle that links humans, documents, and computers.

My rejection of the information processing paradigm of information science is based on views similar to those of Machlup (1983) and Winograd and Flores (1987), who contend that the original definition of 'information' is something that an individual (or a living system) communicates to another individual (or living system). The meaning of information can only be understood if we consider living beings in a social and historical context. Furthermore, I agree with Machlup when he suggests that one cannot define information as that which reduces uncertainty. In fact, some kinds of information will make the receiver more uncertain. But if one knows the social context precisely enough to determine the full spectrum of possible outcomes, then one can use a statistical/entropic information concept as part of the description of the characteristics of a message. I further agree with Searle (1989) that the common link between information processing in humans and machines is not the fact that both follow rules. Machines behave according to causalities, but only conscious beings can choose deliberately to follow rules!

But since the information concept is now firmly rooted in computer informatics and in the information theories of Shannon and Weaver as well of Wienerian cybernetics, another strategy would be to abandon the original human communicative meaning of the concept. This is what I will suggest as a strategy, because this will also make it possible to combine this theory with a semiotic sign concept without any major overlap between subject fields, thus paving the way for an integrative cybersemiotic framework instead of a paradigm competition.

In human language systems there must, furthermore, be an interaction between information and the social and cultural aspects of the inner life of conscious beings. As we shall see from a semiotic perspective, it has been claimed that adequate theories of the communication of signification have been developed. Warner (1990, 20), for instance, points to the importance of semiotics as offering an interdisciplinary unifying framework that does not reduce all communication to scientific laws. He writes especially about the unification of documents and computers from a semiotic perspective, whereas my aim is a bit broader:

> Although the specific aim is to bring documents and computers within a single analytical category and thereby indicate a unifying principle, there are three further related intentions. First, revealing a unifying principle should demonstrate that semiotics can contribute to clarification within the established domains of information science. A second intention is to contribute to the development of information science on a non-scientific model by indicating connections with the broader category of the human, rather than simply the social sciences ... Thirdly a terminologically sound

basis for further intersections between information science and semiotics should be established.

It is thus clear from our analyses of the information processing paradigm and Machlup's phenomenological communication approach that we are seeking principles for establishish unifying principles as well as meaningful distinctions not only between documents and computers, but also between them and human social communicative practices. However, Shannon's theory of information has never addressed the semantic content of messages. Shannon and Weaver (1969, 31–2) write: 'The fundamental problem of communication is that of reproducing at one point either exactly or approximately a message selected at another point. Frequently the messages have meaning; that is they refer to or are correlated according to some system with certain physical or conceptual entities. These semantic aspects of communication are irrelevant to the engineering problem. The significant aspect is that they are selected from a set of possible messages.'

What people and animals treat as 'information' is quite different from what Wiener's theory of information suggests. Stonier[14] therefore makes a sensible discrimination between information and meaning, as information to him is objective structure and organization. This is clear, but we must then realize and acknowledge that the theory has little to do with semantic aspects of cognition or communication between living systems. As von Foerster (1980, 20–1) concludes: 'However, when we look more closely at these theories, it becomes transparently clear that they are not really concerned with information but rather with signals and the reliable transmission of signals over unreliable channels.'

This is surely one aspect of the cognition and communication of living systems, but it is not the central one. In a conclusive analysis summarizing many years of work with the concept of information in the physical sciences and information theory, Christiansen (1984) posits that it is in fact a materialistic reduction to claim that one's theory of information is based on the physical concept of entropy:

In as much as the intentional aspect of entropy is its meaninglessness and uselessness. The measure for information, which was introduced by C. Shannon and N. Wiener, among others, is also in the theory of information designated 'entropy' because it is formally identical with the measure of entropy in statistical mechanics. In the theory of information, one attempts to escape from the oddity that entropy in physics is a measure for missing information about the distribution of energy over the degrees of freedom, by placing a minus sign in front of the entropy measure. 'Information' is thus defined as 'negative entropy' (neg-entropy): i.e., information theory's message to us can be summarized in the following manner: 'You must not at first be interested in meaning, but you will learn to measure the meaningless in a precise way.' In this way one can always learn to understand meaning afterward by changing signs for meaninglessness. [my translation]

Thus, information science in the subject area of living systems and humans will not be able to explain vital aspects of the phenomena of cognition and communication, such as meaning and the constraints of social context. It is also well known that to determine the entropy in a system it is necessary to determine in advance what will qualify as macrostates and the probability of every state. There is no room for the completely unexpected, and therefore the real creative complexity of nature and language is lost. Thus this approach has other limits at its own level.

Quantum mechanics has important implications for the limits of obtaining physical information. Discussions about Heisenberg's indeterminacy principle relating to the problem of measurement in quantum mechanics and Bohr's theory of complementarity (Bohr 1954) reveal some of the cognitive limitations that quantum mechanics sets for the traditional view of objective information gathering in science. They reveal that the final information content is first determined by the process of measurement, and that our choices of equipment and experimental setting greatly influence the information produced.

In the 1980s, Prigogine (1980; see also Prigogine and Stengers 1984) clearly stated further limitations for classical science that spring from thermodynamics' discovery of irreversibility and 'the arrow of time' in physics. Knowledge, including scientific knowledge, is created within time and is about phenomena within time. It is probably not about eternal transcendental laws, but rather statistical laws – or habits of nature, as Peirce would call them. Furthermore, Prigogine claimed that thermodynamics is a more fundamental science than mechanics. This led to a renewed discussion about the relationship between entropy and information. Ultimately, concepts such as time, non-linearity, chaos, and unpredictability became accepted by many as fundamentals in science.

I contend that knowledge – or <u>knowing</u> (to underline the process) – is a far more complicated 'thing' or process than expected by the 'information processing paradigm' described earlier. According to, for instance, Thomas Kuhn's philosophy of science (1970), nature and human mind are not directly connected. Nature does not speak to us. I would also agree, with Maturana and Varela (1980), that nature does not – in the usual meaning of the word – transfer information to us through our observation. I would rather say that we participate through science in a socially, biologically, and psychologically influenced interpretation of the world.

One of the problems with the information processing paradigm is that in spite of that, psychology – the science originally dealing with cognition – is partitioned into four different aspects: the behavioural, the physiological, the phenomenological, and the socio-linguistic, all of which structure the conceptualized part of our 'inner' life. The information processing paradigm in cognitive science sets out to obtain an interdisciplinary and intermethodological integration where the socio-phenomenological perspective is almost completely absent. Despite this, the information processing program offers an integrative paradigm capable of connecting not only the various aspects of psychology, but also studies of mankind with studies of nature and society. For instance, the paradigm of strong AI is attempting to develop computers that will be able to perform human and socially intelligent tasks. This project is underpinned by the rationalistic tradition from Hobbes through Kant (1990) and Leibniz which supports the idea that thought and concepts are governed by rules for logical calculation and derivation. According to this conception, the new scientific object is cognition, which is understood as information processing, including human language communication. I doubt that the information processing paradigm can establish that unity across scientific, social scientific, and phenomenological approaches. I also have doubts about the *functionalistic* thesis that there is a unifying software program level that is relatively independent of the type of hardware or wetware in which it is installed.

This scepticism concerning the basic paradigm in cognitive science is also embraced by Searle (1989), who holds that biology is decisive if we are to understand the structure of thought. He views consciousness and intelligence as emergent phenomena and as functions of how neurons are organized in the nervous system. He compares these phenomena to the relationship between water molecules and water's macroscopic abilities. Thus an individual water molecule is not wet; rather, wetness is an emergent ability of water molecules when they are organized in a certain way. Ice, for example, is not wet. So it is a faulty assumption to postulate the existence of a symbol-manipulating program between the brain and its consciousness. A Peircean biosemiotic has much to say about this, and we shall return to it.

Many biologists and cybernetic-oriented thinkers, such as Humberto Maturana (1988) and Gregory Bateson (1973, 1980), share this scepticism regarding the basic paradigm in cognitive science. The Dreyfus brothers (1986, 1995) also maintain, as Searle does, that a middle level of information processing does not exist. Deacon (1997), who summarizes modern research into the brain, heredity, and the development of the human linguistic capability, argues against a single module for language and reason.

The two other paradigms of cognitive science – weak AI and neural networks – do not build on the assumption that a general program or algorithm lies behind cognition and language. Weak AI tries to simulate intelligence in computers, and neural networks view mental structures – including language – as emergent products of the mass interactions of processors in networks with no central CPU. This dovetails with the critique of the lexical idea of semantics (an idea that is so important in point 10 of the above description of the information processing paradigm). As Dubois (1994, 73) states:

> The question remains open to decide if words as entries in a dictionary are the relevant units in a scientific description of a language, the temptation of defining such a level of segmentation being highly dependent on the written form of (some) languages.
>
> In other words ... I wonder whether the 'mental lexicon' can be considered as a 'genuine' or 'real' psychological object.

It is well known that Wittgenstein originally considered lexical definitions of words and grammatical rules for simplified pedagogical constructions (Blair 1990). Attacks on the idea that words have clear and unique references are also attacks on the idea that universal classification systems are the only solution to the mediating problems that LIS encounters.

Warner (1994) points to the problems that face LIS when the meaning of words must be partially inferred from a socio-linguistic context. It is clear that simply matching query words to index words – no matter how sophisticated a partial match and ranking algorithm one has – will always have a low precision because the semantics are not equally well defined. Wittgenstein and Peirce both offer profound arguments for the socio-pragmatic nature of signification. Hjørland and Albrechtsen (1995) further discuss how knowledge domains and discourse communities function as the vital context for determining the meanings of concepts.

As Winograd and Flores (1986) demonstrate, most of our automatic IR systems and expert systems are built on this simplified idea of signification as denotative atomistic reference. More advanced systems allow for the statistical covariance of certain words. That can be helpful, although it is a primitive (because mechanical) method for modelling the context of a sentence. Furthermore, as hermeneutics has pointed out, the context that determines the meaning of words in a sentence or indexing system is a system of Chinese boxes going from the sentence, through the paragraph and the text as a whole, to the situation and intentions of the writer and the relevant cultural and social context.

From the field of cognitive semantics, Lakoff (1987) offers a profound critique of the epistemology and ontology of the information processing paradigm. He especially criticizes our poor understanding of how human concepts and their semantics are embodied. The computer's inability to account for the cultural context of human semantics seriously limits projects of AI and expert systems.

But the AI that cognitive science would like to build can, of course, be used when what it means to be human is immaterial – for example, in measurement-based medical diagnosis, mineral searching, spectrogram analysis, and chess (Winograd and Flores 1986).

The greatest limitation of these programs is that they cannot learn by themselves. These programs function primarily through a previously incorporated knowledge database constructed from experts' experiences in the given area and expressed in the form of rules and assessments. Independent learning capacity has not been well developed in contemporary computer technology. There are logically structured systems, but not intelligent ones. They are useful because although humans are intelligent, they are seldom consistent over time or domains, their memory is experientially organized, and they have difficulty retaining context-free facts and numbers.

Also, in human/computer interfaces in IR, the complexity of human language raises problems for work with natural language. Rowley (1993, 109) concludes that recent research on information retrieval systems has not considered the indexing language in any detail. Most recent research has focused either on ways of improving the human computer interface (by, for instance, offering the user support in the selection of search terms, possibly through an expert system-based interface) or ways of enhancing natural language as a search device (by investigating ways of identifying how effective certain terms are in representing concepts in documents). Records are ranked in response to a query in the order of decreasing match with a query. Such work takes no account of the detailed text structure of records, and the syntax of sentences; and the structuring of records into fields is usually not exploited, although ranking may be performed on the basis of the contents of specific parts of the record.

AI systems can only handle the most primitive aspects of the signification of words, and LIS deals daily with the most complex scientific and cultural aspects of the meaning of texts. When one uses expert systems in more complex situations, the computer's lack of general (biocultural) knowledge manifests itself. Humans acquire this knowledge through their bodily life in a society. Through life experiences, we have come to know what it is to be a human being; a computer needs a description. This makes it difficult to teach computers to receive, apply, and translate colloquial language. Meaning is not based on a logical coherence, but rather on general human experience within culture. A concept can have several meanings depending on the social context in which it is used, and this complicates the development of automated IR systems.

These are some of the differences between humans and machines that restrict expert systems, which can only function within narrow and well-defined limits, where it is possible to install the relevant background knowledge. Sense is not simply logical thinking: it is a mixture of rationality, instinct, feelings, ethics, and aesthetics. The kinds of tasks that expert systems can usefully perform is more limited than was thought in the early days of AI. Carrington's (1990, 47–8) delineation of what would be an appropriate problem for an expert system in a library clearly shows its limits in relation to normal LIS work situations:

What Is an Appropriate Problem for an Expert System?
The scope and domain should be quite finite and bounded. Rather than try to organize an entire reference collection, start with items which are problematic for patrons and for staff, such as biographical or statistical sources.

The problem and its solution should have a logical structure. It should not require a solution, which is dependent upon the use of common knowledge or everyday know-how. The answer should rest in a set of facts, and not be dependent upon intuitive or serendipitous processes.

The problem should be repetitive, yet sufficiently complicated to warrant the effort to create the program. One conventional measure is to tackle a problem which would require an expert to spend more than five minutes but less than thirty minutes to find a solution. Make sure that there is not another more cost-effective way to offer the information. Very complicated problems should be left to the now-liberated expert.

The solution should be clear cut and not involve opinion. Most people, including other experts, should agree upon the answers, although pure logic may present surprises about conclusions. That is the advantage of using heuristics, or rules of thumb, to incorporate expertise. The facts should be indisputable, but there may be room for interpretation.

The expertise must be available; it will not be created by the program, although understanding may be enhanced in the process of development.

This has not changed very much since. These systems cannot help us with the human-social and linguistic-communicative aspects of LIS work. The work of librarians and documentalists is both complex and dependent on human social knowledge about cultural and domain-specific information; accordingly, LIS has been working towards inter- and trans-disciplinary approaches. It is hoped that these will usefully encompass more of the cultural and socio-phenomenological aspects of signification. This is important, because the crux of the discussions about the correct foundation for an information science between cognitive science-inspired paradigms and alternatives centres on what information is and whether there can be a common denominator for all cognition and communication. I contend that because semantics is so central to the mediation of documents, LIS does not benefit much from an information processing paradigm founded on objective and structural information concepts. Let us consider a few examples.

1.8 The Problem of Language as the Carrier of Information in Document-Mediating Systems

In modern bibliographic IR systems, it is not unusual to have ten million documents in a database available worldwide. Normally a data-

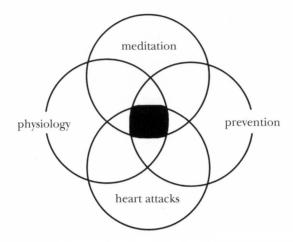

1.5   A Venn diagram of the search for documents characterized by four differ-ent index terms. Each circle represents a set of many thousands of documents. The user seeks only those which combine all four subjects.

base specializes in a particular domain of knowledge (BIOSIS, for example). Documents are created by professionals within the knowl-edge domain, but they are indexed and stored for retrieval by profes-sional librarians and information scientists.

Let us assume that a user who is neither a biologist nor a librarian wishes to use this system online. He wants to find scientific studies on the health benefits of meditation in preventing heart attacks as well as information about the physiological theories behind that benefit. This can be illustrated in a Venn diagram (see Figure 1.5).

Let us say that the database contains ten million documents and that the user's search retrieves one hundred records, of which only fifty are judged truly relevant or useful. It is easy to see that the search precision is only 50 per cent. But the real problem is that the user cannot assess the extent of this 'recall.' That is to say, the user has no direct or con-trolled way of knowing how many documents are in the bibliographic database that might be relevant to his quest. He cannot compute the percentage of the relevant documents he has retrieved. This could be absolutely vital in some types of searches, such as patent searches or searches for relevant documents in connection with a lawsuit. If we call the four different areas A, B, C, and D, he could, of course, continue to create combinations such as $A \lor B \lor C \land not\ D$, $A \lor B \lor D \land not\ C$, or A v C v D ∧ not B, and so on, for a broader view of what is in the supposedly relevant area (Blair 1990). But this is very tedious, and he will have to scan hundreds of documents for relevance. It will take a lot more work than he is willing to do, and he will get a lot of 'noise': the feedback is not very useful relative to the amount of work spent to acquire it. This can be very unsatisfactory for the uninitiated IR searcher. Another approach is to find synonyms for the subject terms in order to find additional relevant documents. But this way the user will also get much noise, and will have to sort through hundreds more documents. He will retrieve additional relevant documents, but he will not learn to retrieve them more efficiently unless he learns exactly how the indexers used the words. So the user returns to the original problem.

In a full-text database this will be even more difficult because there are no ideals or rules for how to use words. In huge databases, free-text searches on full-text documents generate a lot of noise and therefore have a low precision. Blair (1990) has found that nearly all information seekers overestimate their actual recall.

As Blair (ibid.) has shown, one of the biggest problems with subject searching is that the indexer and the searcher do not participate in the same language game! Their work and social environments are different, and therefore their use of words will be different. This means that their subject descriptions will be different: they will mean different things by the same words, or they will use different words for the same thing. There is no 'ultimate' description of a document or of the uses of a subject term. Attempts to make a universal and correct description are pointless because there is no limit to the number of descriptors one could use to characterize a document; semiosis is unlimited (ibid.). To limit the spectrum of meanings in a useful way, the indexer must create descriptions in accordance with certain forms of living (such as trading and research) and their language games, also called discourse communities and their discourses.

From here, it is possible to point to several system-based reasons why the user does not obtain a satisfactory retrieval result and why this problem is so difficult to address. Although the large, domain-specific databases attempt to make the definitions in their classification systems clear and consistent (for example, through thesauri and controlled keywords), there is still the human factor of interpretation. The professional indexer's actual subject-indexing performance is never more than 75 per cent consistent between all indexers on a detailed or 'deep' indexing of a document and is often much less. The likelihood that a user is applying the subject term in the same way as the indexers – even if the user reads the scope notes carefully – is even smaller, say 60 per cent. Figure 1.5 can show the consequences: visualize the limits of the sets getting very fuzzy. Every time one uses a subject term to describe the documents sought, the chances of locating the correct one are 0.75 x 0.60 = 0.45, even when the system is being used to the best of the user's abilities. When one combines four different subject terms to select specific documents, the chances of selecting correctly are then $0.45^4 = 0.04$ = 4 per cent (see ibid., 106, for an even more merciless example). This problem is not addressed by mechanical models of partial match that use probability, weighted factor ranking, vector space, fuzzy sets, or hypertext. All of these are based on the ideal of good and consistent indexing and a perfect match with the user's application of search terms.

Thus one can retrieve only a very small portion of the relevant documents, and a great number of those retrieved will be irrelevant. The more search terms used, the more serious the problem becomes. If one knows the bibliographic base's classification system, there are ways to diminish this problem. But most searchers do not; and even for those who do, their efforts only diminish the problem, they do not eliminate it. Information is stored in such a way that only specialists who can combine subject knowledge with technical retrieval knowledge – investing years of training – really have a chance to retrieve anything up to date and useful for the problem at hand. The system can produce knowledge with the desired precision and scope only for certain groups, and then only to a limited extent. There may be physical access for all, but there is intellectual access only for highly trained specialists.

Librarians, documentalists, and LIS researchers work every day on the social and practical dynamism of signification and how to relate it to the textual representations in computer systems (not to mention the problems of understanding how the different software systems themselves use words). Today, through the Internet, corporate intranets, management information systems, GISs, and file-handling systems, more people are spending more time looking for exponentially increasing numbers of documents. What LIS needs is an interdisciplinary scientific understanding broad and deep enough to encompass the communicational and organizational aspects of computer systems, knowledge producers, and the classification and indexing of documents. Therefore, the theoretical foundations of LIS in the field of IR must be broadened to incorporate the semantic production of meaning if there are to be substantial improvements in the situation.

With regard to the use and meaning of language, earlier in this book I pointed to an interesting convergence between the second-order cybernetics of von Foerster (1993a) and Maturana and Varela (1980), Luhmann's social communication theory (1995), the semiotics of Peirce (1931–1958), the embodied cognitive semantics of Lakoff and Johnson (1999), and the later Wittgenstein's language philosophy of life forms and language games (1958). Second-order cybernetics contends that forms of knowledge spring from the praxis of living and the criteria of validation. Information and meaning in their broadest sense only arise within those self-organized – or in the words of Maturana and Varela (1983), 'autopoietic' – systems which have a practical and historical relationship within a domain of living. Lakoff (1987) shows how important embodiment is for cognitive semantics. In his semiotics, Peirce says that the meaning of a word is all its possible uses in society (practice of living). This fits well with the language philosophy of the later Wittgenstein (1958) who says that the meanings of words are fixed not by definition, but rather through the 'language game' they appear in, such as dialogues, persuasions, or seductions. This is what Wittgenstein calls 'forms of life' – in short, the things humans do. Science is a life form and has its own language games, as does document searching by subject.

A simple way to state the theoretical problem is that there are two basic ways to approach it: (1) A non-semantic, functional, structural, logical, syntactical approach, and (2) a semantic, pragmatic, social approach. Meister (1995, 269) summarizes the non-semantic approach of computer science in this way:

> Computing as a methodology would obviously fall under the numeric paradigm. The latter can be characterized as follows:
> - It is based on a clear differentiation of objects and procedures.
> - It presupposes and/or affects a complete de-semantization of all its objects. In the numeric paradigm we deal with pure signifiers, or rather quantifiers that can be added, multiplied, divided or subtracted irrespective of their potential arguments, their 'content.'
> - In this paradigm the result of any given manipulation and/or processing of data serves to confirm the validity of the procedure as such. As computing procedures, i.e., algorithms, will always produce non-ambiguous and non-contradictory results, such results are effectively nothing but a more or less sophisticated re-formulation (one might even say a 'translation') of the original data input.

This is one end of the spectrum of scientific approaches to the LIS area of IR and document-mediating systems. The other end is the problems of signification and semantics. Signification requires a living social referent. Meister (ibid.) summarizes:

> The semantic paradigm is rather defined as follows:
> - It is based on a constant reciprocal logical link between objects and procedures, and it presupposes the concept of reference between a signifier and a signified.
> - Instead of the procedure (the 'algorithm') de-semanticizing its objects, the object that is manipulated within the semantic paradigm will inadvertently semanticize the very procedure, thus making transparent the epistemological and ideological presuppositions embedded in the algorithm *per se*.
> - Only those results that are different, that happen to question the validity or confinements of the procedures, which produced them, will ultimately be found to be relevant and noteworthy. A result which amounts to nothing but a simple and transparent repetition or permutation of the original input is mostly considered to be redundant.

One of our difficulties is that the adherents of these two approaches understand little of each other's fields and therefore often fear and loathe each other's knowledge. We need a framework that can help them understand each other as contributors to the same interdisciplinary complex of problems.

In spite of intelligent interfaces for manipulating natural language, full-text bases with automatic natural language indexing and searching, bigger databases, CD-ROMs, hypertext, and global Internet connection to any base, the above-mentioned problems are growing instead of declining due to an explosion in the production of documents and the number of users. Computer technology helps us handle and access huge numbers of documents, but it does not offer any profound solutions to the basic cognitive and communicative problems of designing, operating, and mediating document-mediating systems. The basic problem in LIS is that one must perform an intellectual analysis to determine the content of a document in order to achieve precise and useful indexing.

Now, does the indexer determine the objective content of the document? Both practice and hermeneutic theory tell us that the content of a document depends on the context in which it is seen – that is to say, it depends on what those who read it know and what their interests are.

There are at least three ways to determine the content of a document:

1. *From the indexing system* (its thesaurus or classification system). In the best cases this is constructed from a profound knowledge of the domain of knowledge in question. But it is seldom the case that the researcher who wrote the document had the classification system and its concepts in mind when writing the paper. The writer might be inventing some neologisms, a new interdisciplinary subject, or perhaps an entire paradigm that is opposed to the paradigm underlying the present classification system. This book is an excellent example. Finally, the user often does not share the knowledge background of either the system or the author.
2. *From the author's perspective.* One can pick words from the text, and the indexer can give a description with appropriate words. But the determination of this is an interpretation by the indexer. The main interest of a document retrieval system is to ensure that others who need or require the document can find it using their own language game, and this is most likely distinct from those of both the classification system and the indexer.
3. *From the user's perspective.* The problem here is that in most large document retrieval systems there are so many types of users that the indexer can only index in relation to the largest and most formally well-defined knowledge domains.

The hope for transdisciplinary theories in information and communication science is that they will be able to deepen our understanding of human-to-human communication through machine-mediated documents in such a way that we can improve our designs of document-mediating systems. In this light, I will offer a short description of the central subject area of LIS, define basic concepts, and briefly outline cognitivist information processing conceptions. After this, I will derive the reasons for their limitations when it comes to understanding the semantic aspects of human language. Finally, I will outline the broader framework of cybersemiotics and its possible consequences.

1.9 LIS: The Science of Document-Mediating Systems

The generalized concept of a document (Buckland 1991; Vickery and Vickery 1988) is something different from the concepts of data and information. There are some important and profound differences.

I define *data* as given inputs with a structure that the receiver regards as reliable and usable in a given situation. I define a *document* as a human work with communicative intent recorded in a material way.

I want to clarify Buckland's view, which can be construed as considering natural things to be documents in themselves. Some cultural and intentionally communicative act, such as insertion into a classification system, must be performed on natural things before they can be considered documents. Perhaps, then, we can say that all things are potential documents, just as everything is potential information. These become documents when they become interesting for members of a communicative knowledge system. But that requires the object to be placed in a position such that it can be viewed from a certain interest. Latour (1999) demonstrates this process with earth sampling by geologists in a very clear way. As Bateson (1973) says, information is a difference that makes a difference.

Data become meaningful information[15] when they are integrated with a given knowledge process and pre-understanding. They only become meaningful information when they are received and interpreted by a biopsychological-social knowledge system. We shall discuss Luhmann's elegant conceptualization of this fact later.

The difference between knowledge and information is that information is viewed as a minor part of a knowledge system. But both require semiotic interpretation if they are to become meaningful. As Salthe (1993, 17) writes:

> Viewing the previous work in this chapter from the semiotic standpoint, we can note that thermodynamics lent itself to an interpretation (Boltzmann's) that allowed entropy to be connected to the later concept of information (e.g., Brillouin 1956). But if we insist that we will not be concerned with 'information' that is without potential meaning to some observer, and then we make a further extension from thermodynamics to semiotics. I will eschew any notation of information capacity that does not (at least in principle) imply a system of interpretation that could reduce that capacity locally by learning something by way of formulating appropriate interpretants.

I agree with Salthe that one cannot consider the meaning of information without an interpretation. We could add to Wiener's statement that (in itself) 'information is information, neither matter nor energy' – that *information is also not meaning until it has been interpreted by a living system.* I further doubt that we can come to understand interpreting systems from a bottom-up scientific approach alone.

There are various other different aspects of information and meaning that are significant. In his analysis, Buckland (1991, 6) usefully distinguishes among the following:

a) personal knowledge (private, mental),
b) the process of knowing or becoming informed,
c) objective/intersubjective materially registered knowledge (documents) and
d) information/data processing, the mechanical manipulation of signals and symbols.

He summarizes this in Figure 1.6:

	Intangible	Tangible
Entity	*Information-as-knowledge* Knowledge　　　　　1	*Information-as-thing* Data, document, 　　　2 recorded knowledge
Process	*Information-as-process* Becoming informed 　　　　　　　　　3	*Information processing* Data processing, document processing, 　4 knowledge engineering

1.6. Buckland's matrix of different kinds of information (1991, 6) in which he uses the information concept as an overall concept – which will not be our strategy.

I will use similar distinctions: (1) phenomenological knowledge, (2) documents, (3) cognition, and (4) information processing. However, I will not use information as an overall concept, but rather as a difference-based concept that must be interpreted in order to generate meaning for an observer. We shall return to this point again in the discussion of Bateson's development of the cybernetic theory of information and mind.

LIS is concerned with finding suitable rules for the design of systems as well as procedures for collecting, organizing, classifying, indexing, storing, retrieving, and mediating those materials which support data, knowledge, meaning, and experience. As an offshoot of both indexing and communication to users with different requirements, we must study the origins of the various document types, how they are produced, for which users they are created, and under which economic and knowledge domain constraints they are produced.

The producers of documents generally have certain consumers in mind, and these consumers are often part of the group of producers themselves. In this way the system is – from the perspective of a cybernetician – closed in on itself. The LISA bibliographic database, for instance, is a base of information and library science with documents written by librarians and information scientists, to librarians and information scientists, and mediated by librarians and information scientists.

1.10   The Cognitive Perspectives Opening towards a Cybersemiotic Concept of Information in LIS

De May (1980), Belkin (1978), and Ingwersen (1992, 1995, 1996) from the cognitive viewpoint all abandon the information processing paradigm for some of the same reasons as those I have discussed. Inspired by Kuhn's idea of paradigm, they are aware that the semantic network derives a decisive aspect of signification from its inherent world view, which in turn is derived from and develops undefined tacit knowledge of a more complex character. The importance of meaning is rooted in social-historical processes that are mentioned but not explicitly treated by the paradigm and that so far have no specific influence on its conceptual formation. Ingwersen (1992) discusses hermeneutic and semiotic theories of meaning, but a pragmatic description of these has yet to be developed. Some progress has been made by Ingwersen (1996), but his main developments focus on individual types of cognition and search behaviour.

From the cognitive perspective, one underlines the fact that the interpretive function of signification goes beyond the known possibilities of computers. Meaning depends on the structure of knowledge, which builds on an individual context and understanding of the world. In Ingwersen (1992) we encounter a perspective that is gradually opening up to the social and historic-dynamic complexity of cognition and semiosis.

In agreement with Ingwersen (ibid.), one can, as an answer to the humanistic and socially oriented critique, formulate a broader and less objective concept of information than that of the information processing paradigm. According to the cognitive viewpoint, information is the mental phenomenon that documents can cause (and these documents can consist of both signs and text, depending on the state of knowledge of the recipient). The examination of these 'correct circumstances' is an important part of information science. In connection with the design of information systems for businesses and institutions, one can now speak of information quality (Wormell 1990). The cognitive perspective represents three important developments:

1. Information is understood as potential until somebody interprets it.
2. The objective carrier of information is a sign.
3. Interpretation is based on the total semantic network, horizons, world views, and experiences of the individual, including the emotional and social aspects.

The aim is for information created in the user's mind to be understood and to meet social, cultural, or existential needs. This is an important advance over cognitive science, the goal of which is to create an objective theory about information. One can therefore reformulate information science's aim as follows: *LIS devotes itself primarily to the study of systems and methods for classifying, indexing, storing, retrieving, and mediating documents so as to create information in the user's mind.*

The crucial question is this: How does the individual interpret the document in a given organizational or institutional context and in a given historical situation? Ingwersen (1996) describes the information need as arising from a cognitive state (including previous knowledge), a work task, an interest, and a domain.

As Casanova (1990, 43) points out, information is not a constant phenomenon, and neither is quality; both change over time. Relevance is the key word here, and relevance is dependent on the meaning we give to things in relation to our preconceptions. It is these socio-pragmatic circumstances that form the context for us to understand our informational desires and problems. Ingwersen (1996) has developed a matrix with four distinct cognitive forms of information needs relevant for determining search behaviour and types of polyrepresentation.

So far we do not have an explicit theoretical treatment of how varying forms of 'aboutness' come into existence and function in a social context. As information, in this view, develops primarily in an individual mind in front of a document-mediating system, there are no explicit theories about how information develops in social practice.

1.11 Aspects That Must Be Further Developed in the Framework of the Cognitive Viewpoint

The cognitive viewpoint represents an important first step away from the mechanistic information processing paradigm in cognitive science as a foundation for LIS. It is a step towards a theory that encompasses the social and linguistic complexity of LIS and IR in a more realistic way. Librarians and LIS researchers know this complexity empirically from their own experience, and so far research has modelled various limited aspects of it. But we still have difficulties with the construction of a comprehensive theoretical framework, one that would improve the consistency in our use of scientific concepts within LIS, guide our research and development of research methods, and finally, provide the background for interpreting empirical research. The cognitive viewpoint has made some important changes in the basic view of the communication process in LIS and IR – changes that are compatible with modern semiotics and pragmatic language philosophy. Within the cognitive viewpoint there has been empirical research and a theory has been developed about the situation of the individual user with an information need confronting an information system. But further aspects must be developed if the theory is to be comprehensive; more specifically, that theory must be broadened into a general framework for information science.

As in Machlup's theory of information, in the cognitive viewpoint the focus is on the individual. Machlup denies that social systems can communicate. Ingwersen (1995, 1996) is open to the study of the influence of knowledge domains on concept formation and interpretation – a study first launched internationally by Hjørland and Albrechtsen (1995) in *the domain analytic paradigm*. The latter offer theoretical reasons why classification and indexing should be directed towards the ways signification is created in discourse communities related to different knowledge domains, especially within the different fields of science.

This insight points us towards the need for a general semiotic framework of communication and sign processing. We need to open LIS to the results and constructive thinking of a more general theory of how signs – such as words and symbols – acquire their meaning through communication, be it oral or written (Warner 1990). Semiotics not only needs to encompass social and cultural communication, but also should be able to address natural phenomena such as communication within biological systems. It should also have categories for technical information processing. At the same time, this transdisciplinary theory should distinguish among physical, biological, mental-psychological and socio-linguistic levels and not reduce them to the same process of information. So far there is little evidence that a profound and practical understanding of information and communication can be found by reducing either to the mechanical manipulation of material symbols. A theoretical understanding of how signs are interpreted by biological-social systems is necessary if we are to talk about how information is communicated.

This leads us to the third requirement: a theory of the cognition and communication of signification should be able to encompass different types of systems. Neither the objective syntactic approach of the information processing paradigm, nor the personal phenomenological approach of Machlup, can deliver a framework that encompasses communication processes in social, biological, and technical systems. We cannot ignore the cybernetic information science that is behind and embedded in the computer, which has become a general tool for document-mediating systems.

As Buckland (1991) points out, we must draw on systems theory and cybernetics – and with Warner and Blair, I would add semiotics. In the rest of this chapter, I will outline my argument regarding the nature of such a synthesis to give the reader insight into what I will be attempting to accomplish in this book, and also to protect against losing the internal line of argument when I conduct a deeper analysis in subsequent chapters.

1.12 Analysing the Possibility of an Information Science

Science, especially natural science, has a double role as both a developer of technology and a producer of world views (Latour 1993). Science as an instrument for obtaining knowledge is a crucial part of our faith in technology as the correct approach to developing society. Science is also the foundation of 'the modern world view' as indicated by rationalism and physicalism (Walter and Heckmann 2003), and it is embedded in a theory of evolution. Part of our cultural project is to uncover all of the 'laws of nature,' to fulfil the desire to bring to light the ultimate basis for constructing objective, true, and provable knowledge. Stone by stone, we will erect the cathedral of truth and achieve the full realization and control of our own selves and of the nature that surrounds us. In this way we shall liberate the human intellect from natural and material forces. This project – according to our self-understanding – is central to our view of ourselves as 'modern.' It is what separates us from – and raises us above – other human cultures.' Today this idea is embraced by great scientific thinkers such as Stephen Hawking (1989) and E.O. Wilson (1999). However, it is questioned by philosophers and sociologists of science such as Thomas Kuhn (1970) and Bruno Latour. The latter argues that 'we have never been modern' (Latour 1993).

One characteristic of modernity is faith in rationalism as the highest value, and the associated tendency to see science as a 'metanarrative.' Empirical-mathematical science, as formulated by Galileo and others, has come to play a powerful role in our cultural self-understanding and world view. In the mechanical physics that has since developed lies a vision that Laplace clearly articulated regarding the possibility of achieving a complete mathematical description of 'the Laws of Nature' – a 'world formula,' as Prigogine and Stengers (1984) call it.

This belief in science and technology, in which science becomes a 'great story,' has much in common with the myth of dogma-based cultures in which myth defines true knowledge, true values, and real beauty. Instead of becoming true liberating knowledge, science is to a certain degree finding its limited perspective raised to a dogma called 'the scientific world view,' which promises to uncover the algorithms behind language and intelligence and to implement them in the computer.

From the Age of Enlightenment's encyclopedists through Comte's positivism to the Vienna Circle and logical positivism, the idea of information has been interpreted in increasingly rationalistic and materialistic ways. Today this path has ended with the split portrayed by C.P. Snow (1993) between 'the two cultures,' with the modern humanities in their divided specializations and often highly refined aestheticism standing in weak opposition to financial power joined with a scientific-technological system. The humanities have difficulty finding a common ground on which to formulate their value assumptions, since they wish neither to make ethics into religion or science, nor to define human nature beyond socio-linguistic material consciousness. But even the mechanical philosophy of nature's rationality is being undermined within science itself through the so-called paradigm shift.

Here the task of formulating a new quantum mechanics has shown itself to be important. The discussions about Heisenberg's indeterminacy principle, the problems of measurement, and Bohr's complementarity theory relate to the cognitive limitations that quantum mechanics sets for the traditional sciences. In relation to its own self-understanding, science has ended in a series of situations of powerlessness; these should eventually lead to deliberations on the status of scientific knowledge in a highly industrialized society.

Even though more and more theoretical scientists and researchers are acknowledging that scientific knowledge has limits, the Laplacian ideology of science seems nevertheless to be influencing a large part of the system world. It is in this 'market' that researchers must find their grants. Perhaps that is why the 'world formula ideology' continues to influence the headings of a series of larger research projects. These include:

1. The continuing research to shoehorn a united quantum field theoretical formulation of all powers' and particles' basic dynamics into one mathematical description. Not long ago the grand unified theory (GUT) was formulated as 'the heterotic super string theory.'
2. The efforts to find and manipulate 'the fundamental laws of life' by uncovering 'the genetic program.'
3. The assumed connection between the laws of nature, logic, and thought and those of linguistic syntax. This lies behind the project that is attempting to uncover and transfer 'the laws behind human intelligence' to computers in order to create 'artificial intelligence.' This also pertains to the project's more sophisticated continuation in 'cognitive science' and certain forms of 'information science,' which we touched on earlier.

This last project especially points to the severe limitations of the mechanistic view of knowledge, nature, language, and consciousness (see Figure 1.7) – limitations I have already described and analysed.

The information processing paradigm will never succeed in describing the central problems of mediating the semantic content of a message from producer to user because it does not address the social and phenomenological aspects of cognition. Furthermore, it will fail because it is built on a rationalistic epistemology and a mechanistic world view with an unrealistic 'world formula' attitude towards science. Science can deal only with the decidable, and as Gödel has shown, there are undecidables even within mathematics.

The problem for the now-classical functionalistic information processing paradigm is its inability to encompass the role of the observer. It is the human perceptive and cognitive ability to gain knowledge and communicate this in dialogue with others in a common language that is the foundation of science. An awareness of this will lead one to start in

World Formula Thinking

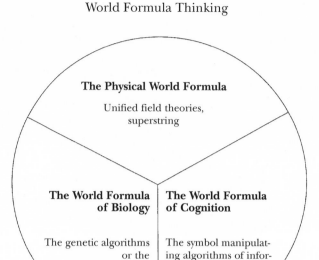

1.7.   An illustration of the three major areas of the sciences and their world formula projects. It is believed that in the future, integration of the algorithmic models of these three areas will fulfil the dream of one common formula. Each is developed with and through a specific technology. They are: nuclear power and weapons, genetic engineering, and artificial intelligence.

the middle instead of at the extremes, to start not with either subject or object, but rather with the process of knowing in living systems. This is precisely what second-order cybernetics and Peircean biosemiotics do.

1.13 The Cybernetic Turn

As one of the founders of second-order cybernetics, Heinz von Foerster is keenly aware of the paradoxes of objectivity, the deterministic mechanicism of classical physics, and even modern quantum physics and relativity thinking. As an answer to these problems, he develops a position from which he can offer dialogic theories of cognition, language, and the creation of reality and meaning in society.

Von Foerster (1984) demonstrates that if an organism is modelled as a machine, it cannot be trivial (that is, there is no deterministic mathematical description of its behaviour). Thus he speaks of living systems as at the very least *non-trivial machines*. The system organizes itself and produces its own parts. The self-organizing ability and the historical dimension of living systems are important reasons why organisms are not trivial machines: they are closed, self-organized systems. But in fact this only makes the whole problem more difficult. If information is not transferred from the environment to a mechanically describable system, what kind of dynamics are we then dealing with?

Von Foerster answers this question of information and dynamics as follows: The organism reacts to disturbances/perturbations in its system through self-referential dynamics (so as to conserve the sort of system it seeks to be). The concept 'outside' is not used, because according to these theories, 'outside' or (objective) 'reality' has no significant objective meaning. As von Foerster (ibid., preface) explains: 'I see the notion of an observer-independent 'Out There,' of 'The Reality,' fading away very much.'

To understand the organization and function of information systems, it is important to appreciate the role played by system-regulated feedback from influential user groups in different parts of the system. This organizational structure includes retrieval systems and user interfaces. These feedback analyses allow us to see information-storing and intermediary systems as self-organizing cybernetic systems in a constant inner interaction, one that includes users as causal parts of the system. Von Foerster (1992a, 310) formulates this basic insight of cybernetics as follows: 'Should one name one central concept, a first principle of cybernetics, it would be circularity – circularity as it appears in the circular flow of signals in organizationally closed systems; or in circular causality, that is, in processes in which ultimately a state reproduces itself.'

Transferred to document-mediating systems, this means that these systems develop in a constant inner exchange between the producers,' indexers,' and users' intellectual horizons.[16] This understanding is inspired by systems science and especially by the new second-order cybernetics (von Foerster 1979, 1981, 1992a), which works intentionally with the integration of the observer's observation process into the actual system description. This promotes our understanding of document-mediating systems and other informational systems as self-organizing processes.

Such systems cannot be controlled exclusively from within or without, and the adequacy of their behaviour and cognition should be judged by their viability rather than by an objective idea of absolute truth. So says another important contributor to second-order cybernetics, the radical constructivist Ernst von Glasersfeld (1992). This places second-order cybernetics on the same pragmatic as Wittgenstein's language philosophy and Peirce's semiotics. Blair (1990) makes use of both these theories in his important book. Hjørland and Albrechtsen (1995) also rely to some degree on pragmatic views of language, although not specifically on Wittgenstein and Peirce.

Cybernetics seeks to describe and explain how the functions of structural constraints influence the development of self-organizing systems, which are now, owing to the work of Maturana and Varela (1980), called autopoietic systems. 'Auto' means self and 'poietic' means creation. Maturana and Varela define an autopoietic system as one that produces its own limits and organization by producing of the elements of which it consists.

It is typical for second-order cyberneticians such as Maturana (1988) and von Glasersfeld (1991) to delve deeper into biology than most humanists. Like Piaget, they descend to biology's prelinguistic creatures. With their concept of autopoiesis, Maturana and Varela (1980) show one of the reasons for this. Maturana's strength is his biological starting point in living systems. Through the concept of autopoiesis he shows that organisms are organizationally closed. The nervous system is also a closed circular system – one that does not accept outside information in any objective sense. Perturbations of the organism's vital organization produce knowledge through structural couplings, but only in relation to the domain of distinctions that the organism has developed in relation to its own domain of living.

Knowledge, therefore, also has a biological foundation. The forms of distinguishing that an observer develops are not 'true' in any universal sense. They acquire, however, an operational effectiveness in relation to the life praxis of the system in question. Viable patterns of differences are then established in the domain of distinction as various kinds of objects. Along the same lines, von Foerster (1992a, 310) explains the bringing forth of objects and concepts as cognitive invariants:

Of interest are circumstances in which the dynamics of a system transforms certain states into these very states, where the domain of states may be numeric values, arrangements (arrays, vectors, configurations, etc.), functions (polynomials, algebraic functions, etc.), functionals, dynamic behaviors, and so on, as attested by the proliferation of books and papers addressing these fascinating developments. Depending on domain and context, these states are in theoretical studies referred to as fixed points, limit cycles, eigenbehaviors, eigenoperators, and so on, and lately also as attractors, a terminology reintroducing teleology in modern dress. Pragmatically, they correspond to the computation of invariants; they may be object constancy, perceptual universals, cognitive invariants, identifications, namings, and so on.

When we look at language as a means of information, it seems clear that a word's metaphorical meaning depends on the organization of the living system (its body) and its context of living. Contrast this with computer language, which is free of context (Lakoff 1987). *Meanings, then, are the result of a coupling process based on joint experiences. This is an important foundation for all languages and all semiosis. Words do not carry meaning; rather, meanings are perceived on the basis of the perceiver's background experience. Percepts and words are not signals; rather, they are perturbations whose effects depend on system cohesion.* After a long period of interaction, a concept acquires a conventional meaning (*Eigenbehavior*) within a certain domain. The perception and interpretation of words force choices that open up opportunities for action and meaning (Luhmann 1990, 32).

This conception is complementary to 'the transmission model,' in which one imagines packages of information sent via language from a sender to a receiver. In the cognitive view, this is modified so as to consider that which is sent as only *potential* information. In second-order cybernetics, biological and social contexts are made explicit through the theory of autopoiesis, and there is a clear understanding of the pragmatic origins of knowledge from different knowledge domains. Von Foerster (1992a, 311) summarizes this position in the following passage:

> Another case of a net with circular organization that cannot be mapped onto a plane is *autopoiesis* ... An autopoietic system consists of interactive components whose interactions produce these very same components. Autopoiesis is thus a special case of self-organizing systems, whose organization is its own *eigenorganization* ... The notion of autopoiesis allows the phenomenon of language to emerge as a consequence, as the *eigenbehavior*, of the recursive interactions of two organisms, each in need of the other for the realization of its own autopoiesis ...

Because language can speak of itself having language, syntax, word, and so forth in its vocabulary, in conversations speakers can speak of themselves, thus preserving their autonomy in a social context by uttering, for example, the first person singular pronoun in the nominative case, 'I,' thus generating the shortest self-referential loop ...

It is precisely at this point that the perspectives of second-order cybernetics can be seen ... Second-order cybernetics invites you to leave Helmholtz's *locus observandi* and to step into the dynamic circularity of human give-and-take by becoming part and partner of the universe of discourse and the discourse on the universe.

In this view, language emerges from a mutual coupling between humans in society (whose consciousness emerges in the self-same process) through a long historical process. Meaning and the semantic level in language are 'sense created in common'; and it is this understanding, and not some direct objective empirical reference, that is language's most important reference. The meaning of a word changes as a consequence of historical drift, which is largely accidental. This development occurs partly because people who communicate never have completely identical 'horizons of understanding,' as Gadamer (1975) expressed it in hermeneutics. The meanings of concepts are created, maintained, and developed within discourse communities – that is, within a given knowledge domain, culture, or society – among biopsychological systems having a material body.

What are the organizational principles (if any) of the observations or cognitions that generate living systems? Organisms are more than dissipative structures; they are also self-organized. As systems they produce their own elements, boundaries, and internal organization. The system, including the nervous system, is organizationally closed. All nerve cells impinge on one another. The senses have no privileged position. *Maturana and Varela contend that there is no 'inside' or 'outside' for the nervous system, but only a maintenance of correlations that are constantly changing. Thus the nervous system does not 'pick up information' from its surroundings; rather, it 'brings forth a world.'* This is accomplished by specifying which perturbations of the sensory surface will lead to changes in the system's behaviour, which in turn is determined by the system's organization. As these interactions are repeated over a period of time, the changes of states that are triggered by the interactions will be adapted by the structure of the nervous system. These repetitions will be conserved as sensorimotor correlations. The repetitions of sensorimotor correlation patterns are conserved as part of the structural dynamics of the network. Structural couplings are established. We shall return to a deeper explanation and exploration of the significance of these concepts.

The problem here is how the scientific community views the connection between nature and mind or between the universe and the world of life, mind, and meaning. In Maturana and Varela's vision, the autopoietic system is closed in its structure-dependent organization. The environment, or a world, is only constructed by another observer. But who is this observer? Is it another autopoietic system that also only exists through the observation of another autopoietic system, observing the observing system and its surroundings? That is, are we confronted with an infinite regress?

The 'picture' of the environment is constructed through a society of observers making structural couplings to the environment and to one another through languaging. Maturana and Varela take biological systems, society, and language for granted, but not the environment. Instead of the usual physicalism, this is a biologistic world view. It is an important step forward; however, it is not a sufficient answer to the basic epistemological and ontological questions of how cognition, information, and communication are possible. This leaves unanswered the question about who made the first distinction between system and environment.

George Spencer-Brown, the philosopher and logician who came to mean so much to second-order cybernetics and autopoiesis theory, was aware of this question. Allow me to quote at length from his lucid description of this problem (1972, 104–5). This formulation is fundamental to his work *Laws of Form*:

> Let us then consider, for a moment, the world as described by the physicist. It consists of a number of particles which, if shot through their own space, appear as waves ... All these appear bound by certain natural laws which indicate the form of their relationship.
>
> Now the physicist himself, who describes all this, is, in his own account, himself constructed of it. He is, in short, made of a conglomeration of the very particles he describes, no more no less, bound together by and obeying such general laws as he himself has managed to find and record.
>
> Thus we cannot escape the fact that the world we know is constructed in order (and thus in such a way to be able) to see itself. This is indeed amazing.

Not so much in view of what it sees, although this may appear fantastic enough, but in respect of the fact that it *can* see *at all.*

But *in order* to do so, evidently it must first cut itself up into at least one state, which sees, and at least one state, which is seen. In this severed and mutilated condition, whatever it sees is *only partially* itself. We may take it that the world undoubtedly is itself (i.e., is indistinct from itself), but, in any attempt to see itself as an object, it must, equally undoubtedly, act so as to make itself distinct from, and therefore false to, itself. In this condition it always partially eludes itself.

It seems hard to find an acceptable answer to the question of how or why the world conceives a desire, and discovers an ability, to see itself, and appears to suffer the process. That it does so is sometimes called the original mystery.

Spencer-Brown poses the metaphysical question quite differently from what is mainstream in the sciences, including the information sciences and cybernetics. But he does so in a way that is important for the problem of the possibility of perception and qualia, cognition and signification and their relation to the meaning production of first-person experiences. *Spencer-Brown includes the process of observing as an important part of basic reality, which, as we shall see later, places him near Peirce, who includes feeling and qualia in his concept of (unmanifest) Firstness.* Both are pointing to a way out of the phenomenological problem of the sciences that Husserl pointed out. Spencer-Brown is also helped by the anthropic principle that knowledge is only possible in universes where creatures like us can evolve and come to see! There may be millions of other universes but nobody is there to see them.

In light of the developments of thermodynamics, chaos theory, and non-linear dynamics, there is a tendency today to change the understanding of metaphysics. Often it is no longer perceived as determined by the laws of mechanics, but rather as the outgrowth of a probabilistic world view. Inspired by system science, more organic views (Gilbert and Sarkar 2000) that include emergence, levels, and wholes that evolve new laws in a non-deterministic philosophy are becoming more widely accepted. Many researchers, however, cling to the mechanistic ideal while accepting the practical impossibility of dealing with large ensembles of atoms in a deterministic way. Such ensembles cannot be modelled except with probabilistic models. Prigogine and Stengers (1984) have shown the inconsistency in such an approach, which rejects chance as something real and views it only as a subjective lack of knowledge. Their point is that objective chance is the source of irreversibility and evolution, and therefore of its products, such as scientists themselves. There is a true metaphysical dilemma in modern physics and information science. If one is a mechanicist and believes that everything – including our brain and cognitive apparatus – is governed by mathematical laws, then all that we are is the expression of a world formula in search of itself. Hawking (1989) sees this dilemma, but backs away from it.

Alternatively, we are the products of chaos and chance, what Richard Dawkins (1987) calls 'the blind watchmaker' of evolution, which is working through 'selfish genes.' No matter what theory one holds, in this metaphysics it will, in the end, only be a product of pure coincidence. Something is epistemologically wrong with this framework and its concepts. This 'wrongness' is what second-order cybernetics attempts to address by developing autology through biological constructivism. Like organicism it is still a materialistic paradigm (Gilbert and Sarkar 2003).

Varela (1975) points to self-reference as the crucial factor in his development of a calculus based on Spencer-Brown's work. But from where can it arise? Some believe that the special quality of constructivism as a scientific paradigm is its avoidance of ontological questions. But in my view, even constructivism cannot avoid stating its preconditions. I speak of course of a radical constructivism that goes beyond the social constructivism that takes nature for granted and as objective, and therefore is not able to incorporate a natural history of observing systems, or that claims that it is realistic but with an 'open ontology,' as Luhmann does. To admit that nature has at least some dynamic structures seems unavoidable.

Even if one were to embrace a 'cookie cutter constructivist viewpoint,' in which one's perception and concept cuts out the form of some basic 'world stuff' – which seems to be Luhmann's position – one would have to say something about the minimum requirement for this 'stuff' to become conscious linguistic systems. As we saw in the above quotation, *Spencer-Brown actually suggests that there is a basic self-referent quality to the world/universe that is the process that started evolution.*

In their discussions of differences and similarities in cognition and problem solving in people and computers, the Dreyfus brothers (1986) and Winograd and Flores (1986) have used Heidegger's (1973) concepts such as 'Dasein,' which underlines the 'throwness' of humans in the world. They use this concept to show that an individual's relationship with the world is fundamentally different from that of a digital computer. Winograd and Flores use Maturana's theory of autopoiesis and the closure of the nervous system to show that this basic condition is common to both people and animals. The basic situation vis-à-vis the environment is not objective and separated. The 'domain of living' – a basic concept from Maturana – is, rather, an integrated part of the structure of the system, and one, furthermore, that predates any cognitive separation between self and non-self. This is quite similar to Latour's claim (1993) that nature and culture were never separated in the way modernity thinks.

Maturana's conclusion is that the world is as we 'see' it in our praxis of living. It is a Multiverse. He never addresses the 'resistance of reality,' though. But why can we not choose to see the world in whatever way we like? He might answer through the antrophic principle (see, for instance, Barrow 1998) that if we did, the world would not be consistent with our existence as living beings. We can see the world only in ways consistent with ourselves as observers. But still, even within these worlds, things seem to have a certain *Eigenvalue*.

The theories and concepts of von Foerster and Maturana lead to a much better grasp of the basic situation of observing and cognition; yet in their radicality, they also seem to have removed too much when they neglect completely 'das Ding an sich.' The problem is that they have attempted to find a scientific solution to a basically philosophical problem. For their part, many social constructivists avoid these basic questions.

Both von Foerster's second-order cybernetics and Maturana's 'bring-forth-ism' are correct to focus our attention on creative processes in perception and cognition. As I have already demonstrated, one cannot resolve the problem of mind and intentionality in an evolutionary philosophy through either mechanical materialism or physical indeterminism. Nor do I believe that this can be accomplished through pure phenomenalistic idealism (there are only phenomena), subjective constructivism (I construct the world), or mentalism (everything is mental), all of which underestimate the importance of the relative stability of the 'outside' world to the possibility of knowledge, communication, and meaning.

This epistemological foundation of second-order cybernetics connects it to important points in Heidegger's phenomenology (Heidegger 1973). The important point from Heidegger is that as observers, we are always already a part of the world when we start to describe it. When we start to describe it, we separate ourselves to a certain degree from the wholeness of the world of our living praxis. This is an important development in second-order cybernetic and system thinking. But it lacks, of course, Heidegger's phenomenological foundation.

Luhmann (1990, 3) continues this development when he summarizes how cybernetics and the concept of autopoiesis in Maturana's definition provide a new way of looking at things. However, he simultaneously maintains a sophisticated realism:

> Autopoietic systems 'are systems that are defined as unities as networks of productions of components that recursively, through their interactions, generate and realize the network that produces them and constitute, in the space in which they exist, the boundaries of the network as components that participate in the realization of the network.'[15] Autopoietic systems, then are not only self-organizing systems, they not only produce and eventually change their own *structures;* their self-reference applies to the production of other *components* as well. This is the decisive conceptual innovation. It adds a turbocharger to the already powerful engine of self-referential machines. Even *elements*, that is, last components (individuals) which are, at least for the system itself, indecomposable, are produced by the system itself. Thus, everything that is used as a unit by the system is produced as a unit by the system itself. This applies to elements, processes, boundaries, and other structures and, last but not least, to the unity of the system itself. Autopoietic systems, then, are sovereign with respect to the constitution of identities and differences. They, of course, do not create a material world of their own. They presuppose other levels of reality, as for example human life presupposes the small span of temperature in which water is liquid. But whatever they use as identities and as differences is of their own making. In other words, they cannot import identities and differences from the outer world; these are forms about which they have to decide themselves.

My concern here has been the function of the concept of 'outside reality' in the analysis of behaviours of autopoietic or 'observing systems.' Although we have rightly abandoned the notion of 'objective reality' in second-order cybernetics, we should not give up the notion of a partly independent 'outside reality.' There is something lacking in the phenomenalistic or idealistic constructivist position that is not corrected by repeatedly referring to 'experienced reality.' We cannot avoid ontological considerations, but these must, of course, be constantly developed through critical epistemological discussions and analysis and an ongoing revision in the light of the experimental results obtained by the sciences. We need to develop a more refined and complex under-standing of the role of the concepts of reality in relation to our under-standing of our own processes of knowing. We need to look closer at von Foerster's way of founding second-order cybernetics, and we will do this later.

Hence, we need a more sophisticated theory of how these identities and differences develop, one that does not resort to the usual material-istic mechanism, eliminative materialistic theories (Churchland 2004), or functionalistic theories of mind that deny any sort of independent reality to human experiences of first person consciousness – and, there-fore, causality as well. But such a theory must be supplemented by a theory of signs and signification, as well as by theories about those bio-logical and social systems for which the difference can make a differ-ence, as cybernetics largely addresses the circularity of differences in self-organized systems. I suggest that to go deeper into an understand-ing of the process, we must analyse the whole process of sign making, as C.S. Peirce does in his semiotics. Let us now take a first brief look at Peirce's semiotic philosophy to get a sense of the plot and its promises and problems.

For at least two hundred years, science has recognized that living beings are an intrinsic part of physical and chemical reality. For more than one hundred years it has been recognized that humans and their culture are an intrinsic part of the biological aspect of reality. Physical and chemical aspects have long been considered basic for the universe, yet only in the past thirty years has it been understood how deeply con-nected our biological aspect is to the entire development of the uni-verse.[16] We are now on the brink of discovering how mind and signifi-cation penetrate the basic levels of our reality, as Peirce has posited.

1.14 Peirce's New List of Categories as the Foundation for a Theory of Cognition and Signification

I will sketch how I see Peirce's work and its value as a transdisciplinary framework for information, communication, and cognitive sciences. Then I will attempt a more detailed analysis to give the reader a pre-liminary understanding of the direction in which I will be moving the arguments.

Peirce has already done important work on this construction of a new framework. Even more importantly, he integrates it both with a transdisciplinary theory of signification in his semiotics and, through his concept of vagueness, with an evolutionary theory of logic.

Following Peirce, I believe that our problem is that we view chaos as the absence of law, which is a negative definition. In fact, we should be viewing it as a continuum of living possibilities and qualities. This understanding is closer to the original Greek definition of Chaos as the origin of the world of time, space, energy, and information (Gaia), where Eros is the creative evolutionary force and mathematics only a means to bond back to the source, not the answer in itself. Abraham (1993) points this out in his attempt to resurrect the Orphic tradition to encompass the knowledge of modern science and chaos theory. Inspired by Abraham and Deely (1990), my thought is that the mechanization and mathematization of nature is the work of classical physics and as such violates the wholeness of the Greeks' Cosmos thinking from which semiotics was originally developed (Deely 2001b). In this process the original Physis concept was reduced, and truth and meaning were separated. Deely (1998, 2001a) is on the same track in his attempt to create (recreate?) a physiosemiotics. I find his work greatly inspiring but still in need of a clear connection to the whole body of scientific knowledge and information science, which is why I attempt to develop a cybersemiotics.

An important difference between modern physics and Peirce's theory lies in the conception of chaos already mentioned and Peirce's unique triadic theory of basic categories. I will not describe or discuss the triadic theory of signification and semiosis at any length here. Instead, I will begin by offering a key quotation from his *Monist* paper 'The Architecture of Theories,' which states clearly the direction and possibilities of Peirce's theory of three metaphysical categories: Firstness, Secondness, and Thirdness (see also Christiansen 1995). Peirce (CP, 6.32–3) writes:

> Three conceptions are perpetually turning up at every point in every theory of logic, and in the most rounded systems they occur in connection with one another. They are conceptions so very broad and consequently indefinite that they are hard to seize and may be easily overlooked. I call them the conception of First, Second, Third. First is the conception of being or existing independent of anything else. Second is the conception of being relative to, the conception of reaction with, something else. Third is the conception of mediation, whereby a first and a second are brought into relation ... The origin of things, considered not as leading to anything, but in itself, contains the idea of First, the end of things that of Second, the

process of mediating between them that of Third ... In psychology Feeling is First, Sense of reaction Second, General conception Third ... In biology, the idea of arbitrary sporting is First, heredity is Second, the process whereby the accidental characters become fixed is Third. Chance is First, Law is second, the tendency to take habits is Third. Mind is First, Matter is Second, Evolution is Third.

Such are the materials out of which chiefly a philosophical theory ought to be built, in order to represent the state of knowledge ... It would be a Cosmogenic Philosophy. It would suppose that in the beginning – infinitely remote – there was a chaos of unpersonalized feeling, which being without connection or regularity would properly be without existence. This feeling, sporting here and there in pure arbitrariness, would have started the germ of a generalizing tendency. Its other sportings would be evanescent, but this would have a growing virtue. Thus, the tendency to take habits would be started; and from this, with the other principles of evolution, all regularities of the universe would be evolved. At any time, however, an element of pure chance survives and will remain until the world becomes an absolutely perfect, rational, and symmetrical system, in which mind is at last crystallized in the infinitely distant future.

This is the 'white elephant' of Peirce's theory, as Appel (1981) calls this crucial metaphysical move in Peirce's semiotics. It is hard to swallow for most mainstream scientists and philosophers. Nevertheless, I will argue that, as mentioned earlier in connection with Spencer-Brown's metaphysics, this is exactly what we need. I further think that it is possible to make it work for science, the humanities, and the social sciences, much along the lines of Deely's (1990) arguments for a semiotics on a Peircean basis, although with some further perspectives from the sciences added.

If one attempts to translate the categories into second-order cybernetic concepts, Secondness is the first distinction made by an observer marked by a primary sign, the Representamen. The observer is Peirce's Interpretant, which belongs to Thirdness. Only through this triadic semiosis can cognition be generated. To become information, differences must be seen as signs for the observer. This happens when they become internally developed Interpretants. See Figure 1.8.

As Peirce writes (1955, 99–100) in his most famous definition of the sign process (in 'A Syllabus of Certain Topics of Logic,' written in 1903): 'A sign, or Representamen, is a First which stands in a genuine triadic relation to a Second, its Object, as to be capable of determining a Third, called its Interpretant, to assume the same triadic relation to its Object

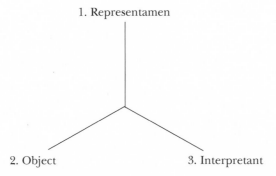

1.8.   The triadic semiosis according to Peirce

in which it stands itself to the same Object ... A Sign is a Representamen with a mental Interpretant.'

The object here is that aspect of reality which the Representamen signifies. In a way, Peirce's Object is also a sign. Peirce's semiotic philosophy pushes cognitive science beyond the limitations of information science and theory, as I and many others have pointed out. It is an Aristotelian golden mean between the mechanicist at the one extreme and the pure (non-ontological) constructivist at the other. Like Aristotle, Peirce is a synechist ('matter' is continuous) and a hylozoist ('matter' has an internal aspect of feeling). From this we arrive at a non-Cartesian cognitive formulation for science with no absolute predistinction between mind and matter, as well as a field view of 'substance' that is compatible with modern quantum field theory and general relativity theory. Most forces are described today by fields, as are subatomic 'particles.' These fields are not actually 'matter' as classical physics perceived it in atomistic mechanics. *Since the rise of quantum mechanics and quantum field theory, science and common sense no longer have a word for the 'stuff' reality is made of.* Peirce offers such a theory. The development of thermodynamics as a fundamental physical theory deploys time and evolution as the bases of physical theory in a way that clearly goes beyond classical mechanistic physics. The concept of irreversible time has become foundational (Prigogine 1996).

When we develop deep scientific theories such as information science, we cannot avoid reflecting on the nature of reality as a prerequisite for our various scientific paradigms. It is far too presumptuous to claim that basic knowledge is expressible in one unified and precise form. There are no 'ideas' or mathematical 'world formulas' waiting to be uncovered in basic reality. Like Peirce, I believe that basic reality or Firstness starts as vagueness and only later develops into distinct forms. No doubt mathematics and logic have much to say about the possibilities and limits of our epistemological situation and is able to connect us back to reality, as Abraham (1993) suggests and as Louis H. Kauffmann describes in his many columns in *Cybernetics and Human Knowing.* Nor can we a priori expect words to fully describe 'the universe' or 'basic reality,' because our investigations show that signs and concepts work on differences in local contexts. Still, there does appear to be intrinsic order in reality, although it may be partly created as an emergent phenomenon by the interactive process of cognition itself.

In ethology one says that ritualized instinctive behaviour becomes sign stimuli in the coordination of behaviour between, for instance, the two genders of a species in their mating play. So – as it is already in the language of ethology – a piece of behaviour or colouration of plumage in movement, for instance, becomes a sign for the coordination of a specific behaviour. The mood and context determine the biological meanings of these signs, which are true triadic signs. Ethology presents a fundamental ecological and evolutionary perspective on cognition and behaviour that dovetails with Peirce's conception of the construction of meaning. Here we see the aptness of Peirce's sign definitions. Peirce (CP, 1.39) writes:

A sign stands for something to the idea which it produces, or modifies. Or, it is a vehicle conveying into the mind something from without. That for which it stands is called its object; that which it conveys, its meaning; and the idea to which it gives rise, its interpretant. The object of representation can be nothing but a representation of which the first representation is the interpretant. But an endless series of representations, each representing the one behind it, may be conceived to have an absolute object at its limit. The meaning of a representation can be nothing but a representation. In fact, it is nothing but the representation itself conceived as stripped of irrelevant clothing. But this clothing never can be completely stripped off; it is only changed for something more diaphanous. So there is an infinite regression here. Finally, the interpretant is nothing but another representation to which the torch of truth is handed along; and as representation, it has its interpretant again. Lo, another infinite series.

There is no final and true object and representation in the present. Both are under constant evolution. The meaning of a sign (a Representamen) is determined by the context. For instance, the red belly of a female stickleback is the Representamen for a male autopoietic system languaging with the female – because she is in a reproductive mood – and creates in him the Interpretant that she is worth mating with. Mating or reproduction is the Object, which is a biosocial construct. It is a context for the play of signs, which in this specific mood of mating attains shared meanings based on a habit established through evolution. Peirce writes: 'In the first place, a 'Representamen,' like a word, – indeed, most words are representamens –, is not a single thing, but is of the nature of a mental habit, it consists in the fact that, something would be' (Peirce 1911, MS 675, 'A Sketch of Logical Critique').

Peirce changed Kant's twelve categories of pure reason to three natural categories bridging mind and nature. As mentioned earlier, he called them Firstness, Secondness, and Thirdness. In Peirce's semiotics, everything in nature is a potential sign. This is a meeting point with Bateson from cybernetics, for whom information is a difference that makes a difference, if one chooses to view every difference as potential information that becomes informative through semiosis. *With Peirce, we can say that differences become information when an interpreter sees them as signs.*

The implication of this is that qualia and 'the inner life' are potentially there from the beginning. However, they require a nervous system to achieve full manifestation. Peirce speaks of the potential qualities of Firstness. The point is that organisms and their nervous systems do not create mind and qualia. The qualia of mind develop through interaction with nervous systems, which living bodies develop into still more manifested forms. Peirce's point is that this manifestation occurs through the development of sign processes.

Second-order cybernetics sees information as an internal creation of an autopoietic system in response to a perturbation. Only in established structural couplings can signs acquire meaning. *Second-order cybernetics brings to semiotics the ideas of closure, structural couplings, interpenetration, and languaging.*

The suggestive value is always working in the context of a life form, both in biology and in human cultural life. The key to the understanding of understanding and communication is that both animals and humans live in self-organized *Umwelten*, which they not only project around themselves but also project deep inside their systems. I call these *signification spheres.* The organization of signs and the meanings they attain through habits of the mind and body follow from the principles of second-order cybernetics, in that they produce their own *Eigenvalues* of signs and meanings, and thereby their own internal mental organization, which is then projected onto the environment.

In humans, these signs are organized into language through social self-conscious communication. Accordingly, our social universe is organized as and through texts. But that is, of course, not an explanation of meaning, but rather an attempt to describe the dynamics of meaning-generating and sharing systems and how they are organized.

Peirce's reflexive or cybernetic definition of the Interpretant points to culture, history, and the never-ending search for truth and knowledge. It considers habits and historical drift – as Maturana and Varela (1980) do – as the social constructors of meaning. Evolutionary science attempts to find relatively stable patterns and dynamic modes (habits); it is not a science of eternal laws. Peirce is close to organicism and general systems theory (Bertalanffy 1976).

In the following chapters I will investigate further the link between second-order cybernetics and the semiotics of C.S. Peirce. I will also analyse the interesting connections among Bateson's concept of information, Maturana's and Varela's autopoietic concept of the knower, Varela's 'Calculus of Self-reference,' and Peirce's triadic and self-referential semiotics.

I will show how the self-referent autopoietic observer in second-order cybernetics can be seen as a further development of the biological understanding of Peirce's concept of the Interpretant. The connection establishes the self-reference of the knower through the time-dependent process of signifying. This process is an ongoing historical drift among the knower, the known, and the process of knowing. Peirce's Tychism is a further development of Prigogine and Stengers's discussion of the objectivity of chance. I will analyse the compatibility of Peirce's semiotic realism based on Tychism and Hylozoism with the world views of Maturana, von Foerster, and Luhmann. Pragmatic language philosophy – especially in relation to Wittgenstein's language philosophy and Lakoff and Johnson's embodied cognitive semantic – will be further analysed to create a cybersemiotics.

1.15 Conclusion

For a long time, cognitive science's 'information processing paradigm,' with the computer as metaphor for cognition and communication, has dominated attempts to develop information and communication science. The limitations of this complexity, randomness, and uncertainty paradigm are mostly seen in its inability to integrate present knowledge of the behaviour of living systems and culture with their creation of signification in language games of communication. Realizing that the ability to obtain knowledge predates science, that knowing requires an autopoietic and languaging system, and that language requires signs and a society to convey meaning, allows one to see the limitations of purely scientific explanations of the phenomenon of information. Knowing is the prerequisite for science. How, then, can knowledge and intelligence ever be expected to be fully explained by a science based on a physicalistic or functionalistic world view?

The two transdisciplinary frameworks of second-order cybernetics and Peirce's triadic semiotics appear promising for developing a dialogue between social systems (Luhmann) and the knowledge of cognition and production of signification in biological systems (autopoiesis and structural couplings). Second-order cybernetics has abandoned the objectivistic idea of information, but it has not yet developed a concept of sign. Semiotics scientifically studies signification as a basic and universal dimension of human reality. Peirce's semiotics also address nonintentional signs and have an evolutionary, process-oriented, second-order triadic sign concept – that is, all parts of semiosis are signs. However, it lacks knowledge of the self-organization of cognition and of the structural coupling of observers. It is suggested that these two frameworks could be integrated through something like Wittgenstein's concept of language games, and that prelanguage biological systems producing signification could be understood as sign games. *Communicative meaning is generated by autopoietic systems in sign and language games. Meaning is generated in the 'flesh' (a concept not limited to a materialistic description apparatus; see Merleau-Ponty 2002). The 'flesh' of any living system is permeated by signs. In humans, 'the flesh' is also permeated with language and culture.*

Meaning is biological, cultural, individually experienced, and situated. It is a biological and phenomenological perspective that reflects observers and their cultural discourse communities. This perspective starts with the living and works from there towards a non-mechanistic unity between science, the humanities, and the social sciences.

In the next chapter I will start by outlining a basic theory of knowledge and knowing that provides the foundation for further analysis. It is only a crude scaffold, but as the theory develops more flesh (so to speak) will be put on the bones of this basic skeleton to develop a self-supporting reflective theory. As shown by the above outline of the problems of an information science and their solutions, the entire concept of an information science touches on the epistemological foundation of science. There is a strange loop in wanting to develop a science of information, cognition, and communication, in that it closely approaches an attempt at the mechanism of that prescientific human knowledge that is the prerequisite for the development of science as a social strategy of knowledge. This is possible only if we release the conception of science from the blend of mechanism, reductionism, and logical empiricism that is still the dominant force in most 'hard' science.

2 The Self-Organization of Knowledge: Paradigms of Knowledge and Their Role in Deciding What Counts as Legitimate Knowledge

2.1 Introduction

This chapter develops a non-reductionist and transdisciplinary view of human knowledge in light of the importance of transdisciplinary practices and sciences. It analyses the difficulties resulting from the lack of a recognized place for and value of phenomenological knowledge in relation to the general physicalistic ontology that is still the generally accepted background for many transdisciplinary scientific frameworks in cognitive science. I promote an epistemology that treats science as only one aspect of our knowledge, and human knowledge as extending beyond language into the hypercomplex. By stipulating hypercomplexity, I assume as little as possible about the nature of the world and reality apart from its capacity to uphold us as self-reflexive, biological, and cultural language-using conscious beings who produce and communicate knowledge and therefore reflect evolution and some kind of dynamic regularities. Next, I will be creating an opening for the phenomenological aspect in a realistic metaphysics. I will then introduce the premise that knowledge consists of self-organized signification systems based on metaphysical frameworks in social practice. The interpretation of signs in a systematized knowledge framework is where the medical sciences started, in the classical Greek tradition of Hippocrates. This non-reductionist framework promises to open a non-Cartesian, transdisciplinary understanding of how knowledge is generated and communicated in society, and without losing what has been gained through the rigor and methods of either the sciences or the logic of philosophical analysis.

2.2 Science and the Development of World Formula Thinking

Aristotle considered Episteme to be the most fundamental knowledge about nature.[1] He employed this term mainly to describe geometrical reasoning and, for instance, the mathematical workings of the heavens. Galileo then brought it down to earth during the Renaissance by laying the foundations for classical physics; he believed that to find the mathematical model behind phenomena such as the pendulum and free fall – sublunary phenomena – would be to contemplate God's laws of nature. Newton's discoveries only strengthened this idea that mathematical laws could unite the descriptions of Heaven and Earth (the sublunary sphere). During the Enlightenment, Laplace's notion of an all-intelligent demon as a transcendent observer and supreme calculator who comprehended Newton's laws carried this idea to the extreme. Knowing the position and impulse of all particles in a 'world,' the demonic or angelic observer – that is, the spirit of the ideal objective observer in natural science – could develop a mathematical formula for the world system in order to predict everything that would happen to the system in the future, and, by reversing the same equations, could calculate the system's history back to the beginning. This was possible because, so this view held, the laws were transcendental.

Prigogine and Stengers (1984) refer to this research program as 'the world formula project.' It assumes that human intelligence and rationality is an instance of, or a reflection of, this transcendental or divine rational and logical world order. This thinking and ethos in science has been most pronounced in physics, but recently it has also been developed in biology and cognitive science. For some time we have looked for the algorithms of genes, of (human) intelligence (AI), and of language (Chomsky's generative grammar and Fodor's 'language of thought').

Since the development of logical empiricism in the late 1930s, many scientists and philosophers have contended that physics is the foundational model-science to which sciences 'at higher levels' should reduce their explanations. This should be accomplished through the construction of mathematical state function models of the systems. In the end, the formulas for linguistics and intelligent behaviour will be integrated with genetic knowledge through physiology and embryology, and the biological formula of genes will be connected to physics through chemistry. A simple model of this idea of the unification of the sciences, the humanities, and the social sciences would be similar to the one shown

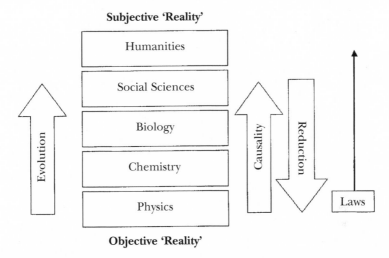

2.1.   The traditional unity-of-the-sciences model from logical empiricism, in which physics is the model science for all other systems of knowledge, to which they can all eventually be reduced. Physics is what comes closest to describing 'objective reality.' The scientific language is mathematics and logic in the form of algorithmic computer models. All causes can eventually be reduced to physical ones. There are many different variations on this model.

in 2.1. Here, physics is seen as the foundational science closest to objective reality. To 'explain' something is to reduce its dynamics to physical laws. All systems in the world are derivations of physical systems; it follows that mental phenomena are either not real or are 'emergent' properties of special ways of organizing physical systems (as is largely believed in systems theory and the biological sciences; the original mechanistic and reductionist philosophy of science, however, does not accept 'emergence.' It is a systemic and organicist term.).

Physics describes the basic laws of reality that determine the real causes of movement and organization in nature. The metaphysics of this paradigm of science presumes that the world started as a physical mathematical system after the Big Bang; thus physics is presumed also to encompass the origins of the universe, the beginnings of the evolution of matter and energy, the evolution of the earth, the origins and development of life and ecosystems, and the cognitive systems that resulted in human nature, consciousness, language, and culture. Through logical empiricism, this philosophy of science has come to view itself as reaching beyond metaphysical assumptions. But as the physicist and Anglican minister John Polkinghorne (1996, 102) writes: 'Every one has a metaphysics – a worldview – just as all people speak prose, whether they are aware of it or not. Science can and should contribute to that worldview, but it should by no means monopolize it. Unless you are one of those ... so flushed with the recent success of your discipline that you are moved to claim that "science is all," you will want to locate scientific understanding within a wider view of knowledge that gives equally serious consideration to other forms of human insight and experience.' This is what I am trying to do with this book.

2.3 Objectivist Metaphysics

Lakoff (1987, 159) has convincingly summarized the most basic metaphysical ideas in an objectivist philosophy about how we can acquire true knowledge of the world and how our cognition and language functions. This is an important foundation for mainstream cognitive science:

> On the objectivist view, reality comes with a unique, correct, complete structure in terms of entities, properties, and relations. This structure exists, independent of any human understanding. Such structuring is necessary in order to get the objectivist view on cognition and language off the ground. If, as objectivists hold, thought is the manipulation of abstract symbols, then such symbols must be made meaningful somehow. The objectivist answer is that symbols (that is, words and mental representations) are made meaningful *in one and only one way*: via a correspondence to entities and categories in either the existing world or in possible worlds.

Accordingly, meaning is defined as the true representation of a preexisting objective world. Any reference to a human inner world of cognition, emotion, and volition is avoided. Representation is seen from a Cartesian dualist perspective and as a logical and mathematical process. But this avoidance of the subjective is paid for with heavy ontological postulates:

> OBJECTIVIST METAPHYSICS: All of reality consists of entities, which have fixed properties and relations holding among them at any instant.
>   Objectivist metaphysics is often found in the company of another metaphysical assumption, essentialism.

ESSENTIALISM: Among the properties that things have, some are essential; that is, they are those properties that make the thing what it is, and without which it would not be that kind of thing. Other properties are accidental – that is, they are properties that things happen to have, not properties that capture the essence of the thing.

The classical theory of categories relates properties of entities to categories containing those entities.

CLASSICAL CATEGORIZATION: All the entities that have a given property or a collection of properties in common form a category. Such properties are necessary and sufficient to define the category. All categories are of this kind. (ibid., 160)

In this way the subjective and socio-cultural element of classification is avoided. To do otherwise might open the door to relativism and social constructivism. So instead, a sort of Aristotelian view of categories is retained; however, it is lifted out of its original consistent and explicit metaphysics and placed in a non-explicit metaphysics of a more Platonic nature, as reflected in the view that mathematics and logic are objectively existing natural languages. Many mathematicians are Platonists. Lakoff (ibid., 162) continues, making this metaphysics explicit:

Given that properties have objective existence, and that properties define categories, it can make sense to speak of categories as having objective existence.

THE DOCTRINE OF OBJECTIVE CATEGORIES: The entities in the world form objectively existing categories based on their shared objective properties. If one adds essentialism one can distinguish a special kind of objective category – one based on shared essential properties, as opposed to shared incidental properties.

THE DOCTRINE OF NATURAL KINDS: There are natural kinds of entities in the world, each kind being a category based on shared essential properties, that is, properties that things have by virtue of their very nature ...

Since the entities of the world fall into objective categories, there are logical relations among those categories – logical relations that are purely objective and independent of any minds, human or otherwise.

OBJECTIVIST Logic: Logical relations exist objectively among the categories of the world.

Thus the world consists of objective categories. Here one sees how logic and mathematics are transported into nature, as already strongly advocated by Galileo. This is further combined with the atomic and essentialistic view that basic undividable properties exist logically and materially:

> Some properties may be made up of logical combinations of other properties; these are complex. Those properties, which have no internal logical structure, are simple, or *atomic.*
> REAL-WORLD ATOMISM: All properties either are atomic or consist of logical combinations of atomic properties. (ibid., 164)

In much of analytical philosophy, these strong ontological postulates lead to logical empiricism and the positions later developed from them. They establish physics, in combination with mathematics, as the most basic science 'closest to reality' and as a model for all other sciences that deal with reality. But this paves the way for a computational view of intelligence and information:

> OBJECTIVIST COGNITION: Thought is the manipulation of abstract symbols. Symbols get their meaning via correspondences to entities and categories in the world. In this way, the mind can represent external reality and be said to 'mirror nature.'
> OBJECTIVIST CONCEPTS: Concepts are symbols that (a) stand in a relation to other concepts in a conceptual system and (b) stand in correspondence to entities and categories in the real world (or possible worlds) ...
> OBJECTIVIST RATIONALITY: Human reason is accurate when it matches objectivist logic, that is, when the symbols used in thought correctly correspond to entities and categories in the world and when the mind reproduces the logical relations that exist objectively among the entities and categories of entities in the world ...
> OBJECTIVIST KNOWLEDGE: Knowledge consists in correctly conceptualizing and categorizing things in the world and grasping the objective connections among those things and those categories. (ibid., 159–63)

This metaphysics indicates that faith in the unlimited possibilities of science's rationality is still an important ideological factor, even though increasing numbers of scientists and philosophers of science are acknowledging the limitations of mathematical-empirical models as candidates for the sort of universal knowledge that Aristotle called Episteme. Knowledge from the natural sciences has authority in today's society, to a certain degree at the cost of other forms of knowledge. This is clear from the importance attached to this form of knowledge in the medical sciences, to the detriment of social-psychological approaches to coping with illness. Philosophy of science is a productive approach to obtaining a reflective understanding of the value of quantitative and natural scientific 'facts,' 'laws,' and 'models' in relation to insights into social and psychological processes. These include ethical and aesthetical opinions when one makes a decision. I want to open up a broader view of knowledge; my hope is that doing so will pave a way to understanding other interdisciplinary strategies and thus increasing our critical insight. We must find a view of knowledge that makes it possible to combine different kinds of knowledge pertaining to specific situations or problems in a reflective and arguable manner.

The late Danish philosopher of science Johannes Witt-Hansen emphasized in his final book (1980) that the 'situations of powerlessness' arising in science and the 'postulates of impotence' they foster are crucial to the development of knowledge. He cites a number of examples in both mathematics and physics. A classic example is the powerlessness of the Pythagoreans' belief that nature's law is based on whole natural numbers. They were faced with the realization that the side and the diagonal of a square are incommensurable because it is impossible to measure the length of the diagonal of a square in units of the side, no matter how small these units are made. Today this relation is called the square root. If the sides were 1, the diagonal would be the square root of 2, which is not a rational number. The Pythagoreans were forced to abandon their philosophy that the universe is governed by harmonic relations between natural numbers. After a delay of two thousand years, this 'powerlessness' was resolved by a fundamental extension of the concept of numbers to include irrational numbers.[2]

In physics, the realization that it is impossible to construct a perpetual motion machine (*perpetuum mobile*) had great importance for the development of thermodynamic concepts of energy and entropy. In quantum mechanics, the recognition of our 'powerlessness' to simultaneously measure a subatomic particle's position and its momentum with an arbitrary precision led to Heisenberg's uncertainty principle and to Bohr's theory of complementarity.

As a consequence of the scientific paradigm shift in the twentieth century, many scientists now acknowledge that all attempts to construct exact models lead to the creation of non-knowledge, or 'blindness.' When we focus on one aspect of the world, the others become blurred: they become 'background' or 'noise.' Every explication, clarification, and formulation must ignore some aspects of reality. However much we exert ourselves, there will always exist some amount of ignorance from a strictly objective, scientific point of view. This leads to a necessary opening towards other scientific and cognitive forms, including an acknowledgment that ethical and aesthetical considerations matter. But this does not provide any real understanding of how these knowledge forms can work together. To understand how, we must move our analysis up one level.

Originally educated as a biologist, I have long been sceptical about research programs based on the belief that mechanism can provide an adequate framework for understanding living systems. Furthermore, from a psychological and semiotic perspective, it does not seem likely that theoretical understandings of the inner world of sensations, feelings, signification, and volition of living systems can emerge from mechanistic or functionalistic algorithmic thinking. A broader framework – both transdisciplinary and non-reductionist – is therefore necessary. This non-reductionist framework should be able to incorporate semiotics, cognitive semantics, and pragmatic linguistics in a theory of signification and semantics without abandoning what we have gained through the rigor and the methods of the sciences and the logic of philosophical analysis. Can we develop a unifying framework for all different knowledge systems that our old mechanistic framework cannot handle without resorting to harmful reductions?

Let me delve deeper into one of these problems in today's research: a scientific explanation of consciousness that does not deny the existence of its phenomenological aspects. How can these two realms be encompassed by the same theory? Or as Petito, Varela, and Roy (1999, xiv) write: 'One of the major concerns behind the investigation of cognitive phenomena today is the construction of a science of cognition that is continuous with the most basic science of nature and, accordingly to understand how a *res externa* could become complex enough through evolution to possess the various attributes of a *res cogitans*.'

This is an example of one formulation of a clear paradox between a scientific program's metaphysical basis and the goal it wants to obtain. The point in Cartesian dualism as a foundation of science is that the two worlds are absolutely and qualitatively separated. This is why science can be built on the basis that nature is like a machine, and that it therefore makes sense to search for the universal laws 'behind it' that were used to create it, and the manipulations of which can control it. Luhmann

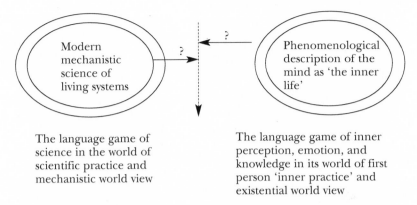

The language game of
science in the world of
scientific practice and
mechanistic world view

The language game of inner
perception, emotion, and
knowledge in its world of first
person 'inner practice' and
existential world view

2.2.   The mechanistic and phenomenological description systems are isolated
from each other and invisible to each other's conceptual worlds. I realize that I
am violating Husserl's thinking by placing phenomenology in a two-world
frame, but here I am using the concept of phenomenology broadly as the study
of the 'inner life' or first-person experiences.

(1995) would say that this is a typical example of how a research school
or paradigm chooses to set a difference to work from, and how this difference masks the connection between the psyche – our first-person
experiences – and the world. Forgetting this original distinction places
the general idea of 'a science of consciousness' in a situation of powerlessness. It cannot overcome the self-same distinction that defined the
research program, which is why the idea of a psychological science has
always been so problematic. It also creates the rift between the two cultures, and makes the distinction between nature and culture almost
absolute. As this distinction is an important foundation for modernity,
Latour (1993) claims that 'we have never been modern.' When science
encounters paradox, the philosophical foundation must be broadened
in order to develop new concepts that explain the empirical data. Niels
Bohr (1954) argued and demonstrated this in quantum mechanics and
the theory of complementarity, and I agree with him.
    The problem lies in our efforts to combine two phenomena from dis-
tinct knowledge systems. Because they reside in two different description systems, they exist in two different worlds that are invisible to each
other because they do not share a common scientific scholarly language, conceptions of knowledge, and methods. See Figure 2.2 for an
illustration.

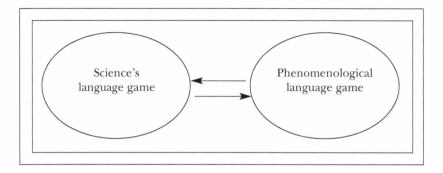

2.3.   How a common conceptual framework for science and phenomenology could make communication possible.

Reductionist, materialistic, and physicalistic paradigms have no scientific concept of mind that includes emotions and qualia; at the same time, phenomenological approaches that describe individual mind content from within have no concept of matter existing independently of mind. If we want to make progress, we shall have to construct a conceptual framework that can incorporate both descriptive systems in a way that allows them to speak to each other (see Figure 2.3).

Can we place these two types of description in the same world? To do this we must look at both descriptions and their foundations. I am aware that social-constructivistic explanations are the preferred solutions to the question of how our concepts of nature and mind came into being as a result of the development of knowledge institutions and their interests. This is an important perspective, and it forms part of the method used here. But it is not a valid explanation as such, in that it either presumes the reality of the two, or (in the more radical version) claims that they are complete social constructions. When we look at the 'inner world description,' it seems fair to say that it was most highly developed in Eastern culture and perhaps influenced Greek mysticism as we see it in Pythagoras, Plato, and later propagators of this theory, such as Plotinus and St Augustine. Then it re-emerges among the great Catholic mystics of the Middle Ages, such as Meister Eckhart, and in the Renaissance in a Neoplatonic mysticism and Hermetics that once again places humans at the centre of the world. But the development of the natural sciences has since the Renaissance been placing mathematical 'laws of nature' at the centre of the world and since the Enlightenment has been placing scientific rationality at the cultural centre. With Darwin from the 1860s, humans became just one product of evolution among many. The 'inner view' has survived in European phenomenology, in existential and hermeneutical philosophy from Kierkegaard through Husserl to Heidegger, Merleau-Ponty, Gadamer, and Wittgenstein. This tradition has not yet made any crucial contributions to the study of the brain or of the behaviour of the organism, although Petito, Varela, and Roy (1999) have made some progress. As we shall see, second-order cybernetics is one of the few traditions to have taken up 'the inner view' in a biological and cognitivistic – albeit still functionalistic – tradition.

This epistemological foundation of second-order cybernetics connects it both with evolutionary epistemology and with important points in Heidegger's phenomenology. A great part of our communication and thinking is not of our own doing. Maturana has posited that there is an ongoing interaction between autopoietic systems and their environments, which co-evolve through a non-deterministic process of 'historical drift.' Organisms that live together become surroundings for one another, coordinating their internal organization. The eventual result is languaging through the coordination of coordinations of behaviour. Still, Maturana says little about the inner life – about the experience of qualia, emotions, and meaning in autopoietic systems. In ethology, Lorenz (esp. 1977) worked with models of motivated perception and learning, but he, too, lacked a phenomenological vocabulary, as we shall see.

There is a complicated psycho-biological development and dynamic-system organization behind cognition and communication. The processes of mind, which can be modelled in classic logical terms, seem to lack any special knowledge about how the system's intentions, goals, and ideas are created. Furthermore, the elementary processes comprising this system seem to be made not of classic mechanistic elements or information processing, but rather of a self-organized semiotic dynamics.

In his elaboration of Hume's arguments, Popper (1972) suggests that no matter how many 'repetitions' of an empirical phenomenon we observe and predict, we can never prove the existence of a universal natural law. Seeing 'something repeat itself' is not objectively free of values, but is based on a judgment of similarity. This judgment is always dependent on assumptions and interests. Repetition-for-us is based on a similarity-for-us experience.

We strive for universal knowledge. At least this is part of the ideal of theology and science. But our knowledge is always contextual and therefore limited to a part of reality. We cannot even offer a simple description of the limits of the truth content in our knowledge (models, theories) in any absolute theoretical way before practical testing and attempts at falsification. The border between the areas within which a given model determines true and untrue statements is not a smooth curve but a fractal one. When we try to generalize knowledge, failure is practically inevitable. This is intrinsic to human knowledge. If we did not know when we are mistaken, our knowledge would not grow. But through our capacity to make distinctions, we are able – by way of logic – to falsify our general models (Popper 1972).

We know that we have some knowledge and that we can obtain more. But we must also admit that we do not have universal knowledge – not in the sciences, and not in theology. Human knowledge is relational and prone to mistakes. It is an ongoing process.

More than a hundred years ago, Peirce (1992) introduced 'abduction' – first called 'retroduction' – as a third kind of 'reasoning,' one that complemented classical deductive and inductive reasoning. Most philosophers and philosophers of science since Hume have not considered induction to be logic in the strict sense. Abduction is even less so, since it is the ability to produce meaningful interpretations from a variety of experiences based on a mixture of perceptions and memory. Hintikke (1998, 13) describes the interaction between abduction, deduction, and induction very clearly:

> The validity of abductive inference is to be judged by strategic principles rather than by definitory (move-by-move) rules in the way that strategic principles differ from other laws by their propensity to lead the person to a desired aim. As we shall see, this in an important principle for both Techne and Phronesis in Aristotle's concept of knowledge. The rules of abduction can thus be helpful in understanding the principles of rational decision, both in science, technology and politics, as abduction originates from perception and cannot use normal mathematical probabilistic for its support. First when the hypothesis is formed, then with the help of deduction predictions can be made. This can be tested by the means of induction. So Peirce views abstraction as an inferential process with the purpose of generating new hypotheses for testing or selecting between various hypotheses. In this way one chooses the hypothesis one wants to invest the time and money to test. Abduction opens up new future possibilities of knowledge acquisition.

Firstness	Representamen	Abduction
Secondness	Object	Deduction
Thirdness	Interpretant	Induction

2.4. Peirce's theory of understanding through his three basic categories and the three aspects of the sign. Abduction works in relation to deduction and induction. Abductive reasoning is the ability to see (establish an Interpretant) a basic or primary difference or quality as a sign for some regularity or pattern (the Object). As such, it is the basic function for establishing signification.

Peirce establishes his pragmaticism on the combination of his three basic and very general categories – Firstness, Secondness, and Thirdness – and connects the three components of the sign process with these. Here abduction is the first discovery of something as a sign, and this discovery relates objects to a more basic kind of regularity (habit) that makes it possible to establish a meaningful understanding (create an Interpretant). See Figure 2.4.

Most of Popper's philosophy of science dovetails with Peirce's schema. But Popper, recognizing this, claims to have read Peirce only late in life. He argues that deduction and induction serve as tools for falsifying and testing a hypothesis or idea about a phenomenon. He calls the ideas or hypotheses created to explain observations – which one wants to test in a systematic way – 'conjectural knowledge.' He thus contends that the process of hypothesis formation as such is outside a philosophy of science and is part of a human being's basic ability to obtain knowledge, and he declares that this ability is still one of the basic mysteries: 'The phenomenon of human knowledge is no doubt the greatest miracle in our universe. It constitutes a problem that will not soon be solved' (Popper 1972, preface).

This is precisely where Peirce inserts the new concept of abduction, the result of the semiotic process of interpretation, which depends on his triadic philosophy. Today it seems unlikely that human knowing will ever be reduced to an outcome of simple logic and algorithmic systems distributed in separate brain modules, or that tacit, scientific, and existential knowledge will be reduced to one another (see arguments in Deacon 1997; Penrose 1995).

2.4 The Turn Away from an Externalist towards an Internalist Realism

The concept of 'paradigms of knowledge' – as opposed to paradigms of science – means that systematized, reflected, and publicly communicated types of knowledge exist besides those normally referred to as science. Religious systems stand historically in opposition to science. They harness existential knowledge of values, meaning, faith, devotion, and interpersonal relations. Practical knowledge involving the use of the body and mind – in medical healing and the construction of things, for instance – is less controversial. Here part of the knowledge is tacit and difficult to express in a systematic way. One needs to have 'the feeling' of it, 'talent,' 'human insight,' or 'skill.' One 'knows how' but not necessarily 'why.'[3] This kind of skilful knowledge is important for a good physician or therapist. Furthermore, much of the knowledge collected and systematized in the arts and humanities is qualitatively different from the knowledge produced in the sciences. Between these two extremes are systematized practices of medicine and health such as family therapy, psychotherapy, zone therapy, yoga, meditation, and spiritual practices. These often have long written traditions and theoretical discussions concerning the reasons why these practices have the desired effects, but their metaphysics often differ from standard scientific objectivistic ones. For instance, therapeutic and existential knowledge might originally have been produced in cultures with distinct metaphysical frameworks of the body, mind, and reality. To our confusion, some of it works – for example, acupuncture, even though its concept of 'energies' and its maps of 'meridians' on the body only partly coincide with something we actually know (such as endorphins). The discovery of acupuncture points may have been phenomenological; in any case, this practice has been further developed through experiments and practice. This highlights our problem of the nature and limits of traditional scientific methods and the knowledge they produce.

The main purpose of this chapter is to suggest that the 'internalist turn' of epistemology can help the philosophy of science contribute to a new framework of how to view different kinds or qualities of knowledge that spring from the human body in its social and communicative practices.

Knowledge begins with ordinary daily human knowledge (represented in everyday language concepts). From there it broadens and is tested (logically and empirically) and refined. Instead of viewing scientific knowledge as approaching the goal of 'final truth,' scientific knowledge can be seen as an island of attempted rationality that is constantly developing against a vast encircling sea of ignorance or potential knowledge, as Kuhn (1970) and Lakoff (1987) suggest. We do not know in which direction we are going, only that the island (our knowledge) becomes larger, more detailed, and more practicable for certain purposes. Yet at the same time, we are constantly discovering that our knowledge is incomplete through praxis, the unexpected 'side effects' our actions have, and our stuttering attempts to use our knowledge in new areas.

Lakoff (1987, 259–60) summarizes the philosopher Putnam's arguments about the need to shift from an externalist to an internalist view:

> In summary, Putnam has shown that existing formal versions of objectivist *epistemology* are inconsistent: there can be no objectively correct *description* of reality from a God's eye point of view. This does not, of course, mean that there is no objective reality – only that we have no *privileged access* to it from an external viewpoint …
>
> The source of the incoherence is what Putnam calls its *externalist* perspective, that one can stand outside reality and find a uniquely correct way to understand reality. Such an understanding, on the view of metaphysical realism, would involve a symbol system standing external to the rest of reality and a reference relation pairing symbols and aspects of reality. The reference relation is assumed to 'give meaning' to the symbols. First, Putnam shows that this is logically impossible, without violating what we mean by 'meaning.' Second, Putnam points out that in order for such an understanding to be unique and correct, the reference relation itself must be part of reality. He then observes that this too is logically impossible.

Like Putnam, I do not want to indulge in solipsistic constructivism about natural phenomena. It is impossible to imagine sign processes without referring to any objects. The precondition for any language is the existence of something 'outside' about which it is concerned. There is a 'background problem' of individual and historical origin. In both physics and psychology (especially the latter), what can be described formally has its background in what is not thus describable: the hypercomplex phenomena that are comprised of the predictable and the regular, as well as the spontaneous, unpredictable, intentional, and individually historical. We always observe and construct knowledge from somewhere within the world, and nobody has a 'God's eye' view:

We are part of it, *in* it. What is needed is not an externalist perspective, but an internalist perspective. It is a perspective that acknowledges that we are organisms functioning as part of reality and that it is impossible for us to ever stand outside it and take the stance of an observer with perfect knowledge, an observer with a God's eye point of view. But that does not mean that knowledge is impossible. We can know reality from the inside, on the basis of our being part of it. It is not the absolute perfect knowledge of the God's eye variety, but that kind of knowledge is logically impossible anyway. What *is* possible is knowledge of another kind: knowledge from a particular point of view, knowledge which includes the awareness that it is from a particular point of view, and knowledge which grants that other points of view can be legitimate. (ibid., 261)

It is not only the 'outside' world that persistently surprises us with its complexity and spontaneity, but also our 'inner' world, the 'subconscious' complexity and spontaneity behind our behaviour, including communication. Freud demonstrated that we do not have absolute control over the impulses generating speech. The conscious 'I' in the sentence 'I said it' is only a part of the 'I' behind the production of the linguistic expression. This basic incompleteness of our knowledge of ourselves, the unknown reasons for our behaviour, and our lack of absolute conscious control over speech, are at the same time prerequisites for our ability to say and cognize something new. Awareness of this will lead one to start in the middle instead of at the extremes of either subject or object, to begin with the process of knowing or signification in the everyday struggle for survival and the need to communicate our intentions. Putnam (1981, 52) writes:

In an internalist view also, signs do not intrinsically correspond to objects, independently of how those signs are employed and by whom. But a sign that is actually employed in a particular way by a particular community of users can correspond to particular objects *within the conceptual scheme of those users*. 'Objects' do not exist independently of conceptual schemes. We cut up the world into objects when we introduce one or another scheme of description. Since objects and the signs are alike *internal* to the scheme of description, it is possible to say what matches what.

Wittgenstein in language philosophy and Peirce in semiotics both argue for this pragmatic point of departure, which coincides with the evolutionary and historical pragmatic perspective on the creation and growth of knowledge. In his system science, Luhmann (1990, 132–3) points out the same idea that ontology is something one posits as a philosophical prerequisite for doing a certain kind of science or search for knowledge:

> The effect of the intervention of systems theory can be described as a de-ontologization of reality. This does not mean that reality is denied, for then there would be nothing that operated – nothing that observed, and nothing on which one would gain a purchase by means of distinctions. It is only the epistemological relevance of an ontological representation of reality that is being called into question. If a knowing system has no entry to its external world, it can be denied that such an external world exists. But we can just as well – and more believably – claim that the external world is as it is. Neither claim can be proved; there is no way of deciding between them. This calls into question, however, not the external world but only the simple distinction being/non-being, which ontology had applied to it. As a consequence, the question arises: Why do we have to begin with precisely this distinction? Why do we wound the world first with this distinction and no other?

There are many arguments – even outside cybernetics and system science – for this philosophy of science and its basic epistemological conceptions, which are, to begin with the observer or the phenomenological position, and thereby acknowledge that humans are knowers, even if we do not know why or how. It is important to acknowledge our existing ignorance regarding what it is to know and how knowledge comes about. We must also acknowledge that we are observers coexisting in language with other humans in culture and society. Our living in nature and in the social world is based on our biological existence as embodied beings with inner conscious worlds – that is, our psyches, in which volition, emotions, and (pre-linguistic) thought are born.

2.5 Developing a Framework to Understand the Relationships among the Sciences and Other Types of Knowledge

It is important for the sciences in general, including interdisciplinary practical sciences such as information and communication science, to realize that the processes of human knowing, language, and meaning are more fundamental than and 'precede' any scientific knowledge. Drawing on the works of Gadamer (1975), Heidegger (1973), and Winograd and Flores (1986), I emphasize that the meaning/information content of a sign is determined by social practice in a historical context, as opposed to the rationalist idea that objective information sits 'out there,' arranged in bits waiting to be picked up. This accords with the views promoted by the pragmaticism semiotics of Peirce and the pragmatic language philosophy of Wittgenstein (1958).

It is also important to understand the consequences of the philosophical insight that science is based on the human ability to gain knowledge by making meaningful distinctions and to signify these through sign creation and communication. Human knowing is the fountainhead of various systems of knowledge. All kinds of knowledge, such as scientific, phenomenological, and practical knowledge, are specializations of basic human knowledge and are based on the ability to make distinctions (and interpret them as meaningful signs) and to communicate them through everyday language. Normally we distinguish between our natural surroundings, our social surroundings, and our own inner life of thoughts, feelings, and will. These can be seen as three qualitatively different aspects of reality, or three different worlds. Nature has a reality that seems to exist almost independently of our social and mental activities. Society, as a product of our cooperation and communication with one another, is a human world created through human interpretations and practice. Finally, our own inner world of feelings, volition, and conscious thought, although dependent in many ways on nature and society, seems also to spring from an independent source, the nature of which science has great difficulty in understanding within the prevalent world view. Let me summarize this in a graphic model (Figure 2.5).

We awaken to a world situated in language with other humans, to a world of our own feelings and tendencies (will, affections, and drives), and to some non-human surroundings: the environment or nature (the notion of our biology will be brought back into this discussion, as a separate issue, shortly). The systematic expansion of knowledge generates three major and qualitatively different knowledge approaches: the sciences, the arts and humanities, and the social sciences. In most cultures each of these subdivisions entails an authorized system of knowledge.

It is important to accept the unique quality of our inner world of emotions, perceptions, memories, theories, and analogies, as well as the fact that at present we can derive this world from neither nature nor society

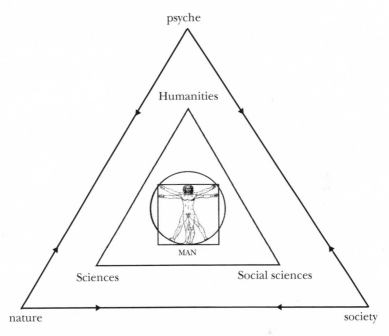

Hermeneutical-Phenomenological Knowledge

2.5.   A graphic model of human knowing. Humans as observers and communicators are placed in the centre, and the pursuit of any systematic knowledge
is seen as a social enterprise. Reality is subdivided into *Nature*, which is our
material surrounding; *Society*, which is our human surroundings, which present
themselves in the field of language and rules of conduct; and *Psyche*, which is
our mind understood as our inner experience of our conscious thoughts, will
power, and feelings. Inspired by Lindström (1974).

nor a combination of these, even though our inner world is clearly
dependent on and formed by elements and processes from all of these
worlds. Still – as Luhmann, inspired by Husserl, suggests – our inner
world and our world of social communication are both self-organized
systems, and furthermore, they are closed to each other. There is a lot
occurring in the psyche for which we do not have words. As Lakoff (1987)
convincingly shows, our major way of ordering, understanding, and predicting events is not logical or statistical; rather, it operates through
bodily motivated categories and connections. Methodologically, we have

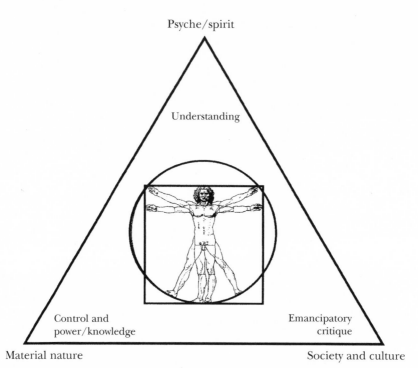

2.6. Inspired by Habermas's work, science, the humanities, and the social sciences are seen as qualitatively different knowledge systems, and based on qualitative differences in subject areas combined with very different knowledge interests. Nature is objective, whereas society and psyche are always interpretative and looking for meaning. I have used Da Vinci's Renaissance man – actually consisting of two humans – to symbolize that we must start from human linguistic and practical knowledge in a context of social cooperation in a culture with history.

no primary access to other people's inner worlds. We have only indirect access through physiology measures, behavioural descriptions, and linguistic narrations that reduce the complexity of inner and outer worlds through our sense making (Luhmann 1990). Thus first-person conscious experience in the form of will and desires is avoided as much as possible as a causal agent in both the natural and the social sciences.

One way to relativize the traditional scientific view of knowledge systems is through Habermas's (1974) idea, based on the Frankfurt

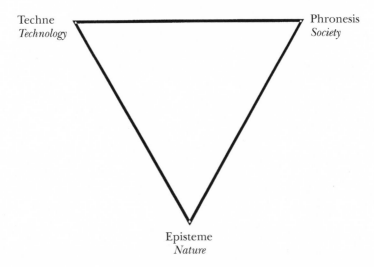

2.7.   Aristotle's three qualitatively different knowledge types based on differences in means, aims, and subject areas, from the *Nicomachean Ethics*. Under each is the modern translation of the subject area.

School, that the sciences, humanities, and social sciences address very different subject areas – nature, society, and our inner world of emotions, volitions, and cognitions – and that the aims of these systematic knowledge systems are distinct. For science it is technological power/knowledge, for the humanities it is understanding, and for the social sciences it is emancipating critique. Figure 2.6 places the embodied community of observers in the centre and notes that the main areas of systematic controllable knowledge systems unfold different types of subject areas.

There are other qualitatively different general systems of knowledge and expertise that intersect with our general subdivisions of scientific knowledge. I will expand on terms from Aristotle's philosophy, because many of our expressions have their roots there. That shows how old this problem is, and I believe Aristotle has good reasons for making this division. To explain this further, I suggest that we reconsider Aristotle's three widely used concepts of knowledge from *The Nicomachean Ethics* (Aristotle 1976): Episteme, Techne, and Phronesis.

In the English version, as already mentioned, Episteme is translated as 'science' (meaning the paradigm of classical mechanical natural science, with its idea of eternal and reversible mathematical laws), Techne is translated as 'art' and productive knowledge (as craftsmanship, technology, and know-how, including aesthetic considerations), and Phronesis as 'prudence' (understood as practical common sense in social matters, such as politics, teaching, therapy, and management, and also as applied or practical philosophy, including ethical considerations). When the goal of Techne is outside itself, then Phronesis has its goal in the good action and the good life in itself. Let us take a close look at Figure 2.7.

The idea of a hidden mathematical order behind the Cosmos springs from the attempts by the Greek nature philosophers to find unifying ordering principles behind 'physics.' Aristotle, inspired by Plato, called this type of knowledge Episteme – that is, knowledge about the eternal and universal features of the world. Mathematical relations can be part of this – for instance, for the movement of the heavens. About epistemic knowledge, Aristotle (1976, 207) writes: 'We all assume that what we know cannot be otherwise than it is, whereas in the case of things that may be otherwise, when they have passed out of view we can no longer tell whether they exist or not. Therefore the object of scientific knowledge is of necessity. Therefore it is eternal … Induction introduces us to first principles and universals, while deduction starts from universals.'

This is the ideal of science originating with Plato, further developed by Descartes and Kant (1990) during the Enlightenment, and continued in modern times by the young Wittgenstein and by logical positivism. It posits that scientific knowledge must be (1) explicitly abstract (not dependent on concrete examples); (2) universal and discrete (composed of context independent elements); and (3) systematic (covering the whole subject area and connecting all independent elements with laws), and able to formulate precise predictions.

Plato's concept of Episteme was rooted in mathematics; he posited that some of the highest ideas behind the Cosmos were mathematical. Aristotle did not possess a theory of transcendental forms, but he still believed that the world functions according some eternal pattern based on the Unmoved Mover – that pure and potential reason (Nous) lies behind the order of the Cosmos.

Techne, often translated as 'art,' is productive craftsmanship or the knowledge and need or wish to construct something. It relies on a blend of reasoned knowledge and know-how, tacit knowledge, and aesthetical knowledge. Aristotle (ibid., 208) writes that 'Every art is concerned with bringing something into being something that is capable either of being or of not being ... For it is not with things that are to come to be *of necessity* that art is concerned nor with natural objects (because they have their origin in themselves).'

Imagine a spectrum with engineering at one pole and theatre at the other. These are concrete, variable, and context-dependent activities that apply practical rationality governed by the conscious goal of producing something artificial, useful, and aesthetically pleasing.

In contrast, Phronesis – often translated as 'prudence' – is practical, social, and aesthetic. It is the ethical knowledge used in teaching, therapy, politics, and leadership. It is a pragmatic and communicative social knowledge, the kind of knowledge contemplated in hermeutics. Aristotle (ibid., 209) suggests that we consider who is called prudent in order to understand the nature of Phronesis:

> It is thought to be the mark of a prudent man to be able to deliberate rightly about what good and advantageous ... But nobody deliberates about things that are invariable ... So ... prudence cannot be science or art; not science because what can be done is variable ... and not art because action and production is generically different. For production aims at an end other than itself but this is impossible in the case of action, because the end is merely doing well. What remains, then, is that it is a true state, reasoned, and capable of action with regard to things that are good or bad for man.

Phronetic action and thinking approaches the conventional idea of wisdom. It is a deep human social rationality that draws not only on systematic knowledge of a scientific and practical character, but also on ethical considerations. It is the phronetic character of social knowledge that makes the social sciences so different from the natural sciences.

Applied phronesis, or practical philosophy, often makes one think of leadership in state and private organizations. But it actually includes all kinds of social practice, including the communication skills required in medical practice to deal with patients and to treat a terminally ill people and their relatives. It demands deliberation, estimation, and experience, and it is context dependent. Aristotle (ibid., 213) writes: 'Prudence is not concerned with universals only; it must also take cognizance of particulars, because it is concerned with conduct, and conduct has its sphere in particular circumstances. That is why some people who do not possess theoretical knowledge are more effective in action (especially if they are experienced) than others who do possess it.'

Phronesis involves social interactions among humans and is therefore an important part of any therapy conducted by humans on humans. Some medical and agricultural practices are clearly Techne, as they bring forth something new and partly artificial. Choices regarding how to treat animals, whether to farm with or without pesticides, and on what kind of economics to base the livelihood of a family are clearly prudential. But we would hope that these forms of practice rested as much as possible on science, social science, and knowledge from the humanities, so as to attain the best possible harmony.

As enlightening as this theory is in shattering the idea that scientific knowledge is the only possible truth about reality, and in placing knowers in the middle and organizing different types around them according to knowledge interests, it does not quite fit what we know about the natural and social sciences. We know that some of the social sciences, such as economics and (at times) sociology, are instrumental and mathematical. Many scientists look on Episteme as true natural laws, as we saw in the earlier section on world formula science. On this basis, I would suggest that we reorganize Figure 2.7 to form Figure 2.8, so that technological power/knowledge is characteristic for some of the sciences and some of the social sciences. In this new figure the emancipatory critique is part of the social sciences and the humanities, and understanding is part of both the humanities and the sciences,[4] as for example in the search for a 'theory of everything' conducted as a foundational understanding of matter, forces, and structure. True, it is basically a mathematical description, but to the scientist it is also an explanation for the creation of the universe, the logic of the living, and the structure and formation of mind in cognitive science.

What was once considered the most basic knowledge of reality in the traditional understanding of the sciences can now – according to this perspective – be viewed as a specific technological power/knowledge. The algorithmic knowledge of a system – especially if organized as a computer model – is a powerful tool for controlling and predicting the behaviour of certain systems. But studies of non-equilibrium, thermodynamics, fractals, chaos theory, and non-linear systems have shown that only a small group of systems can be described sufficiently by a stated function. Our world view is increasingly shifting away from the belief in a simple mathematical order that underlies the complexity we perceive

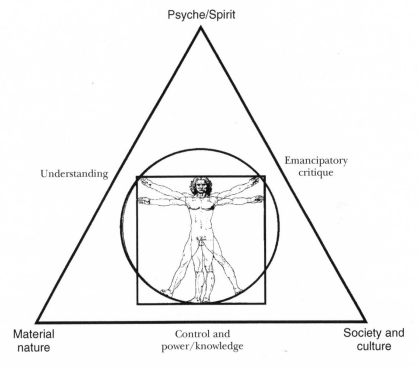

Psyche/Spirit

Understanding

Emancipatory
critique

Material
nature

Control and
power/knowledge

Society and
culture

2.8.   Revising Habermas's view of the knowledge areas of the sciences, the humanities, and the social sciences by moving them between areas so they become one aspect of at least two major domains, but not the essence of the way any single knowledge domain functions.

at a macro level. In deterministic chaos, there are well-known formulas that provide functions that enter and escape chaos in partly regular ways. Some equations generate fractals so complex that they cannot be predicted, but only empirically investigated. Prigogine and Stengers (1984) called thermodynamics the theory of complexity and irreversibility, as one cannot turn time backwards as in classical mechanics. They deny that classical mechanics is a more fundamental science than thermodynamics. Most systems we encounter in nature and technology are non-linear, and often have strange attractors, some of which may be fractal. Thus there is a shift in the ontology of many natural sciences towards a more complex view of nature.

As Peirce argued, we may think more productively about these matters if we consider chaos – understood as a hypercomplex dynamic continuum – to be the basic reality (see also Popper 1972, 212–14; Mathews 1991). Chaos can be viewed as pure chance endowed with what Peirce calls 'the tendency to take habits.' Chance and habit making are thus embedded in each other, and regularities arise from chaos. Chaos can also emerge from order, as for instance in types of deterministic chaos, such as Feigenbaum's tree. There seems to be a complementary enfolding of chaos and regularity. I suggest that we perceive our environment as hypercomplex and as reflecting innumerable differences and regularities of which we can conceptualize and systematize only a few in everyday life and cognition, and in the sciences.

The contexts of life forms and language games are understood within a collective metaphysical framework that is part of a culture. This framework can be of a mythical-animistic nature, such as that of a hunter-gatherer tribe; or the idea of Cosmos, as it was for the Greek philosophers; or the mathematical machine universe of Newton. It does not matter. They are all part of how humans frame nature within a certain society, of the kinds of questions they ask, and of the kind of rationality underpinning their categorizations and classifications of objects. Lakoff's exposition (1987) of the classification system in Dyirbal (an aboriginal language in Australia) is very convincing. His analysis shows a mixture of mythical and gender-ordering principles, combined with related practical principles. Among the Dyirbal, mythical ordering has priority over gender and practical principles. It makes sense, although it does not reflect what we would recognize as an internally consistent logic or rationality. In this way we can see that different frameworks result in different perceptions of nature. Frameworks can develop and change in a culture over time. All frameworks relate to the constraints of reality known by that culture. They are sensitive to the partly independent patterns of nature.

The framework partly determines what a given culture considers rational. It was within such a specific rationality – the Classical Greek – that geometry was established in a general way and accepted as a valuable kind of rationality (Episteme), one that uncovered deep and hidden 'laws' in physics. But algorithmic rationality is only one deep truth within a certain metaphysical framework. Our sciences have to go beyond these frameworks because they can no longer encompass the new things we have discovered, at least not to our satisfaction. For this reason, we have relativized our view of linear algorithmic models from being the deep

Unexplained area (1)

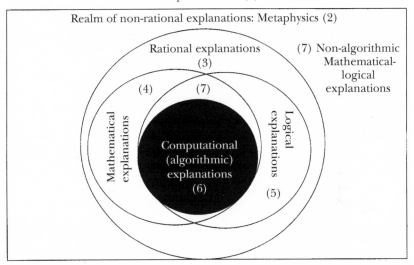

2.9.   Cultural frames of rationality. Because reality as a whole cannot be scientifically explainable, the realm of explanation is only an island in an – in exact terms – unexplainable reality (1). We choose to frame reality by means of a metaphysical framework, often through myth and other narratives (2). What is considered rational is partly determined by the mythical/metaphysical framework (developing from mythos to logos) (3). Some explanations are mathematical (4), and some are logical (5). Some are non-computational (Penrose, von Foerster) (7), and the computational realm of explanations (6) is the overlap of mathematical and logical explanations. These focus on the aspects of nature because we have the most success in handling them, but they represent only a small fraction of existing systems, and therefore cannot be expected to cover everything, like intelligence, consciousness, and meaning, for example.

truth to be powerful instruments to control a small class of systems. Penrose (1995, vi) contends that consciousness clearly has non-computational qualities and that to understand consciousness as a part of the physical world we must 'understand how such non-computational action might arise within scientifically comprehensible physical laws ... I shall argue strongly for a need for a fundamental change, at a certain clearly specified level, in our present quantum-mechanical worldview ... I am suggesting that a physical non-computability – needed for an explanation of the non-computability in our conscious action – enter at this level.'

I created the model in Figure 2.9 as a framework to encompass Penrose's theory, after some discussions with him (at a conference at the Niels Bohr Institute) about the metaphysical prerequisites for his theory of mathematics as a creative human endeavour. My hope is to view nature as hypercomplex, thereby opening a way for Peirce's semiotic metaphysics as a bridge to hermeutics and the social sciences.

This explains why it seems more realistic to place the observer and actor in the middle of Figure 2.8; from there, he or she can create different kinds of knowledge systems as a result of 'being-in-the-world' in an engaged way. Here, different subject areas have different research interests, as Habermas pointed out when he distinguished the sciences from the humanities and the social sciences. I have revised his model of the nature and research interests of these three areas slightly, although I believe that the concerns and goals of his inquiry are still important.

2.6 The Role of the Biology of Embodied Knowledge

In recent times we have come to realize that there is a fourth, qualitatively different subject area. The fact that our bodily existence is a vital element in the process of cognition has only recently been taken seriously. This has happened, for instance, in the evolutionary epistemology initiated by Konrad Lorenz, in second-order cybernetics, in autopoiesis theory, and in Lakoff and Johnson's experientialism. It is now realized that 'embodiment' is the foundation for psychic and socio-communicative systems, as in Maturana and Varela's work with autopoiesis, von Foerster's work with cognition as a product of the communication of non-trivial machines, and somewhat differently in Luhmann's autopoietic systems.

This development has led us to consider biological systems as separate from physics, chemistry, and the social sciences. As more researchers are suggesting today, biology counts. The ability of living systems to embody knowledge is a unique and qualitatively different area of study from physics or chemistry. Lakoff and Johnson's (1999) attempt to build philosophy on embodied metaphors stands out as an important late-modern project. The research program of biosemiotics (Brier 2006) is an attempt to found biosemiotics on a semiotic and communication approach that goes beyond mechanistic conceptions.

If we continue our attempt to build a framework by placing the knowledge systems of different subject areas in relation to one another and the knower as we generate 'scientific' knowledge systems, we can see four qual-

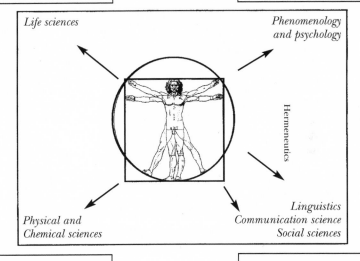

Signifying living
autopoietic
systems

Organizationally closed
thinking – feeling –
volitional systems

Life sciences

*Phenomenology
and psychology*

Hermeneutics

*Physical and
Chemical sciences*

*Linguistics
Communication science
Social sciences*

Physico-chemical
matter-energy open systems
and dissipative systems

Organizationally closed
socio-communicative
systems

2.10. An illustration of the qualitatively different sciences and knowledge types connected to the different subject areas of reality that we see in our search for a socially acceptable intersubjective knowledge. The subject areas are seen as qualitatively different, and subsequently the knowledge systems are connected to them with deliberations on what is believed to be the nature of the subject area.

itatively different major types of systems, which form four subject areas and methodological approaches. These are (1) the physico-chemical systems of matter, energy, and differences; (2) the biological-autopoietic sign-producing systems; (3) the conscious psychological system of feeling, thinking, and volition; and, finally, (4) the socio-communicative system based mainly on language and symbols. See Figure 2.10.

We must acknowledge that the sciences develop and pertain to our needs from our observing position in the world, and that we understand ourselves and the environment through this systematization and conceptualization of lived practices. We derive our own life world and the systems partaking in it from the society with which we interact. We then try to link these systems to form a consistent whole that we call a universe.

By placing human beings and their worlds at the centre of the model, we can only create models of human inner life, physiology, and individual and social behaviour. There is no support for the idea that all human actions can be reduced to logico-mathematical laws. The fact that computer models are based on algorithms does not signify that nature, psyche, or society as such are essentially mathematical, and the soft AI view also realizes this (for discussion, see Searle 1989; Dreyfus and Dreyfus 1995; Lakoff 1987).

The only unity that can be established is the non-fundamentalist, human-centred, pluralistic philosophy that all knowledge systems are both necessary and complementary within a hypercomplex world view. In a hypercomplex world view it is not presumed that any knowledge system can get to 'the bottom of things.' Thus it is not expected that the differences among knowledge systems will ever disappear through 'the development of science.' With Peirce (1992), I believe that the search for 'The Truth' is the most important regulative idea in science, and a part of its ethos as a social project for gaining knowledge that is generally socio-communicative and reliable enough to stimulate common action. But the actual fulfilment of the ideal may lie almost infinitely far in the future.

That I have placed humans at the centre of the figure illustrates what in cognitive science is called 'subsymbolic calculation' (Hofstadter 1983). This idea – now linked to neural networks – is that many cognitive activities are subsymbolic, predating any conscious formulation in symbols and language. The 'tacit knowledge' of Polanyi (1973) and Freud's idea of the unconscious (Andkjær and Køppe 1986) are examples of non- or subsymbolic knowledge. Another way to describe this distinction is in terms of 'declarative' versus 'procedural' knowledge, approximating the difference between 'knowing why' and 'knowing how.' The idea behind declarative knowledge is to describe the 'universe' in objective, atomistic, and context-free facts and to objectively describe the logical connections among those facts, as stated in the young Wittgenstein's *Tractatus Logico-Philosophicus*. But 'know-how,' or procedural knowledge, is connected to the human 'World.' Dreyfus and Dreyfus (1995, 435) point to Heidegger's distinction between a 'universe' and a 'world': 'A set of interrelated facts may constitute a *universe*, like the physical universe, but it does not constitute a world. The latter, like the world of business, the world of theater, or the world of the physicist, is an organized body of objects, purposes, skills, and practices on the basis of which human activities have meaning or make sense. To see the difference one can contrast the *meaningless* physical *universe* with the *meaningful world* of the discipline of physics.'

These different domains of human practice only make sense against the background of the cultural common sense they presuppose. They are elaborations of a general common sense that they feed back into it, thereby contributing to it as the individual mind and its world also do.

As I have already argued, only a small part of our reality lends itself to algorithmic description in all the different knowledge areas: mind, body, culture, nature, and so on. Chaos and order are folded into each other. There are only small windows of fairly simple order, which manifest themselves at different levels, intersected with hypercomplexity. In these areas we can locate differences that are clear, stable, and distinctive enough to establish Interpretants and therefore make sign processes and conceptual understanding. The rest is entangled states and functional relationships that so far have eluded exact science, although some of these we can relate to and act on biologically and psychologically without language. Such knowledge is 'tacit,' following Polanyi (1973).

So far I have been reflecting mainly on the pure sciences and humanities. But there are other systematic but applied forms of knowledge. I will now sum up my view and make a visual model of it. As I have already mentioned, in the *Nicomachean Ethics* Aristotle argued that scientific knowledge (Episteme) aimed at true universal knowledge is qualitatively different from practical constructive knowledge (Techne), which is partly based on craftsmanship and practical experience. Techne is knowledge aimed at producing certain entities or events, such as tools or a theatrical production. Practical wisdom (Phronesis) is qualitatively different from both Episteme and Techne, in that it concerns the highest principles for action within society.

Let us turn to Habermas's idea that scientific knowledge has an interest in control and power. We use what we call algorithmic models to control all linear systems, and we hope in vain that we can also control all non-linear systems. But we can only gain this powerful knowledge over a small class of systems. There is no compelling reason to believe that they are expressions of some deep universal mathematical law

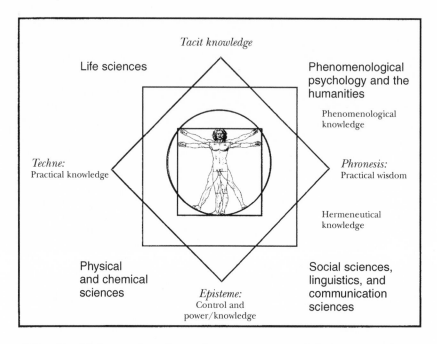

2.11.   Combining previous figures into a summary model, the present figure illustrates that there are qualitatively different knowledge areas and types besides the sciences and the arts. The model suggests a way to view their inter-connectedness. I have already argued that in a modern view, Epistemes are algorithmic models of (mostly linear) systems.

underlying the entire complexity of nature, but it is the most powerful control-knowledge we possess, and it makes possible the development of technology to use these systems to our advantage.

Finally, let us integrate that special kind of silent, linguistically inexpressible knowledge that Polanyi called 'tacit knowledge.' As already mentioned, this refers to skill and abilities at the bio-psychological (but beyond the socio-communicative) level, where knowledge (as in tools or instrument handling) and intuitive pattern recognition are located. Much of our knowledge – for instance, in the form of skills – is not linguistically expressible. As Lakoff and Johnson (1999) suggest, most of our reasoning is unconscious (see Figure 2.11 for a diagrammatic overview of the theories of and relations among the concepts presented thus far).

In this model of the many basic knowledge systems, we must abandon the modern mechanistic belief that episteme is able to uncover absolute principles or laws, and replace it with a model of limited subject areas of systematic, communicated, stable knowledge engaged in a steady process of improvement. Within this field of communicable knowledge, the phenomenology of Heidegger is attempting to understand the place of the human being in the world before the difference between subject and object is created (*Dasein*). This view means abandoning Husserl's view (1977) that a phenomenological analysis of our pure perception will 'get to the bottom of perception in the mind.' I have placed hermeneutics within Gadamer's tradition (Gadamer 1975), which focuses on the social and cultural understanding of texts and on how different 'horizons' change our understandings as part of the social science approach. But we know that in both biology and the physical-chemical sciences we also need a deep understanding of nature in order to supplement technological aspects of our project.

In the next section I will be suggesting a model for describing the functional relationships among traditional science, philosophy, religion, and politics and for explaining how new developments at the end of the twentieth century have changed these into new conceptions and relationships within the ecological utopia of a Third Culture – one that unites Snow's two cultures of the sciences and the humanities.

As already mentioned, the ideal of epistemic knowledge originated with the Pythagoreans, who believed that whole numbers were the basic building blocks of the natural world. Plato used this ideal in his theory when he considered (in *Timaeus*) mathematical ideas as basic to the creation of the natural world. Galileo used the idea of 'mathematics as the language of nature' as one of the major philosophical foundations of the paradigm of natural science; his idea then became part of the mechanistic paradigm. This was developed further by Laplace and later by Einstein, and is seen at its extreme in the superstring project, the gene program idea, the vision of AI, and the cognitive sciences, as well as in much of current economic theorizing. On this basis there have been attempts to reduce human nature and culture to epistemic laws. Such an approach is normally called reductionism and in many ways goes further than both Plato and Aristotle in its contention that a precise formula for human knowledge about the Cosmos is possible. But it is important to note that reductionism is possible from all four corners of Figure 2.11 through claims that there is only one genuine kind of knowledge. Some examples include the study of Psyche (subjective idealism, phenomenalism, and solipsism), the study of society (conventionalism, radical constructivism that includes nature as a social construction, and vulgar or mechanical historical materialism), and the study of nature (scientism, physicalism, and eliminative materialism).

This view comes as a surprise for most researchers in the humanistic and social sciences, who are used to accusing only physics and biology of being reductionistic. My view is that the relativistic and idealistic views of, for instance, radical constructivism – views that reject any kind of realistic perspective on nature and ideas of truth in science – are equally reductionistic in their efforts to explain the complexity of reality. But to explain this complexity, I must claim the possibility of a more general position, one that is not completely under the sway of cultural constructivism.

This is the basic idea behind a philosophy whose goal is to establish some basic prerequisites for human thinking without explaining away the mystery. I consider it a regulative idea (Kant 1990) and an ideal we strive for. As a scientist doing philosophy of science, and thus stepping out of science, this is the only place where I can stand if I want to discuss interdisciplinarity.

We must not be seduced by any of the specific knowledge systems in the corners of Figure 2.11. They represent the temptations of the power of simplicity and fundamentalism. Each of those corners offers important knowledge, but none offers all-encompassing solutions. This is not a perspective that wins you many friends in these knowledge areas. Our experience with both religious and scientific theories and paradigms is that they are useful for certain subject areas for a limited time; but as our experience expands, new phenomena arise that cannot be accounted for in consistent ways. We must then reconsider the philosophical foundation from which we began.

Science, then, is our search for understandable and useful regularities and principles that organize and create natural things – including ourselves. We pursue this endeavour through the social construction of languaging, building on our fundamental gift for making (prescientific) distinctions in our world. We work as methodologically consistently as we can, knowing that there is not one but many scientific methods, knowing that theories and paradigms are important and that therefore we have to make them explicit. We strive to establish objectivity through the collective of researchers. We try to keep all relevant angles and interpretations open for discussion, knowing that science is not so much what the single researcher does as it is the whole collective critical process in the search for truths about the world; it is the ability to foresee and to construct useful technology as well as understand the world and the human condition that drives this social functional specialized system. We know it is human and social. It carries with it all the flaws and mistakes of every human social systems: religion, arts, politics. None of them are logical machines. Nevertheless it is the best we can do. Thus in order to understand science, we must place it in a broader framework of knowledge types. How, then, can we place all systems of knowledge taught at universities within a broader view of knowledge, power, myth, and faith?

2.7 A Suggestion for a Transdisciplinary Framework for the Conception of Knowledge

Let me conclude with a suggestion of how we can model relationships among the various organized knowledge systems in a metaview based on the observer's admittance to reality in a social-linguistic culture. I want to suggest a way to understand the traditional relationships among science (broadly understood), art, religion, and politics as they have established themselves in modernity. I will start by reflecting on the basic metaphysical assumptions that often blend ontological and epistemological considerations.

The first and often unreflected metaphysical decision in any knowledge system involves deciding what exists and what does not. This is the question of being and non-being (compare to the frame of reference in Figure 2.9). The second problem involves determining the part of being that can be accessed through the normal senses, and the part that cannot – that is, between what is manifest (explicate order) and what is not (or implicate order, as Bohm 1983 calls it). See, for instance, Spinoza's deliberations (1996). Culture builds a view of what is real and what is not real, what is manifest and what is not manifest. I have placed these four decisions into a square inspired by Greimas's square (see, for instance, Nöth 1995). We thus begin with real phenomena, some of which can be handled directly and some of which work behind the scenes, such as laws of nature, animal spirits, and 'invisible, blind watchmakers.' See Figure 2.12.[3]

As I have already noted, the decisions in the first inner circle of this figure can generate a mythical framework such as the old Nordic, Classical Greek, or Roman pantheon to explain how the world came about (cosmogony) as well as what exists, such as gods, spirits, magical

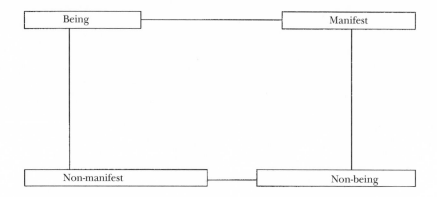

2.12.   The Brier-Christiansen multiple square. The first circle, developed and inspired by Greimas's semiotic square, consists of two pairs of combined opposites. Objects can be characterized by their being and manifestation. True objects have both. Fictional and mythological beings have none.

powers, living conscious linguistic systems, general living systems, and material systems. All cultures have objects as manifest beings. However, not all include spirits, although most cultures have gone through a period of animism and shamanism and many are still in this phase. Western cultures have mainly given up on animism, although there are often relics of this in peasant cultures. In Christian cultures since the Renaissance, the Church and the sciences have cooperated to construct a view of nature as a purposeless machine governed by hidden mathematical laws that to religious people could be God's thoughts (logos) or creation, and to materialistic atheists a product of the Big Bang.

At the next level, the concept of *object* appears (see Figure 2.13). The real and manifest in our culture are primarily considered to be natural 'things' or 'objects' (res). What is not real and not manifest is 'nothing,' or nothing, such as the Godhead, the emptiness, the empty set, zero, the vacuum field, or similar. The Buddhist speaks of the void or emptiness. Physics speaks of vacuum fields beyond the Planck scale. Mathematics operates with the empty set. Many religions speak of one transcendental Godhead (such as the absolute unity of the Holy Trinity). For the Christian mystic Meister Eckhart, the transcendental realm in which the mystical union developed was beyond any personal god. This is also true in Shankara's Advaita Vedanta in the Vedic tradi-

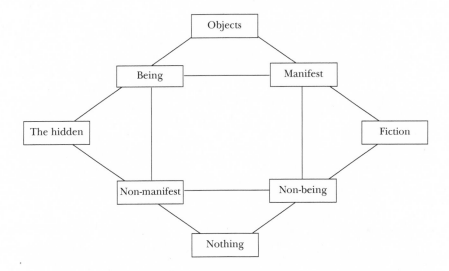

2.13. The Brier-Christiansen multiple square. The second circle produces basic objects in our culture: the real, the fictional, the hidden forces controlling object processes, and finally the zero or negative basis for everything, which can also be viewed as a fullness of potentialities.

tions, and in the Tao of Taoism. I do not posit that they all speak about the same (no-)thing, but I would point out that many of the most highly developed knowledge systems postulate some kind of zero, emptiness, void, or no-thing. The concepts of *nothingness* mentioned here are very different in nature, and some of them are mutually exclusive. Discussions about whether nothingness is emptiness or fullness, whether it is non-rational or super-rational, and whether it is with or without intentions are an important part of metaphysics. I have so far referred to this as a hypercomplexity, which suggests that we should not expect to find any simple form of Logos there (for instance, a mathematical world formula). We will return in a later chapter to Peirce's view on Chance, Firstness, and superorder.

Manifest cultural objects are not real in the way natural objects are – they are fictional. This goes for works of art and the architecture of buildings and machines, although the parts they consist of are natural objects or 'matter.' Real non-manifest phenomena, such as the natural laws and the meaning of life, are 'hidden.' They are to be viewed as immanent rather than as the transcendence of nothingness. Later we

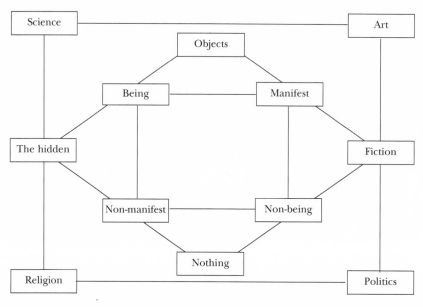

2.14.   The Brier-Christiansen multiple square. The third circle explains the emergence of different kinds of knowledge types related to the kind of objects our culture defines in the world. All are necessary and irreducible. The sciences deal with the hidden order behind the dynamics of objects. Religion is concerned with hidden non-material forces and order, which some presume to govern our existence. Art includes the production of fictional objects. Politics is the creation of a non-material collective of fictional goals, such as democracy or a sustainable society.

shall go into more detail with Peirce's metaphysics, which demonstrates these points very well. Here we stay at the level of generalization.

That which exists but is non-manifest is *the hidden*. The latter includes the laws and powers of nature, or in other cultures spiritual powers, depending on the metaphysical framework. Finally, that which is not being but which nevertheless is manifest is *fiction*. Fiction is an important part of reality (Deely 1997), whether it is literature, movies, sculpture, dance, future plans, visions, or just plain lies. To this construction I add in Figure 2.14 our basic systems of knowledge. Science deals with the hidden laws behind objects and their dynamics (kinematics). Religion deals with the hidden that is no-thing. Art deals with fictional objects, be they manifest or imaginary. Politics deals with fictional nothing phenomena such as democracy, human rights, and free markets, which are human social inventions or constructs.

Different knowledge-generating systems then evolve in relation to these ontological realms; we can see these at the third level. As I have already discussed, they are the sciences, art, religion, and politics/ideology: functional differentiated systems with symbolic generalized media as Luhmann calls them. Classical mechanistic *science* is about discovering the hidden laws behind the movements of objects. *Religion* is about uncovering meaningful connections hidden behind our nothing-ness or mental and spiritual existence. *Politics* is the creation of visions for social coexistence that did not exist beforehand – for example, democracy or a sustainable ecological future. *Art* deals with how to use objects to materialize meaningful patterns and connections not seen before.

These have been the traditional ways to order knowledge systems since the Enlightenment. One could say that religion and science are working respectively on uncovering subjective and objective truth. Art and politics create fictional social objects, such as pieces of art, constitutions, and laws for society (except in the case of fundamentalisms, where either religion sets the framework for 'science,' 'the arts,' and 'the political constitution'; or a political ideology sets the framework for arts, religion, and science, as for instance Lenin's and Stalin's dialectical materialism tried to do; or the sciences dominate all other knowledge systems [which is often called 'scientism'], as in B.F. Skinner's radical behaviorism and E.O. Wilson's sociobiology. Recently evolutionary psychology, especially Dawkins' 'selfish gene' version, has sometimes been accused of scientism).

This is the traditional knowledge organization of modernity. However, a new layer has appeared in the postmodern/postindustrial area (see Figure 2.15). We are developing a Third Culture that promises to go beyond the fundamental split between the world of science and technology and the world of the humanities and the arts (Brockman 1995). This Third Culture reveals that science and art share creative aspects. This is why we now increasingly use the term 'knowledge production' instead of the discovery of truth or facts. Since positivism we have come full circle in our culture by realizing that both religion and science have metaphysical assumptions and frameworks – paradigms, if you like.

Our basic attitude of relating to and caring about reality and the living beings in it (Heidegger's *Sorge*), and the search for meaning and ethics, are fundamental parts of the existence of a conscious individual in a body and a culture. Elaborating the last diamond of Figure 2.15 brings us to the subject that moves us today: *metaphysics*. We have discovered that science, philosophy, and religion cannot eliminate metaphysics (Kuhn 1970) and that neither can Protestant Christianity (Latour 1993, Laszlo 1995, 1996, 2004, Bateson and Bateson 2005, Bohm 1983, Bohm and Weber 1983). Today we must work with metaphysics in a reflective way, as I attempt to do in these models. This has to a certain degree relativized classical mechanistic science and our belief in one institutionalized religion.

New connections between science and religion have opened spaces for broad movements such as New Age and ecological thinking. Let us call it *spirituality*: a new way beyond organized religion and political ideology. We attempt to relate to the basic reality of our own inner worlds, and through this find ways to connect metaphysics, science, art, and lived political practice. Think of the ecophilosophy of Arne Næss (1973), Bertalanffy's general system theory, and other kinds of holistic thinking. All are working towards new utopias: reflecting on our experiences and conceptualizing our metaphysics and ideals, we are creating our own visions of a sustainable future in a world without hunger, natural catastrophes, or other disasters. Finally, politics and the arts have joined forces in our cultural construction of social utopias. Currently, global ecological as well as human and economically sustainable societies are our new utopia, as we worry about our planet's ability to maintain the conditions needed for our survival.

We are moving into a *Third Culture*: using all our knowledge and creative powers, we might be able to create a Third Culture in which art and science work together to create knowledge, a culture beyond the dichotomy separating Snow's (1993) cultures of science, technology, power, and money, on the one hand, and the humanities, the arts, the social sciences, ethics, and aesthetics on the other; as also Hesse envisioned in *Magister Ludi*. As we realize that we depend on metaphysical frameworks and the constructive and creative aspects common to both the sciences and arts, we can begin to work in a more reflective and constructive way with the interplay between metaphysics, methods, goals, and creativity. For example, in Næss's 'deep ecology,' our view of the interrelations among nature, society, science, and technology is changed through a spiritualistic philosophy which suggests that we should develop our society towards an ecological utopia in which we shall live in harmony and peace with nature, other living beings, and ourselves. Freia

Mathews (1991) promotes a more moderate and scientific version of this vision, which we shall return to later. The growing interest in Peirce's semiotic philosophy, which developed into biosemiotics (and for some into pan-semiotics), is also a new way to think about these questions.

Science also must be viewed as a collective narrative that creates possible worlds by producing new concepts and objects within the constraints of nature. It is clear – as von Foerster demonstrates – that scientists and the sciences must take responsibility for the new objects they create and offer to bring into our social reality. They will have to argue for their theories as they relate to a social utopia, including its ethics and aesthetics, as well as for a theory of the existence of humans. Science cannot escape its deep political engagement – through its choices of subject areas, methods, and interactions – with industrial technological development. With Luhmann, we can say that science is a generalized medium that operates according to a simplified code of true and false. In this way it broadly disseminates its message throughout society. Through its interactions with industry and political-economic power (both forms of generalized media), science offers utopian realities built on technologies such as nuclear power, AI, gene therapy, and genetically modified living organisms that grant us energy, food, and better health – but do so at a cost, or at least with some risks. The new modes of knowledge (mode 2) are, for instance, discussed by Gibbons and colleagues (1994); the generalized media's interactions in the public 'agora' of the electronic media are discussed in Nowotny and colleagues (2001).

The present model is only one among many capable of showing, in a transdisciplinary, non-reductionist way, how the inner connections among the diverse – but probably all necessary – knowledge-producing systems in our culture could complement our search for understanding and control, in a way that does not reduce those systems to one foundational knowledge type.

Figure 2.15 illustrates a second-order knowledge, generated from a perspective that recognizes the outer circle as important and that in this way makes metaphysics explicit. I am consciously writing about humanity's fumbling with new utopias – for instance, ecological and systemic ones – and I recognize spirituality as an important factor in the development of a Third Culture. This figure uses the transdisciplinary integration of knowledge from different viewpoints, methods, and subject areas to create a sustainable culture for the next millennium – a culture that does not reduce everything to one principle or law.

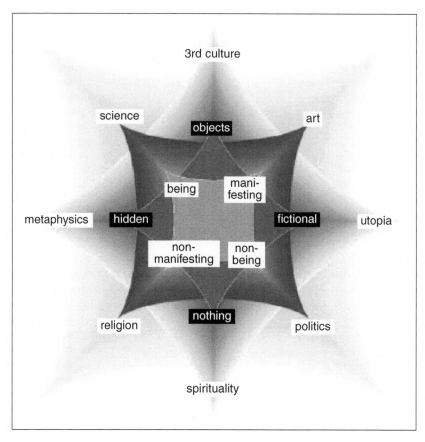

2.15. The Brier-Christensen multiple square (BRICHMU). In this graphic overview of the transdisciplinary self-organizations of different knowledge systems, we begin at the inner or first level, at the basic metaphysical consider-ations of being and manifestations. The second level is the basic ontological realm of the world. The third level is the manifestations of different knowledge production systems. The fourth level shows some of the forms of knowledge that are now growing as we seek foundations for a new understanding of our-selves, our culture and our place in nature. (Figure designed with the help of Pille Bunnell.)

One way to accept the immense differences among knowledge methods and areas without becoming completely relativistic (as in the radical forms of postmodernism and constructivism), while still advancing towards a stance that is truly postmodern (as Deely 2001b argues for and Luntly 1995 also aims at) is to adapt a hypercomplex stance towards reality. This means abandoning the idea that any knowledge system has a direct way to obtain absolute truth on any matter. In abandoning this idea, we are able to avoid becoming radically relativistic or constructivistic, and we open a way to acquire a fairly reliable knowledge of a limited number of aspects and ranges of reality. As I will explore further in later chapters, one way to understand regularities in the world is to see them, as Peirce (1992) did, as habits of a hypercomplex nature developed through evolution (statistical and dynamic regularities). For Peirce, Firstness is a complex and dynamic continuum that cannot be reduced in any way. One can only know Firstness intellectually after the moment has passed by making signs via abductive reasoning, using Secondness and Thirdness. Only then can one use deductive and inductive reasoning to design experiments to search for regularities. Absolute exactness is impossible. All knowledge is partially constructed because a certain limited angle and expectation is always the culturally biased basis for categorization (Lakoff 1987). We are always in need of various kinds of knowledge aspects when trying to understand, map, or make predictive models of a complex area or aspect of life or reality. Peirce offers a new metaphysical framework that includes science. We shall return to this when we discuss the contributions made by biosemiotics to a theory of information, cognition, and communication.

We must also realize that there are many sources of knowledge, types of theoretical knowledge, and types of practices that generate knowledge in different areas of society; classical logic is only one. Knowledge types and forms are constantly interacting. Sometimes the dialogue is constructive, and sometimes authority and power conflict in determining a frame of reference such as the one I have attempted to construct here. The epistemology of this frame always departs from human experience within our four spheres of existence. It is not likely that we, in any near future, shall acquire a scientific explanation for it all. This frame also seeks to include the internal realism of Putnam (1992), which is supported both by the work of Prigogine and Stengers and by that of Lakoff and Johnson. Internal realism is the only realism we can have. But considering how many millions of years our perception has existed and developed, it is fair to say that we are firmly embedded in reality. Our biology places constraints on our possible perceptions.

This is the first constructive draft of the philosophical framework behind my analysis. More details of this epistemological stance will appear when I analyse second-order cybernetics and Peircean biosemiotics. So far, my point of departure has been an internal, non-mechanistic realism that embraces Niels Bohr's general theory of complementarity and Søren Kierkegaard's emphasis on the existential uniqueness of each person's inner life.

This model calls for us to reflect on our own metaphysical framework and its limits in light of the restructuring of our rationality that ecological challenges impose on us. Can we solve these problems using scientific and technological methods, or must we broaden our idea of rationality to include our fellow living species, our ethics, and the view that nature is more than just a machine?

There is no way to prove that any metaphysics is true in the broadest sense of the word. One must, of course, demand that these models not violate the knowledge we consider to be true and in accordance with practical experience. Also, our expanding concepts could include new areas of experience while remaining compatible with previous knowledge. Including quantum phenomena in our scientific world view is no less difficult than accounting for the effects of our 'inner world and bodyhood' on the creation and sharing of information. Both change our views of how the universe and the world are connected.

3 An Ethological Approach to Cognition

3.1 Overview

So far I have constructed a preliminary version of a metaframe model of knowledge systems that can serve as a platform for creating a non-Cartesian information science that includes nature as well as our inner and social worlds. It is already clear that we shall have to make a foundational change in the concepts of both 'information' and 'science' in 'information science' if we are to keep the transdisciplinary goal within sight. To that end, we shall have to change the conceptual framework to which these terms refer.

I have endorsed the non-reductionist view that knowledge always originates from feeling – that is, from a volitional signifying living system with an inner experiential world and with, as well, a body relating to and distinguishing itself from both a natural world and a cultural environment by means of social communication.

Acknowledging the necessity of all four worlds (body, mental, nature, culture), it seems too strong at the outset to suggest that an explanation for any one of these worlds could emerge from any one of the others. I cannot find a way to explain everything as evolving from either a dead mechanical deterministic world, or a completely indeterminate material world that pre-exists all knowing systems, or a radical and social constructivism wherein our 'world' amounts to tapestries of language and concepts, and in which all phenomena – even nature – are merely social constructions.

Pure idealistic solipsism is a black hole from which nothing escapes and from which, it follows, no communication is possible. I contend that a partially independent reality with some structure and dynamics, although hypercomplex, must be assumed even by an internal realism. Internal realism is compatible with Heidegger's view that we find ourselves 'thrown' into a 'world' to which we are emotionally attached (*Sorge*), and that we waken to a partial self-consciousness in language (Heidegger 1973). Furthermore, we live in the 'world,' and the regulative idea of science and its ethos is to find 'the truth,' and an important part of scientific truth is to construct a 'universe,' as it seems logical to assume that there must be some kind of unity in or 'behind' and 'before' it all. The concept of a universe is a regulative idea (Kant 1990), one that attempts consistent discourses and collectively disciplined perceptual practices; but in the end the final truth about the universe and us is probably something that will escape the precise language of science, based as it is on well-defined and measurable differences, or it will make no common human sense.[1]

But let us keep an open mind as to what the nature of this basic reality is, and not assume simplistic models that might limit our possible results. I agree with Maturana that our many knowledge systems cause us to explain, predict, and conduct activities in a 'Multiverse' – or 'Umwelten' as von Uexküll calls them, or 'life worlds,' as the phenomenologists call them. It is from these that we identify, name, and classify 'things.' The later Wittgenstein catches this well with his idea that we live within language games that develop intricately with our life forms – a view that seems to dovetail neatly with Maturana's idea that objects appear in language. But I do not believe that this perceptual and linguistic Multiverse can be upheld as an ontological concept alone. I still think, perhaps naively, that we all live in the same universe.

It is also difficult to deny that as material and cultural beings, we live in irreversible time seen from a thermodynamic perspective (Prigogine and Stengers 1984). When we acknowledge the foundational nature of irreversible time, we are implying that we cannot avoid evolutionary and historical explanations. But we must also remember that these are explorative narratives with no absolute explanatory powers as long as we operate with a single universe. We seem to be caught as individuals in our worlds and as a species in the universe. As Wittgenstein points out, only mystics claim to be capable of being aware of a state before and beyond the universe and therefore beyond words; for this reason we cannot speak clearly about such states – and perhaps therefore should not try to do so. Unless the precise point is that the meaning of 'Life, the universe and everything' is beyond words.

Still, it makes sense that our language and concepts can be understood as having been developed through our attempts to survive as self-organized systems in the world, and must therefore have viable relations to the world and its objects. Biology has a profound influence on our metaphors and classification schemes, as Lakoff and Johnson have pointed out very well, and this accords with ethological thinking and with the biosemiotics of Sebeok. But it is also true that, since our thoughts are formed and carried by language, it is extremely difficult for us to see *beyond* language. To some degree our thinking is *caught* in language. We acquire knowledge through signs (Representamens); out of these we generate Interpretants in order to assume the existence of objects and actions in a world that we project to be 'outside us.' But we still do not know for certain and in specific detail what 'the outside world' is; and even less so we know what or who 'we' are. But Peirce's three categories seems necessary in order to create an evolutionary theory of semiosis.

A biologist by training, I have begun my analysis of cognitive information and communication from the broad mid-level concept of living systems. From this level it is possible, as we shall see, to draw on systems and cybernetics as well as on the biosemiotics of Sebeok. My point of departure is the foundational theories of Lorenz, Tinbergen, and von Uexküll, who founded the discipline of behavioural and cognitive biology now called ethology.

In analysing these scientists' work and asking myself how far their theories can be 'pursued' into the field of human psychology, I found myself inspired to analyse the paradoxes common to those who research human and animal cognition, as presented by the Danish ethologist Iven Reventlow. I have already touched on whether, considering the vast differences between the phenomenological and behavioural approaches, a unified psychological science is possible. I will continue this theme throughout this book.

Several books could be written from a purely philosophical point of view on this perspective alone. But this book is not 'pure' philosophy. It is an attempt to conduct a constructive philosophy of science, one that addresses an interdisciplinary scientific problem encountered on the border between philosophy and science. The debates over information science, are, after all, woven tightly into epistemology and ontological assumptions.

Having sketched the problem and outlined the starting point for a general philosophy of science, I will discuss examples of the problems confronting non-Cartesian evolutionary sciences and interdisciplinary research programs to argue my case. I hope to show whether a non-reductionist analysis can illuminate ways in which these two can be interwoven to provide a new, transdisciplinary framework for information, cognition, and communication studies – one that goes beyond the limits of mechanistic and functionalistic paradigms.

A consistent theory of information, cognition, and communication must embrace the social sciences and the humanities as well as biology and the physicochemical sciences. True transdisciplinariness is necessary if we are to understand information, cognition, and communication in nature and in living, artificial, and social systems. The research program of cybernetics and systems theory attempts to develop a transdisciplinary information science, and so does the 'information processing paradigm' of cognitive science; however, both interdisciplinary paradigms lack a theory of signification and of the 'inner life' of organisms and observers. A theory that connects the internal phenomenological view with a theory of language and epistemology must be developed. We cannot continue with a naive realistic epistemology of mechanistic science while working from an evolutionary basis. Thus we shall start with ethology and its difficulties with becoming 'scientific' in order to see how these problems reveal themselves in the life sciences.

3.2 The Ethological Research Program

The degree to which animal and especially human behaviour can be described and explained according to scientific methods has always been central to discussions of the foundations of psychology. Is there a science of psychology in the Galilean tradition of objective science[2] (Lewin 1935) that includes the phenomenological aspect? Can this science be based on a materialistic realism and its Galilean idea of objective universal mathematical and deterministic laws? Or is it necessary to adopt a more constructivist and organic view of reality that breaks with mechanism?

We are searching for a theory that is neither mechanistic nor subjective-idealistic nor vitalistic in the sense that it believes in some special spiritual power of life – a life force that sets the theory beyond the laws of non-living nature. This was the project of Lorenz and Tinbergen when they founded the discipline of ethology in the 1920s based on three foundations of modern biology: the theory of evolution, ecological theory, and modern population genetics (advanced on a molecular basis in the 1950s), combined with the methods of comparative anatomy as applied to instinctive movements. Lorenz and Tinbergen developed a theory of innate cognition and communication based on a new and differentiated theory of motivation. But in my opinion, they failed to provide a new theoretical foundation for this theory. However, Lorenz introduced evolutionary epistemology by contending that Kant's categories were explainable in an evolutionary sense (see Lorenz 1970–1, esp. his 1943 article 'Die angeborenen Formen möglicher Erfahrung').[3] This is an interesting aspect of epistemology, but it raises the question of what sort of knowledge evolutionary theory is.

When approaching the mechanical foundations of information, it is relevant to discuss the fundamental problems of ethology, since this theory addresses in a general way the cognitive and behavioural interactions between organisms and their surroundings (see Tinbergen 1968, 1973). Ethology observes the interactions between the organisms and their milieu. Ethology is behavioural research with theoretical foundations in biological-natural history; it asks how behaviour has developed phylogenetically and ontogenetically and how it contributes to the survival of the organism both as an individual and as a species – a question not encountered in Wiener's information theory. Ethology's goal is to describe and explain the cognition and behaviour of organisms within an evolutionary ecological framework; it is concerned primarily with the specific innate behaviours of species. Furthermore, ethology addresses the various forms of learning that different instinctive conditions make possible (see Bittermann 1965; Lorenz 1977), partly where they manifest themselves as 'constraints on learning,' and partly where they occur as surprising outbreaks of 'intelligent thinking' – for example, the ability of rats to find the way out of a labyrinth.

The model of reaction and releasing of behaviour, arrived at after sixty years of research into behaviour's internal organization (a motivational model), attempts to 'integrate in a simple way the effect situation, inner motivation and the outer-observable behavior' based on the central concept of the 'innate release response mechanism,' which ethologists believe is located between perception and primarily instinct-guided behaviour (Reventlow 1970).

I will focus on the limits of mechanistic descriptions in the behavioural sciences by evaluating the Danish psychologist Iven Reventlow's ethological approach to psychology. Extending my previous attempts to elaborate Reventlow's work (Brier 1980), I will present at length Reventlow's attempt to discover a common foundation for non-reductionist ethology and phenomenological psychology based on Kurt Lewin's Galilean psychology.[4] I will then elucidate the main theme in Reventlow's pursuit of fundamental functional concepts of psychology – concepts that can reveal psychological laws. Reventlow's analyses present themselves as epistemological deliberations on behavioural analysis, and as the construction of a statistical model of motivation based on classical ethological experiments with sticklebacks. His doctoral thesis (1970) has unfortunately not yet been translated into English; however, there is an English description of the model in Madsen (1974). Other sections of his work can be found in Reventlow (1959, 1961, 1970, 1972, 1973, 1977, 1980).

Finally, I will discuss the limits of this approach. Even in the most stringent presentation, the biopsychological paradigm raises some elementary questions: What is the status of the functional cognitive and informational concepts and laws? Are these laws objective, eternal, and absolute, as often claimed in physics? Must psychology be coupled with a materialistic ontology that considers the use of mental concepts such as intentionality a convenient way to talk about phenomena (Dennett 1983) that, in the future, will be reduced and duplicatable by computer? Reventlow attempts to develop basic methods and concepts for a Galilean, law-determined psychology following Kurt Lewin (1935), through research with animal models in the tradition of ethology. His standard model is the nest-guarding behaviour of the male stickleback – a small fish in a partly self-created world. Reventlow attempts to restrict description, causal analysis, and explanation to the behavioural level. To this end, he works with statistical models, integrating ethological methods with gestalt ideas to obtain new fundamental and functional concepts in behavioural psychology. His ultimate goal is to use these results to analyse human personality and action. In this process, however, he finds that he cannot separate the organism from its environment. It is not possible to carry through either a mechanistic or a dualistic perspective.

But let us first examine the development that led to the use of an evolutionary and biological paradigm to explain human cognition. It shows how analysis of behavioural experiments lead us to the core of semiosis; the abductive creation of a perceptual 'object' or a 'rependium' as Reventlow had called it. Thus there is solid empirical work that leads us into biosemiotics.

3.3 A Selective Historical Summary of the Ethological Science Project

Until the Renaissance, the point of departure for the scientific discussion of the cognition of living systems and what they can reveal about our epistemological situation was a Christian view of the world as a meaningful pattern where God and Satan battled each other. To fight paganism, especially nature-oriented religions and superstitions, Christianity increasingly conceived of nature as 'dead.' When vitalism brought back living nature by incorporating nature-philosophy, the pan-psychic elements in Aristotle's hylozoistic view of substance and form were de-emphasized. Animals were not viewed as possessing individual souls, so they had neither rights to the sacraments nor places in Paradise (or Hell). They did, however, possess divine instincts to help them survive, albeit without realizing that they were participating in God's great plan. As the natural sciences developed after the Renaissance, nature became increasingly mechanized. Descartes (1596–1650) finally declared plants, animals, and the human body to be machines. One of his followers, Malebranche, launched comparative psychology with experiments that did not acknowledge that animals could feel pain. Later, La Metrie and Loeb developed a detailed basis for a mechanistic explanation of animal and human behaviour (Brier 1980).

In the nineteenth century the idea of evolution spread from the social sciences to geology and finally to biology. Lamarck (1744–1829), one of the founders of the biological sciences, saw living systems as a 'stream of life' with a common origin qualitatively different from the physicochemical aspects of nature. Based on his research, the discipline of 'natural history' developed, although it did not attain the status of a science. It was Charles Darwin (1859) who laid the foundation for scientific evolution and who contributed to the founding of ethology with his book *The Expression of the Emotions in Man and Animals* (Darwin 1899). Around the same time, Ernst Haeckel (1834–1919) established the concept of ecology. In the first half of the twentieth century, evolutionary and ecological thinking formed the basis for new ethological explanations of the nature of animal behaviour. This work was supported by the later development of population genetics (Brier 1980).

In the nineteenth century, Carnot (1796–1832), Kelvin (1884–1907), and Clausius (1822–88) developed thermodynamics, which was later statistically interpreted by Boltzmann (1844–1906). The development of a unified concept of energy, which espoused in the first law of thermodynamics that the amount of energy in the universe is constant, was important to this development. In the second law of thermodynamics the physical concepts of irreversibility and time are conceptualized based on the conversion of free energy to entropic energy, by assuming that entropy always increases. This was a physical theory of evolution.

Thermodynamics inspired Lorenz's and Freud's models of the energies of the psyche in animals and humans. Lorenz (1950) based his psycho-hydraulic theory of motivation on the concept of action-specific psychic energy that accumulates until the pressure is intense enough for instinctive movements to be prompted by very low stimulation, or even to occur spontaneously. Sigmund Freud (1856–1939), in his early *Entwurf,* treated the nervous system as akin to a steam engine: psychic energy behaves like steam, accumulating until it forces a way out of its confines (Andkjær and Køppe 1986). Freud also employed an energy model for the id. Psychic energy originating in the basic drives, such as sex, cannot be destroyed but only temporarily suppressed. Eventually it will force its way 'out' – often in the form of neurotic behaviour.

Lorenz conceptualized motivation, or drive, as 'action-specific energy,' a special type of psychic energy created in the nervous system. As I noted earlier, the first law of thermodynamics posits that energy is constant. Energy cannot be destroyed, only transformed. Lorenz developed his psycho-hydraulic model on this basis in order to understand the various motivations and moods of each species, and to comprehend why these drives seem to 'dam specific urges' for instinctive behaviour such as mating and hunting.

Focusing on the concept of information, it is particularly relevant to analyse the innate release mechanism. From the point of view of the human observer, only small parts of the stimuli that usually occur in nature activate the behaviour. These parts have been characterized as 'sign stimuli' – that is, stimuli that without previous learning activate specific behaviours in an organism. Sign stimuli lead to sensations that cooperate with internally motivated conditions so as to release a genetically determined behaviour.

The action-releasing perceptions of these sign stimuli are always connected to definite states of motivation. When von Frisch's studies of the colour sense of bees were published, von Hess denied that bees could differentiate between colours. The experiments von Hess had done on bees' escape behaviour showed that they always flew towards the patch of light with greatest intensity, regardless of colour. Recent studies show that von Hess was correct, but von Frisch was also correct that bees do have a sense of colour, which they employ when seeking food; these were two different innate release response mechanisms, related to flight motivation and the search for food respectively (Lorenz 1977).

The significant result from ethology concerning the relationships among reality, perception, and information is that perception is not a purely mechanical process whereby objective information is passively accepted. On the contrary, perception requires motivation. All of ethology's explanations of release and behavioural functionality build on this concept of action-specific motivation.

From an ethological point of view, this type of process is the primitive starting point of human perception. Our cognition of information is controlled by 'interests' that derive partially from the nature of the perception apparatus (Lorenz 1977) and partly from the innate release response mechanisms in our organisms. In his development of the concept of instinct and motivation, Lorenz struggled with the causal role of the organism's mental experience in the release of behaviour (Brier 1980). Finally, in 1950, he denied that it played any causal role.

But in his later theory of learning based on instinctual structures as foundations of and constraints on the organism's learning abilities, Lorenz again emphasized that experiential–emotional aspects reinforce the trial-and-error process.

Lorenz (1977) discussed the relationships among instinct, motivation, and learning, and realized that there must be some phenomenological reward in the form of pleasurable emotions to make an animal want to repeat a particular behaviour. He had difficulty with the nature of appetite behaviour, since it must include emotions, awareness of a goal, and a fulfilment/reward; the psycho-hydraulic model was therefore inadequate. Although by the 1950s he had developed a neutral monistic theory of the mind and acknowledged that there was a psychological side to the physiologically described phenomenon of drives, he did not ascribe causality to psychic functions per se. But it was unavoidable to ascribe some causality to psychological processes beyond what could be described by physiological models at that time. A choice had to be made between a cybernetic model of a goal-seeking machine with feedback and the intentionality concept stemming from phenomenology. Cybernetic models were accepted, and phenomenological models of causality were rejected.

When organisms must adapt quickly to changes in their environment, in the course of evolution their instincts eventually 'open' different parts of their 'program' towards learning such as the perceptual; this often takes place during 'sensitive periods.' Examples include the 'imprinting' of ducklings, the song learning of many birds, and children's language acquisition. In the culturally based upbringing of children, basic human motivations and needs are developed and differentiated, and feelings are developed together with self-consciousness. From the phylogenetic perspective of evolution, differences that observers register are heavily dictated by biologically and culturally created interests. To some extent, different species and different cultures live in different worlds.

Influenced by mechanistic thinking, ethologists for many years attempted to find physiological explanations for various kinds of motivation and their influence on perception. Under the rubric 'Evidence for drive,' Thorpe (1979, 132) wrote the following passage, which I see as exemplifying the relationship of the English school to the ontological status of the concept of motivation:

> We have shown above that a very real problem is raised by the question of the motivation of particular stereotyped actions. The name used by the pioneer ethologists, following Lorenz, was 'action specific energy.' This was a thoroughly bad term and was later softened to 'specific action potentials' etc. The increase in responsiveness is an outward sign of an internal change, and what most, if not all, ethologists want to discover is the physiological basis for such change. So the very question of the internal motivation of specific acts leads us straight into the general problems of 'drives.'

In a conclusive analysis of the role played by the concept of motivation in ethology and comparative psychology, Hinde (1970) showed this to be a logical category error. Hinde concluded that explanations of motivation are founded on an entirely different descriptive level than are physiological and behavioural descriptions.

One could expand Hinde's perspective by pointing out that the concept of motivation can be said to occupy the same position within ethology as the concept of life in biology, or that of the law of gravity and the attraction of masses in Newton's classical mechanics. In other words, it is an 'occult' basic concept that cannot be explained within the paradigm, but that cannot be ignored either.

The Danish psychologist K.B. Madsen (1978, 9) documented this position of the motivation concept in ethology and other schools of thought within behavioural research in a paper that summarized his many years of research into the concept of motivation:

Under the name of 'instinct,' 'need,' 'motive,' 'tendency,' etc., the motivation variable has been introduced into psychological theories to explain
behavior. Therefore, one does not find the motivation variable in the psychological epochs or schools of thought where psychology's task is looked
upon as the description of consciousness. One cannot find motivation variables in classical experimental psychology (Fechner, Wundt, Ebbinghaus,
etc.). Only with the advent of Freud's psychoanalysis and American learning theory did one attempt to explain behavior by introducing concepts
such as 'drive' and the like (for instance Freud's 'Trieb' and Woodworth's
'drive'). The concept of motivation spread from psychoanalysis to the
theory of personality (for instance, Murray's 'need'). After World War Two,
motivation psychology gradually became an independent psychological
discipline. (my translation)

The concept of motivation would thus seem to be a 'remnant' of the
classical psychology of consciousness in mechanistic behavioural
research. The desire to explain the release of observable behaviour as
dependent on 'inner' motivation, drive, tendencies, or needs appears to
be an attempt to transform the original phenomenological description
level's incentives and intentions into something less subjective and
anthropomorphic. But this does not make a theory of cognition more
scientific. Concepts of consciousness cannot be reduced to physiology.
One can, at most, claim that there is a one-to-one correlation between
mental conditions and (neuro)physiological states. However, when one
claims that they are the same, it is not clear why that is, or how the qualitatively different aspects come into being.

But as Jensen (1973) has shown, such a correlation theory cannot be
maintained. The human brain and the brains of higher mammals are so
complex that it is highly unlikely that any nerve impulse would ever
occur in the same way, even in simple reflexes. Here we face immense
complexity! The complexity of neurophysiological states makes it necessary to classify them based on some sort of interest or point of view.
For Jensen, it is culture through language that conducts this classification of the referrals of the concepts, through the conventions determined by the child's surroundings.

Karl Popper (1972) argued along the same lines, clashing with the
idea that scientific hypotheses via induction emerge spontaneously
from researchers' observations. No matter how many times we predict
and observe an empirical phenomenon, we can never prove the existence of a natural law because the experience of something repeating

itself is not a value-free, absolutely objective observation, but one based on a judgment of similarity. The philosopher Hume is famous for showing that inductive reasoning is not logically compelling. Hume's argument, which Popper develops, is that repetition is based on similarity: repetition-for-us is based on similarity-for-us. That is, we identify the situations as identical. But it is highly unlikely that situations we observe are ever completely identical – they are in fact too numerous and varied in composition and appearance. It can only be a matter of similarity. The Danish psychologist A.F. Petersen (1972, 46), who developed Popper's theories within an ethological perspective, wrote:

> The problem of repetition arises the moment an organism's viewpoint is introduced. The world of phenomena cannot be shown to be repetitive in its own right; we do not know whether the laws of nature that have been revealed to us will apply in the future. The world of phenomena has an objectively historic course, but no one can guarantee that the historic laws we find apply for all time and in every milieu that might arise. This does not mean that the knowledge an organism can possess must be subjective. Figuratively speaking, the organism finds itself in the objective stream of phenomena and by assuming certain attitudes toward this stream of phenomena the organism will perhaps be able to discover phenomena which, seen from its particular perspective, repeat themselves. This will perhaps reveal itself as the first step to understanding certain connections between the phenomena and to explaining the respective connections within the given spatio-temporal region. (my translation)

We can add that things can only be classified and become identical or different in this way – by being placed in relation to the needs or interests of a living system. This rule applies not only to animals but also to humans – even to scientists. So the concept of information is not purely subjective, but neither can it be defined without observers and their motivational selective attentions. How can this problem be solved and psychology still be a real science, as the information processing paradigm of modern cognitive science claims it to be?

3.4 The Necessity of a Galilean Psychology

According to Lorenz, emotions have functions and survival value. Wimmer (1995) further develops this evolutionary theory about the functionality of emotion, which one can also find in Bateson's (1973) work. But it is still a purely functionalistic description and cannot explain how certain things and events become significant for a living system so that it perceives them as a sign for something vital. Reventlow has made some interesting and thorough deliberations on this that bring us a step closer in the analysis.[5]

A famous article by gestalt theorist Kurt Lewin titled 'The Conflict between Aristotelian and Galilean Modes of Thought in Contemporary Psychology' (in Lewin 1935) was an important basis for Reventlow's analysis of complex concepts in psychology. In this article Lewin showed that psychology classes together many things with very slight or unimportant relations, and separates things that are objectively closely related.

Aristotle believed that it is possible to work scientifically only on the basis of constant or almost constant (frequent) recurrences. He argued that laws are constituted in a historical context through frequent and regular occurrences within a geographical area. Seen in this light, the 'less frequent' and the 'rare' become the accidental, the laws for falling stones are distinct from the laws for the harmony of the spheres, and phenomena can be described by 'attributes' that are almost always present. These characteristics, having been summed up, assign the phenomena to a 'class.' These characteristics can then be ascribed to each member of the class as 'attributes' – the essence of the class that determines its entire behaviour. The other characteristic of this classification scheme is that it often works through pairs of absolute opposites: cold/hot, dry/wet, upward-seeking/downward-seeking. Following are examples of Aristotelian laws in psychology.

1. The statistical concept of normality, where developmental psychology attributes certain behavioural norms to specific ages in child development instead of to specific processes.
2. The division of psychological phenomena into 'normal' and 'pathological.'
3. The separation of intelligence, memory, and the impulse to act (will).
4. The classification of emotions and temperaments.
5. The concepts of drive and motivation.

Both Lewin and Reventlow attempted to break away from this oversimplified classification. Regarding the application of theoretical probability models in the analysis of behaviour, Reventlow (1970, 85) wrote in his doctoral thesis:

The question is … whether it is possible that these models will enable psychology to make a leap forward comparable to that which occurred in physics when Galileo and Newton started looking for laws rather than just studying phenomena. In this way one law was enough to explain phenomena as diverse as the fall of an object to the ground and the movements of the planets … It might be that the division of factors into groups such as stimuli, forces of motivation, or learning processes would prove to be far too primitive and will persist only because the effects of these factors have been studied in many experiments.

The results of these explanations, however, have been used solely to explain the conditions of the particular experiment and to create 'laws' from this, while they have only rarely been used to extract simple laws from the many experimental results. (my translation)

This tendency is related to something that Lewin identified in Aristotle: a lack of conviction that the entire field under study is determined or governed by laws (which was the case in the sublunar sphere). Belief in the all-embracing character of natural laws is a cornerstone of the ontology of the exact sciences, but not of the humanities or the social sciences. It is precisely this problem that forms the leitmotif of Reventlow's work. Agreeing with Köhler and other gestalt psychologists, Reventlow accepts phenomenological data as adequate for the study of humans, but avoids as much as possible the use of intentional models and explanations in his theories and models.

3.5 Reventlow's Theoretical and Methodological Background

Reventlow received his education during and after the Second World War. He was active in the Danish Resistance during the German occupation of Denmark and wrote his master's thesis in 1954. One sees clearly in all his works that for him the major divisions in psychology are behaviourism, gestalt psychology, and psychoanalysis with respect to phenomenological studies as well as the phenomenology of the Copenhagen school (especially Tranekjær Rasmussen). Also, through the Danish psychologist Edgar Rubin he was introduced to perceptual experimentation. Reventlow has emphasized experimentation and methodology, but he has always been keenly aware of the importance of his theoretical background. His fascination with the emerging biological science of behaviour added an important element to the research program of ethology.

Lorenz (1970–1) and Tinbergen (1973) founded modern European ethology together, but Reventlow was most influenced by the latter. Combining a gestalt psychological perspective with a respect for statistics rare in an empiricist, Reventlow used Tinbergen's tradition to develop approaches that infuse comparative psychology with new depth.

Reventlow's objective was to examine precisely the complex phenomena of 'everyday life' in natural and simplified situations in order to find meaningful 'basic units' of behaviour that can be used as 'fixed points' for the analysis of more complex psycho-biological phenomena, such as the human personality. His training had focused on the psychology of perception; however, his desire to achieve greater exactitude and objectivity in psychology led him to psycho-biological behavioural research.

The transition from humans to animals was the first simplification undertaken by Reventlow – largely because it is easier to conduct experiments on animals. Also, in animals the personality factor (individuality) does not have a dominant influence over the release and control of behaviour, as it does in humans. Animals have individuality, but this does not conceal the general characteristics of their behavioural release and control, as it does in humans. The less complex an organism one researches, the less individual characteristics will dominate and 'mask' general aspects of behaviour. But to ensure that the results are relevant to human psychology, the animals used in the experiments must have an individuality factor strong enough to be included as a factor when constructing general models of the functional organization of behaviour.

At this point, one might have expected Reventlow to throw himself into experiments with rats and pigeons; for this, there is a time-honoured tradition in psychobiological behavioural research, especially in the United States in comparative psychology and behaviourism. But Reventlow rejected this approach for several reasons. First, his greatest interest lay not with 'arbitrary learning' but rather with the emotional/motivational foundations, the basic 'unconscious' processes that govern much of the behaviour that is relevant to developmental psychology and psychoanalysis/psychiatry. Second, he wanted to work with behaviour in 'everyday life' and with surroundings 'natural' to the behavioural repertoire of organisms. He did not believe that the psychological experiments typically conducted within behaviourism fulfilled this condition:

The behaviorist posits that by having a cat press buttons in a 'puzzle box' it is possible to ascertain something of importance about its behavior. But 'no one could reasonably expect to achieve an understanding of Einstein's thoughts by observing his behavior while he was attempting to solve a very simple cat problem such as catching a mouse in the dark with his bare hands. (1954, 5)

Much later he added that biologically speaking, the white laboratory rat must be viewed as an artificial product:

A living physiological specimen, 1) whose reactions, compared to the wild rat, are relatively independent of emotional factors, 2) which to a great degree is lacking social behaviour 3) which is not very aggressive or anxious 4) which is relatively unaffected by pain and 5) which has an unbelievably small need for mobility – altogether an exceptionally well-adjusted laboratory guinea pig [or rather 'rat'] which can be placed together with fellow members of its species in a very small space, but which on the other hand certainly bears very little resemblance to a wild rat. There remain only rudiments of the wild rat's strength, aggressiveness and social behavior. Levine and Mullins ... conclude that the growth environment of the laboratory rat is so protective that the rats do not develop a complete endocrine system. What we have here is, all in all, an emotionally rather blunted 'personality' compared with the 'wild type.' (1970, 46; my translation)

Finally, Reventlow suggests that, judged in relation to the purpose of uncovering basic functional laws of psychology, behaviourists' efforts to simplify experiments have led to work on far too few forms of motivation (for example, hunger, thirst, and avoiding pain). Working with so few motivations, we can hardly expect to learn anything essential about the behavioural individuality of animals. Oversimplifications by comparative psychologists and behaviourists of experimental designs have been a step in the wrong direction for studying normal motivational and functional organization. For this reason, Reventlow chose male sticklebacks tending their nests as his experimental animals. The stickleback is a wild species with its own natural microcosm in the laboratory.

Insights into learning processes as such are extremely important if we are to understand the emergence of a given organism's behavioural individuality. But it is most expedient to work with types of behaviour in which the learning process does not cast too deep an individual-historical shadow over the motivational structure of behaviour. This is significant in light of our general ignorance regarding the basic structures of behaviour that somehow determine what is learned. It is well known that we learn only that which we are motivated to learn – or need to learn as a matter of survival. Lorenz (1977) also argued in favour of the existence of many more types of learning processes than those with which behaviourists normally work. He argued that the characteristics of these types are largely determined by the basic structures that are their starting points.

If one wishes systematically to include the organism's 'behavioural personality' in one's models of the functional organization of behaviour, then one should not conduct reproducible experiments with several members of the same organism combine the results of all experiments done on different individuals into an average, and then because the individual organism's importance disappears, while the uncertainty surrounding the value of the results as 'general' laws decreases. For this reason, among others, Reventlow thought it important to begin by analysing the functional organization of instinctive reactions. The theoretical basis for his experiments has for the most part been ethological: 'As ethology demands that the examination of the behavior of animals and humans be conducted in relation to their biotopes, and continually strives to understand psychic phenomena on the basis of the relationship between stimuli, motivation and behavior, it becomes one of the broadest psychological theories in existence – or at least, the most ecologically oriented' (1980, 90; my translation).

Ethology interprets and attempts to explain behaviour; it describes the causes underlying behaviour. One method is experimentation with behaviour, both in nature and in the laboratory. On the basis of these observations and experiments, and based on a theory that posits behaviour as a fairly stable, inherited part of an animal's 'survival machinery,' one seeks to formulate models of the inner organization and control of behaviour. The reaction model arrived at for the inner organization of behaviour (a motivation model) is of the utmost importance to the ethologist's approach to observing and interpreting behaviour. In his doctoral dissertation, Reventlow (1970, 21) describes the model shown in Figure 3.1 as follows:

3.1 An illustration of ethology's conception of the release mechanism. (1) denotes the outer world, elements of which can be stimuli, (2a) the senses, (2b) the perceptive part of the nervous system that conveys information from the outside world, (3) the motivating and coordinating part of the nervous system, (4a) the motor centre of the nervous system, (4b) the movements of the muscles, and (5) the total external behaviour. The combination of (2) + (3) is the release mechanism. (4), the effector section, comprises one or more fixed movements, possibly with learned modifications. (2)+(3)+(4) shows the congenital nerve connection, which in conjunction with certain motivating conditions produces certain effects – without prior learning – resulting in the release of the congenital behavioural dispositions. The difference in length between (1) and (2a) illustrates that organisms never register the entire physical reality, and that the concept of sign stimulus emphasizes the selection by each species of a few well defined stimuli from among complex phenomena (after Reventlow 1970).

Looked at as a psychological theory, ethology has the great advantage of offering a comprehensive theory that integrates in a simple fashion the stimulation situation, the inner motivation and the outer observable behavior. The theory can be graphically illustrated as [Figure 3.1], which visualizes the genetically determined connection ('innate releasing mechanism' – usually abbreviated IRM), which ethologists believe exists between perception and behavior. It is characteristic of this inherited connection (IRM) that only certain parts of the stimulus situation normally found in nature are necessary to release the behavior. These parts are called 'sign stimuli' or 'Schlüsselreize.' Sign stimuli give rise to sense perception, which in conjunction with internally motivated conditions works in such a way that the genetically determined behavior is released. Ethology sums up in a simple concept the complex interaction between the environment, the individual and behavior.

At times several IRM's can be arranged in a common system, as Tinbergen (1951), for instance, has pointed out in the case of the male stickleback. (my translation)

In this chapter I will not go into detail regarding Reventlow's methodological conclusions. Instead I will focus on more general psychological conclusions arrived at through his work with the theoretical probability model. His method depends on scrupulous research combined with epistemological reflections, ethological observation, and mathematical-statistical model building and model testing, followed by adjustments. He uses this method in an effort to liberate his thinking from folk psychology concepts. In the next section we shall see how this work has drawn ethology towards biosemiotics.

3.6 The 'Rependium': An Attempt to Construct a Fundamental Galilean Concept in Psychology

Reventlow's work from 1970 to 1977 aimed to find new and more fundamental concepts of psychobiology (later called cognitive science). It culminated in his 1977 paper, in which he launched his 'rependium' concept, concerning the sudden shift in the 'construction' of cognition to see something as significant. This paradigmatic view was his first concrete attempt to

> continue Lewin's endeavors to restructure psychological concepts by analyzing phenomena of apparently different types so as to create a basis for the formation of new concepts reflecting their purely theoretical/functional properties, without undue consideration of their psychological context. The following will serve as an example of how one can work toward finding psychological concepts of a more functional abstract type than those used today. Many psychological concepts are just concepts borrowed from the conceptual world of everyday life. (1977, 130; my translation)

In this attempt to go beyond the normal surface dualism, Reventlow dovetailed systems theory with cybernetics. In this 1977 article he summarized observations from ethology, phenomenological psychology, and gestalt psychology.

Reventlow's first example is a condensation of three key ideas and observations:

I. He compares the ethological concept of sign stimuli with general gestalt principles (for example, the laws of proximity, equality, and the good curve). He offers a common psychological interpretation of sign stimuli as species-specific gestalt principles whose function, unlike common gestalt principles, depends on motivation. Thus, when an animal is not especially motivated to mate, more sign stimuli of a stronger nature are necessary to trigger a reaction.

Reventlow (1972) argues in favour of applying the concept of sexual sign stimuli to humans. This could possibly explain why individuals possessing a strong but unreleased sexual urge experience objects and movements normally not associated with sex as being sexually laden. For example, psychoanalysis uses the term 'sex symbols' when a sword or a candle is seen as an erect penis.

The common element that Reventlow emphasizes arises from a third observation he made during his work with sticklebacks. When a highly motivated male is shown a female dummy with a low release value (having few sign stimuli), it may swim around for a while before suddenly reacting with the characteristic courtship swim (a zigzag dance) followed by prolonged reaction to the dummy. This phenomenon – a sudden, lasting alteration of perception – can also be seen in the experience of gestalt figures and phenomena that have acquired the nature of sex symbols.

II. Reventlow's second example is also taken from ethology: the so-called imprinting known through Konrad Lorenz's experiments with geese and ducks. Lorenz presented himself as the first mobile noisy object in the duckling's life, and in doing so released a pattern of behaviour that after a brief period became irreversible. He was able to induce the ducklings or goslings to follow him everywhere and totally ignore their 'real' mother. Reventlow wrote that the classical concept of imprinting differs from other learning processes in five ways:

1. by occurring very quickly;
2. by requiring only a single exposure and a single reaction by the animal;
3. by occurring only at a certain period in the life of the individual;
4. by its stability after just one occurrence – it can reasonably be termed irreversible; and finally
5. by carrying no other reward than the reaction itself.

Imprinting is very important for the individual's later choice of sexual partner and 'social circle.' Imprinting can be compared to the process that occurs when one looks at a drawing where at first we see only a meaningless jumble of dots, splatters and lines and then suddenly perceive a 'meaningful' figure. In other words, it is a sudden restructuring of the area of perception into a meaningful figure. (1977, 132, my translation)

III. Reventlow's third example consists of so-called kip figures or double figures, one of the best-known examples being 'Rubin's vase,' where one sees either a vase or two human profiles. What distinguishes these phenomena from those mentioned earlier is their reversibility. It is rather like having two equally 'strong,' interchangeable alternatives, although – as in the previous example – one alternative always takes precedence at any given moment.

Köhler's monkeys are Reventlow's fourth example. By a sudden flash of insight, they realized that the poles they had climbed for fun could be used to reach a coveted bunch of bananas. The chimps thus combined three forms of behaviour – instinctive, 'trial and error,' and insight – into one action. Similar 'aha experiences' of sudden insights are known from numerous animal and human experiments. Reventlow tells us: 'It is evident from Duncker's studies that as soon as a person achieves insight, the individual elements that are of relevance to him are integrated in a totally new and stable structure' (ibid., 134, my translation).

What Reventlow suggests is a common 'mechanism' or psychobiological function that causes all of these different phenomena. His Galilean conclusion is this:

> What do the phenomena described above have in common? As far as I can see they share the significant feature that as they emerged, a radical change occurred in the relations between various phenomena in the psychological field. This change was brought about through a discontinuous and at times irreversible process leading to the formation of a new and stable structure where all previous elements are simply effaced. (1977, 135; my translation)

It is this process or function that Reventlow wants to understand. He gives the new psychological function a name:

> Let us ... call this phenomenon a 'rependium' (from Latin repente – the sudden unexpected) – a term that will hopefully make it easier to handle in conjunction with the many other gestalt phenomena.
>
> By the term rependium we are to understand creation through a sudden and discontinuous process of an unforeseen, stable structure which is a decisive departure from previously existing structures that have now, from a psychological viewpoint, vanished. (ibid., my translation)

In the process of perceptual abduction – as Peirce (CP, 5.184) would call it – the perception of a unit of recognizable structure – an object – comes to us like a flash. Peirce writes that it is an act of insight, but a highly fallible one. The perceptual object is a kind of subconsciously developed hypothesis that arises out of perceptual judgment from an uncontrollable process of inference (Innis 1994, 13). Perceptual judgment is 'a judgment absolutely forced upon my acceptance, and that by a process which I am utterly unable to control and consequently unable to criticize' (CP, 5.157). It is a subconscious Thirdness. This is where semiotics and ethology meet, because ethology – and gestalt psychology as well – investigates the subconscious abductive judgments and their development through evolution in the form of sign stimuli.

The new concept of 'repentium' is the culmination of Reventlow's theoretical work and seems to confirm the Galilean paradigm. To the extent that it is leading to detailed work that advances deliberations, empirical observations, and the construction and testing of theoretical probability models limited to simple and well-defined situations, we are witnessing the development of a more unified view of the causes of behaviour. Reventlow is searching for the fundamental function of distinguishing a difference that makes a difference and that is therefore perceptually interpreted as a sign for an object.

In our personal discussions on these topics, Reventlow has reluctantly admitted that the repentium function presupposes mental ability – which means that even a stickleback has intentionality and cognitive experiences. The reaction is not mechanical. Thus there are limits to the mechanical understanding of life and mind, as those who work within an organicist paradigm (Gilbert and Sarkar 2000) point out. The 'stimuli' must often be presented several times before a stickleback 'reacts.' Furthermore, the stickleback must be in a certain motivational state. This implies that motivation is not a simple physiological concept (see for example Hinde 1970). As mentioned earlier, it cannot be explained in physiological terms even though it has physiological aspects. Reventlow seems to be in the same difficult situation as Lorenz. Both began their study of behaviour in dualistic terms, viewing matter and mind as two different worlds. But their evolutionary theory forced them into a theory of continuation between the mental capacities of humans and animals, and to consider mental awareness, emotions, and intentionality as having survival value (or else they would not exist). As is clear in ethology, Reventlow sees that the living system to some extent creates its own *Umwelt* (as Jakob von Uexküll called it, and to which we shall return later).

Some would claim that the perceptual self-organization of 'objects' can today be explained in a 'systemic way' as a phase shift or as a shift from chaos to order. But in which system should these mathematical, physical, and chemical principles apply? Is it in the behavioural, the physiological, or the phenomenological system of the organism? Is it related to the surroundings as something independently objective, or is it a part of the system and distinguished within it? Reventlow (1970) conducts some interesting – and for cybernetics and biosemiotics quite relevant – methodological discussions of this problem, the result of which I find convincing.

3.7 Limitations to a Galilean Psychology

Reventlow's dissertation (1970) was an attempt to conduct motivation research based on purely behavioural conditions without considering either physiological or phenomenological levels. The outcome was a probabilistic model of the tendencies of behaviour of the male stickleback tending its nest:

$$P\{t \geq T\} = e^{-\omega t^A}$$

In this behavioural probabilistic model, P expresses the probability within a certain time span (t) that a male stickleback will contact its nest or – if it is in the nest – will leave it. A is a constant for all male sticklebacks in all situations tending the nest; ω is a parameter characterizing the individual in connection with a single kind of experimental manipulation of the nest – a manipulation that changes with every new experimental situation in the natural logarithm.

In this model, Reventlow finishes his structuring of the model with a parameter (A) common to all fish in all situations (see the formula above), and lastly a parameter unique to the individual fish in the individual experiment (ω). That is, it is a type of *individual environmental factor-combination* (see Madsen 1974 for further details).

From the perspective of objectivism, it should be possible to divide such a factor into an environmental parameter and an individual parameter (which says something about individuality and the 'inner' motivation-physiological parameters.). One of the crucial points in Reventlow's thesis is that it is impossible, given the limits built into psychological scientific investigative methods, to make such a division.

More penetrating studies might make it possible to 'peel' parametric layers away from the individual-environment factor, albeit never to split the factor completely. As Reventlow (1970, 128) writes: 'This is perhaps a necessary cognitive consequence of the fact that we are not able to observe an individual without observing its behavior in a specific environment. In so far as psychology has not yet discovered its ultimate concepts nor a way of measuring them, this seems very important' (my translation).

Let me summarize the history and background to understand the revolutionary significance of this conclusion. In terms of Descartes's philosophy, the works of Galileo and Newton led to an understanding of nature as governed by mathematical-mechanical laws. These were supposed to apply also to animals, which were regarded as insensitive machines. According to Descartes, only the human body was controlled by an immortal soul. Furthermore, the soul could not be described through the mechanical-mathematical sciences. Laplace replaced the dualism of Descartes with a pure materialistic-mechanistic model. The Galilean concept of scientific laws was considered omnipotent. Galileo based his science on the theory that nature was governed entirely by mathematical laws. Nature could be likened to a great book written in the language of mathematics, and in Laplace's philosophy this concept of nature included animal and human minds. Reventlow and Lewin apparently share this belief. Reventlow has in our personal discussions gone so far as to declare that he does not consider it possible to believe in free will and simultaneously to work honestly as a scientific (Galilean) psychologist. This also applies to those who believe that we only have a free 'won't.' Urges to act come from 'inside,' and all we can do is rationally and self-consciously choose not to act on some of them.

I think that here he has pinpointed the paradox of the idea of psychology becoming a Galilean or Newtonian science. It follows that he has also pinpointed the central problem in the research program of pan-information and cognitive science as well as in the 'towards a science of consciousness' research project that has gathered researchers to international conferences for more than thirteen years (review here the back numbers of *Journal of Consciousness Studies*). A new basic understanding of knowledge, science, truth, laws, information, and meaning is necessary. I content that only by formulating a new framework can this understanding be achieved. Through his admirable empirical research, Reventlow has made a foundational discovery that supports the works of Jakob von Uexküll, Husserl, Heidegger, Merleau-Ponty's *Phenomenology* ('lifeworld'), von Foerster, Maturana and Varela, and Luhmann.

From his research we must admit that to a certain extent even the lowest organisms define their surroundings (*Umwelten*) in their own ways. As Maturana and Varela (1980) point out, the organism 'brings forth' a world – an *Umwelt*. But according to Reventlow, this occurs only to a certain extent – a stance that guards us against antirealistic forms of radical constructivism. He is not an idealist: the environment restricts and constrains perception – a problem that von Foerster has thought through, as we shall analyse later.

Reventlow's individual-environment factor leaves him facing a situation that spells powerlessness for a Galilean–Cartesian paradigm of the science of psychology. Here we are dealing with a factor that, for fundamentally epistemological reasons – derived from the measuring problem (just as in quantum mechanics) – refuses to be broken down to allow a final description of the causal relations among separate elements, often called 'subject' and 'object.' Reventlow summarizes his methodological problems in Figure 3.2.

In his analysis of the scientific observer, Reventlow points out that the main difficulty is not determining the relation between 1 (exterior world) and 5 (exterior behaviour), but determining the relation between 2a (the animal's perception of the world) and 6a (the observer's perception of the world), and furthermore the relation of this relation to the relationship between 5 and 6b (the observer's perception of the animal's behaviour). One of the challenges is that we do not have any final knowledge about 1 and 2a. According to Reventlow's results, we shall never have such a final knowledge in causal deterministic terms. Within certain limits, a kind of creative construction is occurring through interpretation.

This result reflects back on the relationship between 1 and 6a. Within certain limits, we also construct what we see. We know that this phenomenon is partly built into our perceptual systems and partly learned during childhood. Furthermore, scientific training (paradigms and so forth) reinforces this tendency. With great (social) effort we can become aware of and partially control it. From a scientific point of view, these basic considerations on the border between science and epistemology set limits for objective scientific knowledge, and therefore also limit the ideas of an objective information concept and an information processing paradigm. These limits are difficult to determine precisely or objectively; they are like the fractal nature of a coastline. Seen from far away it is a line, but the nearer one approaches the more complicated it appears.

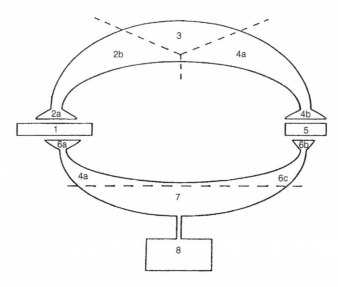

3.2.   This figure 'illustrates the conditions for observation of an individual organism. 1 represents the exterior world, which stimulates/perturbs both the observed individual and the observer. 2, 3, and 4 represent mechanisms in the observed individual (compare with [Figure 3.1]), which cause 5, representing the total exterior behavior, to be brought forth. 6a and b represent the sense organs of the observer, and 6c the other perceptual parts of the nervous system and what further determines 7, which is his experience of the observed behavior. 8 represents the description of the observations, which the observer gives, and which becomes the scientific datum, that is the foundation for the further scientific analysis ... When 6a is not situated symmetrically with 2a, it is because animals most likely sometimes react on stimuli, whose physical properties we do not know ... while we (e.g., through physical measurement apparatuses) can get knowledge about appearances of the physical world that are without significance for the perceptions of animals. In the same way 6b is smaller than 4b and 5, because the animals have behaviors which we do not know and even some that we cannot perceive or measure yet' (Reventlow 1970, 32, my translation).

   Thus there is a fundamental antithesis between the Galilean concept of law and the concept of intentionality in Reventlow's paradigm. The crux of the matter is the relation of motivation, intentionality, and feelings to the perceptual cognitive level. This especially concerns how any kind of mechanistic or functionalistic model for explaining behaviour, perception, and communication can account for the will and emotions of animals and humans. *Somehow, an epistemology and an ontology in which law, intentionality, and free will can simultaneously exist must be described.* This is crucial for the discussion of what information is and what the foundation of information science should be.

As we have analysed, Lorenz struggled with this problem. Motivation cannot be modelled in mechanical terms. He therefore uses an energy or psycho-hydraulic model premised on the idea of emotional energy that must be released. As already mentioned, this is very similar to Freud's thinking, and I view ethology as deepening Freud's concept of the id and as better explaining how projection – which makes one see things as symbols – occurs. But the models do not delve into the nature of motivation, intentionality, or emotions. The algorithmic approach of the information processing paradigm in cognitive science has the same problem.

Cognitive information sciences partly based on first-order cybernetics have also encountered a situation of powerlessness in their attempts to find the algorithms of intelligence, informational meaning, and language. This approach has difficulties with the phenomena of context and signification and the ways in which they interact. They wish to explain everything algorithmically, including consciousness and meaning.

Gregory Bateson (1904–80) was among the first cyberneticians to launch a new development in cybernetics that paved the way for more constructivist approaches, such as autopoiesis theory and second-order cybernetics, and his insights are still broadly used. I will therefore in the next chapter analyse Bateson's development of this new information as 'a difference that makes a difference' concept. It is his attempt to connect ethology on the one hand with cybernetic information science on the other, going from mechanism to cybernetic self-organization and feedback loops carrying differences. But still we shall continue to ask where the subject, free will, meaning, emotions, and qualia all are.

4 Bateson's Concept of Information in Light of the Theory of Autopoiesis

4.1 The Pattern That Connects

One of Gregory Bateson's major projects was explaining the nature of mind on a modern scientific basis, avoiding both the metaphysical dualism of Descartes and the mechanicism of Laplace. Through cybernetics, Bateson offers a new delineation of the concept of information that unites in a more consistent way the scientific and materialistic world views with concepts deriving from the non-mechanistic view of cybernetics. He writes (1973, 428): 'In fact, what we mean by information – the elementary unit of information – is a difference which makes a difference.'

But if one reads this as a classical subject or ego that uses his self-conscious free will to make existentially meaningful selections, one does not fully understand the radicality of the cybernetic framework. For Bateson as well as for Wiener, it is a stochastic process. What happens is that a stream of random events gets coupled with a non-random selective process. This combination causes particular components to survive, or at least last longer than others. The mutually reinforcing forces within a system or organism can, if they work synergistically all in the same direction, increase that organism's stability in a given environment, among other things through feedback mechanisms. But if this turns into rigid patterns and structures, the system's potential to adapt to changes in the environment decreases. The 'happy mean' lies somewhere between complete stability and utter chaos in a dynamic cybernetics recursive complexity at several inclusive levels.

Bateson's world view is scientific and materialistic. But it is not classically mechanistic, because he depends on Wiener's cybernetics. Cybernetics is defined as the science of communication and control; it maps the pathways of information along which systems may either be regulated from outside or regulate themselves from within. As a message loops around in a system, it recursively conveys information about the entire system. Wiener developed the concepts of circular control (feedback) and goal-directed behaviour. This recursive circularity offered alternatives to standard cause-and-effect explanations, thus making possible a theory of circular causal systems as opposed to linear cause-and-effect thinking. This was underpinned by a heavy mathematical apparatus.

Bateson believed that latent in cybernetics exists the means of achieving a new and perhaps more human perspective through a new relational cybernetic pattern. This could be the means for changing our philosophy of control, as well as a means for seeing our own follies in broader perspective. He saw cybernetics as a holistic rather than a linear system for addressing issues of control, recursiveness, and information.

His research crossed the disciplinary boundaries of cybernetics, animal communication, ethnography, psychology, psychiatry, ecology, and biological evolution. He was looking for 'the pattern that connects.' Especially in *Mind and Nature: A Necessary Unity* (1980), he developed a holistic perspective based on cybernetic principles. With this he tried to explain how the world works and how the universe holds together. In a cybernetic way, he saw nature and mind as forming one organism; in this project, he defined 'mind' as cybernetic steps towards a recursive ecology of mind.

Because of the width and depth of Bateson's transdisciplinary project, he never became a central figure in any discipline; however, the value of his work in the transdisciplinary philosophy of science and knowledge is becoming increasingly appreciated as we pass the centennial of his birth. He and his daughter Mary Catherine give a retrospective view and reflection on his work in Bateson and Bateson (2005), which is an important source for their analysis.

Bateson's 'working hypothesis' was that the world's basic constituents are space, time, elementary particles (matter), and energy. But seemingly not information, which he saw as a relational concept. He believed that science would end if we endowed elementary particles with mind qualities (1980, 103). His project was to explain mind as a function of complexity and cybernetic organization. He contended that the strength of cybernetics lay in its capacity to offer a more profound understanding of what the mental is, by incorporating his concept of information into a universal cybernetic ecological philosophy. *Steps to an Ecology of Mind* (1973) and *Mind and Nature* (1980) are the titles of his most influential books. In them, Bateson argued that his cybernetics could provide an understanding of mind that is neither subjectively idealistic nor mechanically materialistic. Deeply interested in anthropology, biology, and psychology, he was on the same track as Lorenz, but he approached the fields of information, cognition, and communication from a cybernetic angle, searching for '*the pattern that connects*': 'What pattern connects the crab to the lobster and the orchid to the primrose and all the four of them to me? And me to you? And all the six of us to the amoeba in one direction and the backward schizophrenic in another?' (1980, 8). This is his famous formulation of his research program. Part of his approach is to take an evolutionary comparative morphological viewpoint.

It turns out that gross anatomy exhibits three levels or logical types of descriptive propositions: 1. The parts of any member of Creatura are to be compared with other parts of the same individual to give first-order connections. 2. Crabs are to be compared with lobsters or men with horses to find similar relations between parts (i.e., to give second-order connections). 3. The comparison between crabs and lobsters is to be compared with the comparison between man and horse to provide third-order connections. We have constructed a ladder of how to think about – about what? Oh, yes, the pattern which connects. My central thesis can now be approached in words: The pattern which connects is a metapattern. It is a pattern of patterns. It is that metapattern which defines the vast generalization that, indeed, it is patterns which connect.' (1980, 11)

Before we explore his theory, let me state briefly how I see Bateson's role in developing the field and the limitations of his answers to the questions I have formulated. Bateson contributed to the development of classical cybernetics into second-order cybernetics by leading cybernetics towards a more ecological, social, and humanistic way of viewing information, cognition, and communication; he came as close to a cybernetic foundation of semiotics as Lorenz did to a biological foundation and has been an important inspiration for the Copenhagen school of biosemiotics, especially Jesper Hoffmeyer. In my opinion, there are two reasons why Bateson did not quite succeed: (1) He was unable to liberate his concept of information from that of Norbert Wiener. Bateson's definition of information seems well suited for second-order cybernetics, but he tied it to the concept of neg-entropy, which lent his theory a physicalistic flavour. (2) He did not develop a satisfactory cybernetic theory of the observer. As such, his concept of mind was empty. It was pure form. He wrote: 'Mind is empty; it is no-thing. It exists only in its ideas, and these again are no-things. Only the ideas are immanent, embodied in their examples. And the examples are, again no-things. The claw, *as an example*, is not the *Ding an sich;* it is precisely *not* the *thing in itself.* Rather, it is what mind makes of it, namely, an *example* of something or other.' (ibid., 11).

But what is the connection then? Where does the 'rependium' and the abuctive sign-making and sign-interpretation come from? Let us take a closer look at this informational, cybernetic concept of mind.

4.2 Mind, Information, and Entropy

For Bateson, mind is a cybernetic phenomenon, a sort of mental ecology. The mental relates to the ability to register differences. It is an intrinsic system property. The elementary, cybernetic system with its messages in circuits is the simplest mental unit, even when the total system does not include living organisms. Every living system has some characteristics that we generally call mental. He summarizes them in the following way:

1. The system shall operate with and upon differences.
2. The system shall consist of closed loops or networks of pathways along which differences and transforms of differences shall be transmitted. (What is transmitted on a neuron is not an impulse, it is news of a difference).
3. Many events within the system shall be energized by the respondent part rather than by impact from the triggering part.
4. The system shall show self-correctiveness in the direction of homeostasis and/or in the direction of runaway. Self-correctiveness implies trial and error. (1973, 458)

Mind is synonymous with the cybernetic system, which comprises a total, self-correcting unit that prepares information. Mind is immanent in this wholeness. When Bateson says that mind is immanent, he means that the mental is immanent in the entire system, in the complete message circuit.

One can therefore say that mind is immanent in the circuits that are complete within the brain. But mind is also immanent in the greater circuits that are complete within the system 'brain plus body.' Finally, mind is immanent in the even greater system 'man plus environment' or – more generally – 'organism plus environment,' which is identical to the elementary unit of evolution, that is, the thinking, acting, and deciding agent:

> The individual mind is immanent, but not only in the body. It is immanent also in pathways and messages outside the body; and there is a larger Mind, of which the individual is only a subsystem. This larger Mind is comparable to God and is perhaps what some people mean by 'God,' but it is still immanent in the total inter-connected social system and planetary ecology. Freudian psychology expanded the concept of mind inward to include the whole communication system within the body – the autonomic, the habitual and the vast range of unconscious processes. What I am saying expands mind outward. And both of these changes reduce the scope of the conscious self. A certain humility becomes appropriate, tempered by the dignity or joy of being part of something bigger. A part – if you will – of God. (1973, 436–7)

As such, Bateson's world view seems biological and organicistic. He sees life and mind as coexisting in an ecological and evolutionary dynamic, integrating the whole biosphere. Bateson clearly sympathizes with the ethologists when he resists the positivistic split between the rational and the emotional in language and thinking that is so important for cognitive science. He acknowledges emotions as an important cognitive process:

> It is the attempt to separate intellect from emotion that is monstrous, and I suggest that it is equally monstrous – and dangerous – to attempt to separate the external mind from the internal. Or to separate mind from body. Blake noted that 'A tear is an intellectual thing,' and Pascal asserted that 'The heart has its reasons of which reason knows nothing.' We need not be put off by the fact that the reasoning of the heart (or of the hypothalamus) are accompanied by sensations of joy or grief. These computations are concerned with matter which are vital to mammals, namely matters of relationship, by which I mean love, hate, respect, dependency, spectatorship, performance, dominance and so on. These are central to the life of any animal, and I see no objection to calling these computations 'thought,' though certainly the units of relational computation are different from the units which we use to compute about isolable things. (1973, 439)

It thus seems obvious that Bateson's 'pattern that connects' includes the phenomenological-emotional dimension in its concept of mind. But it does so, however, only in the form of relational differences circulating in cybernetic loops. I suggest that this cybernetic viewpoint tells us a great deal about motivational and emotional functionality as seen through an ecological and evolutionary framework. It avoids physicalistic explanations. Although Bateson developed his theory far in this direction, he never revisited the first-order cybernetic foundation on which it was built. But as we shall see, one can also ask whether second-order cybernetics, which followed in his footsteps by analysing biological cognitive systems, really managed to change this foundation enough to enable it to encompass concepts of emotions, qualia, free will, signification, and meaning.

4.3 Autopoiesis, Mind, and Information

The first major obstacle for Bateson's theory, in its attempt to become a general theory of information and knowing, relates to the difficulty of determining to whom or what a difference makes a difference.

His concept of mind-system is too general to be the agent to whom the difference makes a difference, as it encompasses everything from the smallest feedback loop in machines to the working cybernetic system of Gaia. Every mind-system or observer is within another observer and is comprised of observing systems, if that is what his mind-systems are. As I understand them, they seem more like information processing systems. He does not realize that 'a materialist system is an organism if and only if it is closed to efficient causation' (Rosen 1991, 244).

The nature of the closure necessary for this to happen, and for agency as such to emerge, is not profoundly grasped in his theory. Although Stuart Kauffman (1995) also saw this early on, Maturana and Varela[1] made the most profound conceptualization of closure with their concept of autopoiesis. They have consistently developed this notion over many years, and I will therefore turn to their work, although I also find their philosophical foundation somewhat inadequate in broader terms.

Maturana and Varela's (1980) definition of the autopoietic system answers the question of to whom the difference makes a difference. It is the autopoietic system that is able to react to differences (perturbations). Maturana (1988, 26) writes about the connection between autopoiesis and life:

> A composite unity whose organization can be described as a closed network of productions of components that through their interactions constitute the network of productions that produce them and specify its extension by constituting its boundaries in their domain of existence, is an autopoietic system; and second, that a living system is an autopoietic system whose components are molecules. Or in other words, we propose that living systems are molecular autopoietic systems and as such they exist in the molecular space as closed networks of molecular productions that specify their own limits.

The autopoietic system does not receive information in an objective physical sense, nor does it respond to the stimuli or information as understood within a mechanistic paradigm. Rather, it is a closed organization, the main concern of which is to stay organized, to survive. It does so by changing its organization whenever its coherence is threatened by perturbations from 'outside' or by spontaneous behaviour from inner parts. We observe this as physiological reactions and behaviour. Through this autopoietic process the organism 'brings forth a world.' This is similar to Jakob von Uexküll's theory of the *Umwelt*, which I will analyse later.

In the next step of developing the theory, Maturana hypothesizes that this is not only a scientific theory of knowledge, but also a general science of knowing. He then applies this theory of knowledge obtained by thinking within a biological frame in a reflexive manner to develop a general self-organizing and self-sufficient epistemology that need not refer to an objective, existing world of ideas and theories: the autopoietic epistemology, called objectivity in parentheses.

The argument is as follows: When one realizes that there is no objective reality for any autopoietic (biological) system, then there is no objective reality for us or for science. We have to place objectivity in parentheses. There are no autopoietic systems without an observer to 'bring them forth.' This means that no theory can refer to objective reality to legitimize its claims of truth. The universe is a Multiverse (Maturana and Varela 1986, Maturana 1988). Through languaging and social practice, we bring forth our worlds. For Maturana, objects are only established in language (see below). This is also the opinion of Deely (1990), but he adds that some objects are things and some (semiotic) objects only refer to human ideas.

Maturana's theory provides a better foundation for Bateson's theory of information because it marks the important point that the autopoietic system does not receive information as such, but only perturbations of its organization. The so-called reaction consists of internal adjustments to preserve the internal organization of the system. In fact, neither Maturana nor Varela wishes to use the concept of information or the concept of sign in a semiotic theoretical context. Therefore they cannot make Deely's move, but seem to lose the reality of things in a radical constructivism.

But Maturana and Varela are as much on cybernetic ground as Bateson, and therefore have only a cybernetic mind concept. Theoretically their work is limited to a biocybernetic theory of the observer as a structure-determined system. Emotions, will, and consciousness are taken for granted; they are not defined on the basis of the autopoietic theory as such. In this still functionalistic theory, there are no defined concepts for the understanding of the 'inner life' of the organism. The theory is still functionalistic, as von Glasersfeld (1991, 68) points out:

> Humberto Maturana is one of the few authors that nowadays engage the construction of a wide, complete, explicatory system comparable to those of Plato or Leibniz. His 'autopoietic' approach includes also the origin of the observer, meant as a methodological *prius* who provides itself a view of the world. Here I try to follow the way Maturana sees the birth of *res cogitans* (entity which gains awareness of what it's doing). I try to demonstrate that the basic activity of distinguishing can certainly lead to the distinction with which the observer is separated from anything observed. But I conclude that – at least for this interpreter – the origin of active consciousness remains obscure, that is, what works as the agent of distinguishing.

Maturana and Varela practise a rather special breed of biocybernetic constructivism. This is an important step forward in the pursuit of 'a pattern that connects to the ecology of mind,' but it also has inherent limitations.

4.4 The Limits of 'Bring-Forth-ism'

Krippendorff (1991) mentions many different kinds of constructivism flourishing within second-order cybernetics, among them Maturana and Varela's 'bring-forth-ism.' Without choosing any of them, he sum-

marizes the essential goal of second-order cybernetics and constructivism: 'The task of constructivism, as I see it, is to describe a system's
operation within its own domain of description and account for the
constitution of its identity and the conditions of its continued persist-
ence in its own terms. Said differently, constructivists need to find a way
of putting the knower into a known that is constructed so as to keep
the knower viable in practice.' This is what I attempted to outline in
chapter 2 as one of the main goals of second-order cybernetics and of
autopoiesis theory within cybernetics.

How do we reflect on the nature and production of knowledge when
knowledge is always produced by somebody? To accomplish that would
– as Nagel (1986, 74) points out – be an important step forward in
objectivity: 'We tend to use our rational capacities to construct theories, without at the same time constructing epistemological accounts of
how those capacities work. Nevertheless, this is an important part of
objectivity.'

It is clear that Maturana and many cybernetic constructivists make
good arguments against physicalism. Behind this position lies the basic
challenge that one cannot talk about reality in itself. It makes no sense
to talk about reality without access to the operations that bring forth
this result (Maturana 1990). In other words, it is illusory to talk about
reality because each of us assumes that we know what the other means
by this. But this is an assumption only. It would be safer for us not to talk
about reality at all. It is more scientific not to talk about autopoietic
systems that have no observer. This has been Maturana's argument in
my many discussions with him.

By envisioning languaging as a coevolution between two or more
autopoietic systems that stabilizes a common domain of distinctions,
Maturana seems to be adhering to a kind of biosocial constructivism
that is a general trend among second-order cyberneticians. Indeed,
most of them deal with social systems without being interested in primarily natural phenomena. But that does not explain the rigid constraints that physical things place on our constructions of 'objects' of
knowledge. Maturana (1988) is aware of the thermodynamic conditions
for the existence of living beings. This leaves us with Maturana's fundamental question of the relationship between the observer and the
observed.

The problem is that although 'bring-forth-ism' and constructivism
reveal something important about the relativity of social concepts,
belief systems, and institutions, it is very difficult to reconcile this view

with the experience of material things. These seem to force themselves upon us with independent necessity, however we perceive or ignore them. Only in mystical (and magical-occult) traditions do we encounter theories about how to change things through mental operations alone and claims that this has been done. Clearly, this is not what Maturana has in mind; nevertheless, he writes that objects are constructed only in language. Maturana has treated the problem of object on several occasions:

> We bring forth a world of distinctions through the changes of state that we undergo as we conserve our structural coupling in the different media in which we become immersed along our lives, and then, using our changes of state as recurrent distinctions in a social domain of coordination of actions (language), we bring forth a world of objects as coordinations of actions with which we describe our coordinations of action. Unfortunately we forget that the object that arises in this manner is a coordination of actions in a social domain, and deluded by the effectiveness of our experience in coordinating our conducts in language, we give the object an external preeminence and validate it in our descriptions as if it had an existence independent from us as observers. (1983, Section H)

Maturana's breed of constructivism (a concept he neither likes nor accepts) is thus more than social; it also includes what we consider to be natural objects and is a general communication theory of how objects are constructed in the human social world:

> Objects arise in language as consensual coordinations of actions that operationally obscure for further recursive consensual coordinations of actions by the observers the consensual coordinations of actions (distinctions) that they coordinate. Objects are, in the process of languaging, consensual coordinations of actions that operate as tokens for the consensual coordinations of actions that they coordinate. Objects do not pre-exist language. (1988, 8.ii.b)

Thus, we see that this is a process philosophy and a radical and social constructivism. Even more interestingly, his claim that objects are constructed only in language has the consequence that animals do not have object perception as such. They do not live in a world of objects as humans do, although they do have cognitive domains:

Objects arise in language as consensual coordinations of actions that in a domain of consensual distinctions are tokens for more basic coordinations of actions, which they obscure. Without language and outside language there are no objects, because objects only arise as consensual coordinations of actions in the recursion of consensual coordinations of actions that languaging is. For living systems that do not operate in language, there are no objects; or in other words, objects are not part of their cognitive domains. (1988b, 9.iv)

The independent existence of objects has been foundational to classical physics as well as to the positivist idea of objectivity and verification, at least in its logical empiricist version. Actually, Albert Einstein had a more reflective and somewhat constructivistic view on the concept of object. But at any rate it is very difficult to establish the same kind of independent reality in the subatomic worlds of quantum mechanics (uncertainty principle, Bohr's theory of complementarity, EPR-paradox, and so on) as exists in the macro-world of classical physics. We have gained knowledge about some of the organizing patterns of the natural macro-world, but we have also been forced to recognize that the knowledge we acquire through experiments – especially when the quantum effects are significant – is not a picture of material mechanisms independent of how we choose our observations in those experiments. The concepts of particle, wave, and field are intermingled with the experimental measurement setup in such a way that the former obscure our previous vision of elementary particles as the simple material building blocks of nature (Bohr 1954).

Nevertheless, quantum mechanics is still objective and precise, the measurement equipment is based on classical physical concepts, and there is no good reason to deny the existence of a partly independent 'natural world.' But the critical question with respect to Maturana's views remain this: How can we catch anything 'out there' that has some general value if there are no mechanisms, structures, or things to be uncovered, and if our concepts are purely social constructs? This question takes precedence over any scientific theory of evolution and natural selection. If we hope to bring forth a basic metaphysics within an ontology for the philosophy of science, we face an unavoidable philosophical obligation to say more about the world than to simply characterize it as a Multiverse. The entire idea of perception will collapse if we do not attribute some independent reality to 'things,' including living languaging 'things,' as a part of the basic distinctions that are prerequisites to the human knowing on which science is built. Therefore I like Deely's concept of objects of which some are things. The final prerequisite for science is language and, it follows, the existence of conscious communicating beings such as ourselves. To accept that the scientific endeavour gives us intersubjective knowledge with survival value, we must accept that living beings with language have and are conscious minds existing relatively independent of our own conscious mind. As von Foerster (1980) states, this is a basic epistemological choice and one that is fundamental for the game called science.

This basic question amounts to a thread running through the rest of the book, as it is fundamental both to present discussions of information theory and to philosophy-of-science discussions about the nature of scientific knowledge.

This brings us to the second shortcoming of Bateson's attempt to build a theory of information and knowing. Like Maturana, he has problems with his world view. But they are of a distinct kind. Bateson attempts to raise his theory on the idea that thermodynamics and information theory are unified. Let us take a closer look at the foundations of his theory.

4.5 Information and Negative Entropy

In *Mind and Nature* (1980, 103), Bateson further develops his criteria for a cybernetic definition of mind:

1. A mind is an aggregate of interacting parts or components.
2. The interaction between parts of mind is triggered by difference, and difference is a non-substantial phenomenon not located in space or time; difference is related to neg-entropy and entropy rather than to energy.
3. Mental processes require collateral energy.
4. Mental processes require circular (or more complex) chains of determination.
5. In mental processes, the effects of difference are to be regarded as transforms (i.e., coded versions) of events preceding them. The rules of such transformation must be comparatively stable (i.e., more stable than the content) but are themselves subject to transformation.

6. The description and classification of these processes of transformation disclose a hierarchy of logical types immanent in the phenomena.

These criteria are famous, and are basic to the cybernetic understanding of mind; and it is in Bateson's work that they reach the fullest development within cybernetics. My critique focuses on the foundation of the second criteria: 'difference is related to neg-entropy and entropy ...' It is problematic that Bateson follows Wiener's idea that the concept 'information' and the concept 'negative entropy' are synonymous, and furthermore, that this insight unites the natural and the social sciences and finally resolves the problems of teleology and the body–mind dichotomy (Ruesch and Bateson 1987 [1967], 177).

To Bateson, cybernetics provides a radical new foundation for a theory of mind and communication, as well as providing cognitive science with a modern expression that unites the natural with the social sciences. Psychology as such is not mentioned.

Shannon's theory of information, however, never had anything to do with the semantic content of messages. In a famous passage, Shannon (Shannon and Weaver 1969, 31–2) writes about this problem with his theory: 'The fundamental problem of communication is that of reproducing at one point either exactly or approximately a message selected at another point. Frequently the messages have *meaning*; that is they refer to or are correlated according to some system with certain physical or conceptual entities. These semantic aspects of communication are irrelevant to the engineering problem. The significant aspect is that they are *selected from a set* of possible messages.'

Therefore, what people and animals conceive as information is quite different from what Shannon and Weaver's theory of information is about. Von Foerster (1980, 20–1) concludes: 'However, when we look more closely at these theories, it becomes transparently clear that they are not really concerned with information but rather with signals and the reliable transmission of signals over unreliable channels.'

In a conclusive analysis summarizing years of work on the concept of information in the physical sciences and information theory, Christiansen (1984) suggests that it is materialistic reductionism to claim that one's theory of information is based on the physical concept of entropy. According to Christiansen (1984), therefore Bateson's theory appears to end in a strange functionalistic and materialistic short circuit. It is well known that to determine the entropy in a system, one must determine in advance what will count as macro-states, and furthermore, one must determine the probability of every state in advance. There is no room for the completely unexpected. But Bateson's original definition would have it that the observing system determines which differences make a difference as the system proceeds in its historical drift.

With this move, a cybernetic concept of mind is created that is free of any first person 'inner world' and qualia. How can one, on this basis, expect to explain will, emotion, and consciousness – not to mention the semantic content of messages?

We now return to the question of what basic assumption we should make about reality and the relationship between the observer and the world – including the theory of evolution – in order to 'find a way of putting the knower into a known that is constructed so as to keep the knower viable in practice,' as Krippendorff put it.

Shannon's information theory is a quantitative theory applied to a set of messages that are presumed to be meaningful. It is a theory about a human tool for social communication. But in Wiener's version, which is the basis of Bateson's development of his 'mind' theory, most of all it is a reification of information (information is information, neither energy nor matter) by connecting it to thermodynamics, and thus it raises foundational epistemological problems that reflect back on the prerequisites for science itself – see also Qvortrup's (1993) analysis. Let us therefore conduct a more careful analysis of the modern development of objective information theory and science.

4.6 The Problems of Order and Chance in Physics

Clausius introduced the concept of energy entropy around 1865. It is an expression of the dissipation of energy as heat into the many degrees of freedom of the movements of the molecules in the surrounding space. The result of this process is not a loss of energy but rather its transformation into a distributed form that cannot be recovered to perform the work that originally defined the concept of energy. A degradation of energy has occurred. Only so-called free energy can do productive work. Based on his reflections, Clausius advanced the two famous dicta of thermodynamics:

1. The total amount of energy in the world is constant.
2. Entropy seeks a maximum.

In this way – and in opposition to the mechanistic idea that the movements of particles are determined by deterministic, mathematically describable, and time-reversible laws – time direction, and thus, evolution, in physics was introduced!

Soon, however, it became apparent that there were divergent views on the epistemological status of thermodynamics, and consequently on the physical concept of entropy. Can thermodynamics be reduced, in principle, to classical mechanics? Or is it a science – irreducible in principle – and so fundamental that mechanics is intrinsic to it? This is also a cardinal point in a century-long discussion about the ontological status of the concept of randomness in physics. Thermodynamics fundamentally breaks with the determinism and time reversibility of mechanics by being a basically statistical theory – a theory of complexity, as Prigogine and Stengers (1984) call it. Indeed, in classical mechanics the direction of time is not a significant parameter, whereas 'the arrow of time' is introduced in and with thermodynamics – if one accepts its fundamental status. It is rather confusing that time is reversible in classic mechanical physics but irreversible in the derived macrophysics of thermodynamics.

On precisely this point, Prigogine and Stengers (1984) intervene with a reflective argument. They point out that our scientific understanding of evolution, life, and human consciousness is not possible without the increasing entropy of irreversibility and an increase in objective randomness. If one believes in evolution and yet insists that this randomness is not objective but only an expression of our limited knowledge, then one is actually insisting that our physical bodies are merely products of our own ignorance!

Notice how closely the mechanical paradigm is connected to the idea of objective materialistic information. Laplace's demon succinctly expresses the idea that the world consists of mathematically describable and completely exhaustible information. If it had knowledge of the position, speed, direction, mass, and acceleration of all the 'particles,' it could compute all the events of the past and the course of the entire future. If this mechanistic world view were true, then reality would be full of objective information waiting 'out there,' independent of any observer. As Stonier (1990, 18, 21), for example, thought: 'In the present work, and it is crucial to the entire analysis, information is considered to be distinct from the system which interprets, or some other way processes, such information. Information exists. It does not need to be perceived to exist. It requires no intelligence to interpret it. It does not have to have meaning to exist. It exists.'

But in the further development of thermodynamics, Boltzmann had to abandon the idea of a simple objective order between the movements of particles in order to comprehend thermodynamic evolution towards states of equilibrium. Laplace's demon is an ideal of classical physics, but in practice it is impossible to initiate the description by noting every single position, speed, and so on, for large populations (ensembles) of particles. It is therefore unrealistic to construct a classical mechanical calculation on this basis. Out of this molecular chaos, however, one is able to define a mathematical density function in phase space, which is a complicated mathematical space with many dimensions. The mathematical model that emerged from the work of Gibbs and others represented a considerable scientific advance and was important to Wiener's cybernetics.

Boltzmann introduced probability as a basic concept in order to explain how systems consisting of large populations of particles eventually 'settle' into stationary conditions within which the mixture of the elements is random. This state is called thermodynamic equilibrium and functions as a general attractor. In other words, if a liquid containing white and blue particles is mixed, the most probable state of rest is not blue particles in one side of the glass and white particles in the other, but a more random mixture with a light blue colour. Once it obtains this state, the probability that it will go back to the separate state is infinitesimally small. The system has 'forgotten' its original state. Boltzmann's principle of order asserts that the system seeks the state in which a large number of micro-events occur simultaneously and – statistically speaking – cancel one another out in such a way that a uniform macro-state occurs. Entropy increases because probability increases (Leff and Rex 1990) and Laplace's demon loses its long-term memory!

Boltzmann's principle of order is based on the assumption that molecules behave independently before they mix and collide. This state is called 'molecular chaos,' and it is a manifestation of the abandonment of Laplace's determinism and Leibniz's 'pre-stabilized harmony.' These were both based on an idealistic assumption that the attainment of total knowledge of every single elementary particle is possible in principle (Prigogine and Stengers 1984).

In this view, Christiansen (1970) shows the impossibility of establishing a materialistic concept of information; he does so demonstrating that it is impossible to register all the connections in a given field of measurements. In the thermodynamic chaos of the micro-world, there is an infinite and unattainable mass of potential information because the microscopic variables are so numerous (a magnitude of about 10 to the power of 23). In principle, it is impossible for humans to achieve more than an infinitesimal fraction of the information necessary to plot the values that determine the Brownian movements of molecules.

The more contemporary, pragmatic conception of physics sees classical deterministic mechanicism and the use of its paradigm in quantum mechanics as an idealistic view of the world, one that has provided useful models for calculation in certain types of systems. But it is not a model of 'reality.' As Prigogine points out, we must accept randomness as a basic property of the physical world, and not just the result of simple ignorance.

Realizing this, Christiansen (ibid.) shows that the starting point for the concept of information must be phenomenological, but still within a realistic – but not necessarily a mechanistic – world view. On this basis, Bateson's definition of information as a difference that makes a difference is still valid. Information is what one receives in reply to a question. One defines the question's limits and area of measurement. From this point one must then work towards the sole form of objectivity that is possible for ordinary people: intersubjectivity. This is an important step towards Peirce's semiotic philosophy that also has a phenomenological and realistic point of departure.

I suggest that the chaos of thermodynamic microcosms can be characterized as *objective ignorance* insofar as the amount of energy and time that would have to be expended in the attempt to attain complete knowledge about it would create such massive amounts of entropy that the world would be considerably altered even before the project was well under way. Therefore it is an irreducible complexity.

Is this a reflective trap? Will our argument for the logical connection between chaos, irreversibility, time, and evolution lead us to the claim that humans, as products of evolution, are the result of this physics-determined chaos? This is still the most common way to comprehend the physical foundation of the neo-Darwinist theory of evolution. Somehow, scientists and philosophers imagine that life and consciousness emerge out of the physical universe. Systems science, cybernetics, and organicism all share this view. Non-equilibrium thermodynamics, dissipative structures, and self-organization are evoked as explanations even by many second-order cyberneticians as creating mind, emotion, and qualia. We thus again enter the discussion of the degree to which deterministic and indeterministic world views are compatible with the epistemological foundations of the science on which they rest.

It is not difficult to pinpoint the inconsistency in efforts to account for human consciousness in terms of physicalistic determinism (which we have already dismissed). If one is this sort of determinist, it cannot be because it is a true philosophy; rather, it must be because one is pre-destined by the physical chain of causes and effects to be one. But if this is so, determinism must inevitably lose its logical and truth dimensions, which supposedly are its underpinnings. Not only do determinists claim to be in accordance with the physical sciences, but they also claim that their determinism is logically valid and true. Such claims, however, require consciousness and knowing, both of which physicalistic determinism rejects.

The questions of origin, the nature of reality, and how to comprehend reality are logically necessary, but it may be impossible to find explicit and final symbolic answers. Such questions seem always to end in self-circularity and paradox. This insight is basic to second-order cybernetics, but by asking these questions we can delimit some of the premises for the possibility of raising the questions at all. A totally paradox-free self-reflection seems impossible in language. There will always be undecidables, as shown by Gödel's incompleteness theorem for mathematics. In von Foerster's (1992b) view, this is where ethics and aesthetics come in. I will analyse von Foerster's theory more thoroughly in the next chapter. But before that I would like to discuss Michael Luntley's perspective on this problem; which also dovetails with our discussion of physicalist determinism.

Since the Enlightenment science has been defined as a striving for universal knowledge. This is the ideal of modern philosophy and science, at least in the version of Michel Luntley (1995, 12):

> The idea of this grand narrative has acquired a number of labels over the years. Sometimes it is called the 'absolute conception' of the world. A more extreme version of this idea has the label of the 'view from nowhere.' Whatever label is employed, what is at issue here is the idea that in seeking truth we are seeking an account of the world that gives a complete unified account of everything. It is tempting to employ deistic metaphors when trying to articulate the idea; hence, 'the God's-eye view.' A secular version

of that label might be 'the world's own story.' That is the term I shall employ from now on. I shall use 'the world's own story' and 'absolute conception' or 'absolute truth' as interchangeable.

The Enlightenment then was a time when philosophers believed that there was such a thing as the world's own story.' It was a religious story. They thought we were beginning to learn what this story was. Modernity proper, I take as the view that the view that the world's own story can be told in a thoroughly ahistorical manner, abstracted from traditional beliefs. For modernists, the world's own story can be put together from the first principles by pure reason and experience alone. That means it must be a secularized story, for the traditions of religion will, like all traditional beliefs, have to be disinherited.

But the fact is that our knowledge is always contextual and therefore limited to a part of reality. We are not even able simply to describe the limits of the truth content of our knowledge (models, theories) in any absolute theoretical way before we conduct practical tests and make attempts at falsification (Popper, 1960). To use a modern image: the border between the areas within which a given model produces true and untrue statements is not a smooth curve, but a fractal one. Science only probes, it does not prove, says Bateson. As Luntley (ibid., 12–13) writes about the basic point of Lyotard and Rorty:

> These postmodernist philosophers are not making a skeptical point about the unavailability of knowledge. They are not saying that knowledge is impossible to get. Rather, they are saying that the idea of the world's own story, the unified picture of reality, is an illusion. There is no such thing as the whole truth. The only stories to be told about the world are local stories and there is no presumption that such stories will have anything in common. The styles of narrative, the very kinds of things talked about in local human stories, may present no more than a patchwork of different approaches that resists unification.

When we try to generalize knowledge, we are always prone to failure. This is intrinsic to what we call human knowing. But if we are unable to recognize when we are mistaken, our knowledge cannot grow. It is through our original ability to make distinctions in particular matters that we are able – by way of logic – to falsify our general models.

We have some knowledge, and we know that we can obtain more. But we must admit that we cannot prove that we have universal knowledge: neither in the physical sciences nor in philosophy. Human knowledge is the meeting point between the subjective (autopoietic) and the objective (partly independent reality) through the intersubjective (language), and so it is relational and prone to mistakes. It is an ongoing process. It is human knowing. As Luntley (ibid., 14–15) writes:

> The Enlightenment believed in the idea of the world's own story, but is also thought that this story was a divine one. The thoroughly modern outlook came about when the idea of the world's own story was secularized into the scientific story of the world. The idea that there is such a thing as the world's own story and that it is the story that is told in the language of the natural sciences is, perhaps, the dominant metaphysics in the world today. Postmodernism challenges the idea of the world's own story and also, therefore, the modern version of that idea that identifies the world's own story with the scientific image.

It is not only the so-called 'outside' world that persists in surprising us with its complexity and spontaneity; this also applies to our so-called 'inner' world, the 'subconscious' complexity and spontaneity underlying our behaviour in the world. This basic incompleteness in our knowledge of ourselves – the reasons for our acting – and our lack of absolute conscious control over speech, are at the same time prerequisites for our abilities to say and to cognize something new, to be in our basic flow of knowing and languaging. That is not the end, but the beginning of science, or rather of second-order science. I agree with Luntley (ibid., 18) when he describes the aim of his work:

> If we can preserve a worthwhile notion of objective truth without the idea of the world's own story, then truth can be made to apply to local human stories. Truth can apply to the perspectives that we enjoy and by which we inhabit the world. If that is so, might it not be possible to show that the truth can apply to our morals and politics? ... If we can legitimise the concepts of truth and rationality without appeal to the idea of the world's own story, then we can have standards of belief other than absolute ones. If this is so, we can have a conception of self other than the absolute and a historical concept inherited from the Enlightenment. That is the prize on offer when we learn to live with concepts of truth and rationality more modest than the idea of the world's own story.

From this perspective, we share the same project. But our roads to suggesting a solution are somewhat different: Luntley's is more purely philosophical, whereas I believe in advancing knowledge through interactions among philosophy, the philosophy of science, and the sciences and the humanities themselves. Nevertheless, his formulation is highly pertinent.

4.7 A Philosophical Reflection on the Concept of Reality in Second-Order Cybernetics

I agree with Bateson (1973) and Maturana (1988) that we must begin our understanding of information with the process of knowing. Bateson's definition of information as a difference that makes a difference is, as mentioned, very fruitful; his problem is that he makes nearly every cybernetic system a communicator and a knower. As in all thinking on cybernetics, there is no theory of qualia and first person experience and awareness.

The main achievement of Maturana and Varela (1980, 1986) is that they have conceptualized the basic limits of living and knowing – namely the autopoietic system – and have shown that there is a basic connection between living and knowing: To live is to know!

But I do think that Maturana and Varela go too far when they claim that there is no world without an observer, that we live in a Multiverse created through our observing and acting, and that we can say nothing meaningful about the world as such. They contend that we should speak only of epistemology and not of ontology. They do admit a world, but it is an infinitely interpreted Multiverse. Even Niklas Luhmann is not willing to go this far. Still, they accept the biological body and life as real. Unfortunately, this apparent inconsistency and lack of realism in expression has discredited their theories in many scientific circles, including biological ones.

Maturana posits that the autopoietic system is closed in its structure-dependent organization. Only another observer constructs surroundings or a world. But who is this observer? Is it another autopoietic system, which also only exists through the observation of another – perhaps the previously mentioned – autopoietic system? Or is it a universal spirit? In the first case we have a strange constructivist loop wherein we create one another and the world through observation, like Baron von Münchhausen extracting himself and his horse out of the swamp by pulling his own hair. As this seems self-refuting, the first observer can then only be Bishop Berkeley's God: things exist only because God observes them all the time (Berkeley 2000). Spencer-Brown (1972) encounters the same problem of who made the first distinction between system and environment. Luhmann imports this problem into his system theory, as we shall see.

On the other hand, one can take a more purely epistemological view: there is still a major difference between making distinctions, descriptions, and explanations of phenomena in the world, and creating these phenomena and objects. When I see the apple tree in the garden, I do not create it as such; I merely create it in my world and give it social signification by fitting it into a recognized classification system. I do create an object in semiosis; if we do not realize this, we can easily fall into a solipsistic idealism.

The problem with solipsism is that it is a black hole. It sucks everything down into itself and denies the independent existence of other human beings with whom the observer/scientist develops language and explanations. It is like saying that every day is Monday, and when somebody asks what Monday is, explaining that it is the day between Sunday and Tuesday. Thus it may be more correct to interpret Maturana and Varela's view within an objective idealism; although at least Maturana would protest. Varela became a Buddhist later in his life and developed a theory of enactment (Varela, Thompson, and Rosch 1992) before he died.

Objective idealists consider mind to be real in its own realm – in contrast, materialists consider mind to be illusory. Objective idealists would argue from this that mind is a foundational aspect of reality and the source of the material aspect of reality (which, in dualism, it is not).

In the old objective idealistic theories of the Vedas, and in Plato's and Plotinus' writings, the material world is seen as 'fallen' from oneness, which can be interpreted as pure mind or spirit. Human souls – with the ability to feel, experience, know, and think – are still a part of the spirit but are seen as trapped in the material flesh (soma – sema), as matter is the 'bottom' of this fall. The creation of the world and of the subject is a partial separation of this original unity. There is no theory of material evolution in older versions of objective idealism. But more modern views have been developed, as we shall see when we look more closely at Peirce's evolutionary objective idealistic philosophy.

Before the nineteenth century the idea of material evolution had not gained a firm foothold in our culture's thinking. But then thinking became so materialistic that great problems arose in attempts to explain how mind came into being. How is it possible that the original 'dead' mechanical world, consisting of 'pure' matter, could develop living and psychic beings or observers? The Nobel laurete and French molecular biologist Jaques Monod (1972), through his mechanistic biology, sees us very consistently as inexplicable strangers in a meaningless world. His book was an important early inspiration for the present work.

From the thermodynamic, systemic, cybernetic, and information-theoretical biological perspective, the mechanics of life are connected to the entire unfolding of the universe in a fundamental way (Kauffman 1995). This is what Bateson (1973) shows in his search for the pattern that connects, which to him is still cybernetic informational, although he is on the brink of becoming a semiotician. But this universal materi-alistic and informationalistic evolutionary theory is still unable to explain the observer and the observing (or rather, the whole cognitive system). This is something of a paradox, since after all it is the observers who through language attempt to explain the origin. This is where the concepts of emergence, wholeness, and organicism are introduced as explanatory tools.

In thermodynamics, cybernetics, and especially second-order cyber-netics, the principle of self-organization – which is also the basis for the concept of autopoiesis – explains evolution and the emergence of new qualities such as life and mind. But understanding the dissipative struc-tures of non-equilibrium thermodynamics is a long way from under-standing living autopoietic systems. We have observed the spontaneous creation of organic molecules in experiments. We have Manfred Eigen and colleagues' (1981) simulations of hypercycles with proteins, RNA, and DNA. We have observed the spontaneous generation of cell mem-brane-like structures in nature and in experiments. But we have not explained the qualitative otherness of life processes as such (Hoffmeyer 1998).

The major philosopher behind second-order cybernetics and Varela's later conception of autopoiesis and (later) enaction theory (Varela, Thompson, and Rosch 1992) was Spencer-Brown. In his 1972 book *Laws of Form*, Spencer-Brown developed a new basic formulation of logical algebra, one that builds on the basic process of distinguishing a differ-ence that makes a difference – the root of information, in Bateson's view – with clear epistemological and ontological intentions. Varela (1975, 6) says of Spencer-Brown's work: 'By succeeding in going deeper than truth, to indication and the laws of its form, he has provided an account of the common ground in which both logic and the structure of any universe are cradled, thus providing a foundation for a genuine theory of general systems.'

Spencer-Brown considered the problem of the observer and knower in the creation of knowledge, and he did so in a way that was not directly linked to biology and evolution. With the concept of autopoiesis, Maturana and Varela made another important advance by grounding this project in the realm of biology.

I see the connection between Spencer-Brown's view and that of Bateson as follows: Spencer-Brown provides a more fundamental philosophical description of the process whereby we create knowledge: by distinguishing differences. This deepens the foundation of Bateson's theory of information. Maturana and Varela's concept of autopoiesis further strengthens our biological understanding of how the knower is established and how the self-organized closure of the living system is crucial to this process of cognition. Bateson (1980, 68–9) is keenly aware that some of the philosophical prerequisites for his theory are not answered.

> It takes at least two somethings to create a difference. To produce news of difference, i.e., information, there must be two entities (real or imagined) such that the difference between them can be immanent in their mutual relationship; and the whole affair must be such that news of their difference can be represented as a difference inside some information-processing entity, such as a brain or, perhaps, a computer. There is a profound and unanswerable question about the nature of those 'at least two' things that between them generate the difference which becomes information by making a difference. Clearly each alone is – for the mind and perception – a non-entity, a non-being. Not different from being, and not different from non-being. An unknowable, a Ding an sich, a sound of one hand clapping.

But to propose a theory of knowledge one must dare to say more about the world than just that it is an infinitely deep, chaotic Multiverse in which we make structures by observing or acting. This is often called an 'open ontology' based on realism. We must further theorize the processes of cognition and communication, beyond their basis in the perturbation of (and between) closed systems, towards a theory of meaning.

With his calculus for self-reference, Varela (1975) developed second-order cybernetics and autopoiesis at a deeper and more general philo-

sophical level. He is aware that it is possible to establish new and intimate connections among epistemology, logic, and ontology:

> The principal idea behind this work can be stated thus: we choose to view
> the form of indication and the world arising from it as containing the two
> obvious dual domains of indicated and void states, and a third, not so
> obvious but distinct domain, of a self-referential autonomous state which
> other laws govern and which cannot be reduced by the laws of the dual
> domains. If we do not incorporate this third domain explicitly in our field
> of view, we force ourselves to find ways to avoid it (as has been traditional)
> and to confront it, when it appears, in paradoxical forms. (ibid., 19)

Varela abandons the dualistic foundations of Spencer-Brown, cybernetics, and Bateson, as well as Maturana and Varela's autopoiesis theory.
Spencer-Brown also lacks a theory of time. Self-reference becomes the
third dynamic element, the one that sets the distinction process in
motion. This triadic dynamic brings autopoiesis theory closer to Peirce's
triadic theory of semiosis. Varela underscores the importance of the
connection between self-reference and time in Spencer-Brown's conception,[2] thus developing an important evolutionary view within this
paradigm:

> True as it is that a cell is both the producer and the produced which
> embodies the producer, this duality can be pictured only when we repre-
> sent for ourselves a sequence of processes of a circular nature in time.
> Apparently our cognition cannot hold both ends of a closing circle simul-
> taneously; it must travel through the circle ceaselessly. Therefore we find a
> peculiar equivalence of self-reference and time, insofar as self-reference
> cannot be conceived outside time, and time comes in whenever self-refer-
> ence is allowed. (ibid., 20)

Varela introduces the link between cognition and evolution and the
arrow of time without basing his theory on Wiener's concept of information as entropy, as Bateson originally did (see Ruesch and Bateson
1963). He thereby establishes a view of cognition that is compatible with
Peirce's semiotics.

Why is this important? Second-order cybernetics has abandoned the
objective view of information, but has yet to develop a theory of
meaning and signification that links the biological realm to the estab-

lishment of an inner world and from there to the social and cultural worlds. But Peirce has done this, and his theory has the same broad, non-disciplinary conceptual character as second-order cybernetics, as well as the same fundamental triadic and reflexive character. Both Varela and Spencer-Brown use signs to make and communicate distinctions. Only through signs can we think and communicate, and if a difference cannot be communicated, it can hardly be said to exist.

To connect Bateson, Reventlow, Maturana, Varela, Spencer-Brown, Deely and Peirce: *A difference cannot become knowledge until it has become so important that an autopoietic observer/knower attaches a sign to it, thus making it an object. Then it will become a rependium and make a difference that makes a difference and therefore is a distinction.* But the ontological basis of this theory is still unclear.

4.8 On Matter and the Universe as the Ultimate Reality

I object to the use of the term 'real' to mean only physical-material. What we can measure intersubjectively is a part of reality, meaning that it has an existence independent of the individual human being. But we do not know whether this existence is completely independent of the existence of conscious beings. When science reifies this substance (that is, declares it to be devoid of life and mind, and subject only to mechanical and statistical laws) and creates a world view in which everything – including life and mind – comes into being through the self-organization of matter through evolution, this move is clearly self-contradictory. It leads to materialism and potentially to fundamentalism in the natural sciences, as evidenced by the term 'universe,' which suggests strongly that there is a single reality that is potentially fully comprehensible by science – the 'world's own story' as Luntley (1995) calls it. Maturana has fought against this trend by offering the alternative concept of a 'Multiverse.' Maturana is reluctant to discuss the prerequisites – besides the need for 'observers' – for this Multiverse. We might agree that we have no certain knowledge of a world 'outside' of the consciousness of a society of observers, but, as I will show in the next chapter, given the relativity principle of Heinz von Foerster, we must accept the existence of other observers as a prerequisite for language, communication, and science. A partially stable environment is also necessary for perception to occur and form the 'substance' of the observers. What is the reality of the observers? What kind of substance do they exist in and by? How is the mind of the observers connected to reality? These are the crucial questions. Here, Peirce makes an interesting intervention with his three basic categories.

A hundred years ago, Peirce gave the old objective idealism a form consistent with modern evolutionary physical, chemical, and biological theory. His semiotic realism delves deep into the relations among mind, matter, natural laws, and the evolution of the universe, and provides a foundation for Spencer-Brown's formulations and for Varela's later developments in autopoietic theory. There is not complete agreement about how to interpret the last stage of Peirce's semiotic philosophy, and if objective idealism is the right concept to characterize it.[3]

Peirce sees the foundations of reality as chaotic, but he develops his concept of chaos a step further than either Maturana's Multiverse or Prigogine's thermodynamic chaos.

Peirce (1891, 1892) theorizes that randomness or chaos must necessarily precede lawfulness and determination in an evolutionary philosophy. In accordance with Christiansen's analysis (mentioned earlier) regarding information defined as neg-entropy, Peirce makes it clear that one cannot base chance on the physical concept of laws in a positive way, because this is only a purely negative definition of the absence of laws or knowledge.

Concurring with modern thermodynamics, and to some degree with quantum field physics, Peirce sees the basic quality of reality as randomness or chaos. But he elucidates some important philosophical ontological consequences from this view: if chaos is basic, one cannot explain it as the absence of law, because chance or randomness precedes law. Thus one must explain law from randomness, not the reverse.

Chaos, chance, and randomness must therefore be understood not only as emptiness but also as fullness, as hypercomplex dynamic processes that include characteristics of mind, matter, and life. He calls this pure spontaneity: 'To undertake to account for anything by saying boldly that it is due to pure chance would indeed be futile. But this I do not do. I make use of chance chiefly to make room for a principle of generalization, or tendency to form habits, which I hold has produced all regularities. The mechanical philosopher leaves the whole specification of the world unaccounted for, which is pretty near as bad as boldly attribute it to chance. I attribute it altogether to chance it is true, but to chance in a form of spontaneity which is to some degree regular' (CP, 6.63).

In order to impart meaning to this philosophy, we must comprehend chaos as spontaneously dynamic and as having the tendency to form habits. 'Symmetry breaking' is the more modern scientific term for the same phenomenon, and is used in both quantum field physics and thermodynamics; 'gestalt' is used in psychology and 'Eigenvalue' in cognition (von Foerster). If we accept that the concept of chaos is as fundamental as that of natural law, then we should not conceive of chaos as the absence of regularity or the absence of the ability to create structures. We should view it, rather, as a hypercomplexity of potential structures and potential information in an infinite, living dynamic. It should thus be possible to transcend the dilemma between determinism and indeterminism.

To explain how law and structure emerge from randomness, Peirce thus endows chaos with one more quality – namely, the tendency to form habits. Evolution of order – its emergence – is a result of this. He avoids saying too much about virtual order in the transcendental, but he also avoids denying the existence of such an order. In this way he approaches David Bohms's (1983) concept of 'the implicate order' in everything, and of an 'ultimate implicate order' in the transcendent (Weber 1972). We shall return to Peirce's use of the somewhat similar conception of Firstness as the source of qualia and pure feeling when we consider his triadic philosophy.

In opposition to most modern scientists, Prigogine among them, Peirce (1892) clearly realizes that his concept of chaos cannot be limited to the mechanistic concepts of a dead and mechanical world. One cannot remove life and mind from the undifferentiated chaos. Fundamental chaos is not the absence of law; it is the *mother* of law. It is not only empty; it is also *full* of possibilities. It is not only 'dead,' it is also *full* of life and mind. Peirce boldly calls this pure spontaneity! It is the spontaneity of pure, living feeling. Peirce then coins a term to explain evolution and the regularities of nature simultaneously; he writes that chaos has a tendency to be 'habit forming.' In modern science we talk about making 'attractors' for diverse processes, even 'strange attractors' as well as self-similar processes such as fractal structures.

With Peirce, one can understand the creation of law from chance as 'habits of the nature.' The laws of nature are precise only in their mathematical descriptions; the measurements on which they are based are always influenced by uncertainties. The laws are only simplified approximate model descriptions of a far richer and more varied reality, one that is spontaneous and living.

Peirce argues that if chaos is the fundamental concept, then law is unusual and unexpected, and therefore is the thing that must be explained. From the perspective of the statistical information of Shannon and Weaver, there is maximal information in chaotic random behaviour. But this is not Peirce's point of view. For him, departures from the random are interesting because they provide knowledge about structures and law-like behaviour. This is also the foundation of Wiener's, Schrödinger's (1967), and Bateson's cybernetic information science.

Peirce's solution to Maturana's problem of the world's existence before and partially independent of the observer is a unique variation of the objective idealistic position, and one that seems consistent with Spencer-Brown's ontology: 'The only intelligible theory of the universe is that of objective idealism, that matter is effete mind, inveterate habits becoming physical laws' (CP, 6.25). But it is a version of objective idealism – if that is what it is – that is different from Plato's, Plotinus's, or Hegel's.

It is precisely the mechanistic scientific paradigm's idea of the absolute and deterministic nature of physical law that Peirce disputes. He provides an alternative that mediates between traditional objective idealism and physicalistic deterministic mechanism and that at the same time offers a better foundation to information science if it is to become part of a broader theory of communication that includes meaning and pragmatic semantics. He has an exceptionally deep insight here that was too advanced for its time. The issues modern science has uncovered, however, show us how precisely he put his finger on the basic problems. He writes:

> The law of habit exhibits a striking contrast to all physical laws in the character of its commands. A physical law is absolute. What it requires is an exact relation. Thus, a physical force introduces into a motion a component motion to be combined with the rest by the parallelogram of forces; but the component motion must actually take place exactly as required by the law of force. On the other hand, no exact conformity is required by the mental law. Nay, exact conformity would be in downright conflict with the law; since it would instantly crystallize thought and prevent all further formation of habit. The law of mind only makes a given feeling *more likely* to arise. It thus resembles the 'non-conservative' forces of physics, such as viscosity and the like, which are due to statistical uniformities in the chance encounters of trillions of molecules.
>
> The old dualistic notion of mind and matter, so prominent in Carte-

sianism, as two radically different kinds of substance, will hardly find defenders to-day. Rejecting this, we are driven to some form of hylopathy, otherwise called monism. (1891, 321; CP, 6.23–4)

By positing that law emerges from the random and that cosmos emerges from chaos as the habits of the universe come into being, Peirce is melding together the creation of the universe and that of our own world in a way that the new cybernetics and constructivism have been pursuing for some time. Hylopathy or the hylozoistic view does not see matter as dead or inert but as potentially alive. As Peirce noted, one must transcend the useless antagonism between idealism and material-ism. When one perceives that deterministic mechanics has no proven scientific ontological status, one understands that this presupposition about reality is not justifiable, and the way is paved for a more compre-hensive view: 'On the other hand, by supposing the rigid exactitude of causation to yield, I care not how little it be but a strictly infinitesimal amount – we gain room to insert mind into our scheme, and put it in the place where it is needed, into the position which, as the sole self-intelligible thing, it is entitled to occupy, that of the fountain of exis-tence; and in so doing we resolve the problem of the connection of soul and body' (1892a, 335).

Since Descartes, the dualistic philosophy of mechanism has been driving the mind from the world and the world from the mind and, as a result, has encountered fearful problems in its efforts to reunite them through various concepts of cognition and knowledge.

Peirce provides us with a basic world view that unites a form of realism with Maturana and Varela's biologically inspired concept of autopoiesis and the theory of the social construction of knowledge. In this way he creates a conscious myth, a new framework for knowledge. Peirce realizes that such an ontology must include a view of the 'creation of the world' that does not conflict with our present scientific knowledge:

It would suppose that in the beginning – infinitely remote – there was a chaos of unpersonalized feeling, which being without connection or regu-larity would properly be without existence. This feeling, sporting here and there in pure arbitrariness, would have started the germ of a generalizing tendency. Its other sportings would be evanescent, but this would have a growing virtue. Thus, the tendency to habit would be started; and from this with the other principles of evolution all the regularities of the universe would be evolved. At any time, however, an element of pure chance survives and will remain until the world becomes an absolutely perfect, rational, and symmetrical system, in which mind is at last crystallized in the infinitely distant future. (1891, 170)

This statement agrees with classical equilibrium thermodynamics and modern physical cosmology – Big Bang theory and the superstring theory – which theorize the universe as arising from a random sporting in the vacuum field. It begins very small but expands rapidly, thereby unfolding space-time. Radiation and matter form through symmetry breaking. Through dissipative structures, matter self-organizes into more complicated structures. The difference between Peirce's perspective and that of modern science is that most modern physicists contend that chaos is non-living and non-mental. They have a physicalistic world view (Walter and Heckmann 2003). But Peirce introduces 'living feeling' as a basic part of reality, because physicalism is far too narrow a frame to solve the problems of signification, consciousness, and communication.

For this reason I believe that Peirce's theory of basic reality as a hyper-complexity of living feeling with the tendency to form habits is a good supplement (or vice versa) to Bateson, Maturana, and Varela's theories of information, communication, knowing, and languaging. I see here a theoretical connection between second-order cybernetics and semiotics that will strengthen both theories.

4.9 Conclusions

I agree with Bateson (1973) that we must begin our understanding of information with the process of knowing. Bateson's definition of information as a difference that makes a difference is profound. His problem is that he makes nearly every cybernetic system a communicator and a knower.

The main achievement of Maturana (1983, 1988) and Maturana and Varela (1980, 1986) is that they have conceptualized one requirement for a system to be living and knowing: to be autopoietic. They underscore an important aspect of Bateson's theory of information by emphasizing that the autopoietic system does not receive information, but only perturbations to its organization. The so-called reaction comprises internal adjustments aimed at preserving the internal organization of the system. This underlines the distinction between (1) the world as it consists of differences (potential information) and (2) the information processing of autopoietic systems.

Maturana and Varela's theory of autopoiesis and knowing is not standard physicalism, informationalism, or idealism. But they say so little of the world and the independent structures within it that it seems as if observers create the physical world – or at least all its objects – entirely by themselves through language, although this probably does not reflect their actual perspective. Cyberneticians must work with this philosophical gap in the theoretical foundations of autopoiesis theory, or at least with its formulations.

In accordance with modern thermodynamics, cybernetics, and to some degree with quantum field physics, Peirce sees the basic quality of reality as randomness or chaos. One must explain law from randomness, not the other way around. Chaos, chance, and randomness must be understood not only as emptiness but also as fullness, as hypercomplex dynamic processes that include characteristics of mind, matter, and life.

Because Peirce does not begin by eliminating mind, living, and knowing from reality, he avoids reinventing them later by 'changing signs for meaninglessness.' He thus creates a non-reductionistic philosophical foundation for the theories of Bateson, Maturana, Varela, and von Foerster, and more generally speaking, for second-order cybernetics.

From the above analysis it is possible to outline a consistent and meaningful foundation for Bateson's concept of information. This will make it possible to include the entire range of Peirce's semiotic reflections; it will also be reconcilable with the important extensions of Bateson's modes of thought that have been made by Maturana and Varela. We shall return later to Peirce's triadic, pragmatic semiotics, which spells out his epistemology and theory of cognition and communication.

Let me summarize from an epistemological point of view. We cannot say that the world we live in has no structures, nor can we say that our process of knowing has no influence on these structures. We cannot claim that the world is basically logical and/or deterministic, nor that it is absolutely irrational and chaotic. We cannot say that reality is basically simple (and logical), nor that it is too complex to be even partially understood. We cannot claim that reality is basically 'dead' material, nor that it is basically 'pure spirit.' Our theory of knowledge and knowing must be located between these positions to be able to put the knower into a framework that can encompass both the world, the knower, and the process of knowledge.

A closer look at the stance of second-order cybernetics as developed by von Foerster will bring us deeper into these problem areas and pinpoint the intricate connections I have only begun to develop here.

5 A Cybersemiotic Re-entry into von Foerster's Construction of Second-Order Cybernetics

5.1 Introduction

Heinz von Foerster has initiated and completed foundational work in second-order cybernetics throughout his research career and has contributed important elements to its basic philosophy. These must be integrated into our current project for a further reason – namely that they are an important part of Luhmann's system theory. In the present chapter I will investigate the basic philosophical assumptions underlying von Foerster's second-order cybernetics, their relations to autopoiesis theory, and their use in Luhmann's theory of social communicative autopoiesis. Finally, I will consider how these theories relate to the concept of signification in Peirce's semiotics.

5.2 From First- to Second-Order Cybernetics

For some years researchers have been working to clarify the limits of the development of knowledge within the first-order cybernetics of Wiener, Shannon, and von Neumann. Norbert Wiener (1961 and 1988) hoped to develop a science of control and communication in humans, animals, and machines. But except for the biological use of the concepts of homeostasis and feedback control, cybernetics never really, before Bateson, released itself from the computer as a paradigm. A concept of objective information has been developed, as has a unit known as the 'bit,' and as have computer and goal-directed steering mechanisms in all kinds of artefacts from washing machines to intercontinental rockets. Finally, attempts have been made to create artificial intelligence (AI) and 'expert systems.' But advances in the understanding of how the nervous systems of animals – not to mention humans – function in relation to cognition have encountered roadblocks. Gerd Sommerhoff[1] (1991, 91) summarizes the difficulty that classical or first-order cybernetics encounters when dealing with the biological system's unique way of functioning:

> The significance of 'information' in goal-directed activities was one of the factors which motivated Wiener and his followers in the development of a branch of studies which they called cybernetics. The name, first introduced by Wiener in 1948, derives from the Greek for 'steersman.' Wiener and a group of scientists around Rosenblueth were aware of the essential unity of the problems centering on control and communication. It was unfortunate, therefore, that they fell short of factoring out the formal structure of the space-time relationships in which this unity resides, the formal structure of goal-directedness. In consequence cybernetics remained, as someone said, 'a unifying name in search of a unifying concept' ...
>
> Moreover Wiener's followers had settled in a trend which looked at machines in the first instance and at the living organism only derivatively. Thus cybernetics came to increase the biologist's dependence on engineering concepts instead of diminishing it, as it might have done had it lived up to its original promise. Meanwhile, of course, control and communication engineering had developed as major disciplines. In consequence, 'cybernetics' is now often used merely as a collective name for these disciplines or, in a more restricted sense, for the study of the basic scientific principles on which they depend.

From a biological point of view, Sommerhoff locates precisely the weakness of first-order cybernetics. The question of the degree to which animal and especially human behaviour can be described and explained satisfactorily according to scientific methods has been raised before and has always had a central place in discussions of the foundations of psychology. For instance, in 1935 Kurt Lewin asked if one can actually talk about a science of psychology (in the Galilean tradition of objective science) that includes a phenomenological aspect. Can this science be based on a materialistic realism and its Galilean idea of objective, universal, mathematical, and deterministic laws? Today we can again ask: Is cognitive science's 'information-processing paradigm' – with its intimations of a deep level of algorithmic symbol manipulation as the essential cause behind all cognition and language – a true transdisciplinary research program for psychology? Or must we adopt a more constructivistic and organic view of reality – one that diverges from mechanicism – which is the approach taken by the project of second-order cybernetics and autopoiesis? Sommerhoff (1991, 92) characterizes precisely these present problems within our research into living intelligence, which calls for the development of new concepts within the new second-order cybernetics:

> Owing to its failure to start with a unifying concept cybernetics has failed to bring about a concerted endeavor to come to grips with the common elements in all teleological processes and to develop a general theory which would cover both the form in which they occur in nature and the form in which we can achieve them in man-made machines.
>
> Attempts to develop artifacts which imitate the performance of living organisms, and then to reason from the machine to the living prototype, have largely failed ... We now have machines capable of displaying the superficial appearances of instincts, taxes and kinesis, machines capable of trial-and-error learning, self-correcting and self-optimizing machines and many other 'brain-like' devices. But most of this work has remained on the level of performance imitation without shedding light on the physical or physiological organization which accounts for these capabilities in the living prototypes ... just as hydraulic systems can imitate muscle performance but shed no light on muscle organization.
>
> The gulf between organism and machine is immense ... Organic activities are not typified by discrete and unrelated sets of directive correlations, but by integral hierarchies of directive correlations in which phylogenetic, ontogenetic and executive correlations combine to produce a self-regulating, self-reproducing, self-repairing and self-maintaining, stable and yet flexible entity. No machine has as yet been designed to emulate these features of organic integration, nor are we likely to meet one in the foreseeable future.

These problems are central to second-order cybernetics (von Foerster 1984; Maturana and Varela 1980, 1986), which is primarily a project about how cognition, information, and communication arise from living systems' self-organizing activities, thereby organizing their lived realities or 'Umwelten.' This new cybernetics includes the observer as a cybernetic system also under study. The view is that at the level of the biological system, the observer is already self-organized through feedback mechanisms; moreover, the primary goal of the organism is to survive, which means that its goals are internal at the level of the individual as well as at the species level. Autonomy is essential to biological existence. The basic goal of an organism's behaviour is to maintain its own organization, its identity, which emerges from the existence of the system. From the biologically basic entity to the multicellular human body with its specialized nervous system, these systems are autopoietic (self-creating and self-organizing). Information is generated internally in the system by re-entry – in other words, by internal changes that maintain the organization of the system. Life equals cognition, as Varela expresses it. Von Foerster addresses this in his own profound way.

5.3 The Ontology of Constructivism and Its Concept of Knowledge

For von Foerster the basic problem of cognition turns back on science itself. What kind of knowledge does science offer with regard to our own cognition and communication? What is wrong with the view that classical science has of its own knowledge? Von Foerster (1981, 102) writes:

> The fundamental problem of a biologist, of a brain theoretician, of a social scientist, is from a classical, or let's say from a standard scientific point of view, that *nolens volens* the theoretician, or the describer of the system he is going to describe, is himself an element of the system. The social scientist excludes himself from the society of which he would like to make a theory. This is not a social theory because he is separated, and he can't handle *himself* in the theory. If he is a brain scientist exploring the functioning of the brain, he will find that in the most standard description of the operation of the brain it is always the *other* brain which is being discussed, but not one's own brain. Usually, developing a theory of the brain is very easy: I cut off the top and open up somebody else's skull, I put the electrodes into somebody else, then I wiggle something in front of his eyes, and then I see what the brain is doing inside, and then I see and know how the brain reacts. Unfortunately, it is only the *other* brain that I watch. So, the problem is: how can a brain scientist develop a theory of the brain when the theory of the brain is written in such a fashion that *it writes itself?*

This is an important critique of the central ideas of functionalistic cognitive science. Information and meaning in their broadest sense arise only from those self-organized systems which we call living, and which have a practical and historical relationship with the domain of the living. There is no information without mind, but there is no mind without body, no body without nature, and no linguistic meaning without society and culture. There is a 'strange loop paradox' involved when we depend on information and brain research alone for the foundations of a transdisciplinary 'cognitive science' – a paradox that leaves the other mentioned foundations in the dark.

Here, von Foerster (1989, 224) expresses the consequences of this view for cognitive and biological theory, as well as for epistemology: 'My nervous system does not, indeed, cannot, tell me what is 'out there,' not because of mechanical but because of logico-semantical reasons. My nervous system cannot tell me anything because it is 'me': I am the activity of my nervous system; all my nervous system talks about is its own state of sensory-motor activity.'

The acknowledgement of this circularity is the epistemological core of second-order cybernetics as encountered in the writings of von Foerster and as further developed by Maturana and Varela through their concept of autopoiesis, which von Foerster explicitly embraces but never explicitly develops in his theories.[2] His perspective on cognition – which he shares with Maturana, Varela, and others – is that it is a *self-organizing process that creates or brings forth a reality*. In this materialistic, emergentist form, it seems to be a version of organicism.

His challenge to AI and cognitive science researchers and implementers is that as long as computers do not function with second-order self-organization, we cannot even approach making machines that are cognitive or that have memory and intelligence. Let me document his opinion with a few quotes:

> We romanticize what appears to be the intellectual functions of the machines. We talk about their 'memories,' we say that these machines store and retrieve 'information,' they 'solve problems,' 'prove theorems,' etc. Apparently, one is dealing here with quite intelligent chaps, and there are even some attempts made to design an AI.Q., an 'artificial intelligence quotient' to carry over into this new field of 'artificial intelligence' with efficacy and authority the misconceptions that are still today quite popular among some prominent behaviorists. (1970, 27–8)

Researchers in AI now realize that there was much truth in von Foerster's early warnings about the radically different organizational principles of living systems and computers. As he remarks below, *machines are not problem solvers because by nature they do not have any problems*. We use them to solve our problems, but that does not make them cognitive entities. Von Foerster continues his critique:

> It is *our* problems they help us solve like any other useful tool, say, a hammer which may be dubbed a 'problem solver' for driving nails into a board. The danger in this subtle semantic twist by which the responsibility for action is shifted from man to a machine lies in making us lose sight of the problem of cognition. By making us believe that the issue is how to find solutions to some well defined problems, we may forget to ask first what constitutes a 'problem,' what is its 'solution,' and – when a problem is identified – what makes us want to solve it. (ibid., 30)

This is well in accordance with points made by Winograd and Flores (1986) in their famous book *Understanding Computers and Cognition*, in which they use both the theory of autopoiesis as well as Heideggerian phenomenology and Searle's speech act theory to analyse these problems. This critique is also valid for the concept of information. Von Foerster delivers a fatal blow to the prevalent idea that a cognitive science can be built upon an objective information science. Such an information science would include the library and information sciences that focus on creating and organizing document retrieval systems. About this idea of objective information, he writes:

> Another case of pathological semantics is the widespread abuse of the term 'information.' This poor thing is nowadays 'processed,' 'stored,' 'retrieved,' 'compressed,' 'chopped,' etc., as if it were hamburger meat. Since the case history of this modern disease may easily fill an entire volume, I only shall pick on the so-called 'information storage and retrieval systems' which in the form of some advanced library search and retrieval systems, computer based data processing systems, the nationwide Educational Resources Information Center (ERIC), etc., have been seriously suggested to serve as analogies for the workings of the brain.
>
> Of course, these systems do not store information, they store books, tapes, microfiche or other sorts of documents, and it is again these books, tapes, microfiche or other documents that are retrieved which only if looked upon by a human mind may yield the desired information. Calling these collections of documents 'information storage and retrieval systems' is tantamount to calling a garage a 'transportation storage and retrieval system.' By confusing *vehicles* for potential information with *information*,

one puts again the problem of cognition nicely into one's blind spot of intellectual vision, and the problem conveniently disappears. (von Foerster, 1970, 30)

The use of the term 'potential information' for what is retrieved from a document is gaining ground in library and information science (Ingwersen 1992, 1996), but it is still uncommon to distinguish between information retrieval and document retrieval, and this leads to a denial of the complicated semiotic and socio-linguistic problems connected with subject searching in document databases. Von Foerster makes some salient points here – he identifies the basic problem as a reductionist and physicalistic approach to the process of cognition. He identifies the problem in the lack of understanding of the biological systemic wholeness that underlies the phenomenon of cognition. This becomes his major research focus:

On the other hand, this reluctance to adopt a conceptual framework in which apparently separable higher mental faculties as for example, 'to learn,' 'to remember,' 'to perceive,' 'to recall,' 'to predict,' etc., are seen as various manifestations of a single, more inclusive phenomenon, namely, 'cognition,' is quite understandable. It would mean abandoning the comfortable position in which these faculties can be treated in isolation and thus can be reduced to rather trivial mechanisms. Memory, for instance, contemplated in isolation is reduced to 'recording,' learning to 'change,' perception to 'input,' etc. in other words by separating these functions from the totality of cognitive processes one has abandoned the original problem and now searches for mechanisms that implement entirely different functions that may or may not have any semblance with some processes that are, as Maturana pointed out, subservient to the maintenance of the integrity of the organism as a functioning unit. (von Foerster 1970, 39)

A very fundamental characteristic of second-order cybernetics is that it is open to the biological as well as to the social in its theories of cognition and communication. This is a sort of biosocial constructivism, which one can also see developing in the work of the French thinker Edgar Morin (1992). Biosocial constructivism – in Maturana and Varela's version, 'bring-forth-ism' – is central to second-order cybernetics. Through its attention to the autonomy of observers and their existence in conversation, the new second-order cybernetics attempts to bridge the gaps among the natural sciences, the arts, and the social sciences in a non-reductionist way. Von Foerster (1981, 104) comments:

> Our cybernetics which was essentially beginning with a theory of observing – I would like to call it cybernetics of the first order – is a cybernetics of observed system. I look at the whole thing: what is the system doing? Can I make an interpretation for it, can I make an interpretation in the sense of what is the purpose of that system etc. etc.?
>
> But a second later one asks oneself: how come that I am observing this thing? What are the necessary requirements for observation? What are the functions of observing? So second-order cybernetics became then the 'cybernetics of observing systems.' Now, in making that statement there is a pun because it can mean two things: cybernetics of observing systems in the sense that I look at that thing and it is an observer, and what is the theory of an observer?
>
> The second thing that I see: I have the theory of observing, I am myself an observer, so I am doing the observing, I am including myself into the loop of argumentation. And in which way can I handle that? So, my proposition here is now that in the second phase of cybernetic evolution a serious attempt was made to cope with the epistemological and the methodological *Grundlagen* (foundational) propositions that appear if you begin seriously to include the observer in the descriptions of his observations. With the first appearance of Maturana's autopoietic system for us all who were working in this field the suggestion was immediately made that for the first time we can start here with a biological theory of autonomy, because if we do not stipulate autonomy, observation is not an act of interaction or something like that, observation would just be a transducer kind of an idea, the concept of observation will not appear, only the concept of a transducer, a recorder.

As you can see, second-order cybernetics and autopoiesis theory clearly attempt to address the problems of an observer scientifically observing other observing systems. This is central to the entire range of ethology, comparative psychology, and cognitive studies. Reventlow (1970) very clearly formulated these problems as basic to any behavioural cognitive science of information, signification, and communication.

Von Foerster (1984) suggests that if one insists that the behaviour of an organism can be deterministically modelled as a machine, then one is in trouble. Organisms are not trivial machines – if they are machines at all, they are non-trivial machines. Non-trivial machines change their state (way of computing) every time they comprehend a computation. This makes them transcomputational to an outside observer (a behaviourist). One can say that second-order cybernetics may still be functionalistic – Maturana and Varela (1980 and 1986) discuss the structural dependency of the autopoietic system at length – but it is a non-trivial mechanical system. In other words, there is no possibility for mathematical determinism in a trivial Laplacian way. If this is so, what strategic possibilities are the sciences then left with? Von Foerster (1991, 71) explains:

> When asked, all my friends consider themselves to be like non-trivial machines, and some of them think likewise of others. These friends and all the others who populate the world create the most fundamental epistemological problem, because the world, seen as a large non-trivial machine, is thus history dependent, analytically indeterminable, and unpredictable, How shall we go about it?
>
> I can see three strategies that are currently applied to alleviate this situation: ignore the problem; trivialize the world; develop an epistemology of non-triviality.
>
> The most popular version of attacking this problem is of course to ignore it, but the method of universal trivialization follows not too far behind. One may call it the 'Laplacian solution,' for it was he who eliminated from his considerations all elements that could cause trouble for his theory, himself, his contemporaries, and other non-trivial annoyances, and then pronounced the universe to be a trivial machine (La Place 1814): if for a superhuman intelligence the present condition of all particles in the universe were known 'nothing would be uncertain and the future and the past would be present to his eyes. The human mind offers, in the perfection which it has been able to give to astronomy, a feeble idea of this intelligence.'

Thus von Foerster accuses classical science of trivializing the world and I agree. As an alternative, he offers a second-order research program that pursues an epistemology of non-trivial machines. It is an epistemology as self-organized as the observer and the observing systems that are observed. This is a fundamentally different metaphysics from either mechanical materialism or those who believe that classical linear logic is the essence of human intelligence. For a description, please review Lakoff's analysis of objectivism.

With their concept of autopoiesis, Maturana and Varela (1980) demonstrate why triviality and linearity are insufficient for understanding living systems. The system organizes itself and produces its own parts. The self-organizing abilities and historical dimensions of the living are important reasons why organisms are not trivial machines and why an organicistic world view is a step forward. Von Foerster and Maturana answer the question on information and dynamics as follows: the organism reacts to disturbances and perturbations of its system through a self-referential dynamic (so as to conserve the sort of system it is). The idea of an objective 'outside' is inapplicable, because according to these theories the concept of 'outside' or (objective) reality has no significant objective meaning inasmuch as no one has access to the objective true reality with which the observations of other systems can be compared. Having demonstrated how illusions and blind spots function, von Foerster (1988, 81) summarizes his position as follows:

> In these experiments I have cited instances in which we see or hear what is not 'there,' or in which we do not see or hear what is 'there' unless coordination of sensation and movement allows us to 'grasp' what appears to be there. Let me strengthen this observation by citing now the 'principle of undifferentiated encoding':
>
> The response of a nerve cell does *not* encode the physical nature of the agents that caused its response. Encoded is only 'how much' at this point on my body, but not 'what.'

This is a basic philosophical problem where epistemology and neuropsychology meet: the problem of qualia or how perceptual qualities emerge as experiences. Why do certain nervous impulses make us see and others make us hear, even though we cannot measure any qualitative difference between them when we open somebody's scalp and register nervous impulses? It seems that only the destination in the cortex determines the quality of perception we experience. In the traditional first-order disciplines working with these problems, we currently have no clue what turns quantity and destination in the nervous system into qualitative perception of a world 'out there.' Von Foerster (ibid., 81–2) summarizes this central problem of cognition in a way similar to that of Galileo:

> The same is true for any other sensory receptor, may it be the taste buds, the touch receptors, and all the other receptors that are associated with the sensations of smell, heat and cold, sound, and so on: they are all 'blind' as to the quality of their stimulation, responsive only as to their quantity.
>
> Although surprising, this should not come as a surprise, for indeed 'out there' there is no light and no color, there are only electromagnetic waves;

'out there' there is no sound and no music, there are only periodic variations of the air pressure; 'out there' there is no heat and no cold, there are
only moving molecules with more or less mean kinetic energy, and so on.
Finally, for sure, 'out there' there is no pain.

Since the physical nature of the stimulus – its *quality* – is not encoded
into nervous activity, the fundamental question arises as to how our brain
conjures up the tremendous variety of this colorful world as we experience
it any moment while awake, and sometimes in dreams while asleep. This is
the 'problem of cognition,' the search for an understanding of the cognitive processes.

The way in which a question is asked determines the way in which an
answer may be found. Thus it is upon me to paraphrase the 'problem of cognition' in such a way that the conceptual tools that are today at our disposal
may become fully effective. To this end let me paraphrase (⌐⌐) 'cognition'
in the following way:

Cognition ⌐⌐ computing a reality.

It appears that von Foerster contradicts himself when he claims to tell
us with objective certainty what is not out there. Thus he ascribes qualia
only to living cognitive systems. This assertion is one of the central
postulates in second-order cybernetics and autopoiesis theory, to which
von Foerster contributes,[3] and it must be combined with Varela's life =
cognition. The result is that *to be living is to compute a reality* – or to bring
it forth – to use Maturana and Varela's words. This view – as I will analyse
in a later chapter – brings second-order cybernetics and autopoiesis
theory close to Jakob von Uexküll's *Umweltlehre,* and thereby also to the
new biosemiotics that emerges from a Peircean reinterpretation of von
Uexküll's theories.

But is von Foerster's view just another of the numerous rationalistic
and functionalistic 'computer philosophies'? Not quite. Von Foerster
has a more basic definition of computation in mind than the usual
symbol-manipulating machine. Von Foerster (1988, 82) explains his
basic conception of computing as follows: 'Harmlessly enough, computing (from *com-putare*) literally means to reflect, to contemplate
(*putare*) things in concert (*com*), without any explicit reference to
numerical quantities. Indeed, I shall use this term in this most general
sense to indicate any operation (not necessarily numerical) that transforms, modifies, rearranges, orders, and so on, observed physical entities ('objects') or their representations ('symbols').'

This is an interesting broadening and demathematizing of the computational concept into a more basic term that precedes any machine, even the abstract Turing machine that often serves as the basis for the definition of computation. His epistemological theory goes beyond mechanistic and dualistic world views to embrace biology.

Von Foerster then raises one of the most basic philosophical and metaphysical questions, one that is yet to be answered. His choice here shows how his view differs from classical mechanistic and dualistic science, and how it is similar to Maturana's choice between objectivity and objectivity in parenthesis. These are the important, but as of yet unanswerable, questions he asks (1991, 65):

(1) Here is one pair of questions:
     Am I apart from the universe?
     (That is, whenever I look, I'm looking as through a peephole upon an unfolding universe).

Or

     Am I a part of the universe?
     (That is, whenever I act, I'm changing myself and the universe).

(2) And here the other pair:
     Is the world the primary cause?
     (That is, my experience is the consequence.)

Or

     Is my experience the primary cause?
     (That is, the world is the consequence).

Why are these questions undecidable in principle? Simply because if they were decidable, a framework must have been chosen within which they are decidable. But since choosing a framework is, in itself, deciding an undecidable question, we can take the decisions on these questions as devices for generating the appropriate framework.

Thus we must make these basic decisions ourselves and accept the responsibility for the world we bring forth as a result, which is what von Foerster attempts with second-order cybernetics and I with cybersemiotics. The framework from which we choose to examine these questions may be decisive for our future and for the kind of beings we shall become. I refer back to those introductory steps of framing already accomplished.

The metaphysics of von Foerster posits that we, as cognitive systems, are part of the universe and that our distinctions and experiences are the primary causes. This is a constructivist and cognitivist world view and some-what phenomenological in that it takes its departure in the way things emerge in awareness, although its somewhat naturalistic and scientific background distinguishes it from standard continental phenomenology.

But this is not scientific, would be one counter-argument. Yes, it is not scientific, precisely because science cannot explain why science should be the only definer of truth and reality. Rationality cannot explain the choice of following rationality, other than from an utilitaristic stance. This problem, as von Foerster – with Kant (1990) – understands it, is a metaphysical choice:

> For instance, questions about the origin of the universe are in principle undecidable. This is apparent by the many different answers that are given to these questions. Some claim that the origin of the universe was a singular act of creation; others say that there was never a beginning: the universe is a perpetually self-regenerating system in an eternal dynamic equilibrium. Still others insist that what appears to us now as our universe are the remnants of a 'Big Bang' that occurred perhaps 10 or 20 billion years ago, whose faint echo one is supposed to 'hear' over large radio antennas. (von Foerster 1991, 64)

Von Foerster thus does not take the modern scientific Big Bang and evolutionary theory of the universe to be the one and only rational explanation of the world. He grasps that the concept of 'universe' is less scientific than metaphysical. This has interesting consequences for the concept of reality, which von Foerster has continued to develop throughout his work. Maturana abandons the concept of reality as belonging to objectivistic epistemology and ontology, and instead uses the concept of a Multiverse; in contrast, von Foerster continues to speak – as does Luhmann – of *a* universe (not *the* universe) in which every cognitive system computes 'a reality.' This 'a' position is very close to Maturana's idea of objectivity in parentheses creating a Multiverse:

> I shall now turn to the defense of my use of the indefinite article in the

noun phrase 'a reality.' I could, of course, shield myself behind the logical argument that solving for the general case, implied by the 'a,' I would also have solved any specific case denoted by the use of 'the.' However, my motivation lies much deeper. In fact, there is a deep hiatus that separates the 'the' school of thought from the 'a' school of thought in which, respectively, the distinct concepts of 'confirmation' and 'correlation' are taken as explanatory paradigms for perceptions. The 'the' school: my sensation of touch is *confirmation* for my visual sensation that here is a table. The 'a' school: my sensation of touch in *correlation* with my visual sensation generates an experience that I may describe by 'here is a table.'

I am rejecting the 'the' position on epistemological grounds, for in this way the whole problem of cognition is safely put away in one's own cognitive blind spot: even its absence can no longer be seen ...

In summary, I propose to interpret cognitive processes as never-ending recursive processes of computation. (von Foerster 1988, 82–3)

One way to interpret von Foerster is that questions of origins, the nature of reality, and how to comprehend reality are logically necessary but cannot – owing to our epistemological position in the world – provide universal, explicit, definitive, symbolic, rational, and consistent answers (hypercomplexity). Like Thomas Kuhn, he sees that one must start by choosing a framework – or, formulated in a Spencer-Brownian and Luhmanian way, that one must to choose a distinction as the basis for observation. Kant (1990) also realizes this and speaks in philosophy and philosophy of science of 'regulative ideas.' We inherit this framework partly from biology and partly from our culture (Lorenz). However, we are able to reflect on this from within philosophy. By asking questions, we delineate the premises for the possibility of raising questions at all. As shown in Gödel's incompleteness theorem for mathematics, there will always be undecidables. Von Foerster (1991, 64) explains the significance of extrapolating the mathematical-logical concept of undecidables into the area of epistemology and the philosophy of science and of reintroducing the fundamental significance of human and cultural choice to the reality of reality:

The difference between decidable and in principle undecidable questions should now be sufficiently clear for me to introduce the following theorem (von Foerster 1989):
Only *those* questions that are in principle undecidable, *we* can decide. Why?

Simply because all decidable questions are already decided by the choice of the relational framework within which these questions have been posed, together with the rules that connect any proposition (say, 'the question'), with any other proposition (say, 'the answer') within the framework.

This is a wonderfully rhetorical way of showing the reality beyond the decidability of logic and mathematics, and of making clear that the mechanical world view and objectivism are chosen views or ways of observing. As we have already shown, frameworks have a substantial influence on what is considered rational.

What is von Foerster suggesting as a new framework, besides the fact that cognition – and thus the construction of reality – is a never-ending process? Is he suggesting a new 'non-ontology' such as the Multiverse of Maturana[4]? Although both locate ethics in human responsibility for the creations of their own realities, von Foerster (1991, 64) intervenes in a slightly – but importantly – different way: 'But we are under no compulsion, not even under that of logic, when we are making decisions about in principle undecidable questions. However, with this freedom gained, we have assumed the responsibility of our decision. This shows that the complement to necessity is not chance (Monod 1972) but choice.'

Like Prigogine, von Foerster directs his dialogue towards Jacques Monod's careful analysis of the limitations and consequences of a mechanistic biology. In developing his philosophy of choice, von Foerster understands that mechanical metaphysics only offers a choice between law-determinism and chance (defined as the absence of law). Like Spencer-Brown (1972) and Luhmann, who builds on Spencer-Brown, he chooses a basic characteristic of mind – the ability to choose a distinction from a variety of possibilities – as his founding philosophical operation. As we shall see, this choice takes mind for granted and as such is actually a kind of phenomenology.

As Mittelstrass (1974, 75–6) states, one of the prerequisites for science is the human ability to make (prescientific) distinctions and observations. Science is built on the foundation of human perception and the cognitive ability to acquire knowledge. To be aware of this will lead one to start in the middle instead of at the extremes, to begin with neither the subject nor the object but rather with the process of knowing within the project of living. This is a sound point of departure in my view. Spencer-Brown (1972) called this the fundamental ability to make a distinction that is the starting point for any knowledge process. Spencer-

Brown begins his book with these words: 'We take as given the idea of distinction and the idea of indication, and that we cannot make an indication without drawing a distinction.'

The distinction between the system and its surroundings is the first act of cognition. This is an act of observing – or, to use a more modern concept, an act of basic cognition. In that act, the difference between the reference to the environment and the reference to the (autopoietic) system is made; and if this difference is again introduced into the system, a conscious awareness of the observing is created when this difference is reflected in the system – this is called a *re-entry*. Through this operation the system becomes autological. *Autology* indicates the condition by which the knowing system becomes one of the objects for its own observation. In his essay 'Sickness to Death' (1964), Kierkegaard points to the same idea by arguing that mind (or spirit) is not the relation, but the fact that the relation relates to itself. In biosemiotics we would say that this is where humans become aware that they are sign-users.

Von Foerster is formulating cybernetics from this position. In some of his papers (see fig. 7 [5.1] in the following quotation) he creates a model of the nervous system as a matrix where squares represent nervous cells and in between are synaptic gaps filled with transmitters. To the left are sensors and to the right are motor neurons that provide feedback to the sensors, forming a closed circular network, a non-trivial machine that changes states with every operation. The hormonal system further changes the states of the nervous system. These two non-trivial machines both act on each other.[5] Von Foerster makes a torus from this model to reach a vision of the nervous system and its dynamics (see his fig. 7 [5.1] below):

> [In] referring to the sensorimotor system. Let us consider the square in figure [5.1] ... The small black squares represent aggregates of immediately adjacent fibers, which project out through the motor system. What happens when you move a hand, for example, is that, through the retina, you can observe your changes, which are then immediately fed back into the system through the receptors and in this way return to the motor system. But there is a second loop, or closure, and it is of course the one affecting the synapses by means of the hormones secreted by the hypophysis. The hypophysis, which is thickly innervated, generates a certain quantity of hormones that act on the synapses so that there is a double closure. This double loop can be represented by a figure called a torus (a doughnut). Here, the synaptic cleft between the motor and the sensory surface

is represented by the striped meridian at the center of the anterior surface, while the hypophysis is represented by the dotted equator and represents the second loop.

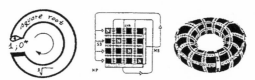

5.1.   Von Foerster's fig. 7: Autonomy (von Foerster 1993b, 102–3)

Thus the nervous system feeds back on itself, creating a closed system. This is illustrated as the system of squares in the middle of his fig. 7. The system again feeds back on itself through hormones, forming a double closure. Von Foerster employs this torus model to explain his basic concepts of cognition and autonomy and their consequences for our responsibility as autonomous beings:

> The computations within this torus are subject to a nontrivial constraint, and this is expressed in the postulate of cognitive homeostasis:
>
> The nervous system is organized (or organizes itself) so that it computes a stable reality.
>
> This postulate stipulates 'autonomy,' that is, 'self-regulation,' for every living organism ... 'autonomy' becomes synonymous with 'regulation of regulation.' This is precisely what the doubly closed, recursively computing torus does: it regulates its own regulation ...
>
> It may be strange in times like these to stipulate autonomy, for autonomy implies responsibility: if I am the only one who decides how I act, then I am responsible for my action. Since the rule of the most popular game played today is to make someone else responsible for *my* acts – the name of the game is 'heteronomy' – my arguments make, I understand, a most unpopular claim. One way of slipping it under the rug is to dismiss it as just another attempt to rescue 'solipsism,' the view that this world is only in my imagination and the only reality is the imagining 'I.' (von Foerster 1988 [1973], 92)

It follows that choice and responsibility become fundamental to von Foerster's philosophy, including his philosophy of science and cognitive theory. But how does this relate to traditional positions? Second-order cybernetics seem to have – in its most completely developed form, devised by Maturana – an epistemological stance closely resembling phenomenology in one aspect; and classical Wienerian information theory (such as Bateson builds on) in another. This generates a paradox in second-order cybernetics, even when it becomes as phenomenological as that of von Foerster. The two aspects do not fit together in a consistent theory. Luhmann (1985, 101) hints strongly at this when he, much more reflectively, develops his theory of meaning and acknowledges Husserl as his inspiration. 'The best way to approach the meaning of meaning might well be the phenomenological method. This is by no means equivalent to taking a subjective or even psychological stance. On the contrary, phenomenology means: taking the world as it appears without asking ontological or metaphysical questions.'

This is how phenomenology began; Husserl, Heidegger, and Merleau-Ponty worked hard thereafter to develop a full philosophical framework for it, but in my opinion never finished the task – and neither has Luhmann. Peirce also starts from a phenomenological position but manages to develop his triadic semiotic framework from it. Luhmann's very short and clear presentation of the phenomenological stance makes it clear why it presents a problem for the kind of – 'traditional'? – philosophy and philosophy of science my approach represents. This is because one cannot avoid asking about the epistemological and ontological presumptions behind this approach, which seems overly naive in its belief that things are as they appear to us and which does not offer deeper reasons why it leads us to things in themselves. Husserl (1977) does ask about this, and he ends with a transcendental idealistic theory that can hardly be claimed to make any contact with the reality of the world of the natural sciences. In a later development of phenomenology and embodiment, Merleau-Ponty (2002) admits in his foreword that phenomenology is not a full-fledged philosophy. I agree, and I believe – as does Deely (1997) – that Peircean semiotics can deliver the missing philosophical framework.

Thus, being in conflict with the phenomenological stance towards philosophy, I cannot help asking the ontological question about the metaphysics of the primary distinction. It seems that some kind of world substratum must be recognized as that from which the observer and the environment emerge. In phenomenology it is human experience that is taken as the given reality, but this makes it difficult to establish the outer world as real; in cybernetics it is the informational world of form (as Bateson puts it), which is again based in a material physical and chemical world substratum understood fundamentally in terms of classical thermodynamics, which as Hayles (1999) clearly sees, leads to a kind of post-human philosophy. The subject is gone! This is also the consequence of Luhmann's systems theory. It is clear that none of these scholars can provide a theory of meaning that relates to embodied praxis in social interaction as well as to actions in an outer natural and artificial cultural environment, because phenomenology lacks concepts for the environment, and cybernetics lacks concepts for first-person experiences and for how language influences them and makes re-entry and self-consciousness possible.

Von Foerster (1986, 86) attempts to overcome this when he writes about how the nervous system's organization permits integration of all sensory input into our internal conscientia: 'The structure of this fabric must permit some cross talk between the senses, not only in terms of associations, but also in terms of integration. If this structure permits the ear to witness what the eye sees and the eye to witness what the ear hears then there is again "together-knowledge," *conscientiae*, but here we call it consciousness.'

Von Foerster's is an original and interesting move in this cybernetic area. However, consciousness and mind – including qualia – are actually not theoretical concepts in his framework; in other words, such concepts have no intrinsic and/or logical connection to the metaphysical prerequisites of either first or second order cybernetics and system theory (Luhmann).

But I am also critical of the American pragmatism of Dewey (1991) and Rorty (1982), which gives up the ontological question just like the phenomenology, but from another position – namely, that of social practice in pursuit of the betterment of human conditions – and then ends up in the problems of utilitarian ethics about how to define happiness and human quality of life (Gustavsson 2001, 150–1). I believe that we need to have the courage to suggest new frameworks, knowing that each is only a stepping stone on the way to a better one.

When we look at Luhmann's work we realize that he is also working functionalistically and not really being true to the phenomenological dimension. This is because, as he likes to point out, from a sociological point of view meaning cannot be seen – it can only be inferred as dynamics. But functionalism and its differentiations are working strategies, not actual philosophies, as we for instance see in Åkerstrøm (2003) and Leydesdorff (2005). I do not believe that one can be a functionalist except within a metaphysical framework. If such a framework is not made clear, functionalism is at best an immanent tactic; in other words it is not made clear and explicit so that it can be rationally reflected on.

Thyssen (2006) analyses the lack of a philosophically consistent frame-work in Luhmann's system theory. When reading Spencer-Brown care-fully, we also see a framework not completely developed.

Functionalistic meaning can probably be described for certain uses as an operator. I contend, though, that meaning and value arise from our existential awareness that we are embodied social semiotic beings in irreversible time. I know it blows a hole in much of the present day's sociological self-understanding that biology matters for signification; but biology and its genetic, evolutionary, and ecological theory is as much a science as mathematics, physics, or chemistry. They all repre-sent our attempts to come to terms with ontological levels of reality and questions of time, irreversibility, evolution, and self-organization. And that is where the information concept comes in – potentially already at the physical level, but much more manifest at the chemical level, which is all about pattern fitting. Above that level, biology is foundational to any theory of meaning and signification. That was what Tom Sebeok noted when he founded biosemiotics! Embodiment has both scientific and phenomenological sides. Merleau-Ponty saw this and he worked on it until his death. Ole Fogh Kirkeby (1994, 1997) has continued part of this work.

Which reduces to an interesting fight between sociology (of knowl-edge) and evolution theory (including evolutionary epistemology) over ontological and epistemological hegemony. Yet evolution is a much bigger thing than the history and sociology of human society and actually provides the foundation for both. But this does not threaten the independence of sociology. As we can see from the soci-ology of science, sociology also teaches us about the origins, function, limits of scientific explanations such as evolutionary theory. This does not mean that you can avoid including them in your foundation. All of the sciences are entangled with one another, build upon one another's results, and interact with one another's metaphysical foun-dations. I do not believe in a pure philosophy. I believe that philoso-phy and the sciences are all imperfect and need to be in a constant dialogue; in this way can be created the metaphysical framework that constitutes the web of our present culture in its attempts to optimize health, wealth, meaning and happiness and to make politics 'to the best of our knowledge.'

Having made a few things clear, I hope, let us now return to von Foer-ster's attempt to solve some of these problems in cybernetics. One problem he attempts to solve is the problem of how to accept the reality of the other psyches when you work from a combined scientistic/constructivist mode. He calls this 'das fremdenpsychologische Problem,' and suggests a solution through his *principle of relativity,* which he explains in slightly different ways in several articles. I consider the next quotation – which follows the above quotation – to be his most successful attempt. His argument (1988, 92–4) leads to the view, outlined earlier, that all knowledge seeking originates in a community of biologically based conscious observers with a linguistic communication system that originates in a culture:

'But I was talking only about a single organism. The situation is quite different when there are two, as I shall demonstrate with the aid of the gentleman with the bowler hat [Figure 5.2].'

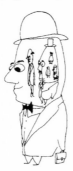

5.2.   Das fremdenpsychologische Problem

He insists that he is the sole reality, while everything else appears only in his imagination. However, he cannot deny that his imaginary universe is populated with apparitions that are not unlike himself. Hence he has to concede that they themselves may insist that they are the sole reality and everything else is only a concoction of their imagination. In that case their imaginary universe will be populated with apparitions, one of which may be *he,* the gentleman with the bowler hat.

According to the principle of relativity, which rejects a hypothesis when it does not hold for two instances together, although it holds for each instance separately (Earthlings and Venusians may be consistent in claiming to be in the centre of the universe, but their claims fall to pieces if they should ever get together), the solipsistic claim falls to pieces when besides me I invent another autonomous organism. However, it should be noted that since the principle of relativity is not a logical necessity – nor is it a proposition that can be proven to be either true or false – the crucial point to be recognized here is that I am free to choose either to adopt this principle or to reject it. If I reject it, I am the centre of the universe, my reality is my dreams and my nightmares, my language is monologue, and my logic monologic. If I adopt it, neither I nor the other can be the centre of the universe. As in the heliocentric system, there must be a third that is the central reference. It is the relation between thou and I, and this relation is *identity:*

reality = community.

Thus our world is created in communication with others, within a discourse community with its own language game connected to its specific life form, as Wittgenstein would say. There is an interesting connection here between the thinking of these two related Austrians,[6] which should be worked out in more depth. Wittgenstein's pragmatic language game theory might serve as a link between Luhmann's and Peirce's theories of communication. Anyway, von Foerster does establish one of our minimal requirements for philosophy of science – namely, the reflective awareness that science starts in a community of embodied real observers. And he then goes on to his next point – that these observers must be connected by sign or language games.

Having accepted this, the epistemological stance of second-order cybernetics moves towards social constructivism through its metaphysical choices. The most developed version of this point is to be found in Klaus von Krippendorff's communication theories (1991, 1993), and is taken up in a special way in Luhmann's theories of socio-communication (1989, 1992, 1995). Von Foerster (1986, 84–5) moves cybernetics into the reality of the social world, and he demonstrates that through the choice of the other as kin in consciousness, we avoid solipsism and acquire reality: 'With this the circle of contradiction is closed, for if one assumes to be the sole reality, it turns out he is the imagination of someone else who, in turn, insists that *he* is the sole reality. The resolution of this paradox establishes "environment" through stipulating a second observer. Reality is what can be witnessed, hence, rests on "together-knowledge," that is, *conscientiae*: Reality is conscience.'

Looking back, one can find that von Foerster had by 1979 recognized the need to acknowledge communication through signs in order to be able to compute a common world. In this respect, in the key quotation below he distinguishes his point of view from that of Maturana. Here we see the conflicts in explanations between the natural and social sciences: Do closure and embodiment come before language, or are language and culture necessary prerequisites for establishing those sciences? He writes (von Foerster 1976, 5–6):

> Here is Maturana's proposition, which I shall now baptize 'Humberto Maturana's Theorem Number One':
>
> 'Anything said is said *by* an observer'...
>
> I would like to add to Maturana's Theorem a corollary, which, in all modesty, I shall call 'Heinz von Foerster's Corollary Number One':
>
> 'Anything said is said *to* an observer.'
>
> With these two propositions a nontrivial connection between three concepts has been established. First, that of an *observer* who is characterized by being able to make descriptions. This is because of Theorem 1. Of course, what an observer says is a description. The second concept is that of *language*. Theorem 1 and Corollary 1 connect two observers through language. But, in turn, by this connection we have established the third concept I wish to consider ... namely that of *society*: the two observers constitute the elementary nucleus for a society. Let me repeat the three concepts that are in a triadic fashion connected to each other. They are: first, the observers; second, the language they use; and third, the society they form by the use of their language. This interrelationship can be compared, perhaps, with the interrelationship between the chicken, and the egg, and the rooster. You cannot say who was first and you cannot say who was last. You need all three in order to have all three.

It is difficult to speak about humans without including language and culture. It is a compelling theory that human self-conscious existence is created as an integrative product of the human cognitive biological system and its ability to communicate socially with language. It is a sound claim in second-order cybernetics that the origin of the observer and the origin of the world are closely linked through language and through society's production of meaning and information. However, science cannot tell us which came first. But still, how are we to relate to a reality that is in part independent of human social consciousness born of language?

As I attempted to show in an earlier chapter, one cannot solve problems of mind and intentionality in an evolutionary philosophy either through mechanical materialism or through physical indeterminism.

Nor can this be accomplished through pure phenomenalistic idealism, subjective constructivism, or mentalism, which underestimates the importance of the relative stability of the 'outside' world for the possibility of knowledge, communication, and truth. One of the deep understandings of modern times – and in second-order cybernetics as well – is that we are biological beings and that human existence is not possible without this foundation.

Second-order cybernetics accepts the biological level of existence, but how can it establish the physicality of things? Von Foerster has devoted a great deal of thought to this and has invented an innovative conception of how we establish the constancy of what we call 'things.' This has been a major problem in epistemology ever since the Greeks began their philosophy by contemplating 'the order of things' (*res*). In several places, von Foerster (e.g., 1980) has employed the mathematical idea of *Eigenvalues* (also used in quantum physics) to provide a model of how objects ('of reaction') are manifested in living, sensing autopoietic systems. *Eigenvalues* are all those values of a function that, when operated on, produce themselves. This is a circular causality. From an example with square roots, he concludes (1980, 23, 26):

> Thus, independent of primary values, the values for A and B created by applying recursively the square root converge to the single equilibrial value 1, the eigenvalue of the 'square root.'
>
> The eigenvalue 'test' states that an operation applied to its eigenvalue must yield this eigenvalue. And indeed: $\sqrt{1} = 1$
>
> This insight (or 'solution') helps us understand the organism which recursively readjusts its behavior (operates on its motor activity) in accordance with limiting 'objections' until a stable behavior is obtained.
>
> An observer watching this entire process, who has no access to the organism's sensations of the constraints on its movements, will report that the organism has learned to manipulate a particular *object* successfully. The organism itself may believe that it now *understands* (or has mastered the manipulation of) this object. However, since through its nervous activity, it has knowledge of its *behavior* only, strictly speaking these 'objects' are tokens for the organism's various 'eigenbehavior.' This suggests that objects are not primary entities, but subject-dependent skills which must be learned and hence may even be altered by the cultural context as well.

These *Eigenvalues* and objects arise in what Maturana[7] and Luhmann call structural couplings between the environment and an autopoietic system. Ethologists call some of these 'sign stimuli.' Reventlow (1977) speaks of a 'rependium' as a 'sudden restructuring of the perceptual field.' Von Uexküll (1934, 1973, 1986), in his 'Funktionskreis,' agrees with von Foerster that objects are constructed in the *Umwelten* of animals through a stable interaction between the perceptual and motor parts of the nervous system. There are underlying connections here between several bioconstructive approaches. I will return to von Uexküll's cybernetics-inspired approach later.

The process of human knowing is the process whereby we, through languaging, create the difference between the world and ourselves, between the self and the non-self, and to some extent create the world by creating ourselves. But my argument is that we accomplish all of this by relating to a common reality that precedes the moment when the difference between 'the world' and 'ourselves' makes a difference. The world divides, as Spencer-Brown put it. Furthermore, as Plato and Aristotle saw, we achieve this based on the implicit belief in a basic, underlying unfolded order. It does not make sense to argue that the world exists completely independently of us. But neither does it make sense to argue that the world is the pure product of our explanations or conscious imagination.

Von Foerster's position is interesting because his claims go further than those of most constructivists in second-order cybernetics as to the nature of 'the outside world.' Quantum physics has made it clear that science cannot claim that 'the world' exists completely independently of our actions. But it is also clear that we do not create trees and mountains through our experience or conversation alone – although Maturana is close to claiming that we do when he says that objects are established only in language. Von Foerster is more aware of the philosophical challenges facing a new epistemological position: that one must address the problem of solipsism and pure social constructivism.

The position we have constructed from von Foerster's writings allows a new critical and socially reflected understanding of understanding and of the cultural production of knowledge; however, it accords with neither our everyday experience of matter and nature, nor with the experiences of the natural scientist regarding the reality and stability of natural things (what some philosophers call 'natural kinds'). The *Eigen*-functions cannot simply emerge randomly out of the blue. There must be some kind of connection to the world, as Peirce noted in his work with the basic categories and as Lorenz also noted in his development of evolutionary epistemology to explain Kant's categories by way of the evolution of cognitive systems. In some dimly understood ways, the existence of nature and its 'things' and our existence as cognitive and conscious beings, are complexly intertwined. Von Foerster (1984, 4) understands that accepting the reality of the biological system of an observer leads to acceptance of the structure of the surrounding environment: 'I propose to continue the use of the term "self-organizing system," whilst being aware of the fact that this term becomes meaningless, unless the system is in close contact with an environment, *which possesses available energy and order*, and with which our system is in a state of perpetual interaction, such that it somehow manages to "live" on the expenses of this environment.'

Both the self-organizing system, and the energy and order of the environment, must be given some objective reality for this viewpoint to function. Von Foerster is unusually clear on this point. I have not come across any other writer in second-order cybernetics, autopoiesis, or Luhmanian system theory who has made the following point, which I find highly convincing. Later in the same article, while discussing the consequences of thermodynamics, von Foerster (ibid., 8) explains:

> To show that there is some structure in our environment ... by pointing out that we are obviously not in the dreadful state of Boltzmann's 'Heat Death.' Hence presently still the entropy increases, which means that there must be some order – at least now – otherwise we could not lose it.
>
> Let me briefly summarize the points I have made until now:
> (1) By a self-organizing system I mean that part of a system that eats energy and order from its environment.
> (2) There is a reality of the environment in a sense suggested by the acceptance of the principle of relativity.
> (3) The environment has structure.

As soon as we choose to abandon solipsism, accept the relativity principle, and acknowledge the reality of human beings, we are led to accept as real also their languaging, cognitive abilities, and necessary biological autopoietic structures. But these systems, as we have defined them, cannot exist in an environment unless they have energy, order, and material structure. We must accept some kind of structure of the world/reality. Peirce (to whom we shall return) talks of habits and Thirdness to characterize this element of reality. How much order, and how real, is a problem to be discussed later. The paradox is that it is difficult to explain the world without relating to it in a way that assumes an inexplicable precondition for being. This is what I call hypercomplexity.

Von Foerster considers the claims of Galileo and Descartes that the outside world is constructed of measurable things such as molecules and pressure. In line with Wiener, to a thermodynamical and cybernetic understanding of order he adds energy, entropy, and neg-entropy as order. But it seems that he does not go as far as Prigogine's science of complexity. I am certain that von Foerster also accepts the need for the concepts of space and time, and – since he accepts entropy and thermodynamics – the concept of evolution as well. But we have not yet investigated what kind(s) of evolution, and we have as yet no indications as to the reality and emergence of qualia. As I have pointed out, it seems very difficult to explain the emergence of an inner world of feeling and first-person consciousness from a mechanistic world view, or even from a Wienerian information-thermodynamically cybernetic world view.

From a modern biological perspective, the mechanics of life are fundamentally connected to the entire unfolding of the universe, which has it that basic atoms and molecules were created in the stars some time after the Big Bang (the heavy elements even later) and that exploding supernovas then created atoms heavier than iron and spread them over the whole galaxy. But this is still basically a universal materialistic evolutionary theory, one based primarily on thermodynamics and unable to explain the observer and the observing (or rather, the entire cognitive system). One could call it a grand narrative or metaphysics to explain the structure of the material world. But as such it is confronted with theories rooted in the observer's semiotic social-communicative practice of the creation of scientific knowledge. We have learned from von Foerster that we must make a basic choice: Do we view the universe as our ultimate origin and environment – understood as outside and before us – or as a construct, computed through our cognition and languaging? We must make a distinction from which to observe.

My focus here is on the function of 'outside reality' in the analysis of behaviours of autopoietic or 'observing' systems. Although the notion of 'objective reality' has been abandoned by second-order cybernetics, one should not eliminate the notion of a partly independent 'outside reality.' That would mean that Maturana's 'objectivity in parenthesis' and the Multiverse it constructs must be seen as possible true aspects of the same rich reality. To forge such an alliance between perspectivism and realism, one would require a complex view of reality (as Prigogine suggests), perhaps even a hypercomplex view (as I would suggest). That means that we cannot expect to find and be able to describe precisely in a consistent universal way a simpler order behind, below, or above it all. The order would have to hyperdynamic and hypercomplex, and the categories – those being the ideas of Plato or the forms of Aristotle – would have to be vague and unmanifest in the beginning. Peirce perceives this as a kind of Firstness; but unlike both Plato and Aristotle, his philosophical framework accepts evolution as a basic feature. We cannot avoid ontological considerations, but we must constantly develop them through critical epistemological discussions and analysis. We need a more refined and complex understanding of the role that concepts of reality play in our processes of knowing. Varela, who worked with von Foerster, made progress in this direction with his calculus of self-reference, which is an extension of Spencer-Brown's work. Varela has thereby established a view of cognition that von Foerster supports in a foreword and that appears compatible with Peirce's triadic semiotics (to which we shall return later).

Why is this important? Second-order cybernetics has abandoned an objective view of information, but it still has not developed a theory of meaning and signification that links the biological and cultural realms. A difference that makes a difference cannot become information until it has become so important to an observer or knower that a sign is attached to it to make it communicable. Cybernetics and systems require a semiotic framework in which to function. This is the minimum required to construct a social reality through cognition and language. Neither Maturana nor von Foerster has developed a systematic concept of society or its communicative and cognitive processes, although von Foerster has laid some foundations and Maturana has elaborated his theory of languaging. Luhmann has conducted further work on autopoiesis theory and second-order cybernetics, integrating crucial points from the theories of von Foerster, Maturana, and Varela with a theory of social communication built on the concept of autopoiesis. In this way Luhmann has integrated a sociological viewpoint with his theory, and at the same time has integrated the other theoretical developments in the research project into a greater whole.

5.4 Luhmann's Theory of Socio-Communicative Systems

Allow me to recount briefly the development of information, perception, and communication within second-order cybernetics – a development that one can see as leading to Luhmann's work. Bateson was the first to diverge from an objectivist concept of information by defining information in cybernetic systems as a difference that makes a difference and by developing a cybernetic and ecological theory of distinctions. In Maturana and Varela's theory, the concept of information is not accepted per se, except as something an observer ascribes to other observing systems. Here, information is a difference created within the autopoietic system by a perturbation from a constructed 'outside.' This theory is somewhat solipsistic. Qvortrup (1993, 12) summarizes this critique:

> If observing systems are closed, and if their operations are based on references to themselves, then the concepts of communication and information must be changed. One possibility is to conceptualize communication as systemic coupling, as we have seen. More drastically, however, one might claim that for a self-referential system, the environment only exists as something constructed by the closed, 'observing' system, any observation being self-observation. Then, information is neither a 'thing' nor 'difference' in the external world, nor is it a difference which makes a difference. Rather, information becomes a mental construction. The human being constructs a mental difference, and through this the world is brought forth.

But von Foerster's and Luhmann's theories tend towards an understanding of information as a difference (created inside) that finds a difference outside (ibid.), or that selects a difference outside with which it can establish a correspondence through an *Eigenvalue* function. Von Foerster (1984, 263) writes: 'The information associated with a description depends on an observer's ability to draw inferences from this description ... the environment contains no information; the environment is as it is.'

Thus observers select differences based on their own abilities to draw information from them. When von Foerster (ibid.) writes about *Eigenvalues* as those stable modes of dynamics which a biological system drifts into when repeatedly perturbed in the same way, it is an attempt to show how representation occurs in a biological system. Maturana and Varela (1980) call the steady connection through which *Eigenvalues* can be established 'structural couplings.' As already noted, these concepts describe well the habits and dynamics underlying the phenomena that ethologists call sign stimuli. These are generated by an innate response mechanism in the instinctive actions of animals. Although the idea of structural determinism is still mechanistic, this is still an important shift from genetic and physiological structures towards organizational cybernetic dynamics. The meaning of information is dependent on the system's own autopoietic organization, its historical drift, and its coevolution with the environment and other observing systems around it. Further recursive structural couplings also occur between organisms. Maturana and Varela (1980, 20) write that 'in this coupling, the autopoietic conduct of an organism A becomes a source of deformation for an organism B, and the compensatory behavior of organism B acts, in turn, as a source of deformation of organism A, whose compensatory behavior acts again as a source of deformation of B, and so on recursively until the coupling is interrupted.'

Therefore, when observing autopoietic systems are forced by circumstances to be part of one another's surroundings for an extended period of time during evolution, mutual structural couplings develop. But this is not – as it is usually understood from a cognitive or a 'logic of language' point of view – an exchange of information or codes: 'Notions such as coding and transmission of information do not enter in the realization of a concrete autopoietic system because they do not refer to actual processes in it ... The notion of coding is a cognitive notion which represents the interactions of the observer, not a phenomenon operative in the observed domain' (ibid., 90).

The way I understand this, they mean that animals are not aware of coding as humans are, and therefore they do not consciously make new codes as we, for instance, do in subcultures. The further development of these organizational processes leads to what Maturana calls 'languaging.' This process of languaging I understand to be the biological foundation of any co-generation of meaning between biological systems – an interpretation that Maturana seemed to accept when faced with my summing up during a conference at the London School of Economics about the way his theory relates to the sociological level. Thus it is important to note that his theory does not specifically address the function of language in cultural communication. Here, Luhmann expands on von Foerster's and Maturana and Varela's ideas, with his theory of social communication.

Luhmann (1990, 2) developed a generalized version of the second-order biocybernetic understanding of perception, generation, and communication of information by generalizing the concept of autopoiesis:

> If we abstract from life and define autopoiesis as a general form of system building using self-referential closure, we would have to admit that there

are non-living autopoietic systems, different modes of autopoietic repro-duction, and that there are general principles of autopoietic organization that materialize as life, but also in other modes of circularity and self-reproduction. In other words, if we find non-living autopoietic systems in our world, then and only then will we need a truly general theory of autopoiesis that carefully avoids references that hold true only for living systems.

Luhmann is not claiming that computers are autopoietic; rather, he is claiming that systems exist that are not primarily biological but autopoietic, such as the psychic and social-communicative systems. But as far as we know, these can only function if based on a biological autopoietic system. As a biologist and a biosemiotician, I believe that Luhmann fails to take this fact seriously enough, and that he therefore fails to develop a theory of embodied meaning. This is why I want to integrate his theory with biosemiotics.

An important aspect of Luhmann's theory is that he defines the three levels as closed systems also towards one another. Although all three are present and function simultaneously in human beings, there are no direct 'inner connections' among them as systems; they communicate only through interpenetration. This is an elegant cybernetic formula-tion of the organizational reasons behind the difficulty of integrating the autopoiesis of self-consciousness, the body–mind, and social com-munication through language. For instance, there are parts of my body's inner organs and processes that I cannot feel. There are also feel-ings I cannot or find difficult to express in words. Poets perhaps have this ability, but I have not yet developed a cultural understanding of these feelings that makes it possible for me to classify them with well-known concepts. As Luhmann understands it, human bodies and psy-ches are the environment of socio-communicative systems. This con-fronts us with the problem of how to establish an integrative individual subject or self, as such a one does not exist in Luhmann's systems theory. In this respect he faces the same type of problem as all cyber-netics, which we analysed in Bateson's ecology of mind, although Bateson's systems were open and Luhmann's are closed.

Luhmann distinguishes among the three systems in order to create what has so far only been partially developed in the theories of von Foerster and Maturana: a psychological and social theory of meaning and communication. Luhmann (1990, 2) further explains the differ-ences between the systems in this way: 'It leads to a sharp distinction

between meaning and life as different kinds of autopoietic organization, and meaning-using systems again have to be distinguished according to whether they use consciousness or communication as a mode of
meaning-based reproduction. On the one hand, then, a psychological
and sociological theory has to be developed that meets these requirements. On the other hand, the concept of autopoiesis has to be
abstracted from biological connotations.'

Luhmann wants to distinguish, but not explain, these different levels
of autopoiesis and to characterize the basic differences in their way of
functioning. He wants to underline that there are psychic as well as and
social-communicative autopoietic systems that are qualitatively different. So in a general theory of autopoiesis, he makes the model in his
own fig. 14 (my Figure 5.3):

It distinguishes a general theory of self-referential autopoietic systems and
a more concrete level at which we may distinguish living systems (cells,
brains, organisms, etc.), psychic systems, and social systems (societies,
organizations, interactions) as different kinds of autopoietic systems (see
Figure [5.3]).

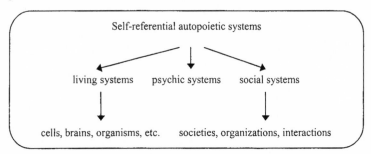

5.3.   Luhmann's self-referential autopoietic system

This scheme is not to be understood as describing an internal system's differentiation. It is a scheme not for the operations of systems, but for their
observation. It differentiates different types of systems or different modes
of realization of autopoiesis. (ibid., 29)

Therefore it is important to understand that communicative systems
are autonomous and have their own intrinsic form of closed organization, aspects of which transcend both biological and psychological
autopoiesis. This leads to Luhmann's theory of social communication

systems as autopoietic systems: 'Social systems use communication as their particular mode of autopoietic reproduction. Their elements are communications that are recursively produced and reproduced by a network of communications and that cannot exist outside of such a network. Communications are not "living" units, they are not "conscious" units, they are not "actions"' (ibid., 3).

Thus, communicative process units have their own special qualities. It is important for Luhmann to explain the human phenomenon of communication and the concept of meaning as reductive representations of complexity. This allows him to define meaning as a system quality that gives access to all potential topics of communication: 'Communication systems develop a special way to deal with complexity, i.e., introducing a representation of the complexity of the world into the system. I call this representation of complexity "meaning" thus avoiding all subjective, psychological, or transcendental connotations of this term. The function of meaning is to provide access to all possible topics of communication' (cited in Qvortrup 1993, 13).

In this way Luhmann is able to introduce the concept of meaning in a fundamental system-theoretical way, without having to work with a transcendental subject. Instead, meaning becomes a strategy in perception, thinking, and communicating: 'Meaning is a representation of complexity. Meaning is not an image or a model of complexity used by a conscious or a social system, but simply a new and powerful form of coping with complexity under the unavoidable condition of enforced selectivity' (Luhmann 1990, 84).

It is only possible to have meaningful communication within the social structural couplings created through the history of society. But not even in this setting can one speak of an exchange of information. Rather, *communication is a shared actualization of meaning that can inform at least one of the participants*:

> *Communication* is not at all what the commonly held view (and quite often the ill-considered scientific use) of this concept takes is to be, viz. a process of 'transferring' meaning or information ... it is a shared actualization of meaning that is able to inform at least one of the participants ... The notion of such a 'transfer' already runs into trouble by assuming the identity of what is to be transferred and thus that possession is relinquished when this transfer takes place, i.e., by assuming some form of zero sum. What remains identical in communication, however, is not a transmitted, but a common underlying meaning structure that allows the reciprocal

regulation of surprises. That this meaning foundation is itself historical in nature, i.e., that it arises within the history of experience and communicative processes, is another matter altogether and does not contradict my thesis that communication does not transmit or transfer meaning, but rather requires it as pre-given and as forming a shared background against which informative surprises may be articulated. (ibid., 32).

To Luhmann (1995), communication is a sequence of selection of (1) information, (2) utterance, and (3) understanding. The first two are created by what we traditionally call 'the sender,' whereas the third is created by 'the receiver,' who chooses an understanding of the signs produced. One could contend that a message is produced when the receiver says something that the sender chooses to understand as confirmation of what the receiver understands of the initial message. Figure 5.4 illustrates a model of the interplay among these three selections. Finally, a fourth selection – the message – is connected to present practice, and either accepted or rejected (Luhmann 1995, 149).

Luhmann's view of information is based partly on Bateson's concept, but despite its Wienerian base Luhmann's definition does not address its own applicability outside of human social communication. Luhmann applies his view of information only as a quantitative aspect of surprise within a meaningful human context, always combining the information concept with utterance and understanding. He stresses that both sender and receiver must make choices about 'information' (related to the subject matter), 'utterance' (pertaining to the way to say something), and 'understanding' (the interpretation of the listener dependent on an evaluation of the human context), in order to produce a meaningful message. Information is not information if it is not meaningful; therefore Luhmann is close to McKay's information concept, which he also mentions in *Social Systems*. But in his further writing it seems to be mostly Bateson's information concept, accepted at surface value, that he uses (Luhmann 1995, 46).

The social-communicative construction of meaning could connect Luhmann's theory to semiotics. Luhmann (1995, 71) says that 'meaning is the foundational matter: A sign must have meaning to be able to fulfil its function, but meaning is not a sign. Meaning focuses the context in which all signs are determined.' This is close to Peirce's pragmaticism, but we must remember that there is no subject and no ontology of qualia and emotions in Luhmann's philosophical framework, although he sometimes imports both into his theory in their

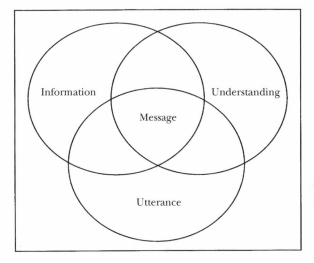

5.4.   Socio-communication: A model of how Luhmann understands the components of the communicative message. Both the sender and the receiver must make choices – or selections, as Luhmann calls them – in all three areas in order to produce a message.

commonsense meaning, which is somewhat inconsistent. But how do you relate the results of a theory that does not accept subjects and individuals as real systems back into a political and juridical system that is based on individuals with free will who are deemed responsible for their actions?

Luhmann refers to Husserl's (1999) phenomenology to indicate that the notion of meaning always occurs within a horizon of possible meanings. But on that basis, the following quote brings Luhmann (ibid., 60) even closer to Peirce's pragmaticism:

The phenomenon of meaning appears as a surplus of references to other possibilities of experience and actions ... Reference actualizes itself as the standpoint of reality. It refers however, not only to what is real (or presumably real), but also to what is possible (conditionally real) and what is negative (unreal, impossible). The totality of references presented by a meaningfully intended object offers more to hand that can in fact be actualized in any moment. Thus the form of meaning through its referential structure, *forces* the next step, to *selection*. This inevitability of selection enters into consciousness of meaning, and for social systems, into communication about what is meaningful.

Luhmann makes it clear that if there are such things as subjects, then they are not systems as he conceives them. Still, he seems to accept that the reality of experiencing oneself as a subject is real from a phenomenological point of view:

> Therefore, to cite an extreme case, no system unity can exist between mechanical and conscious operations, between chemical operations and those that communicate meaning. There are machines, chemical systems, living systems, conscious systems, and (social) systems that communicate via meaning: but no system unities encompass all these at once. A human being may appear to himself or to an observer as a unity, but he is not a system ... The living system is inaccessible to the psychic system; it must itch, hurt, or in some other way attract attention in order to stir another level of system information – the consciousness of the psychic system – into operation. (ibid., 39–40)

Thus bodies (our animal) do not communicate – but they itch and thus perceive – and neither do the psyches. They only think. As with all other systems and cybernetic frameworks, a theory of emotions, qualia, and free will based in a conscious subject seems not to have been developed within the framework. These things seem to be taken for granted or imported as commonsense concepts. But Luhmann's focus is primarily on society as communication, as the setting where the embodied mind is simply taken for granted. Nevertheless, his basic ideas of meaning and intersubjectivity seem to be imported from Husserl, albeit taken out of his transcendental philosophy and transplanted into his cybernetic system science to produce the idea of the closed, partly independent 'intersubjective' socio-communication system. Luhmann (ibid., 6) writes that his move was to 'replace the traditional difference between *whole and part* with that between *system and environment.*' But he also replaces the difference between subject and object with the differences between the biological, the psychological, and the communicative autopoietic systems and their environments. It seems to me that he loses Husserl's reference of meaning in Noema and provides no alternative, perhaps because he reads Husserl through the eyes of Merleau-Ponty, who transfers his theory of meaning into a social and embodied personal awareness. But this cannot be part of Luhmann's theory, as it is two different systems. So it seems there is an inconsistency in the transferral of the concepts that renders Luhmann's concept of meaning blurred – or perhaps even missing from the basic framework. 'Luhmann tends to treat the development of meaning as culturally given. Meaning is no longer considered as constructed in communication, but meaning processing proceeds and controls communication as an independent variable' (Leydesdorff 2007, 1). As Habermas (1987, 385) points out, 'then subject-centered reason is replaced by system rationality' and the usual subject-object metaphysics is turned into a sort of metabiological discourse that processes meaning without intentionality, as Leydesdorff points out. It is a scientific objectification of meaning. It is building on the fact that 'Husserl considered the external referent of communications as a horizon of a potential variety of meanings' (Lydesdorff 2007). But in Luhmann's use of Husserl's philosophy in his system science, the 'transcendental intersubjectivity' is replaced by 'communication' as an autopoietic system based on a double contingency working on difference in a given field of meaning.

Furthermore, it is very clear that Luhmann's system science, like all cybernetics, cannot support a theory of the subject as an intentional observer with a free will. In Bertalanffy's general system theory, this is still theoretically possible as an emergent phenomenon. Yet it is interesting that neither Bateson, with his open inclusive cybernetic mind systems, nor Luhmann with his mutual system closure, mutual structural coupling, and interpenetrations, can support in their respective systems the idea of a conscious subject. Neither can modern neuro- and brain physiology as such (which is in line with Reventlow's analysis as a consequence, if it is based on a Galilean science). Peirce at least has a subject theory, although he sees the individual as a sign or a kind of metasign – which is also unsatisfactory for many. To me, it seems fair to perceive the subject as a symbol and therefore as an ongoing interpretative process, the signs of which – seen from Peirce's semiotics – are part of the interactions of all three autopoietic systems. Peirce's theory of Firstness also offers a different ontological framework than the one of cybernetics and hard-core, thermodynamically based system theory.

One can declare that science – including system science – has spoken, that our self-conscious understanding (folk psychology) is false, and that the subject is a hallucination. But I admit that I am not 'mature enough' for that. I feel connected to my self, my free will, my emotions, and my existential choices, and furthermore, I live in and support a culture that has been erected upon the belief in the personal and political emancipation of the individual (Kant) and the individual's juridical and moral responsibility for his actions. I choose to see the lack of a theory of the subject as a limitation in Luhmann's approach and also in the entirety of informational theory and science. But I think that both von Foerster and Luhmann have made progress in framing the informational aspect of a message – especially Luhmann, who connects it with interpretation and utterance in a true triadic function. We merely need to clear up the concept of meaning on which it is based.

In Luhmann's theory, information is a context-dependent conception. He uses several of von Foerster's insights as building blocks for his theories, and these two men have been conferring together for many years. In a paper celebrating Luhmann's birthday, von Foerster extended his theory of cognitive objects as *Eigenvalues* by offering the following formulation, which connects his own theory with Luhmann's: 'Communication is the Eigenrelation in a recursively operating, double closure system' (1993a, 84; my translation).

This is the languaging 'dance' whereby two closed autopoietic systems become each other's surroundings to such a degree that they form a two-way structural coupling. Neither system can 'see' the other's interior or inner world and organization, nor can it see its own entire inner world. At any rate, we do not have access to other people's inner world of thought and emotions or to their biological self-perceptions. In this way the model provides an excellent picture of the strange conditions for human communication. *I talk to my imperfect model of the other from my own imperfect model of myself. Together, we interact like black boxes, without any metalanguage to provide 'objective' verdicts about what is occurring.* Our common world is created through the meanings that emerge out of this interaction. In the following quote, von Foerster (1980, 27) elaborates on his position regarding communication, although he still embraces the concept of individuals:

> If we take this as a metaphor for the interaction of two subjects, then the interaction becomes communicative if, and only if, each of the two sees himself through the eyes of the other. Note that in this perspective of communicative competence, concepts such as 'agreement' and 'consensus' do not appear and, moreover, need not appear (and this is as it should be, since in order for 'consent' and 'agreement' to be reached, communication must already prevail). These concepts, however, may very well appear in the vocabulary of an observer, who, outside the recursive loop watching the communicative interactions between the two subjects, sees no other

way of explaining their concerted actions. But we should also note that, on the other hand, from this perspective, in which consciousness is attained only through conscience (that is, by identifying oneself with the other), communication, ethics, and love converge into the same domain.

In this way, von Foerster's theory of choice, dialogue, and social constructivism in undecidable and non-trivial machines elucidates a perspective in which the common roots of consciousness, communication, ethics, and love are revealed in a self-reflective philosophy of science that focuses on the prerequisites for cognition and communication. This forces us to consider the basic prerequisites for cognition and communication in a metaphysical framework, which in turn brings us to the point of departure for Peirce's semiotics. This is a positive convergence, since there are limits to von Foerster's project even when we integrate it into Luhmann's theory complex. I cannot, for example, see that von Foerster has a theoretical concept of love, ethics, and responsibility. Luhmann wrote a whole book about these things, but it is not clear to me how it connects to his theory of meaning and communication. It is of course a second-order theory; nevertheless, it needs a first-order metaphysical framework to build on, as von Foerster did realize.

In trying to understand Luhmann, it is important to remember that he distinguishes communication from consciousness. This forces us to approach communication in terms of *Eigenvalues* and *Eigendynamics* of communication. His references for this are Husserl's phenomenology of meaning on the one hand, and on the other a paradigm such as that of Ruesch and Bateson (1987), which we have already criticized for lacking a theory of first-person experiences, qualia, and meaning.

Luhmann defined social systems as consisting of communications and their attributions as action. Communications reproduce themselves by linking themselves to other communications over time. Communications are operations, which cannot directly be observed; pragmatically, it follows that actions serve as the observables of the system (Luhmann 1995, 164). Thus one makes inferences about the meaning of communication on the basis of the observable interactions among the agents because communications and agents are structurally coupled. Therefore the states of the agents can be used as indicators of the evolving communication processes among them. But Luhmann is not a simple pragmatist; he did, after all, define agents in terms of consciousness, which in his theory is part of the psychic system and thus related to meaning. The states of the agents should not be identified with behaviour. Here Luhmann is close to Peirce, who defines the meaning of a sign as all the possible meanings and actions it can give rise to in the future.

Luhmann's systemic sociology thus departs from the subject-oriented philosophical sociological tradition in a very radical way. His theory of self-reference makes it necessary for us to distinguish a given social system from its social environment (society) on the one hand, and on the other from its psychic (prelinguistic consciousnesses systems) and biological (the embodiment of the mental) environments. Intriguingly, his theory then focuses on communication as a system that is self-organizing and self-differentiating. In order to process increasing amounts of complexity, the communication system tends to develop functionally differentiated systems such as science, politics, economics, intimate relations, the arts, and religion which draw on symbolically generalized media of communication such as truth, power, money, love and faith; these use special codes in the communication such as, for science, true and false.

But from where does meaning arise that makes a difference make a difference, as Bateson so well put it? Leydesdorff (2005, 1.3) writes very precisely about Luhmann's conception:

> Interactions at the social level provide meaning to actions. According to Luhmann's ... theory of social systems, meaning processing can be considered as providing social and psychic systems with the ability to distinguish between actual and possible states of the system in terms of expectations. The communication of meaning is not a biological, but a cultural phenomenon ... Using Luhmann's definitions, however, there can be no meaningless information in meaning-processing systems. Information is defined by Luhmann ... as a selection by the system, and not as uncertainty ... The system, however, is defined as an operation at an interface with an environment.

In Luhmann's system theory selections are in meaning. As I pointed out earlier, there is a problem with Bateson's theory of information and meaning: he based his theory on Wiener's pan-informational theory, in which information is neg-entropy and has nothing to do with meaning, and he is not able theoretically to show which system it is that decides what difference makes a difference. The theory of autopoiesis helps very much here, and von Foerster seems to understand this. Bateson fits well into Luhmann's system, which adds a concept of meaning – one originally based on Husserl – which Bateson does not present in any systematic way. For Bateson it is 'the pattern that connects.' But I think he failed when he made that pattern only cybernetic, although he was on the brink of a semiotic theory.

I see a paradox here: no cybernetic theory, including Luhmann's, can support a self-conscious embodied existential subject from which meaning and selections can emerge in symbolic interaction when it tries to determine its place in society, nature, and irreversible time. This is the subject that in practice, in philosophy, and in religion is pondering whether there is an intrinsic meaning to life, or whether there is a system above and beyond it that determines meaning and justice, or whether these are only established in society through the individuals' communicative exchanges with other individuals through the symbolic generalized media in the agora. I do see that in this case meaning is also a socio-communicative self-organized phenomenon or force. I agree with Gadamer (1995) that meaning and understanding develops as a deep tradition of pre-understanding in the history of a culture and this creates a horizon that the subject will place itself in as an evident doxa. But I also agree with Bourdieu (2005a, 2005b) that the individual subject or person can, as the insights of the social sciences demonstrate, empower his or her own free will and become more conscious about the 'habitus' induced in one by the cultural upbringing.

Neither a pure structuralism nor a pure systemic analysis can catch will, emotions, and qualia and their dynamics in the models and concepts. I still think it needs those self-consciously embodied subjects to grasp theoretically the important dynamic and experimental aspects of human meaning, action, and communication. Thus I have trouble understanding what that concept of meaning is that is used in Luhmann's theory of the message as consisting in information, utterance, and understanding. He writes (Luhmann 1995, 157): 'We cannot use intentionality and linguisticality to define the concept of communication. Instead we focus on the consciousness of difference; the difference between information and utterance built into all communication.' He goes on (ibid., 67–9):

> By information we mean *an event that selects system states* ... Information presupposes structure, yet is not itself a structure, but rather an event ... elements fixed as points in time ... elementary units of processes ... A piece of information that is repeated is no longer information. It retains its meaning ... but loses its value as information ... It has changed the state of the system and has thereby left a structural effect ... All meaning reproduction occurs via information ... and all information has meaning. Infor-

mation is always information for a system ... Information reduces complexity ... appears as a selection of possibilities ... As soon as meaning and
information are available as evolutionary achievements, an evolution of
meaning as such can be set going that tests which schemata of acquisition
and information processing will prove themselves (above all for prediction
and action) in their quality of making connections ... meaning itself
acquires form and structure.

The observation of the selection of a message in the context of the set
of possible other messages is performed by an observer. This is the very
starting point of a sociological theory of communication. One is
tempted to say that this is not sociology in the normal sense at all. There
are no individuals in it, only recursive self-organizing patterns of communication. Luhmann writes (1995, 69): 'no meaning constituting
system can escape the meaningfulness of its own processes ... The circular closure of these references appears in its unity as the ultimate
horizon on all meaning as the world.'
System science cannot deal with individuals at all. That is the special
angle of system science and the reason why it can produce new knowledge. The environmental basis for communication is the biological and
psychological autopoiesis system, which holds the potential to become
a human being, just like a baby does but like a chimpanzee (for
instance) still does not.
But a human body-mind is not really a human being – if there is such
a thing in system theory? – without language. It is language that creates
the reflective self-consciousness that lifts us out of animal awareness. If
you accept that the biological and the psychological autopoietic systems
are so strongly coupled that they become a single new system, then it is
an animal that has the potential to become a human by being programmed with language. But I doubt that system science should accept
this. As I understand it, there are no individual animal or human
observers in system science, as we would understand it in common
sense, if it stays consistent. Luhmann (1995, 69) chose to understand
the original idea of an extramundane subject '(which everyone would
know existing in oneself as consciousness) ... as the self-description of
the world.' This is very close to Spencer-Brown and seems to refer to an
objective idealism of some sort. Luhmann has not entirely escaped
Hegel and Husserl! A mechanical world on the other hand cannot
produce meaning and consciousness. I have argued further that neither
can a systematic view based on thermodynamics, the objective informa-

tion theory of Schrödinger and Wiener's cybernetics, complexity, and system science, even if it extends to a second order and includes autopoiesis and the basic distinction between system and environment as its point of departure. Who, after all, makes the first distinction in an objective, material, and dead world? In some ways Luhmann has never left Husserl's phenomenology behind, although he wants us to believe otherwise. He writes (ibid., 70): 'Thus in each specific performance the world functions as the "lifeworld"'; immediately before this he had written 'that for every system the world is the unity of its own difference between system and environment.' It is all in conscious experience, perhaps even in a collective transcendental intersubjective one. Information is a difference that makes a difference because it is a selection based on meaning, which on the one hand comes from the psychological system and on the other hand comes from the selection between various meaningful messages. Luhmann's system is not interested in explaining how meaning arises in body–mind systems. It is just taken for granted that it does arise. Only the systemic aspects of making choices and distinctions are reflected on, not the phenomenological and existential aspects of meaning and observing as they emerge.

As we have seen, there are two levels of meaning: the prelinguistic psychological level, and the communicative level as the possible other messages to which a specific communication relates and which gives it (relational) meaning.

I do think it is problematic to claim that there are observations and agency without subjects. As Qvortrup (2004) suggests, one could argue that the psychological and socio-communicative systems are so closely woven together by interpenetration and structural couplings that they represent what is normally called the subject or person. But Luhmann did not do this. Instead, he tends to smuggle a non-theoretically argued 'commonsense embodied person' into the explanatory system when explaining what this systemic sociology is and how it relates to individuals and to society.

But we also have the ethological evolutionary understanding of how meaning is built up in psychobiological systems, as well as Uexküll's theory of how such systems form an *Umwelt*. And we also have theories of how the human being achieves self-awareness and free will through language (see Deacon 1997), based on another framework (biology and semiotics). And we also have the phenomenological understanding of our experiential life world established on yet another basis. But they are not integrated into one framework. To integrate these I suggest a biosemiotic approach enlarged with a theory of cybernetic information, which I call cybersemiotics.

My question is whether the system of inter-human communications and control is analytically distinguished from the carrying agents, in a way that points to another level of meaning at the level of the experiences of the self-conscious, qualia-feeling subject (carrying agent) – a level that Luhmann does not address because his theoretical foundation does not allow him to do so. But the two systems can be 'structurally coupled'! Thus I want to see whether it is possible to couple systems theory with Peirce's triadic and pragmaticistic semiotics.

The tripartition of autopoiesis into biological, psychic, and social systems seems warranted in order to define a fundamental scientific and operational concept of meaning and social communication; but doing so will not tell us much about how these systems evolved. Luhmann does not integrate evolutionary ecological thought about the cognitive biological development of our categories and perceptual schemes in a functional way (which is what Bateson, Maturana and Varela, and von Foerster all attempt). Furthermore, we do not learn much about *what* the systems exchange when they communicate without transferring information. It is this unity of information, understanding, and utterance in the form of difference that makes a difference in a pre-established field or horizon of meaning. Luhmann (1995, 71) writes: 'The reference to the world immanent in all meaning prevents one from defining meaning as a *sign*. One must carefully distinguish between the structure of reference and the structure of signs ... meaning is the foundational matter: a sign must have meaning to be able to fulfill its function, but meaning is not a sign. Meaning forms the context in which all signs are determined.' Luhmann (ibid., 61) explains meaning 'as a surplus of references to other possibilities of experience and action.' He sees (ibid., 60)

psychic systems constituted on the basis of a unified (self-referential) nexus of conscious states, and social systems constituted on the basis of a unified (self-referential) nexus of communications ... psychic and social systems have evolved together. At any time the one kind of system is the necessary environment of the other. This necessity is grounded in the evolution that makes these kinds of systems possible. Persons cannot emerge and continue to exist without social systems. Both kinds of systems are ordered according to it, and for both it is binding as the indispensable, undeniable form of their complexity and self-reference. We call this evolutionary achievement 'meaning.'

This makes it clear that Luhmann needs the common sense concepts of 'person' and 'sign' to establish his theory. Luhmann's explanation here of meaning as evolutionary survival valve shows clearly that so far we have not been able to describe or grasp the human core of emotions or the existential aspects of meaning, speech, and the motivational drive, or the emotioning of exchanging signs in systems and cybernetics. But it must be possible to enrich this second-order cybernetic theory with knowledge about how signs function among living systems and how meaning is founded in the embodied mind. The earlier quote from von Foerster indicates that he wants to move in this direction.

Information and meaning in their broadest sense arise only from autopoietic systems. Luhmann (1990) has developed a general autopoietic theory of meaning as a prerequisite for human knowing and language communication that encompasses social systems. In this way he has also developed a general theory of communication, one that moves from the biological system level over to the psychological and the sociological levels, and does so in ways that may be made compatible with semiotics.[8] We need a theory of something that can stand for something else based on interpretation, or social convention, or both. In short, we require a theory for how signification functions in cognition and communication. Warner (1990, 17) realizes this and has written the following about the relationship of LIS to semiotics:

> Information science would seem to have some affinities with semiotics. The storage, retrieval and transmission of the products, particularly, although not exclusively, the written products, of the semiotic faculty have been among its principal, if not unifying, concerns. In cognate fields, bibliographers and cataloguers have shown a semiotic impulse in their concern to impose order on otherwise chaotic primary literature and have developed sophisticated codes for translating signs from one system, from the title and other pages of a document, into another, as entries in a catalogue or bibliography. Aspects of information science, such as information retrieval and citation analysis, are also concerned with expression to concept relations, from word to meaning and from a citation to its significance.

From the present analysis, it is clear that a central theme of LIS and IR revolves around the way meaning is generated, represented, and controlled in written media in different social contexts. Gardin (1973) studied document analysis from a linguistic perspective; but except for his work, semiotics has never really 'caught on' in LIS. Warner (ibid.) analyses why semiotics has not been used in LIS, and concludes:

> An explanation for the absence of connections from information science to semiotics can be derived from differences in provenance, language and disciplinary affiliation. The literature of information science has been predominantly Anglo-American in provenance and English in language. Partly as consequences of its early development in scientific communication and telecommunications and the prevalence of non-social scientific research backgrounds, information science has tended to align itself with the physical sciences and with technology and to use methods of study modeled on those employed in those fields.

But a semiotics connected to the natural sciences and natural phenomena does exist. It is based on a full-fledged philosophy, including ontological considerations, and it has the potential to develop the new foundation sought by Maturana, Varela, and von Foerster. We now turn to Peirce.

5.5 Semiosis and Second-Order Cybernetics

Von Foerster, Luhmann, and Maturana all casually use the concept 'symbol,' but I have not encountered in these scholars any reflections on signs and how they acquire meaning in social communication, except in Luhmann's short paper on 'Zeichen als Form' (1993). But even Luhmann has taken only the first steps towards developing a theoretical concept of the sign as a vehicle of communication to be integrated into second-order cybernetics; thus he has missed some deeper points in Peirce's semiotics. In 1999, *Cybernetics and Human Knowing* (vol. 6, no. 3) published an English version of Luhmann's article under the title 'Signs as Form.' Here, Luhmann tried to show that Peirce's semiotics dissolve into his (Luhmann's) theory of form and differences. This article was followed in the same issue by a critical analysis by Nina Ort and Markus Peter. They pointed out that Luhmann's difficulties in grasping Peirce's theory lay in the fact that the theory was triadic, whereas Luhmann's was not. Furthermore, Luhmann's knowledge about Peirce's semiotic philosophy was not profound, according to semioticians. No wonder, here was a theoretician who had written even more pages than Luhmann himself.

About a hundred years ago, while he was developing a basic semiotics, Peirce did some fundamental thinking about the necessary relationship between the subject, the sign or Representamen, and the Object, and the minimum of qualities that were necessary to ascribe to them in order to formulate a model of the process of knowing and sign making.

Peirce's definition of sign is in some respects cybernetic and self-organized but triadic. It is so reflexive that it is completely second-order, since all parts of semiosis are signs. The semiotic web of interrelated processes of meaning is what creates meaning. Usually researchers in autopoiesis theory and second-order cybernetics distance themselves from 'symbolism' and reference theories such as analytical language philosophy, logical positivistic reference theory with empty logic symbols, or the like. But Peirce's semiotics is quite different.

Peirce's semiotics is triadic, process-oriented, fundamentally evolutionary, and based on a continuum view of basic reality. Peirce, in his partly phenomenological theory, goes beyond both Husserl's and Luhmann's foundations when he endows Firstness with the basic qualities of both mind and matter in a chaotic complexity with a tendency to form habits. The Representamen originate here. Secondness is force, volition, and individual existence in a dyadic relation to something else – the Object in semiosis. Thirdness has regularity, habit, law, and understanding as the Interpretant. This theory promises to be broad and deep enough to provide a theory of meaning and cognition for framing a non-physicalistic theory of consciousness, meaning, and communication. It is a relational theory.

Signification is never simply a relation between a sign and the object to which it refers. The sign can only signify through a process of interpretation, and thus the Interpretant is a necessary part of the sign. I believe this is where Peirce, von Foerster, and Maturana meet. Peirce provides a very broad definition of the Representamen when he underscores that the Interpretant need not be more than potential. In fact, anything can be interpreted as a sign. In accordance with Bateson, *we might say that we interpret differences as signs when they truly make a difference for both communicators – that is to say, when they establish a shared meaning.*

Peirce's reflexive or cybernetic definition of the Interpretant points to culture, history, and the never-ending search for truth and knowledge (Peirce 1893). It emphasizes habits and historical drift – as Maturana and Varela's (1980) definition does – as crucial to the construction of meaning. But it is a drift, not a causally law-determined event. But to Peirce it is a tendency to form habits and regularities as in Lamarckian evolutionary theory. This is where he also differs from the cyberneticians.

From this it follows that signification, meaning, rationality, and logic are not born fully formed, but gradually crystallize from vague beginnings through the historical drift of praxis and the dance of languaging.

We must further accept signs and concepts as just as fundamental a part of reality as material objects are. They are, to use von Foerster's words, an *Eigenvalue* established through communication.

Peirce's concept of habit offers a more substantial foundation for how systems self-organize realities through cognition. These *Umwelten* I refer to as *signification spheres*, in the modern semiotic reinterpretation of von Uexküll. Living systems exist in a sphere of signification of their own making, in an informational world or reality. Von Foerster developed some interesting ideas about the dual evolution of the biological system and the world it computes – ideas that fit well with Bateson's cybernetic mind ecology. This is some of the most refined biological thinking that von Foerster has ever accomplished. It approaches Maturana's idea of the coevolution of the autopoietic system and its environment, which Luhmann embraces, but it takes an interesting epistemological and ontological turn. Von Foerster (1986, 82) writes:

> An organism that is matched to its environment possesses in some way or another means for detecting the order and the regularities of this environment. Perhaps the most fundamental principle involved in this registration is the correspondence between the *neighborhood relationships* that determine environmental structures, and the *neighborhood logics* that are incorporated into neural connectivity, which determine the 'whether' and 'where' of certain environmental properties.
>
> This suggests two levels of 'computation.' First, computation on the grand scale of evolutionary differentiation that incorporates the environmental constraints into the structure of neural networks that, on the second level, computes within the limits of their structure spatio-temporal quantities of useful universal parameters. The first level refers to the species, the second to the specimen. It is on the first level that the notion of 'Platonic Ideas' arises.

This epistemological foundation of second-order cybernetics dovetails with important points in Heidegger's phenomenology. The important point from Heidegger (1973) is that as observers we are always already a part of the world when we begin to describe it. When we start to describe it, we separate ourselves to a certain degree from the wholeness of the world of our living praxis. One can then add that from a biological *and* psychological point of view, a great part of our communication and thinking is not of our own (self-conscious) doing; rather, biological evolution and cultural history 'ideas' and schematas are signifying through us. Like Lorenz (1970–1), von Foerster realizes that our overall way of structuring cognition is already constructed through evolution and makes us the species we are. He hints at an evolutionary origin of the 'Platonic ideas' of cognition, along the same line of reasoning as Lorenz's evolutionary epistemology explaining Kant's categories and Peirce's habits of nature. In accordance with von Uexküll's work with *Umwelten* (which I analyse further later in this book), von Foerster grasps that the species constructs its world of living and perceiving (what I term its signification sphere). In accordance with this thinking, von Foerster (1986, 83) continues his evolutionary thought regarding how realities are carved from the universe:

> The dual interdependence of organism-environment permits a dual interpretation of the tree of evolution ... Instead of interpreting points on this graph as *species of organisms*, one may interpret them as *species of environments*. Thus viewed, this chart represents the evolution of environments that were successively carved out of the physical universe. These environments evolved from simple, almost deterministic ones, to extremely complex ones, where large numbers of constraints regulate the flow of events ... Figure [5.5] sketches the circular flow of information in the environment–organism system. In the environment constraints generate structure. Structural information is received by the organism that, in turn, computes the constraints. These are finally tested against the environment by the actions of the organism.

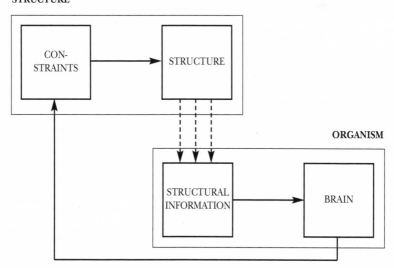

5.5.   Information flow in the organism–environment (O–E) system.

Just as we cannot speak of an absolute time or absolute space in the physical theory of general relativity, we cannot discuss an absolute reality or absolute environment in von Foerster's biopsychological theory of cognitive systems. Both theories retain the idea of one universe, although it is something of a Kantian 'thing in itself.' One might conclude that the theory of the universe is a metaphysical construct that humans extrapolate out of their common experiences and the rationale of their cognition. Von Foerster (ibid., 87–8) describes it as the development of a common world through the process of finding common ground for communication; Peirce would see this as the as the goal of science to develop a rational theory of the universe in the long term.

The urge to obtain communicability is a prerequisite for establishing a common environment. Only a system that achieves stable behaviour and communication habits will survive as a collectivity. This closely approaches Peirce's idea of habit forming. Only through established structural couplings can signs acquire meaning. Maturana has suggested an ongoing interaction between the autopoietic system and its environment: they coevolve in a non-deterministic historical drift. Organisms that live together become surroundings for one another, coordinate their internal organization, and finally create languaging to coordinate their coordinations of behaviour.

There is, therefore, a complicated psychobiological development and dynamic system organization underlying cognition and communication. The elementary processes of this system are not made of classical mechanistic information processing, or logical inferences, but rather out of a self-organized evolutionary semiotic dynamics. Leydesdorff (2005) makes it clear how Luhmann's distinctions between various functionally differentiated systems offer several advantages for analysis at the social level and for understanding the function of science:

- The possibility of functional differentiation of the communication. Since the communication system is considered as a system different from the carrying action systems (which Luhmann preferred to call 'consciousness systems' in order to stress the priority of meaning processing), the differentiation can be expected to carry functions for the social system that differ from those functional for action ...
- These functions are carried by the symbolically generalized media of communication. These media operate by codifying the communication

with potentially different meanings. Thus, using natural languages can be considered as a 'primitive' (since natural) form of communication, notably, one that is not yet codified by using symbolic media. Prices, for example, enable us to speed up the economic process with an order of magnitude on compared with bargaining at a market.

- Consequently, communication and language can be further distinguished. Within scientific discourses, for example, communication is governed by code which determines whether or not the communication can be considered as 'true.' The code of communication closes the specificity of a scientific paradigm and thus a next-order jargon can be developed ...

- In addition to the functional differentiation, Luhmann (1985, 2000) suggested a systemic differentiation in social communication between the levels of interaction, organization, and society. While the first two levels can be considered as specific formats for the integration, the level of society can evolve into a dynamics of functional differentiation and the self-organization of meaning processing. The dynamics between the functional and the institutional layer drive the system potentially in the higher gear of a knowledge-based system.

This dovetails with Wittgenstein (1959), who explains that human speech origins and individual meanings can never be explained in a classic scientific way. Humans had speech, meaning, and knowledge before they created science. But they also had bodies before they had speech and concepts. Luhmann tends to bypass the consequences of our embodiment and therefore the biological and psychological prerequisites for signification. But animals are already semiotic beings. Because animals do not have language with syntax and generative grammars, I call what they do *sign games*. I am extending Wittgenstein's 'life form' concept into the animal kingdom by taking seriously his claim that forms of life are a part of our natural history. For instance, the structural coupling of mating creates the sign game of the mating game life form. But many scholars would say that this is stretching Wittgenstein a bit too far and that a more proper concept would be 'cognitive frame' or 'conceptual scheme' (Davidson 1984). Still, I would argue that animal conceptual schemes arise from special motivations connected with certain important situations – for instance, with cognitive learning situations such as imprinting, and with essential communication situations such as mating play – which I then see further differentiated culturally, as I shall argue later. To combine the theories of Peirce and Wittgenstein by adding Wittgenstein to the Peircean framework and turning his pragmatism into pragmaticism, I further emphasize that unlimited semiosis means that the Interpretants of signs are created through evolution, as the history of the species, *and* through cultural history, *and* through the individual lifetime. The habits of Peirce, which are the meanings of the signs in his pragmatic semiotics, are equivalent to Wittgenstein's life forms in this context. Seen from ethology, second-order cybernetics and biosemiotics reveal some of the processes whereby sign games are created in our natural history. Ethology calls these habits instincts. These instincts can be combined in different degrees with individual learning to make the communicative act possible, as happens in birdsong.

What second-order cybernetics gives to biosemiotics are ideas of closure, structural couplings, and languaging. To develop the semantic aspect of the latter concept, I prefer to integrate it with the Wittgenstein-inspired concept of the sign game. This emphasizes the biological foundation of language without claiming that animals actually have language. The concept of the sign game can also be connected to Peirce's second-order theory of signs. I thus combine second-order cybernetics and Peirce's triadic second-order semiotics to form what I call cybersemiotics. This cybersemiotic frame of thinking takes us forward in understanding how signs gain meaning and produce information within communicative systems. *Communication is the actualized meaning in shared sign or language games.*

The epistemology in Luhmann's system theory is, as mentioned earlier, based on Spencer-Brown's 'laws of forms,' a logical-mathematical system that deals with the emergence of anything from the void through the basic process of making a distinction in a continuum. Spencer-Brown's work is the logical underpinning for all second-order cybernetics; his theory also fits with autopoiesis theory (Varela 1975). When we analyse Luhmann's attempt to integrate Peirce's triadic semiotic system into his own dyadic system, it becomes clear that even this profound system has limits. As mentioned earlier, Ort and Peter (1999) have diagnosed the limitation of Luhmann's theory to be its basis in two-valued logic. This is important, because Luhmann collects and integrates essential points from Bateson, von Foerster, Maturana, and Varela. Only Varela – in my opinion – perceived the depth of the problem and made the connection to Peirce's theory – specifically, through his calculus of self-reference.

Since Spencer-Brown is building a basis for the entire Boolean algebra, it is not unreasonable to say that his thinking can be seen as a later formalized basis for all of the functionalistic distinction thinking in second-order cybernetics, from von Foerster through Bateson to Varela and Luhmann. None of them, however, went so far as to discuss the basic distinction the way Spencer-Brown does. Bateson's definition of information as a difference that makes a difference is similar to Spencer-Brown's idea of making a basic distinction. All of cybernetics and information science theory is basically binary. This may be why it is insufficient to grasp the 'logic of the living,' which I contend is *also* semiotic.

What is the limitation of Spencer-Brown's philosophy, where he sees the world as splitting itself into a system and an environment in the continuum so as to observe itself? As Varela assessed in 1975, it is the lack of stabilizing self-reference over time – or as Peirce would have said, Thirdness. It is Thirdness that makes it possible to establish an Interpretant that is the foundation for semiosis, understanding, mediation, and habit formation. Varela (1975) sees self-reference as implicit in the cybernetic loop and as that which introduces time into the processing of the loop. But it is more than that. As in models of autopoiesis theory, the organizational closing of a system makes the establishment of individual identity possible because a core of organization is conserved. The system then develops an interest in conserving its own structure, and in so doing it values its own being higher than that of other beings. Living autopoietic and semiotic systems produce meaning and value by introducing the individual stance and subjective cognition. These beings lived and experienced the creation of space, time, and meaning in their own signification spheres!

The question of whether or not Luhmann found a way to build on difference without ontology is crucial for my view of the need to connect his theory to Peirce's semiotic philosophy. Luhmann often remarks that his distinction between system and environment is more or less arbitrary. We just have to start drawing a distinction corresponding to Spencer-Brown's imperative, 'Draw a distinction.'

Looking at Spencer-Brown's model, we realize that the first distinction already presupposes a unity, which refers back to an unintelligible and primary horizon or universe. Although it is not until chapter 12 in Spencer-Brown's book that the observer is introduced, he/she/it was of course there all along, being foundational to the first predistinction's arbitrary desire to distinguish. He writes: 'The conception of the form lies in the desire to distinguish. Granted this desire, we cannot escape the form, although we can see it any way we please.' This is an interesting fact that Spencer-Brown does not discuss owing to his abstract universe of logic and form. But the ethologist, von Foerster, and Maturana and Varela would point to the evolution of living systems that lead to the human body and nervous system. While the calculus is based on difference, surely it presupposes an ontology – namely, the world, whatever that may be. Spencer-Brown writes in his notes to chapter 12: 'The world we know is constructed in order ... to see itself.'

This is a most interesting reflective remark, one that dovetails with the antrophic cosmological principle, which in its most general form states that the universe is tailor-made for the existence of life. We see the universe the way it is, because if it were different, we would not be here to see it. Any valid theory of the universe must be consistent with our existence as carbon-based human beings, if not permanently then at least at this particular time and place in the universe. The universe appears to be 'fine-tuned' to allow the existence of life as we know it. See for instance Hawkings (1989), who asks: 'What is it that breathes fire into the equations and makes a universe for them to describe ... Why does the universe go to all the bother of existing?' Hawkings cannot see past his equations to the deep problem of how life, consciousness, qualia, free will, and meaning arose in a 'physical universe.' I find that doubting the existence of a universe as well as denying mind as real not only is futile, but also reveals a self-implicative fallacy, which it seems that neither Spencer-Brown nor Peirce commits. But Peirce's theory of Firstness goes much further than Spencer-Brown's logical reflections.

I would suggest that Spencer-Brown's void or complex continuum is equivalent to Peirce's Firstness of possibility and qualia or perhaps even to the void behind it. He discusses this in the later development of his theory. I will return to this issue. Peirce's Secondness is defined as the first distinction between a system and its environment, a distinction that thereby creates differences, constraints, and forces. Varela's self-reference is Peirce's Thirdness of mediating, habit forming, and interpreting that establishes the system's realization of itself, its subjectivity, its self-value, and its semiosis. But when we observe the theories from Peirce's metaphysics, it is an observer who draws the distinctions so fundamental to second-order cybernetics, autopoiesis theory, and Luhmann's system theory. It is only when the Interpretant is established in the autopoietic semiotic system that the observation of habits (relatively stable laws) is possible through the world of signs. This happens evolutionarily and ethologically – first in reflective reactions to signals, then in instinctive reactions to signs in motivated sign games, and finally through conscious language games in human society.

But apart from presupposing a world that desires to observe itself, the calculus makes no further ontological or metaphysical assumptions. Thus the conclusion is that Luhmann's theory is based on an ontology (the unity of difference between system and environment is the form of the world), and that the social construction of the forms in the world is in accordance with that basic reality. But we cannot talk about this reality in itself; we can only talk about it by using our semiotic constructions. Through evolution we have at every moment of time a belief in how the world is in itself. We only see what is made possible by the systems, by the society. Consequently we cannot follow the natural sciences in their insistence on seeing basic reality as mechanical and dead at the core. We cannot know that. It may be convenient for the natural sciences to operate within such a framework, but already in biology it has clearly become too narrow and reductionistic.

5.6 Cybersemiotics

I have introduced this first outline of a framework to deepen our understanding of the relations among observing, anticipation, cognition, signification, and communication in what we call information, cognition, and communication sciences. I hope this brings us closer to the nature of cognition and the structural dynamics of living anticipatory systems. I believe that the pragmaticist, evolutionary, psycho-biological framework I have shown is necessary to progress in this field. Let me conclude with a figure summarizing the proposed integration between second-order cybernetics and Peirce's triadic semiosis. In Figure 5.6 I show how the concepts of second-order cybernetics fit into the basic semiosis model of Peirce's triadic philosophy. I also show that to a certain extent, the three basic elements of semiosis that Peirce deduces from his triadic philosophy can be found in the conceptual apparatus of second-order cybernetics and autopoiesis theory. But Peirce developed this model from a deep philosophy and theory of sign processes that furthers our understanding of cognition and communication.

By joining the efforts of the latest developments of cybernetics and ethology with Peirce's transdisciplinary semiotics, and uniting them with Wittgenstein's pragmatic language game theory, we arrive at a

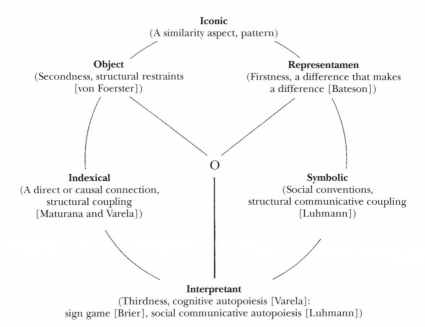

5.6. The model represents the basic structure of the triadic sign process of Peirce's semiotics: Representamen, Object, and Interpretant. In the parentheses, the category from Peirce's philosophy is followed by a concept from second-order cybernetics that addresses the same aspect of reality. It is followed, in square brackets, by the name of the scientist(s) who coined the term. I have also added Peirce's concepts of Icon, Index, and Symbol – which will be explained more in the next chapter – and suggested similarities between second-order cybernetics and Luhmann's system theory, to sum up some of the bridges we have discussed.

framework that is even more transdisciplinary and that conceptualizes the anticipatory dynamics of all cognition. There is an active anticipatory element in all perception and recognition, one that is deeply connected to the self-organizing dynamics of living systems and to their special ability to be individuals.

The key to the understanding of understanding and communication is that both animals and humans live in self-organized signification spheres that they not only project around themselves, but also project deep inside their systems. Von Uexküll calls this *Innenwelt*. The organization of signs and the meanings they attain through the habits of mind and body closely follow the principles of second-order cybernetics, in that they produce their own *Eigenvalues* of sign and meaning and thereby create their own internal mental organization. That is why I call this realm of possible sign processes the signification sphere. In humans, these signs are further organized into language through social self-conscious communication, and accordingly our universe is also organized as and through texts. But this does not explain meaning and consciousness.

6 Foundations of Cybersemiotics

6.1 The Complexity View

Many scientists have failed to note that mechanicist metaphysics does not fit within a basic evolutionary viewpoint. This is one of the reasons behind the great anger towards Prigogine and Stengers's (1984) argument that thermodynamics, as a science of complexity and definer of the physical time arrow, is more fundamental than classical mechanics. Mechanics cannot explain thermodynamics, and especially not non-equilibrium thermodynamics, as state functions only work for systems in thermodynamic equilibrium. Special relativity theory's view of time and the limitations of mechanicism in quantum dynamics further demonstrate that mechanicism is no longer an adequate metaphysics for all science. But there is at this time no consensus over a more comprehensive framework. As I have already argued, when working from an evolutionary basis, epistemologically we cannot continue to embrace the naive realistic epistemology hoped for by logical empiricism which could then be combined with rationalism and atomistic mechanicism – the view that Lakoff (1987, 9) refers to as objectivism and describes so well in his book that we will use it here:

- Meaning is based on truth and reference; it concerns the relationship between symbols and things in the world.
- Biological species are natural kinds, defined by common essential properties.
- The mind is separate from, and independent of, the body.
- Emotion has no conceptual content.
- Grammar is a matter of pure form.

- Reason is transcendental, in that it transcends – goes beyond – the way human beings, or any other kinds of beings, happen to think. It concerns the inferential relationships among all possible concepts in this universe or any other. Mathematics is a form of transcendental reason.
- There is a correct, God's eye view of the world – a single correct way of understanding what is and is not true.
- All people think using the same conceptual system.

These ideas have been part of the superstructure of Western intellectual life for two thousand years. They are tied, in one way or another, to the classical concept of a category. When that concept is left behind, the others will be too. They need to be replaced by ideas that are not only more accurate, but more humane.

I agree wholeheartedly. Lakoff's book is a very competent analysis and critique of this paradigm from the linguistic perspective of cognitive semantics. He employs convincing examples that establish an experientialist alternative wherein cognition and categorization are ultimately based on bodily metaphors and metonymy is extended into more abstract domains of thought. This approximates Lorenz's thinking on evolutionary epistemology (Lorenz 1970–1).

Prigogine and Stengers (1984) emphasize that we must accept chance and complexity as basic concepts in science – but as Peirce already demonstrated, one cannot build a metaphysics of science on the understanding of chance as the mere absence of law.

For his part, Peirce perceives chance and chaos not only as encompassing all possibilities, but also as endowed with the tendency to form habits and regular behavioural patterns, which we then, in science, identify as laws. His 'Chaos' – or 'Firstness' – also encompasses spontaneous feelings and potential basic qualities (qualia) producing qualisigns. He accepts Darwinian evolution as one form of evolution, that of *Tychastic* evolution based on random variation and natural selection. But he accepts two other forms as well: the Anachastic and the Agapastic forms of evolution. *Anachastic* evolution is a mechanically determined necessity, and *Agapastic* evolution is nature's tendency to form habits. He also calls the latter 'evolutionary love,' or agapism. This broad evolutionary frame of understanding connects his framework very well with the ethological view of evolutionary epistemology.

Lorenz and Tinbergen developed a theory of genetic preprogrammed behaviour and learning that theorized how perception

depends on species-specific, partly self-energizing motivations regulated by age, sex, physiological needs, and the time of year. But the
concept of motivation, and its relation to emotions and consciousness,
has not found broad acceptance (Hinde 1970; Reventlow 1970; Brier
1980).

As I noted earlier, the first law of thermodynamics posits that energy
is constant. Energy cannot be destroyed, it can only be transformed.
Lorenz developed his psycho-hydraulic model for action-specific
psychic energy (motivation) in order to understand the many different
types of motivations or moods in each species, and to understand why
these drives seem to 'dam specific urges' for instinctual behaviour such
as mating or hunting. Later, Lorenz (1966) launched this model for the
'aggression drive' (Brier 1980) as something building up and then
having an urge to be released.

It is generally accepted in ethology that most living systems perceive
their surroundings only in terms of their needs. Gibson (1966) later
introduced the concept of 'affordances' to explain this. Jakob von
Uexküll used the concept of *Umwelt* to describe how animals live in a
cognitive world of their own construction, perceiving it through 'tones.'

On the one hand, we have Shannon's information theory (Shannon
and Weaver 1969), which when combined with Wiener's cybernetics
(Wiener 1961) connects to thermodynamics when one redefines information as neg-entropy. Cybernetics integrates the ideas of computing –
formalized by Allan Turing (1912–54) – and other concepts of AI and
functionalist information. This mixture is often employed in the cognitive sciences. Today these trends are united under the information processing paradigm, which still seems to be the basic framework for cognitive science.

On the other hand, we have existential philosophy, phenomenology,
and hermeneutics. These are the traditional humanistic disciplines of
meaning, signification, interpretation, and cultural consciousness.
Their conceptual foundations do not allow them to encompass the
fields of science, not even that of biology.

But cognitive information sciences have encountered unexpected
great difficulties in uncovering the expected algorithms of intelligence,
informational meaning, and language (Winograd and Flores 1986;
Dreyfus and Dreyfus 1995). As Bohr (1954) noted, when one runs up
against such limitations in the foundation of one's scientific framework,
the moment has arrived for a further development of the conceptual
foundation. I contend that Peirce's semiotics is capable of forming the

foundation for biosemiotics (Hoffmeyer 1997) and that it can establish a new, transdisciplinary foundation that integrates into cybersemiotics new results from other disciplines such as second-order cybernetics, cognitive semantics, and pragmatic language philosophy.

Peirce was sceptical about there being a mechanistic foundation for a philosophy of science. He believed there was a continuum between mind and matter, between the internal world of emotion, will, and thinking and the external world of matter, energy, and laws. The process that united all of these was semiosis, the process of significa-tion. Peirce (CP, 7.463) writes: 'The present writer holds that in advance of positive knowledge, the presumption ought to be that there is such a unity in the universe that the difference between mental and natural phenomena is only a difference of degree. Pre-sumably, the same elements are in both, and if so, there is no essential difference in their intelligibility.' This is how Peirce bridges the two cultures of Snow. I have already argued that Peirce seems to be pro-pounding a second-order theory of signification, one that is compati-ble with second-order cybernetics, ethology, and autopoiesis theory, even though it is inherently phenomenological.

Ethologists have never deliberated on the foundations of the sign concept they employ in theories. Even so, I believe that Peirce pro-vides the most suitable model because instinctive sign stimuli are not established in a completely arbitrary way. Signs exist in communicative societies. Biosemiotics demonstrates that this includes animal com-munities such as anthills, beehives, and schools of fish. Furthermore, the Interpretant is generally created through ongoing dynamic social practical processes with communicative systems such as these. Hof-stadter (1983, 276) offers a description of the complexity of social meaningful practice: 'It takes an immense amount of richness for something to represent something else. The letter *I* does not in and of itself stand for the person I am or for the concept of selfhood. That quality comes to it from the way that the word behaves in the totality of the English language. It comes from a massively complex set of usages and patterns and regularities, ones that are regular enough for babies to be able to detect, so that they, too, eventually come to say 'I' to talk about themselves.'

Hofstadter is referring here to the semiotic net and to the various aspects or contexts within which a sign can be used. The sign becomes a mediator, which is included in the Interpretant because it can only be recognized as such through the creation of an Interpretant.

Peirce operates with a 'dynamical object' – sometimes called the 'ultimate object' – that is the ideal limit of all 'immediate objects' created through Interpretants and Interpretants' Interpretants. The Interpretant is created through a specific 'ground' that determines the aspect of the dynamical object that is of immediate interest in a given situation. In his central definition of the sign and its function, Peirce uses the concept of 'ground' to represent the context of interpretation in the central definition of the sign and the way its dynamics function.

The sign represents the immediate object that contains some aspect of the dynamical object that has the observers interest. The immediate object is what the sign 'selects' from the dynamical object and what it mediates to the Interpretant based on the ground. From an ethological point of view, it is the innate motivation, and thus the entire Innate Release Mechanism, that determines the ground, as in Freud for whom this motivation is also the repressed drive that determines how an entity or a situation is interpreted. But in the end there exists a reality with certain constraints, and through this reality evolution and history may lead to the final Interpretant of the dynamic object.

6.2 Peirce's Philosophical Framework for Semiotics

To develop this semiotic theory, Peirce established an alternative to both the dualism of rationalism and the materialistic monism of empirical science. He combined realism with idealism to form a new kind of objective idealism which contained synechism, an evolutionary perspective, and a pragmatic(istic) epistemology. Synechism posits that the basic 'stuff' of reality is continuous and unexhaustible – like the number line. Today we would contend that this is a field view (or a 'plenum' view), not an atomistic view. This field view now pervades quantum field theory and Einstein's general relativity theory, even though these are different types of fields. See for instance Mathews (1991), who develops a modern evolutionary, systemic field theory of reality.

In Peirce's synechistic philosophy, Chaos exists before Cosmos, and chance is before order. But chance is not assumed to be the absence of the concept of law. Rather, chance is considered to be a First, a part of Firstness in which pure feeling also resides.

In modern cybernetics and systems theory we now talk of the self-organizing universe, in which existing complex systems tend to be self-organized and living systems tend to be autopoietic. In Peirce's view, the habits of the universe are what we call laws in physics. They are never absolutely precise, as is often assumed in mechanistic physics. For

Peirce, laws are emergent phenomena. New laws will appear as the universe evolves. Laws are created by the universe – not the other way around, except for the tendency to take habits. This is in accordance with Prigogine and Stengers's acknowledgment of complexity as real and with their declaration that thermodynamics is the science of complexity. Concurring with this view of nature, the Danish physicist Holger Bech Nielsen (1989, 1991; Nielsen and Rugh 1992) has developed a theory of 'chance dynamics,' in which he abandons the mechanistic idea that nature was originally mathematically simple. Instead he posits a basic hypercomplexity from which laws as we know them emerge as the universe expands and cools.

In cybernetics, 'second-order' denotes a level of science that accounts for both the observer and the process of observation in its methods and concepts, but without subscribing to either subjective idealism or naive realism. What kind of world view can form the basis for such a science? In the previous chapter I showed that neither second-order cybernetics nor autopoiesis had developed a full metaphysical framework but could in their most advanced forms be made compatible with Peirce's basic conceptualizations, which we will go deeper into in the following.

We cannot escape the ontological presumption that a sign must refer to something in order to be a sign. The Object in Peirce's semiotics is a sign, and so is the Interpretant. I contend that this is what makes him second-order. I see an important difference between Peirce's Object and our usual unrefined realistic concept of 'thing.' Only some semiotic Objects refer to things, but all objects refer to 'some thing.' John Deely (1990, 54–5) writes:

> Whatever is objective exists through an actual representation, that is, as cognized or known. If what exists as known also happens to exist, in whole or in part, physically as well, that is, independently of the cognizing, then we say that it is, besides being an object, also a thing – a case of a 'physical object' ... Things, in this most general sense, are whatever in my experience is experienced as not reducing to my experience of it, and as having an embodiment, moreover, in the environmental structures such that it is not merely a figment of thought or imagination, but has also an existence proper to itself that is physical or 'real' in the sense that it obtains apart from my thinking of it. Things have bodies, in a word ...
>
> Objects are more than things, even when – which is not always the case – they are also things. Objects always involve a 'relation to an observer' so to speak, or, more exactly, to an organism experiencing.

Peirce's pragmatic view is a realistic type of social constructivism, but one that acknowledges the reality of Secondness as forces, will, and resistance. Reality is what affects our world of social signification and places limits on its own free development. Peirce is a conceptual realist. The same applies to laws. If something is so persistent that we refer to it as an object or thing, there must be stable habits ('laws') supporting its existence for it to be able to bear its qualities.

In the sciences today – for instance, in quantum mechanics – the reality of materialistic atomistic or field/plenum theory is built on matter/energy patterns. But Peirce's synechism is not simply materialistic; it is, rather, a special form of objective idealism, one in which matter and mind and, ultimately, even the three categories arise from the same source. Firstness consists of random emotions and qualities with the tendency to form habits, and this field is both inside and outside the observing systems. Pure feeling, mathematical qualities, relations, and the basic qualia, are there in an unmanifest and vague form as possibilities of Firsts, just like the quantum phenomenon before it is measured with a specific instrument in a specific experimental context (Bohr 1954, Bohm 1983). The concept of the object is only secondary in Peirce's theory; for him, only some objects are things. To some degree, the perceiver must create objects through the process of semiosis, not out of nothing, but rather out of Firstness through Secondness and Thirdness, which is not only 'out there' but also 'inside us.' Through the triadic 'leap,' (Reventlow's 'rependium') our experienced objective reality comes into being as signs. Some of these signs come from a partly independent world outside of us, some from our body, and some from inside our mind.

Thus in one way, reality is dividing itself in order to be able to look at itself; it is creating our world through its desire to see and make signs (so wrote Spencer-Brown regarding the reason for the first distinction). Peirce and Spencer-Brown are amazingly close to each other's formulations around this Firstness, but Peirce has by far the more developed philosophy. The meaning of a sign, says Peirce, lies in its power to determine all the possibilities regarding how observers of the sign will interpret it in their social activity in the future. This is not far from how Luhmann defined meaning, but Luhmann lacked Peirce's more developed metaphysical theory – which includes qualia, feeling, the tendency to take habits, and the subject or person as a sign – to give weight to his concepts. The real, then, is that which eventually results in information and reasoning. Therefore there can be an incorrect interpretation of signs. Short (1982, 287) writes:

> Since goals can often be obtained only by taking risks, there will be some fallible grounds of interpretation. This makes it possible for there to be false or misleading signs. These have significance or grounded interpretability, yet what they signify is not. That is, their immediate objects form no part of their dynamic objects. A sign is inaccurate when its immediate does not fit its dynamic object precisely enough, relative to the goal of interpretation. A sign will be true and accurate but incomplete or inadequate when, relative to the goal of interpretation it does not convey enough about its dynamic object; in this case the immediate is an aspect of the dynamic object. We can thus discriminate several different types of mistaken interpretation. One is where there is no ground that justifies the interpretation: something is taken to be a sign which it is not. Another is where a false or inaccurate sign is taken at face value. In that case the significance of the sign itself ought to be corrected. A third is where an inadequacy goes unrecognized.

Thus this view does not support 'everything goes.' Let us now dig a little deeper in the semiotic philosophy. Afterwards, we shall turn to a more detailed description of categories.

6.3 One, Two, Three ... Eternity

Firstness has, among other things, monadic qualities and predicates: immediate sensory qualities, simple and uncompounded forms and feelings, possibilities that exist without reference to any other thing, and the potentiality of being and of pure quality. A pure monad is a quality that is itself without parts, without any features, and without embodiment. Firstness is perception; it is latent and vague because it does not in itself stand in a relation to anything else. In this way Peirce establishes a phenomenological basis for his philosophy; however, he differs from Husserl, Heidegger, and Merleau-Ponty in that he establishes it in a much more classical philosophical framework – one, however, that is at the same time a renewal of this tradition. (Deely [2001b, 614] calls him the first of the real postmoderns.) Some examples of monadic qualities are red, bitter, hard, and noble, all of which are qualities of things and events. Firstness is thus contained in the world. Abduction is Firstness.

One might say that it is an immanence and not a transcendence, in that Peirce (CP, 6.490) also operates within a transcendental void 'behind' time, space, and the categories, from which spring the three basic categories – or 'worlds,' as he calls them.

Secondness is a dyadic quality by which something has a relation to something else without any dependence on a third thing. Secondness is a category for the characteristics of objects; it is what makes it possible to know and identify objects independently of concepts – in other words, by pointing at them and saying 'this/that.' For example, indexes are signs that stand for things without describing them. Secondness is the subject in logic. It is resistance, breaks, separateness, quantity. Whereas Firstness is possibility, Secondness is necessity, such as local causality. Deduction is Secondness. Secondness is defined as a dyadic relation between the sign and its Object. Consider Peirce's (CP, 1.328) definition of the dyad: 'Thirdness, in the sense of category, is the same as mediation. For that reason, pure dualism is an act of arbitrary will or of blind force ... The dyad is an individual fact, as it existentially is; and it has no generality in it. The being of a monadic quality is a mere potentiality, without existence. Existence is purely dyadic.'

The relation is dyadic – that is, something 'else' exists in a binary relation to something, such as a force, a will, a corresponding unwillingness, or the like. Secondness is the category of qualities of objects that makes them recognizable and identifiable independently from concepts. The relation between Firstness and Secondness is dialectically related in the sense that the quality in and of itself does not constitute the fact, but rather is tied to the fact: thus, feeling is Firstness, volition is Secondness, but cognition is Thirdness.

Thirdness is the triadic quality that exists only because it brings second and third things into relation with each other. This is the category of generality and understandability, of rationality and lawfulness, and also of the sign and of logical inference. From a human perspective, Firstness is feeling and Secondness is concrete experience. Thirdness is the generation of a biological, cultural, or linguistic habit that elevates us above Firstness's universe of possibilities and Secondness's innumerable incidents into generality and understanding. Thirdness unifies quality and quantity to form a relation parallel to logical inference, such as in science. Induction is Thirdness.

Thirdness is defined as the category for generality, comprehensibility, rationality, and regularity. The concept of 'force of habit' is central to Peirce's theories; thus he believes that natural laws are manifestations of habit formation in nature. Thirdness is the mediator between Firstness and Secondness. Thirdness completes the triadic relation. The triadic sign is thus more than a mere binary relation; the triad is non-reducible. Peirce (CP, 1.337) describes the relationship between Thirdness on the one hand and Firstness and Secondness on the other in the following way:

> By the third, I mean the medium or connecting bond between the absolute first and last. The beginning is first, the end second, the middle third. The end is second, the means third. The thread of life is a third; the fate that snips it, its second. A fork in a road is a third, it supposes three ways; a straight road, considered merely as a connection between two places is second, but so far as it implies passing through intermediate places it is third. Position is first, velocity or the relation of two successive positions second, acceleration or the relation of three successive positions third. But velocity in so far as it is continuous also involves a third. Continuity represents Thirdness almost to perfection. Every process comes under that head. Moderation is a kind of Thirdness. The positive degree of an adjective is first, the superlative second, the comparative third. All exaggerated language, 'supreme,' 'utter,' 'matchless,' 'root or branch,' is the furniture of minds which think of seconds and forget thirds. Action is second, but conduct is third. Law as an active force is second, but order and legislation are third. Sympathy, flesh and blood, that by which I feel my neighbor's feelings, is third.

In semiotics, Thirdness is identical to the Interpretant of the sign. For a sign to have meaning, it must have some regularity. This regularity might be a social habit – a reaction to the sign – or the sign might designate a regularity in nature.

In the bulk of human experience, we reach Firstness and Secondness only through Thirdness. Peirce considers non-conceptual direct experiences possible but rare. Firstness includes all the qualities we know such as blue, hardness, sweetness, and forms, but only as potentials. These qualities must manifest themselves in 'thing-ness' or difference in order to come into existence, and to be known they must be interpreted by a system that can recognize them as signs for habits or regularities that create an Interpretant within themselves. Within our usual time frame, we only know this to occur in living systems. Maturana and Varela (1980) suggest that the autopoietic character of living systems is what makes it possible for them to create structural couplings. Through these structural couplings it is possible to establish *Eigenvalues* of cognition, as von Foerster (1984) calls them: stable systems of recursive processing that stabilize in the mind and cause us to (re)cognize things. I posit that this is among the things that Peirce calls the Interpretant: the signs in our minds that make us see and recognize something as an object.

In conclusion, Peirce is neither a materialist nor a mechanicist, nor even an atomist. Rather, he agrees with Aristotle that the substance of reality is continuous. He further believes that signs and regularities are real and that humans cannot eliminate the mental or the emotional from basic reality since we are connected to it (Nature) just as it is connected to us (Mind). But unlike Aristotle, Peirce is an evolutionist who does not believe that classical logic penetrates to the ultimate depths of reality. As in the Ancient Greek myth of creation, Peirce believes that Chaos (Firstness) is the cradle of order (Thirdness), and not the other way round. Basic ideas and forms exist only as potentials in a sea of spontaneously complex dynamics, including emotions, basic qualities, and mathematical forms. Peirce sees topology as the most basic of the mathematics; he is thus an evolutionary, some sort of objective idealist as well as a non-reductionist pragmaticist.

Through this theoretical combination we can now posit one overarching evolutionary narrative for the history of human languaging. We have abandoned the mechanical-atomistic and deterministic ontology and its epistemology of the possibility of total knowledge, also called 'world formula thinking.' This is in accordance with Peirce, who sees absolute truth as the ideal but unobtainable goal for science and logic. Meanwhile, evolutionary science is attempting to find relatively stable patterns and dynamical modes (habits). It is not a science of eternal laws. It is a science of the habits of evolution and the meaning they come to have for the living systems created in the process. Peirce's idea of Firstness is that it is a complex, and even chaotic continuity. It encompasses the primary qualitative aspect of both the 'inner' and 'outer' worlds. His world view is thus fundamentally antireductionist, antimechanistic, and truly evolutionary. In the following quote (1891, 175), he powerfully summarizes how these three categories work with his ontology and epistemology: 'In psychology Feeling is First, Sense of reaction Second, General conception Third, or mediation. In biology, the idea of arbitrary sporting is First, heredity is Second, the process whereby the accidental becomes fixed is Third. Chance is First, Law is Second, the tendency to form habits is Third. Mind is First, Matter is Second, Evolution is Third.'

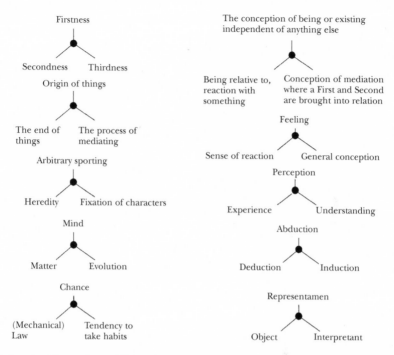

6.1. An illustration of Peirce's triadic philosophy in epistemology, ontology, evolutionistic theory, psychology, and semiotics.

It is Peirce's notion that 'mind is first,' combined with his realism, that makes it tempting to call him an objective idealist, which is what he sometimes calls himself. In Figure 6.1, I summarize the relation between the triadic philosophy and Peirce's semiotics to show how Peirce integrates emotions and qualia into his metaphysics, thereby avoiding the present problems facing the sciences. Many scientists are ruled without knowing it by the basic ontology of a mechanical reality based on an eternal mathematical order. From this perspective, meaning, emotion, and volition can only be given functionalistic explanations, and in the final instance they must be determined to be hallucinatory phenomenological processes. How the quality of consciousness should be integrated into this paradigm is beyond my imagination; I find supervenience theories on this basis inconsistent. It has never been established that mechanicism is an adequate philosophy for either biology in general, or ethology in particular.

The implication of Peirce's philosophy and method is that qualia and 'the inner life' potentially exist from the beginning but require a nervous system in order to achieve their full manifestations. Organisms and their nervous systems do not create mind and qualia as such. The qualia of mind emerge from the nervous systems that living bodies develop, thus creating still more self-organized manifested forms. Peirce's point is that this manifestation occurs through the triadic semiosis. According to the new cybersemiotic view, we can add that we become conscious through the semiotic development of living systems and their autopoietic semiospheres in the form of sign games for shared communication, which eventually evolve into human language games. This is the new foundation I suggest – and it is one that allows for biosemiotics and evolutionary epistemology to integrate recent developments from ethology, second-order cybernetics, cognitive semantics, and pragmatic linguistics in a fruitful way to forge a new transdisciplinary view of cognition and communication.

In combining the ethological, autopoietic, and semiotic, one can say the following: meaning is habits established as structural couplings between the living autopoietic system and the hypercomplexity that we call environment (including other living systems). 'Objects' are cognized within the environment – through abduction – by ascribing sign habits to them that relate to activities of survival such as eating, mating, fighting, and nursing – what we, extending Wittgenstein's concept, call 'life forms' in a human or animal society. With the reflective linguistic consciousness of human beings in a culture, the concept of meaning expands beyond the body and its immediate needs.

We thus take a step forward in our understanding of how signs acquire meanings and produce information within communicative systems when we theorize signification as actualized meaning in shared sign or language games without leaving a realist world view – the knowledge of the world provided by the sciences and the insights of social constructivism.

6.4 Sign Trigonometries and Classes

Having defined the concept of the sign and its philosophical foundation in Peirce's phenomenology, we now have an understanding of Peirce's pragmatic semiotics, in which the meaning of a sign is usually the possible social habits it can create. I now wish to elucidate Peirce's semiotics a bit more by discussing the development of the first basic

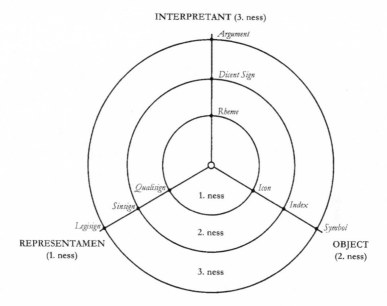

INTERPRETANT (3. ness)

Argument

Dicent Sign

Rheme

1. ness

Qualisign   Icon

Sinsign   Index

Legisign   Symbol

2. ness

REPRESENTAMEN   OBJECT
(1. ness)   (2. ness)

3. ness

6.2.   This is my own figure, which shows how the basic sign types relate to First-ness, Secondness, and Thirdness. Each radial line from the centre corresponds to parts of the sign relation: Representamen, Object, and Interpretant. Each leg is then made subject to triadic analysis. Firstness is closest to the centre, Secondness in the middle, and Thirdness farthest away from the centre.

types of signs and how he develops his ten basic classes of signs, the use of which I[1] will demonstrate with an example from LIS.

According to Peirce, the sign can be divided into three trigonometries for each of the basic categories of Firstness, Secondness, and Thirdness (I have developed a new way to illustrate this in Figure 6.2).

It is important to realize that these types are ideal analytical classifications that are seldom represented purely in reality, as they are only one leg of the triadic sign. It is their combination in triads that gives the basic different sign types, of which there are ten, as we shall see. Peirce (MS, 599) writes: 'They are like chemical elements. To a certain degree one could say that the very laws of chemical reaction prohibit us from obtaining in absolute purity. But the approximate purification gives us a tolerably accurate idea of their nature, and which present themselves habitually in such a degree of purity, that we have no hesitation in saying, this is gold, that silver, and the other copper.'

Below I briefly explain each of the three trigonometries, beginning with the trigonometry of Firstness, which is the inner circle in the figure. Peirce (CP, 2.243) explains how 'first, according as the sign in itself is a mere quality, is an actual existent, or is a general law; secondly, according as the relation of the sign to its object consists in the sign's having some character in itself, or in some existential relation to that object, or in its relation to an interpretant; thirdly, according as its Interpretant represents it as a sign of possibility or as a sign of fact or a sign of reason.'

What Peirce mentions secondly relates to the second circle, what he mentions thirdly to the third or outer circle in my figure. The first division of the sign trigonometries is thus within the category of Firstness, which in the sign triad is the Representamen and consists of the Qualisign, the Sinsign, and the Legisign. The Qualisign is defined as a quality of a sign. Before the manifestation of the Qualisign, its quality must be carried by another sign, since it is positively contained within itself. Since quality can only describe an object through some resemblance or a shared element, a Qualisign must necessarily be an Icon. When a quality is a logical possibility, the Qualisign can only be interpreted as a sign of being, in other words, as a Rheme. The experience of the colour blue must, of course, be transmitted via a thing or event (Secondness).

Therefore, the first kind of fundamental complex sign is the Rhematic Iconic Qualisign. (See Figure 6.3 for a model of Peirce's ten basic sign types.) This is the first of Peirce's ten basic classes of signs that I will describe below, along with the other trigonometries from which Rheme and Icon originate.

The Sinsign comes after the Qualisign in the first trichotomy. The Sinsign is an actual thing or event as a sign. The Sinsign exists only through its qualities, and thus often contains and transmits several Qualisigns (Peirce 1994, 99). But it can also be combined with other sign types at the same level. There are thus several combinations of Sinsigns: a Rhematic Iconic Sinsign, a Rhematic Indexical Sinsign, and a Dicent Indexical Sinsign.

The Legisign is the third type in the first trigonometry. Peirce defines the Legisign as a law that is also a sign. Its lawfulness is defined and determined by its users. The Legisign is a conventionalized sign. Peirce states that the Legisign is not a particular object that transmits an agreed-upon meaning, but rather a general type. Here, we are still within the Representamen part of the triadic sign. To give an example of the differences between Qualisign, Sinsign, and Legisign: the letter B can be interpreted as black strokes (Qualisign), as a successful example of a type in a composing room (Sinsign), or as a representative for the class we call 'the letter B' (Legisign). Thus the sign types give us a classification of cognition types in terms of signification forms.

The next trigonometry of signs relating to Secondness and the Object consists of the Icon, Index and Symbol. This trigonometry builds upon Representamen–Object relations, or how Secondness is expressed in the sign through the Icon, Index, and Symbol. Peirce (CP, 2.247) writes that the Icon is a sign 'which refers to the Object, that is, it denotes merely by virtue of characters of its own, and which it possesses, just the same, whether any such Object actually exists or not.'

The Icon is a sign that resembles the Object it represents. Common examples of Iconic Signs are photographs, since they resemble the Object (that is, the model) they depict. Thus a photograph is an Icon, although it is also sometimes an Index when the photograph has a causal relation to the Object it depicts. Maps and metaphors are also iconic. The receiver determines how exactly they are iconic.

Index encompasses a class constituted of signs that have a causal relation to the Objects they describe. The sign refers to the Object that it describes by virtue of the fact that the sign causes the Object, as smoke is an Index for fire. An Index sign thus stands for its Object by virtue of its direct causal reference to the Object, for example, as footsteps point to a person who has recently walked past.

A Symbol is a sign that refers to an Object that it denotes by virtue of law. Peirce clarifies this by stating that the law is an association of common ideas whereby the Symbol will be interpreted as pointing to the Object. Thus the Symbol is a sign that has meaning by virtue of rules and conventions. A 'conventionalized' sign has meaning that is agreed upon by a large number of users. Letters, words, and numbers are examples of Symbolic Signs.

The third trigonometry of signs consists of the Rheme, Dicent sign, and Argument, and describes the relation between the sign and the Interpretant/Thirdness. The Rheme is 'a Sign which, for its Interpretant, is a Sign of qualitative Possibility, that is, is understood as representing such and such a kind of possible Object. Any Rheme, perhaps, will afford some information; but it is not interpreted as doing so' (CP, 2.250).

Examples of Rhemes include nouns that refer to possible Objects. As Umberto Eco (1979) writes, signs are the prerequisites for lying, because the Object does not have to be present at the same moment as the Representamen and because they do not have to be materially real but can be fictional or mythical like the unicorn. So the Objects referred to are only possible objects.

Dicent Signs are signs of actual existence. For that reason the Dicent Sign cannot also be an Icon. The Icon does not provide an opportunity for interpretation. A Dicent Sign must contain a Rheme in order to describe the case to which it is interpreted as referring. One example of a Dicent Sign is a complete sentence.

The Argument represents its Object in its capacity as a sign – in other words, something is being stated about the sign. One example of an Argument is whole passages of text, in other words, meaningful links of Dicent Signs.

These are the combinations of the nine basic pure types of signs. The pure forms comprise only one aspect of the triadic sign. Living signs, however, are characterized by the quality of the connections between these.

6.5 The Ten Fundamental Sign Classes

It is interesting that Peirce – from the 3 x 3 types of signs – creates ten classes of signs and not twenty-seven (3 x 3 x 3). The ten classes result from the logical exclusion of classes, as already explained. For example, a Qualisign will always be a Rhematic Iconical Sign, and a Symbol will always be a Legisign, and an Argument will always be a Symbolic Legisign. Each of the ten classes of signs can be said to correspond to a distinct triadic relation between the categories of Firstness, Secondness, and Thirdness.

Figure 6.3 shows the organization of Peirce's ten basic classes of signs. Two classes separated by a thin line share two similarities. For example, Indexical Sinsigns (III, IV) can be either Iconic or Rhematic. Where the thick black line divides the classes, such as between II and VI, VI and IX, and III and VII, this is not the case. The classes have been given the most concise names possible to distinguish them. The names of the classes are in bold. Classes cannot share similarities if they do not share a border.

Distinguishing among sign classes is useful because some of these classes refer to Objects in ways that elucidate the informational strength of the index term. For instance, the Dicent Indexical Legisign contains more information about the Object it denotes than does the Rhematic Indexical Legisign. This is something I will return to later. First I will dwell on the characterization of the different sign types shown in Figure 6.3.

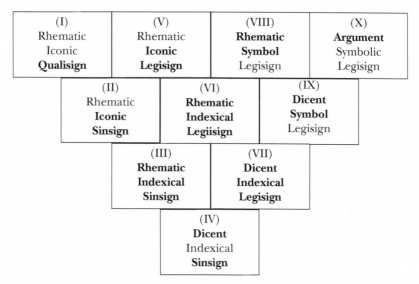

6.3. Peirce's ten basic classes of sign types (CP, 2.264)

(I) A Qualisign is any quality that is also a sign. Peirce defines the Qualisign as iconic because the quality can only denote an Object through some similarity. Furthermore, Peirce writes that the quality is a mere logical possibility – in other words, a Rheme. The Icon is a sign purely by likeness – thus it can only be interpreted as a sign of possible essence, in other words, as a Rheme embodying a Qualisign. This is the Rhematic, Iconic, Qualisign, such as a feeling of redness.

(II) Peirce defines the Sinsign as 'any object of experience in so far as some quality of it makes it determine the idea of an object' (CP, 2.255). Thus this is the Rhematic, Iconic, Sinsign – for example, a photograph or a diagram is a representation or likeness of an actually existing thing or event.

(III) Peirce defines the Rhematic Indexical Sinsign as 'any object of direct experience so far as it directs attention to an Object by which its presence is caused. It necessarily involves an Iconic Sinsign of a peculiar kind, yet is quite different since it brings the attention of the interpreter to the very Object denoted' (CP, 2.256). One example would be a spontaneous scream, as it directs attention to the screaming person.

(IV) Peirce states that the Dicent Indexical Sinsign can only offer information about actual fact: 'A Dicent Sinsign … is any object of direct experience, in so far as it is a sign, and, as such, affords information concerning its Object. This it can only do by being really affected by its Object' (CP, 2.257). As an example of a Dicent Sinsign, Peirce suggests a weathervane that provides information about the direction of the wind by being causally influenced by the wind. This is therefore also indexical in nature.

(V) Peirce defines a Rhematic Iconic Legisign as 'any general law or type, in so far as it requires each instance of it to embody a definite quality, which renders it fit to call up in the mind the idea of a like object. Being an Icon, it must be a Rheme. Being a Legisign, its mode of being is that of governing single Replicas, each of which will be an Iconic Sinsign of a peculiar kind' (CP, 2.258).

(VI) Peirce defines a Rhematic Indexical Legisign as any general type or law, however it might be established, that directs attention to an object (CP, 2.259). Peirce gives the example of a demonstrative pronoun. Its function is to stand for the noun it refers to. Thus, 'it' can stand for a 'car,' in reference to a previously mentioned car in the same text. 'It' alone offers no further information about the car: 'The Dicent Indexical Legisign is any general type or law, however established, and which requires each instance of it to be affected by its Object in such a manner as to furnish definite information concerning that Object' (CP, 2.260).

(VII) When discussing the Rhematic Indexical Legisign, we know nothing of the Object that the sign refers to. 'It' can refer to any thinkable noun without providing any additional information about the noun. But the Dicent Indexical Legisign offers information about its Object – here a street cry could be a cry for help, in which case the cry tells us that the 'crier' might be in danger: 'A Rhematic Symbol or Symbolic Rheme ... is a sign connected with its object by an association of general ideas such that its Replica calls up an image in the mind which image, owing to certain habits or dispositions of that mind, tends to produce a general concept, and the Replica is interpreted as a Sign of an Object that is an instance of that concept' (CP, 2.261).

(VIII) The difference between the Rhematic Indexical Legisign and the Rhematic Symbol is that the sign as a Rhematic Indexical Legisign denotes a specific object. Through an interpretation of the sign, the Rhematic Symbol can refer to a single class, which is an Object. Using the car example to illustrate the Rhematic Symbol, we can see that when reading about 'a car' without reference to a specific car, the idea of a car becomes a sign defined by a Rhematic Symbol.

(IX) About the Dicent Symbol, Peirce wrote 'A Dicent Symbol or ordinary Proposition, is a sign connected with its object by an association of general ideas, and acting like a Rhematic Symbol, except that its intended interpretant represents the Dicent Symbol as being, in respect to what it signifies, really affected by its Object, so that the existence or law which it calls to mind must be actually connected with the indicated Object' (CP, 2.262).

This is to say that the Interpretant denotes the Dicent Symbol as a Dicent Indexical Legisign. The difference between the two is that the Dicent Indexical Legisign offers information about a single case within a bigger class – that is, one must interpret the sign as belonging to a class of signs. This is not necessarily perceived by the Interpretant, who instead tends to see the Dicent Symbol as a Dicent Indexical Legisign, and consequently as referring to a certain Object.

(X) 'An Argument is a sign whose interpretant represents its object as being an ulterior sign through a law, namely, the law that the passage from all such premises to such conclusions tends to the truth. Manifestly, then, its object must be general; that is, the Argument must be a Symbol. As a Symbol it must, further, be a Legisign. Its Replica is a Dicent Sinsign' (CP, 2.263).

An Argument is a meaningful combination of sentences that form a text. An Argument will always be a Symbol because the meaning within the Object is conventionalized, and it will always be a Legisign because its meanings are determined through laws. Thus the tenth class is Argument, Symbol, Legisigns.

The ten classes of signs are Peirce's basic tools for characterizing and distinguishing among different qualities of signs. The classification table thus shows that:

I.   Qualisigns correspond to the relation of Firstness–Firstness–Firstness,

II.   Iconic Sinsigns correspond to the relation of Firstness–Firstness–Secondness,

III.   Rhematic Indexical Sinsigns correspond to the relation of Firstness–Secondness–Secondness,

IV.   Dicent Sinsigns correspond to the relation of Secondness–Secondness–Secondness,

V.   Iconic Legisigns correspond to the relation of Firstness–Firstness–Thirdness,

VI.   Rhematic Indexical Legisigns correspond to the relation of Firstness–Secondness–Thirdness,

VII.   Dicent Indexical Legisigns correspond to the relation of Secondness–Secondness–Thirdness,

VIII. Rhematic Symbols correspond to the relation of Firstness–
       Thirdness–Thirdness,
IX.   Dicent Symbols correspond to the relation of Secondness–
       Thirdness–Thirdness, and finally,
X.   Arguments correspond to the relation of Thirdness–Thirdness–
       Thirdness.

For Peirce, signs always consist of a primary sign (Representamen),
the object that is referred to (Object), and an interpreter (Interpretant)
who deciphers the sign in relation to the historical processes of life and
culture. The sign is a unit of the three. The Interpretant is not the interpreter; rather it is the sign formed in the mind of the individual interpreting a sign within a certain internal/external context. The Object is
not a Kantian object, a 'thing in itself,' but rather an aspect of that
reality which the Representamen brought into focus in the specific situation. So we find that semiosis is made out of signs, but Object might
refer to things! In other words, semiotics is a second-order theory compatible with second-order cybernetics. But unlike second-order cybernetics, Peirce never loses sight of reality. The dynamical object, in its
Secondness, is an inescapable part of the triadic semiosis.

The triadic sign is part of a network; thus the Representamen in one
sign triad can be the Object in the other if we are discussing the meaning
of an indexing term. The Interpretant can also become the Representamen for another triad. The user's understanding (Interpretant) of an
index term (Representamen) can be a Representamen for an LIS
researcher analysing the information retrieval (IR) processes in a particular system. The way a user utilizes a particular word can be a Representamen for the librarian to understand a system or a knowledge domain,
or both. Signs must be triadic, and they can only exist within a network
of sign relations: *the semiotic net.* This network of meanings is the alternative that the theory of signs offers to the knowledge-structure theory of
cognitive science. The act of human interpretation (the Interpretant)
can be considered a type of sign in itself, and it must then understand
itself through a 'semiotic web' of a culture and its knowledge domains.
Consider, for example, for how many thousands of years humanity has
attempted to interpret what the Representamen 'I' stands for.

6.6 The Usefulness of Peirce's Approach in LIS

This is all very abstract. Let us therefore consider its usefulness to LIS
in order to demonstrate what this conceptualization does to help us in

one sort of practice – one we have already introduced. According to the semiotic view, the interpreting process can never be completed, and neither can scientific knowledge that seeks 'the truth.' Peirce refers to this as unlimited semiosis. Signs are woven into meanings, which are linked to societal–cultural communicative praxis and history. Lexical denotations do not define the meaning of signs; these are defined by their use in social life, such as in a language game. Blair (1990, 137–8) points out the significance for LIS of this fundamental understanding of the signification processes:

> In terms of inquiry, the notion of unlimited Semiosis has important con-sequences for the representation of texts. First of all, there can be no nec-essary and sufficient (i.e., complete) representation of a text (other than the entire text itself and even this may not be sufficient for retrieval pur-poses ...). *Secondly, the standard to be used to judge the usefulness of a particular textual description is not that of 'correctness,' but one of 'appropriateness.'* In other words, a textual description is neither correct nor incorrect, but, rather, more or less appropriate for a given task and situation.

The compatibility between Blair's 'appropriateness' and Glasersfeld's 'viability' is obvious. Glasersfeld also thinks in terms of different tasks within society; this relates to the 'work task/interest' of Ingwersen (1996) and the domains of Hjørland and Albrechtsen (1995). The meaning of words is created through the cultural-historical background of language and through the social-communicative praxis among individuals, each of whom has a unique subjective historical access to the meanings of a sign. People are never in complete agreement about all the meanings of a word or concept, but through the development of customs they may reach an agreement on its meaning in situations experienced jointly. This is significant in various domains of science and the humanities, in which long traditions have fixed the meaning of specific concepts, and in the practice of law, which also has developed its own special terminology. The pragmatic-semiotic approach is important because it is these connections which constitute the individual's understanding and ability to:

1. decipher the document's signs,
2. decipher the document as a sign in itself, *and*
3. evaluate the relation and value of the sign in the actual situation.

As Blair (1990, 137) points out, one must base the organization of document-mediating systems on conventional uses of concepts:

In short, Peirce is pointing out that there can never be a necessary and sufficient explanation or description of the meaning of a sign/expression. In the sense of meaning which we have developed here, this means that there can never be a complete description of the kinds of allowable uses that can be made of a given expression. But this is not a despairing observation; in fact, it puts our analysis into a more thoughtful context. Instead of concerning ourselves with definitive uses of expressions, we can recognize this endless regression of meaning/signification and concentrate on elucidating conventional uses of expressions, realizing that new and creative uses of these expressions are inevitable ... What is important, then, is not just the uses of an expression, but the conventional uses of that expression in relation to some situation or task at hand.

Peirce is both a phenomenalist and a realist. His theoretical rhetoric is the science of how signs become effective in a constantly evolving historical and social context in which there are no final referents. Blair (1990, 169) draws the following conclusions for the understanding of indexing in LIS from this semiotic view of meaning:

In the first place, there is an unlimited number of unique documents which a single subject description can be used to represent. In the second place, there are an unlimited number of subject descriptions that reasonably could be applied to any one document. Traditional indexing theory, though aware of the ambiguity and inconsistency in the assignment of subject descriptions, has never demonstrated a full awareness of the magnitude of this problem, preferring to think of such difficulties as temporary aberrations rather than the first waves of a rising tide of difficulties.

This provides a theoretical understanding of the enormous practical problems that have faced classifiers and indexers for centuries. The ongoing evolution of signification poses a major difficulty for all document-mediating systems. Every classification system implicitly attempts to define the specific meanings of words, and after a few years this becomes a problem for all dynamic knowledge systems. It is essential for LIS to be able to adjust classification and indexing systems quickly to follow changes in the meanings of language, while at the same time keeping track of past records. Since these adjustments are semantic and related to social practice, we do not yet have a mechanical way to accomplish this. Ideally, any document database that uses words as classification and index terms should have its documents reindexed every five years to stay in accordance with the present meaning of the words. Furthermore, it would be ideal to have specific classifications and indices for different user groups with different interpretations of keywords, to account for their different educations, sciences, and practices. This is presently not economically feasible, nor is it possible to do it automatically.

Some would argue that Peirce's semiotics does not tell us much about texts and language. But as Blair notes, Peirce is in general agreement with Wittgenstein, who in Section 43 of his *Philosophical Investigations* (1958) says that 'for a *large* class of cases – though not for all – in which we employ the word 'meaning' it can be defined thus: the meaning of a word is its use in the language.' This suggests that the meaning of a word is equivalent to its use within a specific 'language game' within a 'life form' (*Lebensform*), as noted earlier. Language games, forms of life, and rule following shape the meaning of every word. It is a matter of what we do with our language in social practice. It is not something hidden inside anyone's mind or brain. Words, gestures, and expressions come alive only within a language game, a culture, a form of life. For example, if a picture means something, then its meaning is not an objective property of the picture in the way that its size and shape are: it means something to somebody. The same goes for any mental picture. Mankind lives in cultural communities or forms of life, which are self-sustaining, self-legitimating, and, in a way, logically and normatively final. (Actually, Wittgenstein also mentioned 'being a Lion' as a life form, when he was explaining why we would not be able to understand a lion if it could talk.)

Blair has attempted to integrate the crucial insights from Peirce's semiotics with Wittgenstein's pragmatic language philosophy in order to examine the problems of IR and LIS in a new light. He argues that the semantic socio-pragmatic basis for meaning is a fundamental aspect of Peirce's 'unlimited semiosis,' and he demonstrates how essential it is for LIS to realize that in order to comprehend a concept's meaning, indexers and classifiers must understand its use for a given producer, in a given specific knowledge domain and for a given user group. I suggest that this fundamental semiotic and socio-linguistic knowledge is the theoretical foundation behind the domain analysis of Hjørland and Albrechtsen (1995) as well as behind the cognitive viewpoint that employs concepts of 'about-ness.'

But it is not enough to understand the language game of the knowledge domain from which a document originates. One must also understand the language game of which the IR process is a part. One aspect of this is the knowledge domain from which the user comes, but just as important are the intentions and social expectations that users have of the system as determined by their own understandings of their tasks. Blair (1990, 158) writes:

> Various kinds of activities (Forms of Life) can serve as a context for the retrieval of subject material. Activities such as defending or prosecuting a lawsuit, patent searching, conducting research, making a business decision, etc., all may make use of subject searching at various times and at various levels of intensity. The nature of the activity being pursued influences subject searching in two important ways: In the first place, the language of the activity, its jargon or cant, will determine which words will be used to describe and ask for subjects. Some activities have or use information that breaks down readily into subject areas, such as academic disciplines (especially the 'harder' or more formal ones), while others have and use information that may not be as readily classifiable (think of activities that deal with new or innovative products or processes, such as new marketing, engineering or medical techniques, to name only a few). The other way in which the nature of an activity can influence retrieval is in determining the level of exhaustivity needed for satisfactory retrieval. Patent searching, the defense of a lawsuit, or searching to support original research all demand that the information retrieval which supports their activity be as exhaustive as possible. The activities of 'Just keeping informed,' browsing, or introducing oneself to a new field require less exhaustive searches to be conducted.

As we shall see, even more language games are actually in play in the IR process; this is already understood according to the cognitive perspective, with its multiple uses of the concept of 'about-ness' (Ingwersen 1992). In my view, the concept of a language game provides both a theoretical and a pragmatic framework for understanding about-ness and provides, as well, an important link between this idea and broader social-pragmatic theories of language and cognition that are of importance for LIS.

Language games are connected not only to the searches by users for documents, but also to the overall design and maintenance of the system and the intentions behind the production of documents. Figure 6.4 illustrates some of the language game systems involved in IR for a document-mediating system.

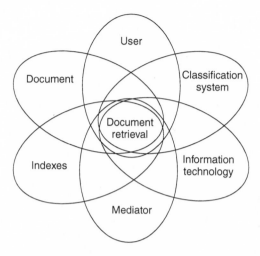

6.4.   The different language games involved in IR for a document-mediating system. A substantial number of the challenges facing LIS are not so much technical as socio-linguistic: How can concepts be made to communicate within and across different types of language games? The user has his own language game but must also handle documents with a language game of their own determined by their authors, ordered by the language game of a classification system, indexed according to the language game of the indexer, and searched for in the language game of the search language. If the user has someone to help, then this problem will be further interpreted through the language game of the mediator (often the librarian or documentalist).

In the sciences one deliberately attempts, within certain knowledge domains (such as those of professions, schools of thought, or other collective knowledge structures) to fix the meaning of key ideas through explicit definitions. Since science is complex and dynamic, such efforts never fully succeed; there is constant historical development. Studies of the communication patterns of professional knowledge domains (Gardin 1973; Hjørland and Albrechtsen 1995) have special relevance to information science and should be central to the research and practice of documentation precisely because the discourse communities of professional knowledge domains are always actively forming conventions for concepts used within their domains. Philosophy of science's analyses of paradigms and preparadigms of competing subgroups, and of how these change the meanings of concepts, can be a very important tool. For example, do the concepts of space and time mean different things in ordinary language, in classical Newtonian mechanics, and in general relativity physics. Sociological studies of communication patterns and of how concepts are used in various discourse communities become an important tool, as I will discuss further below. As Warner (1991, 18) writes: 'Recourse to the sociology of knowledge is justified by a recognition that the established domains of information science are social not natural. Information transactions typically involve interactions of individuals with individuals or with socially constructed information systems, within a social framework. Methodologies for investigation modeled on the physical sciences and technology, either by explicit derivation or as an accepted inheritance, are therefore radically misplaced, and have not been productive.'

Thomas Kuhn (1970), among others, demonstrated how scientific concepts and understandings of method are the results of the common praxis of the scientific community. It is not the individual, but rather the scientific group, that is the functional unit for the establishment of a professional specialized conception. Within any hermeneutic expression, the professional group forms a preunderstanding, which all of those who communicate with it must respect, and to which all information systems that handle its professional knowledge must adjust. It becomes the intermediary's (usually the librarian's) role to fuse these understandings into the domain-specific concepts of information systems, which are rarely quite up to date. The concept of a language game and the conventional meaning of a concept are obviously simplifications, since a user can participate in several language games simultaneously or shift among them. Furthermore, the borders separating language games are complex and dynamic, like family relations, as Wittgenstein suggested.

The librarian's task of mediating among different language games is a complicated one and is becoming increasingly so every year. Because the number of documents and users is growing exponentially, economic considerations are forcing us to seek automated solutions to these problems. It is crucial to research how to achieve the most productive integration between machine and human skills. But the economic requirement to use machines should not obscure the fact that the central challenges facing LIS often relate to the interface between socio-pragmatic linguistic processing that humans perform and the logic or algorithmic processing of sign vehicles that computers perform.

6.7 Indexing in Light of Semiotics

Indexing is vital for information storage and retrieval. The indexer allows a descriptor to represent something else – such as a document – so that it can be found by means of something else, on the basis that these entities in some respect share the same content or idea. This description parallels the description of the sign.

In order to understand these relations as signs, it is necessary to identify the sign relations between descriptors and documents and to recognize that the signs can alter sign categories – in other words, the sign alters nature according to the person who is interpreting it. While librarians already know this, Peirce's sign categories offer theory-based concepts to characterize these differences and thus to connect theory and practice in a systematic way.

I can now emphasize the insight that sign categories provide new methods for distinguishing among categories of indexing. Let us take a closer look at the relationship between the descriptor and the document.

When one assigns descriptors to a document in an IR system, these descriptors are chosen because the words (signs) describe the idea or content of the document in a way that makes document retrieval possible from a certain point of view. The descriptor becomes a sign – something that stands for something else – of the document or the class to which it refers. Here we can use Peirce's sign categories.

The Representamen of the descriptor cannot be a Qualisign, as this refers only to the pure qualities of the sign. The Sinsign refers to actual things and events, but we are here dealing with classes of similar objects, and therefore the Representamen of the descriptor can only be a Legisign. As previously discussed, the Legisign is characteristically conventionalized.[2] Descriptors are language, language is conventionalized, and thus descriptors must be Legisigns.

In relation to the Object, the descriptor cannot be an Icon. There is no resemblance between the Object and the Representamen. The descriptor does not figuratively resemble the idea to which it refers. The index term is not indexical, because it refers to a document without having any physical relationship to the Object. The descriptor is mostly symbolic, as the interpretation of the index term is based on social and cultural conventions.

Moving on to the Interpretant, the descriptor cannot be an Argument. The Argument is a meaningful connection of sentences that forms a text; and we cannot claim that the descriptor is a text. The descriptor is Rhematic in the sense that it provides a certain amount of information about its Object and necessarily requires an interpretation. The Rhemes presuppose a minimum of information in order to create an interpretation.

The descriptor can also be a Dicent Sign if the descriptor is itself meaningful and does not merely refer to its object. This means that a descriptor is a

Rhematic Indexical Legisign (VI), or
a Dicent Indexical Legisign (VII), or
a Rhematical Symbol (VIII), or
a Dicent Symbol (IX).

When the descriptor is a Rhematical Indexical Legisign, it directs the attention of the user to a number of documents without providing any information about their content. For example, the decimal classification code 14.8 refers to a group of documents, but for the layperson it offers no information about the content of the group.

If the users are librarians or indexers, then the decimal classification code 14.8 does provide information to the users by way of their professional knowledge, and hence they will be able to interpret the sign. For the librarian, this descriptor becomes a Dicent Indexical Legisign characterizing a group of documents in a regular, describable way. Thus the Dicent Indexical Legisign refers to the document by indication. The descriptor only provides the specific information to those who know what the descriptor is referring to. There is no information offered about the content of any individual document. The Peircean sign classes thus provide a theory for distinguishing these differences in interpretation.

To summarize, in most cases descriptors are Dicent Indexical Legisigns, because they provide information about a single object within a larger class. The indexer interprets the document as an example of the class under which the indexer classifies the document. The users interpret descriptors on the basis of their own semantic/semiotic webs, which are not necessarily equivalent to the semantic/semiotic web of the indexer.

It is interesting to note, however, that signs can alter sign categories according to the knowledge that users or indexers possess about the subject. When users have little knowledge of a particular classification code, the decimal classification code is changed from a Rhematic Indexical Legisign to a Dicent Indexical Legisign, whereas the opposite is true if the users, librarians, or indexers have specific knowledge about the classification code.

After expanding the discussion of the sign categories to include ordinary descriptors (and not merely classification codes), I believe that the most serious difficulties in indexing are here. It may be that a descriptor provides information to the user by referring to a class of documents containing similar ideas, but when the bibliographic base is intended to be generally accessible – for example via the Internet – then the descriptor as sign is detached from its context/discourse, which consists of the discourse within the document as well as the context of which the indexer is a part and in which he or she operates. In this way the sign is separated from its ground, allowing for diverse and conflicting interpretations – with vast consequences for the results of document seeking.

In the process of indexing, this is not apparent. Nevertheless, users must interpret the descriptor as a sign and use their own knowledge to interpret the sign, even though the idea anchored in the document will be lost. If, on the contrary, the users know both the descriptors and the discourse of which the documents form a part – here I have a knowledge domain in mind – then the descriptor will contain a greater information value and the sign reference will be clearer to the users. Problems may, of course, arise if the librarian has poor knowledge about the discourse in which the users' knowledge is anchored, and from which their questions derive.

In this rather abstract semiotic discussion of analysis and indexing, my hope has been to clarify and emphasize the fact that understanding the relation between the descriptor and the document is essential if we are to recognize what happens during indexing and retrieval. Through a semiotic discussion of this relationship, it is possible to describe the nature of descriptors from the users' level of knowledge. We have included the user in the descriptor–document relation. However, we have seen that there are also other semiotic webs involved in the user–descriptor–document relationship – namely, the semiotic webs of the indexers and the semiotic webs of the authors. If information retrieval is to succeed, these semiotic webs must approximate one another. How we can make these semiotic webs more identical in practice will be explored in the upcoming discussion of two concepts: *basic level* and *signification–effect level* from Lakoff's cognitive semantics. I will define the central concepts of cognitive semantics in the following chapter before I relate cognitive semantics to the challenges of indexing.

7 Cognitive Semantics: Embodied Metaphors, Basic Level, and Motivation

7.1 Cognitive Semantics

Cognitive semantics emanates from traditional cognition research and its vision of a scientific description of cognition across cultures, species, and machines. It is often accompanied by a belief that an algorithmic information processing program or module is found in both brain and machine, and that this will explain the cognitive act discussed earlier in this book. Lakoff (1987, xii) describes the objectivistic 'mind-as-computer paradigm' succinctly:

Among the more specific objectivist views are the following:

Thought is the mechanical manipulation of abstract symbols.

The mind is an abstract machine, manipulating symbols essentially in the way a computer does, that is, by algorithmic computation.

Symbols (e.g., words and mental representations) get their meaning via correspondences to things in the external world. All meaning is of this character.

Symbols that correspond to the external world are internal representations of external reality.

Abstract symbols may stand in correspondence to things in the world independent of the peculiar properties of any organisms.

Since the human mind makes use of internal representations of external reality, the mind is a mirror of nature, and correct reason mirrors the logic of the external world.

It is thus incidental to the nature of meaningful concepts and reason that human beings have the bodies they have and function in their environment in the way they do. Human bodies may play a role in choosing which concepts and which modes of transcendental reason human beings actually employ, but they play no essential role in characterizing what constitutes a concept and what constitutes reason.

Lakoff does not begin from a semiotic foundation; therefore his concept of the symbol is less specific than that of Peirce. But this does not negate the usefulness of his and Johnson's work on the role played by embodiment in categorization and conceptualization – or signification, as we would label it from a semiotic point of view. Lakoff (ibid., xiii) continues this description of the 'mind-as-computer paradigm':

> Thought is abstract and disembodied, since it is independent of any limitations of the human body, the human perceptual system, and the human nervous system.
> Machines that do no more than mechanically manipulate symbols that correspond to things in the world are capable of meaningful thought and reason.
> Thought is atomistic, in that it can be completely broken down into simple 'building blocks' – the symbols used in thought – which are combined into complexes and manipulated by rule.
> Thought is logical in the narrow technical sense used by philosophical logicians; that is, it can be modeled accurately by systems of the sort used in mathematical logic. These are abstract symbol systems defined by general principles of symbol manipulation and mechanisms for interpreting such symbols in terms of 'models of the world.'

This describes the strong 'logical form' in twentieth-century philosophy and linguistics that laid the foundation for artificial intelligence (AI). Lakoff, however, draws our attention to the fact that the entire field of cognitive research cannot be anchored in the paradigmatic theoretical background mentioned earlier if it is to express something profound with regard to the signification and communication of living systems. Nonetheless, it is the declared theoretical epistemological background for the majority of cognitive research and the development of AI and IR.

The crucial limitation of this paradigm is its more or less conscious basis in an unembodied rationalistic world view, one in which all thinking fits some natural kinds – be they transcendent Platonic ideas or Aristotelian forms – but in a seemingly mechanistic ontology, without really considering evolution. This view lacks any contribution from modern biology – especially ecology and evolution – that living beings manifest knowledge in autopoietic systems based on experiences with nature accumulated over billions of years. But Peirce, ethologists, and researchers of second-order cybernetics and autopoiesis theory embrace this biological perspective. In linguistics, Lakoff and Johnson have pioneered this biological perspective in cognitive semantics. Yet they have done so without drawing on knowledge and concepts from ethology, semiotics, or autopoiesis. I contend that these results can in fact be integrated with the broader foundation of cybersemiotics, as it is neither Cartesian nor focused on a pure or pan-information processing paradigm.

Lakoff (ibid., xiv) diverges from the mentioned mind-as-computer paradigm with his argument that reasoning, and therefore communication, is embodied and metaphorical and that it has ecological structures:

> Thought is embodied, that is, the structures used to put together our conceptual systems grow out of bodily experience and make sense in terms of it; moreover, the core of our conceptual systems is directly grounded in perception, body movement, and experience of a physical and social character.
>
> Thought is imaginative, in that those concepts that are not directly grounded in experience employ metaphor, metonymy, and mental imagery – all of which go beyond the literal mirroring, or representation, of external reality. It is this imaginative capacity that allows for 'abstract' thought and takes the mind beyond what we can see and feel. The imaginative capacity is also embodied – indirectly – since the metaphors, metonymies, and images are based on experience, often bodily experience. Thought is also imaginative in a less obvious way: every time we categorize something in a way that does not mirror nature, we are using general human imaginative capacities.

Clearly, Lakoff and Johnson view thinking as much more than logic cognition and as originating in the body's connotative and emotional experiences. Their work is well known, so I will mention only some of their central tenets to illustrate how their theory fits with the cybersemiotic perspective:

> Thought has gestalt properties and is thus not atomistic; concepts have an overall structure that goes beyond merely putting together conceptual 'building blocks' by general rules.
>
> Thought has an ecological structure. The efficiency of cognitive pro-

cessing, as in learning and memory, depends on the overall structure of the conceptual system and on what the concepts mean. Thought is thus more than just the mechanical manipulation of abstract symbols.

Conceptual structure can be described using cognitive models that have the above properties.

The theory of cognitive models incorporates what was right about the traditional view of categorization, meaning, and reason, while accounting for the empirical data on categorization and fitting the new view overall. (ibid., xv)

On this basis, embodied cognitive semantics makes a fundamental break with the objectivistic tradition.

Embodied cognitive semantics is a universal human epistemology, so it must also be applicable to classification and indexing, because these concepts express the self-understanding of humans and the place of humans in their world (Lakoff and Johnson 1980, 1999). Moreover, embodied cognitive semantics diverges from the idea that syntax is the staple and decisive level of meaning – as is assumed with the generative grammar of Chomsky (1994). Embodied cognitive semantics posits that the content of language results from cognitive problems, and that thus there is a general level where language, thought, and perception meet. It follows that language must be studied as a cognitive competence. Language is viewed as a privileged source for cognitive research because it displays those cognitive structures to which one has only introspective access.

A key concept in Lakoff's cognitive semantics is that of basic-level categorization, which adds a pragmatic aspect to embodied cognitive semantics. This is an important part of his embodiment concept, in which thinking is understood as based on our body's relations and experiences and as anchored in our self-understanding as biological beings. From a phenomenological point of view, it is interesting that embodiment is seen as both preconceptual and prelinguistic, and therefore as decisive to experience, reasoning, and the comprehension of categorization. Merleau-Ponty (2002) saw it the same way, albeit from a phenomenological life-world point of view. Let us explore the consequences of Lakoff's view and see how it works in LIS.

7.2 Basic-Level Categorization

When one assigns a descriptor to something, the descriptor is always assigned in relation to something else. This 'something else' is the relation created between the concepts and is a manifestation of what Lakoff refers to as a confluence of gestalt perception – the capacity for bodily movement and the ability to form rich mental images. In semiotics this is known as sign relations: the ability to relate one or more objects to a sign by creating a context. One conveys meaning from one structure (known as a descriptor) to another structure (such as a document) in order to create the connection – that is, the user's interpretation.

The image of mental space is often used to express the metaphor's ability to transfer meaning from one structure to another. Useful here is the concept of 'basic levelness' offered by Rosch and Lakoff (Lakoff 1987, 46). Rosch's basic-level categories are defined by the following:

The highest level at which category members have similarly perceived overall shapes.

The highest level at which a single mental image can reflect the entire category.

The highest level at which a person uses similar motor actions for interacting with category members.

The level at which subjects are fastest at identifying category members.

The level with the most commonly used labels for category members.

The first level named and understood by children.

The first level to enter the lexicon of a language.

The level with the shortest primary lexemes.

The level at which terms are used in neutral context. For example, there's a dog on the porch can be used in a neutral context, whereas special contexts are needed for there's a mammal on the porch or there's a wire-haired terrier on the porch.

The level at which most of our knowledge is organized.

The concepts of 'dog' and 'chair' fit the above-mentioned definition, whereas concepts such as 'mammal' and 'furniture' are more difficult to conceptualize because at this higher (superordinate) level they cannot create mental images that can integrate this superordinate level into one mental image. Instead, one chooses a piece of prototypical furniture, such as a chair, to represent the 'superordinate' level. Likewise, when a sign is able to represent a number of objects, or a number of documents, at the lower (subordinate) level, more specialized knowledge is required to form a mental image of, for example, a rocking chair. Svend Østergård (1997, 178) makes this observation clear: 'Suppose that I and another person see a vague shape appear in the horizon, and I am asked what I see. If I answer, "It is a dog," then it is clear that my answer puts brackets around the specific details of my perception. The empirical dog is still able to assume an infinity of concrete forms, but "dog" does not denote a single one of them, and yet the lexeme "dog" is released by the appearance of a concrete form' (my translation).

Peirce would say that the present dog is a token of the type *dog*. Østergård describes the basic-level concept in a clear and precise way, and furthermore he connects the basic-level concept with semiotics.

Once the dog, a dachshund for instance, is categorized by its race instead of its species, it is no longer a basic-level concept; it is a subordinate concept. Basic-level categorization calls for the interpreter's knowledge about the sign; without this knowledge, the concept 'dog' cannot exist as a basic-level concept in the life world of the interpreter.

Lakoff appropriates Rosch's concept of the basic level, but adds this: the fact that basic-level categorized objects have most natural attributes in common does not emanate from the categorized objects in themselves, but rather is a result of the categorization. To a large degree it is the human process of categorization – and not essential qualities – that determines these common qualities. Categorization is part of the cognitive mechanisms.

Rosch suggests that an understanding of the world is first acquired through a basic-level understanding and with the aid of 'additional processing.' It is as if one looks up a word in an internal thesaurus (sign structure) and then classifies the concepts within a context determined by one's intellectual level.

The way in which we interact with objects (chairs, tables, beds, and so on) is conditioned by the use of objects. Strictly speaking, we do not use a bed as a table or a chair as a bed. Each type of furniture prescribes a different sequence of body movements. Rosch (1978, 33) writes that 'when performing the action of sitting down on a chair, a sequence of body and muscle movements are typically made that are inseparable from the nature of the attributes of chairs – legs, seat, back etc.'

Rosch conducted experiments in which she asked a person to describe in detail which motor movements took place when the subject sat down in a chair. Rosch (ibid.) found that 'there are few motor programs we carry out to items of furniture in general and several specific motor programs carried out in regard to sitting down on chairs, but we sit on kitchen and living room chairs using essentially the same motor programs.'

This demonstrates that many common qualities do not emanate from categorized objects, but rather from the process of categorization itself. This is why, from the perspective of the body, we understand the surrounding world from a basic level; why interactions with objects also take place at the basic level; and why we transfer the motor movements between types of furniture within the same category. On this basis we can make a sound argument that basic-level categorization permeates how we act in relation to our life world, both bodily and intellectually.

If our understanding, and thus our categorization, of the surrounding world occurs at the basic level, then the language by which we 'arrange' the world must also emanate from the basic level. It follows that this categorization will be expressed through our communication with the surrounding world. Lakoff stresses that the basic level is the level first understood and used by children; furthermore, this is the level where they begin to learn a language. Lakoff (1987, 47) summarizes basic-level categories as being characterized by the following:

1. Perception: Overall perceived shape; single mental image; fast identification.
2. Function: General motor program.
3. Communication: Shortest, most commonly used and contextually neutral words first learned by children and first to enter the lexicon.
4. Knowledge Organization: Most attributes of category members are stored at this level.

Applying the basic-level category, Lakoff and Rosch illustrate how the relations of concepts are experienced at the level from which we conceptualize the world during the usual course of living. I propose the following hypothesis: since the user of library systems normally experiences, arranges, and organizes the world from the basic level, the indexing of documents must also be done from the basic level, because indexing is a way to categorize and classify 'the world.' Semiotically speaking, indexing allows something to represent something else. The indexer must therefore index with the basic-level understanding of potential users in mind.

Lakoff makes another interesting observation. All human beings are equipped with the same cognitive apparatus and are grounded in the same embodiment, but the surrounding world determines the basic level because those surroundings determine what a culture defines as basic. A fisherman has a different understanding of what is the basic level than a farmer. Researchers from different knowledge domains have different basic-level understandings of the same concepts. Thus even the concept of 'information' is used and understood differently across knowledge domains, such as the humanities and the natural sciences. Within the same knowledge domain there can also be differences in understanding the same concept. We might call these different 'dialects.' Intentionality is cognitively tied to a life world, not just to the context of the concept within a knowledge domain. Intentionality also forms part of the knowledge domain into which the concept is woven and from which it derives meaning.

During her research, Rosch introduced the concept 'prototype effect' to explain how some members of a class, such as animals, are more typical for their class than others. The blackbird is more prototypical for the class of birds than the ostrich or the penguin. Rosch, however, quickly abandons the idea that categories are organized from a prototype from which other elements in the class derive. According to Rosch and Lakoff, prototype effect is not a basic quality of categories, but rather a consequence of the fact that language is built on mixed and not necessarily uniform life experiences. Prototypicality is thus itself a sign of categorization.

7.3 Kinaesthetic Image-Schemas

The second part of the embodiment concept is the theory about kinaesthetic image-schemas. Kinaesthetic image-schemas should be understood as gestalt schemas through which one perceives the world as defined via basic-level categories, and perceives how one subsequently acts in this life world. Basic-level concepts are grounded in embodiment; kinaesthetic image-schemas are understood bodily and transferred through metaphors, metonymies, and radial structures. Lakoff's cognitive semantics takes a powerful biological turn once he introduces kinaesthetic image-schemas: 'Kinesthetic image-schematic structure: Image schemas are relatively simple structures that constantly recur in our everyday bodily experience: CONTAINER-PATHS, LINKS, FORCES, BALANCE, and in various orientations and relations: UP-DOWN, FRONT-BACK, PART-WHOLE, CENTER-PERIPHERY, etc.' (1987, 267).

Kinaesthetic image-schemas serve as preconceptual archetypes. They can be used to comprehend complicated and not fully understood phenomenological occurrences. They are most often of a spatial nature. We understand the phenomenological world in the way we bodily move around in it, and we use kinaesthetic image-schemas to systematize and categorize the world into basic-level objects.

From a semiotic point of view we can then say that kinaesthetic image-schemas are the tool that our intellectual ability uses to understand the connection between sign and object. They constitute the basic mechanism by which we create our Interpretants. Thereafter this mechanism is able to transfer meaning through the concept of metaphor, metonymy, and radial structures, all of which are mediators of kinaesthetic image-schemas.

7.4 Metaphors, Metonymy, and Radial Structures

According to the ordinary use and comprehension of the concept of metaphor, it is a word with no direct relationship to basic-level representations in reality. The connection between the sign and reality is conventionalized. A white pigeon is a metaphorical expression for peace, even though pigeons are known to fight among themselves.

Lakoff understands metaphor as a central tool for thought. Thinking projects structures from one mental space into another. Metaphors are preformed thoughts and can later be read into language. This is central to how thinking works.

The mental space that Lakoff hypothesizes is the ability to metaphorize – that is, to transfer a perceived phenomenological world into one's cognitive structures through kinaesthetic image-schemas. The metaphor is no longer just an expression of poetic fantasy or pure stylistics; it is a cognitive activity of great importance. It is essential to understand this new function, because metaphor transfers what we sense and recreates it according to our individual semiotic web. We understand and conceptualize the world through the mediation of kinaesthetic image-schemas between the world and the embodied self, and within the aforementioned mental space via metaphors, metonymies, and radial structures. This also applies when we classify, index, and search for information in databases. Semiotically, all of this tells us how the symbolic function came into existence.

Like metaphor, metonymy possesses a mediating quality that transfers meaning from a part to a whole, thus allowing us to recognize the part in the whole and the whole in the part. The transfer takes place within that cognitive activity which identifies the metonymy as what semiotics calls an indexical sign. The metonymy as a sign contains symbolical, iconical, and indexical qualities. Lakoff emphasizes that the metaphor is also able to transfer parts of structures from one mental image to another. With this in mind, it would seem reasonable to draw an analogy to Peirce's semiotics, but Lakoff is not inclined to do this.

Lakoff discusses a third important transfer structure: the radial structure based on both metaphorical and metonymical qualities. According to Lakoff (1987, 84), a radial structure is 'one where there is a central case and conventionalized variations on it which cannot be predicted by general rules.'

Radial structures contain ideal members of the category only in the centre. Other members can be identified only through social rules, conventions, and metaphorical and metonymical motivations. This means that radial structures are conventionalized and must be learned: they are cultural phenomena. One typical example of a radial structure is the 'mother' concept. Lakoff (ibid., 83) describes the central, ideal content in this structure as follows: 'The central case, where all the models converge, includes a mother who is and always has been female, and who gave birth to her child, is married to the father, is one generation older than the child, and is the child's legal guardian.'

Lakoff provides a multitude of degrees of motherhood: stepmother, adoptive mother, birth mother, natural mother, unwed mother, and so on – all of whom diverge from this ideal content but are mother types nonetheless. The presence of well-defined subgroups makes the concept of 'mother' a radial structure. Lakoff, however, points out that not all possible variations exist as categories: 'There is no category of mothers who are legal guardians but who don't personally supply nurturance, but hire someone else to do it. There is no category of transsexuals who gave birth but have since had a sex-change operation' (ibid.).

The synthesis between basic-level categories and kinaesthetic image-schemas is Lakoff's fundamental tool for mediating between language and reality. Lakoff refers to such synthesis as idealized cognitive models (ICMs), which share qualities with Peirce's ground and the innate release response mechanism (IRM). Ethologists posit that the latter determine meaningful conceptions linked to essential biological life forms, such as hunting and mating. I see it this way: part of our inner world consists of the entanglement of all the ICMs that define us as individuals. Behind these are the biopsychological IRMs and the drives and emotions connected to them. After developing his theory of classes of sign type, Peirce did not use the concept 'ground' very often, as the class specifies the aspect of semiosis alluded to through the concept of ground.

7.5 Idealized Cognitive Models

By lived human context is meant the practical social context through which concepts are defined and from which they gain their meanings. The encounter between these contexts defines meaning as it is experienced. Semiotically, this means that one meets the world in terms of the premises outlined by Secondness and in accordance with how one's semiotic web is biologically, psychologically, and culturally structured. I will return later to how these levels can be described when they are combined with Luhmann's autopoiesis theory.

With respect to understanding and categorizing concepts, this suggests that people differ in their understandings of them because they use concepts in multiple ways depending on their situational perception, intentions, and motivations. Still, I believe that in a defined culture there is an intersubjective understanding of concepts that controls the development of the meanings people assign. This ensures that cognitive semantics and pragmatic semiotics do not become purely mentalist theories. Nevertheless, no two individuals ever understand the same concept in exactly the same way in all its applications.

The individual defines and understands symbols by knowing the appropriate ICM. The ICM concept is determined by culture and embodiment. Lakoff's arch-example of an ICM is the understanding of the concept 'bachelor.' One cannot answer the question of whether the Pope is a bachelor because the concept bachelor 'is defined with respect to an ICM in which there is a human society with (typically monogamous) marriage, and a typical marriageable age. The idealized model says nothing about the existence of priests, "long-term unmarried couplings," homosexuality, Moslems who are permitted four wives and only have three' (ibid., 70).

The bachelor concept is especially relevant to women looking for a suitable mate with whom to start a family. Biological sexual and procreative urges play an important role in the motivational drive of the bachelor ICM. Until some decades ago, after a man went through puberty, was able to mate, and then received an education in order to obtain a steady job with an income that could provide for a family, he was expected to marry and have children. When a man entered this period in his life – this combined biological and cultural state – and had not yet married he was a bachelor. Since these social expectations do not apply to the Pope, he cannot be a bachelor. The bachelor ICM must motivate the use of the category of bachelor.

Lakoff states that the ICM structure is a gestalt that cannot be broken down into smaller meaningful components without losing its wholeness. The idea of wholeness is important for understanding the complexity of ICM situation philosophy. The situations are not identical but are variations on a theme; the theme is the ICM and the variations are different cognitive structures derived from the ICM. Since we are discussing variations that share similarities with the theme, we can recognize the situations and thereby register them as variations on the theme.

As we consider theme variations, it seems that the ICM does not always fit precisely with reality. Its background assumptions are oversimplified. Nevertheless, one immediately knows what is meant when the topic is a bachelor. The meaning is created in the encounter between two contexts: the preunderstanding of the concept, and the context of which the concept is a part.

This is analogous to Peirce's sign. The sentence is a sign with three relations: the concept or sign (the word bachelor), the imagined object (that is suspected to fall into the category), and an Interpretant that interprets the sign as a quality of the Object. One must know the Object before a relation between sign and Object can be created through the Interpretant. Otherwise there is no logical relation. This is underlined in one of Peirce's last definitions of the sign relation from 1910 (MS 654, 8): 'By a sign I mean anything whatever, real or fictive, which is capable of a sensible form, is applicable to something other than itself, that is already known, and is capable of being so interpreted in another sign which I call its Interpretant as to communicate something that may not have been previously known about its object. There is thus a triadic relation between any Sign, and Object and an Interpretant.'

I mentioned earlier that it is possible for more than one ICM to function at the same time. Lakoff referred to this as 'cluster models.' These are complex models that combine a string of individual cognitive models to form a cluster. In the cluster there is no central model in which the radials form subcategories.

It is important to be aware that a concept can be defined through many ICMs. This is analogous to Peirce's semiotic web and the unlimited semiosis in which signs create meaning and constantly change. The semiotic web develops continuously and there is no final answer to the meaning of concepts.

7.6 The Concept of Motivation in the Theory of Embodied Cognitive Semantics

In cognitive semantics, especially in Lakoff and Johnson's work, there is an understanding that semantics is based on embodied metaphors. Lakoff (1987, xi) elucidates how this new research program in cognitive semantics diverges from past thinking:

> The traditional account claims that the capacity for meaningful thought and for reason is abstract and not necessarily embodied in any organism. Thus, meaningful concepts and rationality are transcendental, in the sense that they transcend, or go beyond, the physical limitations of any organism. Meaningful concepts and abstract reason may happen to be embodied in human beings, or in machines, or in other organisms – but they exist abstractly, independent of any particular embodiment. In the new view, meaning is a matter of what is meaningful to thinking, functioning beings. The nature of the thinking organism and the way it functions in its environment are of central concern to the study of reason.

This is highly applicable to the biosemiotic approach. Lakoff and Johnson ground cognitive functions in the embodiment of words, concepts, and categories because they believe that most of our thinking – including our choice of concepts in spoken language – is unconscious. Their theory agrees with phenomenology. But contrary to Husserl,[1] they believe that our perception and choice of categorical concepts and metaphors for understanding a sign are driven by a combination of our bodily structure of perception and cultural classifications – as, for instance, with colour classification:

> The Kay-McDaniel theory has important consequences for human categorization in general. It claims that colors are not objectively 'out there in the world' independent of any beings. Color concepts are *embodied* in that focal colors are partly determined by human biology. Color categorization makes use of <u>human biology</u>, but color categories are more than merely a consequence of the nature of the world plus human biology. Color categories result from the world plus human biology plus a cognitive mecha-

nism that has some of the characteristics of fuzzy set theory plus a culture-specific choice of which basic color categories there are. (ibid., 29)

Lakoff then demonstrates that our way of perceiving a situation is determined by how we unconsciously categorize events or things in that situation. A blend of biological propensities, social conventions, and expectations has become unconscious in our daily thinking.

The ICMs are often a product of social expectations that determine the framework and language game within which the concept acquires meaning. But ICMs are based on embodiment, and – as a consequence – on instinctive forms of motivation. From an evolutionary perspective it seems obvious to connect the two kinds of motivation and to posit that embodied linguistic metaphorical motivation is based in part on the motivational processes developed in the living system through the process of evolution. These are foundational to the capacity of living systems to create signification. Lakoff (ibid., 291) ties language and cognition together in a way I can only describe as semiotic:

> In summary, linguistic expressions get their meanings via (a) being associated directly with ICMs and (b) having the elements of the ICMs either be directly understood in terms of preconceptual structures in experience, or indirectly understood in terms of directly understood concepts plus structural relations.
>
> Language is thus based on cognition. The structure of language uses the same devices used to structure cognitive models–image schemas, which are understood in terms of bodily functioning. Language is made meaningful because it is directly tied to meaningful thought and depends upon the nature of thought. Thought is made meaningful via two direct connections to preconceptual bodily functioning, which is in turn highly constrained, but by no means totally constrained, by the nature of the world that we function within.

From a semiotic perspective, Lakoff is saying that cognition is semiosis. He further argues that the biological body plays a significant role in the conceptualization of object and event in the environment of the living system. One of the key claims made by biosemiotics is that semiosis is basic to the way living systems function, and that it is through the creation of Interpretants that the perceptual world of the organism is constructed. Living systems live in spheres of signification, as I call them. I will later analyse this phenomenon in detail.

Lakoff (ibid., 267–8) summarizes his and Johnson's experiential theory of embodied categorization:

> There are at least two kinds of structure in our preconceptual experiences:
> A. Basic-level structure: Basic-level categories are defined by the convergence of our gestalt perception, our capacity for bodily movement, and our ability to form rich mental images.
> B. Kinesthetic image-schematic structure: Image schemas are relatively simple structures that constantly recur in our everyday bodily experience: CONTAINERS, PATHS, LINKS, FORCES, BALANCE, and in various orientations and relations: UP-DOWN, FRONT-BACK, PART-WHOLE, CENTER-PERIPHERY, etc.
> These structures are directly meaningful, first, because they are directly and repeatedly experienced because of the nature of the body and its mode of functioning in our environment ...
> 2. There are two ways in which abstract conceptual structure arises from basic-level and image-schematic structure:
> A. By metaphorical projection from the domain of the physical to abstract domains.
> B. By the projection from basic-level categories to superordinate and subordinate categories.

Lakoff and Johnson[2] extend the metaphorical and metonymical motivations so as to depend on the (usually) unconscious ICMs that are based on embodiment. This is where I insert ethological knowledge of motivation into a biosemiotic interpretation. One of the basic theoretical claims of Lakoff and Johnson's work (Lakoff 1987; Lakoff and Johnson 1999) is that *the use of metaphors is neither logical nor possibilistic, but motivated*:

> We will describe the extensions of a central model as being *motivated* by the central model plus certain general principles of extension. Much of the rest of this volume will be concerned with the concept of *motivation* and with the kinds of general principles of extension that govern the structure of radial categories ...
>   Of these principles, motivation is perhaps the least obvious and is worth some discussion. There is a big difference between giving principles that *motivate*, or *make sense* of, a system, and giving principles that *generate*, or *predict*, the system ...
> Finally, the fact that extensions from the center of categories are neither

predictable nor arbitrary, but instead are motivated, demonstrates the ecological character of the human mind. I am using the term 'ecological' in
the sense of a system with an overall structure, where effects cannot be
localized – that is, where something in one part of the system affects things
elsewhere in the system. Motivation depends on overall characteristics of
the conceptual system, not just local characteristics of the category at
hand. (Lakoff 1987, 91–113)

It is remarkable how close to biological thinking – especially to ethological thinking – Lakoff (1987) and Lakoff and Johnson (1999)
approach without ever using the models developed in ethology. When I
first read their work on embodied categorization, on how central motivation is contained in the structures of categorical classes, and on how
categorization is used metaphorically in other domains, I immediately
thought in ethological terms.

I later realized that their use of the concept of motivation was purely
linguistic. In linguistics and semiotics many types of motivation are
accepted, as with different types of iconicity. Phonetic motivation (ono-
matopoeia) is one type of motivation; it contradicts claims of arbitrariness between phonetic sounds and the meanings of words. Semantic
motivation occurs in figurative language, especially with metaphors and
metonymies whose motivational basis is similarity and contiguity. Basically they are – from a semiotic perspective – based on the function of
iconicity. See Figure 7.1 for an illustration.

From an evolutionary perspective, it seems obvious that there are
connections among the linguistic use of motivation in categorization,
the use of metaphors, and the ethological use of motivation in cognitive
behavioural science. This helps explain how animals selectively react to
those parts of their environment we refer to as sign stimuli.

Based on ethology and biosemiotics, I contend that our cognition
manifests itself as embodied semiosis motivated by biological, psychological, and social interests, which are powerful generators of structure
and meaning in our spheres of signification. Most animal behaviour is
considered to be unconscious – like our linguistic categorizations and
uses of metaphors. Still, ethologists have realized that motivation is not
a physiological concept (Hinde 1970). In cybersemiotics, concepts are
now understood – owing to the inspiration of Maturana and Varela's
autopoiesis theory (1980) and von Uexküll's *Umweltlehre* (1957) – as
arising in a space of interaction for semiotic processes occurring in the

ICONS		

Images	Diagrams	Metaphors
Photographic or sound picture similarity.	Symbolic representations of rationally related objects. Types are materially manifested as tokens of representation.	Mapping signs or concepts from one area of experience or knowledge domain to another that is often more abstract.

7.1.   Iconicity functions mostly through three channels: images, diagrams, and metaphors. There is iconic content in all symbols. As such, iconicity is a strong semiotic type of motivation.

living system as it perceives, orients towards, and reacts to 'objects' in its environment. As this is one of the most important bases of ethology, I will give a short exposition of the ethological model of signification, cognition, and motivation and illustrate how, through second-order cybernetics, autopoiesis theory, and von Uexküll's phenomenological biology, it can be integrated into biosemiotics.

8 The Cybersemiotic Integration of *Umweltlehre,* Ethology, Autopoiesis Theory, Second-Order Cybernetics, and Peircean Biosemiotics

8.1 The Mechanistic Quest for Basic Order

If we return to the roots of natural philosophy and science, we find that both the Greek natural philosophers and the founding fathers of classical (mechanistic) physics assumed that the world was based on either transcendental or immanent natural laws of a mathematical form comprehensible by the human mind. Both Plato and Aristotle assumed that the logical-mathematical structure of the world was also the basis of human reason (*nous*), and that it explained the epistemological mystery of how humans could acquire true knowledge of the world through either reason alone or a combination of perception and reason. Still, Aristotle had a hylozoic conception of matter as a continuum, the inside of which was filled with life and mind-like qualities. Aristotle believed that things moved towards their 'natural place,' and that the movement and growth of animate things – such as a seed growing into a tree – tended to fulfil the form immanent within them. Everything attempted to find and fill its place in the divine order.[1]

During the Renaissance, Galileo believed that through scientific inquiry the human mind could contemplate God's mathematical laws of the universe. Later, Descartes believed that animal and human bodies were mechanical systems, but that only human rational minds were imbued with divine ideas – similar to Plato's view. Descartes thus declared that the animate world and its systems – such as human bodies – were non-intentional machines and for that reason were open to Galileo's vision. This rationalistic thought flourished in France; meanwhile, in England, empiricists argued that only sensory experience could lead to true knowledge, although the mind was nevertheless imbued with a universal rationality founded in classical logic. Newton's system convinced most scientists that all movements could be sufficiently explained by a mechanistic framework; this was combined with the claims of Descartes and the Catholic Church that animals do not have souls. The pursuit of a mechanistic model of animal behaviour and cognition became the dominant research program in comparative psychology and behaviourism (Jaynes 1969). Modern epistemology and philosophy of science began when Kant (1990) abandoned the idea of absolute truth in science and instead united empiricism and rationalism by arguing that space, time, and the twelve categories of perception and thinking – such as causality, reality, negation, and necessity – were the innate tools of cognition. Kant also argued that we always work with the thing as we see it. We can never reach the thing in itself. He perceived that living systems are self-organizing systems, yet he never integrated this with his own epistemology. But Konrad Lorenz did.

8.2 The Biological-Evolutionary View of the Roots of Cognition

In 1941, Konrad Lorenz – the father of ethology – posited that if humans utilized Kantian categories of perception and thinking, then they must have developed them through evolution as a part of their system of survival (1970–1). In this way, evolutionary epistemology was born. The belief that perceptual categories developed through the evolution of living systems is today influencing epistemological discussions of the human ability to distinguish 'natural kinds' (Bird 1998). It is not possible to prove directly that the world is actually partitioned as we perceive it. But from an evolutionary perspective, one can argue that a certain realism pertains to the perceptual apparatus, since this is a product of natural selection within a shared environment. As previously discussed, Lorenz's use of evolutionary biological epistemology was hampered by his inability to formulate a theoretical foundation that could encompass both phenomenological and emotional aspects of living systems. Also, he was caught up in a Descartian dualism. It is interesting that Lorenz was influenced early on by Jakob von Uexküll but later abandoned many of his views. In this, perhaps, is the key that connects ethology with a broader Peircean semiotic framework? Sebeok attempted to forge this link through his biosemiotic reconceptualization of von Uexküll (Sebeok 1972, 1989).

Lorenz[2] mentions von Uexküll's *Umwelt* in 'The Companions as Factors in the Bird's Environment' (1935), in which he emphasizes his use of the concept. His more historical paper, 'Methods of Approach to the Problems of Behavior' (1958) describes the influence of von Uexküll on the ethological paradigm. Here Lorenz devotes a section to von Uexküll, despite calling him a 'dyed-in-the-wool vitalist.' But Lorenz also admits that notwithstanding their philosophical disagreements, von Uexküll was one of his most important teachers. He writes (1970–1, 274) that the one

> who first consciously applied that method of 'analysis on a broad front': Jakob von Uexküll, whom, in spite of fundamental philosophical dissension, I regard as one of my most important teachers. The point of departure, in all his investigations, is a complex of observational, empirical facts representing a *system* in which the organism and its environment are found to stand in a relationship of multiple, mutual interactions. Analysis invariably has to begin with the question: Which, among the many data of environment, are the ones that, on the one hand, have a releasing effect on certain behavior patterns of the animal and are, on the other hand, influenced and changed, by the activity thus released, in such a manner that their change has, in its turn, a repercussion on the organism's response?

There is no doubt that von Uexküll exerted great influence over the development of early ethology, especially before the Second World War. But how did Lorenz use von Uexküll's theories when they differed so greatly from his own philosophical outlook? This quotation from 'The Companion as Factor in the Bird's Environment,' which is dedicated to von Uexküll, points to Lorenz's preoccupation with von Uexküll's concept of object:

> The concept of an *object* in our environment arises from a process of compilation of stimuli emanating from one given thing, by means of which we relate the assembled stimuli to that particular source of stimulation (the 'thing'). This also involves projection of the perceived stimuli outwards into the space surrounding us, in order to localize the object. The image of the sun formed on the retina of the human eye by the lens is not perceived simply as 'light' in the same way that we perceive the image of the sun projected onto our skin with a magnifying glass as 'heat.' We in fact *see* the sun up in the sky, a long way from our bodies. This localization effect is a product of our perceptive mechanism and not an achievement dependent upon some conscious process.

Thus, in the realization of the presence of objects in our environment, we are dependent upon those senses whose perceptive mechanisms permit us to localize things in the surrounding *space*. It is only in this way that we are able to recognize the inherent spatial correspondence of the individual stimuli, which defines the concrete unity of the object and which provides the basis for Uexküll's simple definition of an object: 'An object is that which moves as a unitary whole.' (1970–1, 101)

Already Lorenz is twisting von Uexküll. One of von Uexküll's major claims regarding the ability of sensory organs to project images into space was that this clearly illustrated that their function was not mechanical. This fundamental point is underlined in many of von Uexküll's writings. The subjectivity of the objects in the *Umwelt* relates to 'real' objects, but these are never their entire reality:

There are, then, purely subjective realities in the *Umwelten*; and even the things that exist objectively in the environment never appear there as their objective selves. They are always transformed into perceptual cues or perceptual images and invested with a functional tone. This alone makes them into real objects, although no element of the functional tone is actually present in the stimuli.

And finally, the simple functional cycle teaches us that both receptor and effector cues are the subject's manifestations, and that the qualities of objects included in the functional cycle can be regarded as their bearers only. Thus we ultimately reach the conclusion that each subject lives in a world composed of subjective realities alone, and that even the *Umwelten* themselves represent only subjective realities.

Whoever denies the existence of subjective realities, has failed to recognize the foundations of his own Umwelt. (Von Uexküll 1957, 72)

Here one is reminded of Peirce's differentiation between the immediate object and the dynamical object. Lorenz transforms von Uexküll's concept of 'tone' into his own concept of 'motivation.' Both these concepts fit well into Peirce's early semiotic concept of 'ground,' which highlights his interest in a perception wherein only specific features of an object are singled out by the Interpretant. The varieties of their function was later described through the concept of sign types.

Reading Lorenz's papers, one has the impression that Oscar Heinroth (1871–1945) was Lorenz's most important predecessor. But when one reads von Uexküll's books, it becomes clear that he is as important a founder of ethology as Heinroth, albeit perhaps only on the conceptual side. About von Uexküll's work, Lorenz (1970–71, 275–6) does admit in 'The Methods of Approach to the Problems of Behaviour' (1958) that 'the research program mapped out in Uexküll's work is pretty nearly identical with that of ethology, very many of the provisional, more or less operational concepts of part functions are the same, even if semantics are different ... Although the starting point and frame of reference for all his considerations always was the animal as *subject*, the method of his research was objectivistic to the extreme.'

Von Uexküll's *Umwelt* concept had a major impact on Lorenz's development of the ethological model of animal cognition and behaviour and on the evolutionary epistemology that stemmed from it (see, for instance, Franck 1999). Like von Uexküll, Lorenz wanted to avoid both mechanicism and vitalism. To contend that animals are subjects is, in my opinion, not sufficient to label von Uexküll a vitalist, as many have done. Judging from his other writings, he is the biological version of a Platonic idealist. About the subjectivity of animals, von Uexküll (1957, 6) wrote:

> Now we might assume that an animal is nothing but a collection of perceptual and effector tools, connected by an integrating apparatus which, though still a mechanism, is yet fit to carry on the life functions. This is indeed the position of all mechanistic theorists, whether their analogies are in terms of rigid mechanics or more plastic dynamics. They brand animals as mere objects. The proponents of such theories forget that, from the first, they have overlooked the most important thing, the subject which uses the tools, perceives and functions with their aid.

Like von Uexküll, Lorenz realized that animals are sentient beings; however, he did not want to use souls or spiritual powers as explanatory principles. Thus he was forced to develop a behavioural and physiological model of the inner world of animals. His investigations of jackdaws – which he shared with von Uexküll – clearly demonstrated that animals have species-specific conceptions of their surroundings and that they are divided according to their functionalities and motivations. He was inspired by von Uexküll's *Funktionskreis* (functional circle). This is how von Uexküll himself (1957, 10–11) described this concept:

> The object participates in the action only to the extent that it must possess certain qualities that can serve as perceptual cue-bearers on the one hand

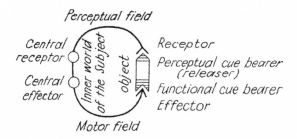

8.1. Von Uexküll's functional circle [Fig. 3]

and as functional cue-bearers on the other; and these must be linked by connecting counterstructure. The relations between subject and object are best shown by the diagram of the functional cycle (Fig. 3 [8.1]). This illustrates how the subject and the object are dovetailed into one another to constitute a systematic whole. If we further consider that a subject is related to the same or to different objects by several functional cycles, we shall gain insight into the first principle of *Umwelt* theory: all animals, from the simplest to the most complex, are fitted into their unique worlds with equal completeness. A simple world corresponds to a simple animal, a well-articulated world to a complex one.

Von Uexküll introduced a profound cybernetic view of perception and cognition, similar to the ideas generated by Bateson, Maturana and Varela, and von Foerster. One reason I call my framework 'cybersemiotics' is that cybernetic researchers have made important progress on these ideas that must be incorporated into modern biosemiotics. Lorenz departed most strongly from von Uexküll in his rejection of evolutionary theory. Von Uexküll contended that all organisms are equally well adapted, based on a pre-existing, pre-established *Bauplan* (blueprint) of organic and environmental structures and functions. These preformational views – which coincide with Leibniz' monadology – and von Uexküll's rejection of any extrasubjective reality outside the *Umwelten* of living systems led Lorenz to disassociate himself from these theories. Today, Maturana and Varela's autopoiesis theory takes the same monadological perspective founded on an evolutionary basis; thus it denies the existence of a universe and promotes the theory of a Multiverse.

Lorenz posits that the functional circle must accept the existence of something external to the *Umwelt* that makes the sign within the *Umwelt* possible. He offers the now famous example from Uexküll of the *Umwelt* of the tick that presumes coordination with an external world of another species, even though the effector cues can be artificially created. However, Lorenz (1970–1, 277) admitted that 'ethology, this young science, certainly owes more to his teaching than any other school of behavioral study,' and he was the first to demonstrate that

(1) causation and survival function of behavior are two points of view which not only can be, but have to be considered simultaneously;

(2) subjective interpretation and physiological analysis of behavior are compatible, though the two aspects must never be confounded or mixed;

(3) The realization that organisms and their behavior are forming, together with their environment, a 'whole' or *system is not an obstacle at all to the attempt to explain that system on the basis of natural laws.*

Von Uexküll developed what he conceptualized as 'theoretical biology,' which Thomas Sebeok and Thure von Uexküll later identified as the basis of biosemiotics. For his part, Lorenz cooperated with Tinbergen, consciously working his way into mainstream biology. Lorenz and Tinbergen eventually won a Nobel Prize for medicine in 1973, which they shared with Karl von Frisch for his studies on the behaviour of bees.

In von Uexküll's writings, one can see the importance of the concept of the *Bauplan.* This concept, which was developed by Cuvièr and Geoffrey-Saint-Hilliare in the eighteenth century, was essential to Linnaeus' idea of classification systems developed in the same century. Probably inspired by Leibniz's philosophy, von Uexküll moved the *Bauplan* into an idealistic setting far from Lorenz's theoretical perspective. Lorenz (ibid., 108) made his debt to von Uexküll clear:

For most birds, we can confidently assume that the conspecific represents, with each functional system (*Funktionskreis* in von Uexküll's terminology) in which it appears as a reciprocating object, a separate object in the environment of the subject. The particular role which the conspecific thus plays in the bird's environment has been neatly described by J. von Uexküll as that of a 'companion.' By 'companion' we of course understand a fellow human being to whom we are bound only by the links of a single functional system, which themselves have little to do with higher emotional impulses, as is the case with a drinking or (at the outside) a hunting companion.

The 'companion' in the bird's environment is interesting not only from the standpoint of environmental research, as is to be conducted here, but also because of its special sociological importance, which I believe merits closer investigation.

I owe to the personal encouragement of professor Dr Jakob von Uexküll the courage necessary to at least attempt to set out the exceedingly complex matter contained in the following passages.

In von Uexküll's writings one finds the roots of important concepts, such as sign stimuli, innate release mechanisms, and motivation, which Lorenz later utilized in his ethological research program. As previously discussed, von Uexküll's 'tone' becomes Lorenz's 'motivation,' the 'subjectively defined object' becomes the 'sign stimuli' in ethology, and the 'functional relation between receptors and effectors' becomes the 'IRM.' But it is clear that von Uexküll's concepts differ from the biocybernetic and partially mechanistic framework encountered in the theoretical foundation of Lorenz's and Tinbergen's articles from around 1950. About tone, von Uexküll (1957, 49) writes the following: 'The *Umwelt* only acquires its admirable surety for animals if we include the functional tones in our contemplation of it. We may say that the number of objects that an animal can distinguish in its own world equals the number of functions it can carry out. If, along with few functions, it possesses few functional images, its world, too, will consist of few objects. As a result its world is indeed poorer, but all the more secure.'

Von Uexküll's 'tone' concept – that the animal sees things in a different light according to its intentional acts – is at the root of Lorenz's specific motivation. However, it seems more closely related to Gibson's affordances, although it is unclear whether Gibson ever read von Uexküll.

Lorenz moved into more energy-causal explanatory models, coining pseudo-physical concepts such as 'action-specific psychological energy' in 'psycho-hydraulic models' to explain the 'mechanics' of the ethological explanation of species-specific cognition and instinctive reaction. See Figure 8.2.

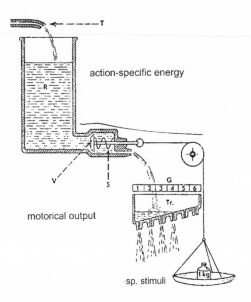

action-specific energy

motorical output

sp. stimuli

8.2. Lorenz's psychohydraulic model. The tap supplying a constant flow of liquid represents the endogenous production of action-specific energy; the liquid accumulated in the reservoir represents the amount of this energy which is at the disposal of the organism at a given moment; the elevation attained by its upper level corresponds, at an inverse ratio, to the momentary threshold of the reaction. The cone-valve represents the releasing mechanism, the inhibitory function of the higher [nerve] centers being symbolized by the spring. The scale-pan which is connected with the valve-shaft by a string acting over a pulley represents the perceptual sector of the releasing mechanism, the weight applied corresponds to the impinging stimulation' (Lorenz 1970–1, 26). The spout symbolizes activity. The distance the jet springs shows the intensity of the reaction. The perforated trough represents the intensity of different activities, from purely intentional movements to completely instinctive reactions: 'This contraption is, of course, still a very crude simplification of the real processes it is symbolizing, but experience has taught us that even the crudest simplisms often prove a valuable stimulus to investigation' (ibid., 28).

An animal's urges to perform certain species-preserving, preprogrammed behaviours, such as mating, preying, and defending territory and rank, are explained here by the accumulation of action-specific energy that lowers the stimulus threshold to a level where the smallest incident can elicit the behaviour.

Both Lorenz and Freud were inspired by thermodynamic considerations regarding the transformation of physical energy into psychic energy, which then races around the confined compartments of the psyche, where basic drives and affective needs fuel the mind. Lorenz worked functionalistically with the role of drives in animal cognition, whereas Freud saw drives in an emotional context. In other words, one could say that Lorenz studied the animal aspects of Freud's id. Both were inspired by their medical backgrounds. Like Freud, Lorenz was fascinated by the concept of the energetic-thermodynamic paradigm and believed that instinctive drives produced specific neural energy. The accumulation of action-specific motivational psychic energy had to be released, in the same way that Freud posited for basic urges and drives in humans, especially the sex drive. Like physical energy, psychic energy cannot be destroyed, and if not released in a natural way it surfaces in unnatural and destructive ways – in neurotic behaviour, for example. As Reventlow (1972) emphasizes, Lorenz's idea of *Lehrlaufen* in animals – in which the motivation is so strong that the animal perceives almost anything as a relevant stimulus – is very similar to Freud's 'psychoanalytic symbols,' in which the patient sees irrelevant things as symbols – for instance, as sex symbols – when this drive has gone unfulfilled for too long. It seems clear that as animals have emotions, they also interpret certain innate signs – such as those of a mate in heat, intraspecies aggression, and submission – and instinctively create Interpretants for them on which they act, presumably unreflectively. It is sign interpretation created by motivated instinctive perception and behaviour.

In a paper from 1963, 'Do Animals Have Subjective Experience?' Lorenz (1970–1) admitted that it is likely that animals have subjective experience, but that most of their instinctive behaviours can be understood as subconscious computations. He thus refrains from giving a final answer to the body–mind problem. Lorenz (1973) later raises the question of how emotions in animal behaviour – especially appetitive behaviour – form an internal reward for the living system that fulfils innate behaviours vital to the survival of the species. He realizes that the appetitive behaviour, where the animal searches for a stimulus to release its pent-up urge for sex or aggression, must be some reward in itself for the animal to want to repeat the behaviour. When considering humans, it is often simple biological behaviours – such as eating, sex, hunting, and for some even aggression – that afford most of our pleasures. This is the reward for using intelligence with the appetitive behaviour to find the right stimuli. Thus intelligence is driven by psycho-biologically motivated needs. Lorenz is not proposing a neutral monistic mind–body theory with his theoretical development of ethology; he does, however, allow feelings a functional role in cognition and the fulfilment of behaviour. Nevertheless, he has trouble fitting this within his theoretical framework that should be neither mechanistic nor vitalistic but biological. The problem was that such a framework did not exist at the time. Biosemiotics has now made it possible.

When one considers these conflicts between mechanistic-cybernetic-functionalist explanations and phenomenological ones, they seem insurmountable. When one reads von Uexküll's philosophical and methodological statements, it is quite clear that his phenomenological perspective positions him as a precursor to the biosemiotic view in the behavioural sciences, rather than as an advocate for mechanicism.

Even where von Uexküll appears to be offering cybernetic graphic models, his explanations are attempts to 'see' the experiental world on the animal's behalf. There was a fruitful research interaction between him and Lorenz precisely because both men took an antimechanistic stance towards the foundations of biology. So to some extent, Lorenz agreed with von Uexküll when the latter (1957, 6) wrote: 'We no longer regard animals as mere machines, but as subjects whose essential activity consists of perceiving and acting. We thus unlock the gates that lead to other realms, for all that a subject perceives becomes his perceptual world and all that he does, his effector world. Perceptual and effector worlds together form a closed unit, the *Umwelt*.'

But where von Uexküll was tempted to allow for the independent existence of animals' phenomenological *Umwelten*, Lorenz sought more functionalist explanations, coining terms such as 'psychic energy' and 'sign stimuli' to explain the modern concept of instinct within an evolutionary, ecological, physiological, and genetic framework (Lorenz 1970–1; Brier 1980). Lorenz and Tinbergen's ethological science created a biological theory of innate cognition and communication based on a new evolutionary theory; it posited that specific motivations fuel an innate release-response mechanism, which then reacts to certain environmental features as sign stimuli. Although Lorenz (1970–1) attempted to avoid it, his theory became physical and mechanistic because he had failed to provide a non-mechanistic philosophical foundation for his theory. Uexküll on the hand did not have a materialistic evolutionary theory and therefore could not connect to one of the basic elements in the biological framework.

Lorenz continued to develop his theory of innate release mechanisms in animals and its significance for human cognition throughout the

1970s. Still, he had difficulty linking his functionalistic explanations, which were partly based on cybernetic ideas, to a phenomenological approach to how feelings and volitions function (Lorenz 1977). He realized that emotions must reward animals for learning and using intelligence with the 'appetitive behavior' that leads the organism to fulfil its innate behaviour. But he could not account theoretically for emotionality and signification as von Uexküll did, although von Uexküll went too far towards idealism and anti-evolutionism.

In the behavioural sciences, both von Uexküll and later Reventlow (1970) proposed that the cognition of living systems partially creates the 'reality' they live in through the development of receptors and effectors. In other words, cognitive systems project their perceptions onto the environment, thereby creating objects of perception. Von Uexküll (1957, 9–10) described it this way:

> The clusters of receptor cells fill the 'receptor organs' [*Merkorgan*] of the brain, and the clusters of effector cells make up the contents of its 'effector organs' [*Wirkorgan*].
>
> The individual cells of the perceptor organ, whatever their activity, remain as spatially separate units. The units of information which they separately convey would also remain isolated, if it were not possible for them to be fused into new units which are independent of the spatial characters of the receptor organ. This possibility does, in fact, exist. The receptor signs of a group of receptor cells are combined outside the receptor organ, indeed outside the animal, into units that become the properties of external objects. This projection of sensory impressions is a self-evident fact. All our human sensations, which represent our specific receptor signs, unite into perceptual cues [*Merkmal*] which constitute the attributes of external objects and serve as the real basis of our actions. The sensation 'blue' becomes the 'blueness' of the sky and the sensation 'green,' the 'greenness' of the lawn. These are the cues by which we recognize the objects: blue, the sky; green, the lawn.
>
> A similar process takes place in the effector organ. The isolated effector cells are organized into well-articulated groups according to their effector signs or impulses. The isolated impulses are coordinated into units, and these self-contained motor impulses or rhythmical impulse melodies act upon the muscles subordinated to them. And the limbs or other organs activated by the separate muscles imprint upon the external objects their effector cue or functional signification [*Wirkmal*] ...
>
> Figuratively speaking, every animal grasps its object with two arms of a

forceps, receptor and effector. With the one it invests the object with a receptor cue or perceptual meaning. But since all of the traits of an object are structurally interconnected, the traits given operational meaning must affect those bearing perceptual meaning through the object, and so change the object itself.

This intimate relation between receptors and effectors creates objects within a living system's 'signification sphere.' Reventlow described this for the stickleback (a small fish) through a well-tested statistical behavioural model. Lorenz realized that the animal responded only to certain features or differences in its environment and then made interpretations that caused behaviours with survival value. He never discarded this naïve, realistic world view to contemplate the constructive aspects of the phenomenology of living systems' cognition.

Reventlow (1977), studying instinctive responses, notes how peculiar it is that the environment, under the right conditions, can suddenly reorganize the organism's cognitive field into an 'aha-experience' that allows it to see its surroundings as meaningful. He argues that a general cognitive phenomenon appears to take place, be it imprinting or intelligent learning. Differences in the environment are suddenly seen as something that he calls a 'rependium.' It is at this moment that an Interpretant is created through the process of signification and that something is 'recognized.' How does this *Eigenvalue* appear as an object established in the body–mind? This we do not really know. Von Uexküll (1973, 71) has emphasized that every object belongs to a subject as a part of its *Umwelt*: 'Each object ... not only changes its meaning quality from one *Umwelt* to another, but the structure of all its material and formal properties also changes ... The constancy of subjects is substantiated far better than the constancy of the objects.'

While Lorenz was preoccupied with the creation of object constancy, von Uexküll emphasized the role of 'the observer' as we understand it in the modern constructivist, cognitive biology of von Foerster's second-order cybernetics, and in Maturana and Varela's autopoiesis theory. Their approaches problematize – as does von Uexküll's – how the perception of non-anticipated things and objects can occur at all. In the little story below, von Uexküll (1957, 62) illustrated how difficult it can be for us to see something unexpected:

Again I begin with two personal experiences, which will best illustrate what is meant by the search image, a factor of great importance in the *Umwelt*.

When I spent some time at the house of a friend, an earthenware water pitcher used to be placed before my seat at luncheon. One day the butler had broken the clay pitcher and put a glass water bottle in its place. When I looked for the pitcher during the meal, I failed to see the glass carafe. Only when my friend assured me that the water was standing in its usual place, did various bright lights that had lain scattered on knives and plates flock together through the air and form the water bottle.

Von Uexküll further wrote that the search image annihilates the perceptual image. The search image has become an important ethological concept for understanding the behaviour of hunting animals. Maturana and Varela (1980) have coined the term 'structural couplings' to emphasize the unique connections that must be created between a system and its environment in order for anything to be systematically sensed.

From the perspective of the philosophy of language, Wittgenstein (1958) addresses the same problem by underlining how closely integrated 'language games' must be with 'life forms' for meaning to appear. His statement that even if a lion could speak, we would not be able to understand it because we do not share its life form or *Umwelt*, underscores how important living practice is to the phenomenological concept of meaning. It is my theory – based on ethology, von Uexküll's observations, Maturana and Varela, and von Foerster's second-order cybernetics – that the semantic capacity of a living system to assign meaning to differences that perturb its self-organization is a prerequisite to the phenomena of communication, language, and consciousness. This concurs with Luhmann's idea that the combined biological and psychological autopoiesis systems constitute the environment of the human social-communicative system within the hypercomplex structure of the environment itself.

8.3 The Cybernetics Theory of Information and Cognition

The new cybernetics of Gregory Bateson, where 'information is a difference that makes a difference' (1973); the development of his theory into Maturana and Varela's autopoiesis; von Foerster's 'second-order cybernetics' of cognition and 'non-trivial machines'; and Luhmann's system theory have all been useful for finding new concepts with which to address the paradoxical problem of the subjectivity of 'real objects' and for moving ethology away from the mechanistic approach that Lorenz developed when he diverged from von Uexküll's ideas. In this new second-order cybernetics, information is perceived as something that an outside observer would note as a creation within the living system, one that occurs when an autopoietic system creates structural couplings in reaction to constant perturbation from the environment.

This is a clear move away from the objectivistic denotative and logical theories of information and language, and towards constructivist theories that go beyond social constructivism and towards biology into a kind of meta-biology. I will call this 'bio-constructivism,' as this theory encompasses all living systems, psychological systems, and social systems despite their different conceptualizations. Second-order cybernetics and autopoiesis dovetail neatly with von Uexküll's *Umwelt* concept, demonstrated here by his example (1957, 70) of the reality of the innate way animals have of following a familiar path: 'To the uninitiated observer a familiar path in a foreign *Umwelt* is just as invisible as is the innate path. And if we assume that the familiar pathway becomes manifest to the foreign subject in his own *Umwelt* – of which there is no doubt – then there is no reason to deny the phenomenon of the innate pathway; since it is composed of identical elements, the projected perceptual and functional signs. In the one case they are elicited by sensory stimuli, in the other they chime in harmonious succession, like an inborn melody.'

Cybernetic and autopoietic theories fail to elucidate the phenomenological reality of perception and cognition – especially that of animals. So von Uexküll uses examples like the one above to highlight the difference between mechanistic and phenomenological approaches to the behavioural science of living systems.

In the 1960s, Gregory Bateson (1973) theorized that humans are cybernetic mind-ecological systems evolving towards a fit relationship with an environment in which they had become inhabitants – a world of information. Bateson contended that the link between the material world of matter and energy and the informational world of living systems is that the latter reacts to the material world of differences only when it is important to the survival of the living system. Information consists only of those differences that impact on the system. This is very similar to the view of von Uexküll (ibid., 13): 'The *Umwelt* of any animal that we wish to investigate is only a section carved out of the environment which we see spread around it – and this environment is nothing but our own human world. The first task of *Umwelt* research is to identify each animal's perceptual cues among all the stimuli in its environment and to build up the animal's specific world with them.'

Ethologists have attempted to identify all the animals' perceptual clues from an evolutionary and ecological angle by composing the *ethogram*. Maturana and Varela's autopoiesis theory is usually taken as a continued development of Bateson's rethinking of Wiener's cybernetics, although Maturana told me personally that he had not read Bateson before he arrived at his theory. Maturana and Varela argue that the concept of information is irrelevant to organisms under observation, as these do not extract information from the environment. Their environment manifests itself only as perturbations, to which they must then adapt in order to survive. Maturana and Varela refer to enduring adaptations to regular environmental perturbations as 'structural couplings.' Only perturbations and differences that occur within a structural coupling can affect an organism. From the point of view of an outside observer, this becomes information in the autopoietic system. It is worth noting that they are objecting to the notion that objective information in the environment is transferred objectively through sense perceptions into the mind/brain. Bateson's information concept is much closer to their conception.

As previously mentioned, Lorenz realized in the 1970s that he required a concept of emotion if he was to understand the reactions and appetitive behaviours of animals that lead them to repeatedly seek the same specific sign stimuli. But he never managed to link his materialistic theory of evolution to a phenomenological view of the organism. Bateson realized that the survival value of emotions was a 'logic of relationship,' but he did not theorize their non-mechanical qualia aspects. Maturana and Varela accepted the usefulness of the biophenomenological view of the organism, but they never developed true phenomenological concepts of signification.

Maturana and Varela's epistemology is as follows: scientists and philosophers observe a system, its limits, and its world, and recognize it as a sentient being such as themselves. As scientists, they choose biology to describe the living system in a functionalistic way. They are members of a society of observers, but they are also an important part of a social-communicative system – or, to employ Wittgenstein's pragmatic concept, language games. One of the shortcomings of Maturana and Varela's theories is that they take for granted consciousness – that is, the inner world of perceptions, cognitions, emotions, and volitions – and theorize on it only in a biological materialistic fashion. Maturana later developed a biological theory of love and emotioning to describe the biological foundation of society, but he has not yet been able to integrate these concepts into his theoretical foundation, in the profound way that Peirce managed to do with his concept of Firstness and evolutionary love.

Maturana and Varela have attempted to reflect on both the observer and observing, but they offer only biobehaviourist explanations of the observer. Their point of departure is somewhat similar to that of von Uexküll; however, their paradigm lacks a phenomenological stance on the *Eigenvalue* or even the *Eigengenese* of the psyche. In contrast, von Uexküll's framework seems to involve some sort of Platonic objective idealism in the psyche, which does not fit well with the modern natural and social sciences. The position taken by Maturana and Varela does not permit them to develop a theory of psychological and cultural meanings that could serve as the basis for a pragmatic theory of signification, despite their biological pragmatic position. But in his general theory of autopoiesis in biological, psychological, and social systems, Luhmann (1995) uses meaning as a tool to reduce complexity, which remedies this to a certain extent.

8.4 Luhmann's Generalization of the Theory of Autopoiesis

Second-order cybernetics and autopoiesis theory are based on the logical discrimination and computation of differences. According to Spencer-Brown's *Laws of Form* (1972), second-order cybernetics and autopoiesis theory distinguish between system and environment as well as between structure and organization. With this two-valued logic, Luhmann (1990, 1995) has developed a theoretical model of systems of social communication by importing elements of second-order cybernetics and autopoiesis theories of cognition as well as Husserl's phenomenological theory of intersubjectivity. He then transplants them to his social-communicative autopoietic system, thus shifting it from its original Husserlian transcendental phenomenology framework into something else – to precisely what, is not too clear from a philosophy of science point of view. He is not building a phenomenological sociology. He generalizes autopoiesis to encompass the psyche and the social-communicative system, including language. Luhmann develops a generalized version of the second-order biocybernetic understanding of perception, generation, and the communication of information into what he calls 'systems theory.'

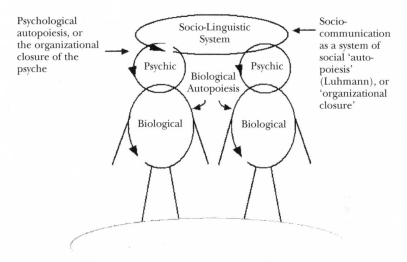

8.3.   Illustrates Luhmann's three autopoietic systems, in which silent biological and psychological systems form the basis for socio-communicative autopoiesis. It is doubtful whether one can label psychic and social-communicative systems truly autopoietic, as they do not create their own membranes or limits. Regardless of this, they are organizationally closed, which is the most important factor.

Luhmann posits that systems exist which are not primarily biological but which are autopoietic – especially, for example, psychological and social-communicative systems. He wants to distinguish (although not explain) these different levels of autopoiesis and characterize their basic ways of functioning. He emphasizes that psychological and social-communicative autopoiesis are qualitatively different. Figure 8.3 is the first in a series of figures or models I will be creating to illustrate the cybersemiotic frameworks and the models that can be developed under it.

The tripartitioning of autopoiesis into biological, psychological, and social systems seems warranted for defining a fundamental scientific and operational concept of meaning and social communication. However, Luhmann does not integrate evolutionary ecological thinking in a profound theoretical way, as this level is not his primary focus. Still, his thinking is very historical-evolutionary.

Maturana and Varela theorize that autopoietic living systems are closed in spatial and temporal organization and reproduction, and that they are only open to the world through structural couplings. Multicellular organisms are second-order couplings between cells, and societies are third-order couplings between organisms. Luhmann transforms this into a theory of social organizations as autopoietic systems created through communication. Communicative systems have an intrinsic form of organization that, although building on biological individuals with organizationally closed psychological systems, has aspects that transcend the biological sphere. According to our current understanding, they can function only on the basis of a biological autopoietic system.

As a biologist I do not believe that Luhmann takes this seriously enough, and many researchers of the arts and social sciences also feel that Luhmann does not take the uniqueness of individual humans and their use of language seriously enough. It is true that Luhmann does not develop a phenomenological theory of cognition, meaning, and signification (Keller 1999). As Fogh Kirkeby (1997) argues, there is no true theory of signification with a reflective phenomenological theory of the self and its existentiality, will, and emotions in Luhmann's work.

Although Luhmann's theory is partly based on that of Husserl, it excludes his idea of a transcendental ego and is only partially phenomenological when seen from the points of view of, for instance, Heidegger, Sartre, Wittgenstein, or Merleau-Ponty. Although Fogh Kirkeby criticizes Luhmann for his lack of a phenomenological philosophical basis, he agrees with him that the psyche itself is silent. The psyche – including Freud's unconscious – only produces non-verbal thoughts within its own closed system. It is this system and the life-world that it produces that von Uexküll insists must be theorized, and this is the place from which biosemiotics is developed.

One could argue that language is an infection – a parasite – on the Umwelt of the psychic system. Language preys on the phenomenological world of primary emotions, perceptions, and motivational qualities, thereby assigning meaning and intentions to signs, words, and sentences. Language has its own closed system of syntax and semantics related to a web of signs, meanings, and social practices, which are in turn related to cultural evolution. As psycho-biological beings we live in symbiosis with the closed socio-communicative system that creates culture and the intersubjective knowledge systems.

It is important that Luhmann conceptualized the biological, psychological, and socio-communicative levels as closed systems. Although all are present in the human being and function simultaneously, there is no direct 'inner connection' between them. They can only communicate through interpenetration. This is an elegant cybernetic formulation of the organizational difficulty of integrating self-consciousness and the body-mind through language.

Later discussions of Varela, summarized in Mingers (1995), have convinced me that, as neither the psychic nor the social-communicative systems produce their own limits (unlike the cell with its membrane), they are not truly autopoietic but merely organizationally closed. Closure is an aspect that von Uexküll underlines as an important element of order in the Umwelts, which makes him compatible with Luhmann's theory:

> The fact that the body structure is ordered according to a plan (*Planmäs-sigkeit*) seems to contradict the idea that the Umwelt structure is also ordered according to a plan (*Planmässigkeit*).
>
> One must not be under the illusion that the plan to which the Umwelt structure accords is less systematically complete than the plan according to which the body structure is ordered.
>
> Each Umwelt forms a closed unit in itself, which is governed, in all its parts, by the meaning it has for the subject. According to its meaning for the animal, the stage on which it plays its life roles (*Lebensbühne*) embraces a wider or narrower space. (von Uexküll 1982, 30)

Maturana and Varela both appear to believe that a grand theory of life, cognition, and communication is possible, but have no theory of how signification is created that includes a first person view of qualia, free will, and emotion. But Peirce did.

8.5 The Relevance of Peirce's Semiotics as a Framework for Biosemiotics

To develop his fundamental holistic theory of Semiosis, Peirce designed an alternate philosophy to both the dualism of rationalism and the materialistic monism of most empirical science. He combined realism and idealism into an evolutionary objective idealism that is still very different from Hegel's and Luhmann's, because he then combined this with synechism, the view that the basic 'stuff' of reality is continuous – and a pragmatic(istic) epistemology. As mentioned earlier, we would say today that this is a field-view rather than an atomistic view. This field-view now pervades theories as distinct as quantum field theory and Einstein's general relativity. Prigogine and Stengers (1984) underline chance and complexity as basic concepts in science – but one cannot build a metaphysics of science by understanding chance as the mere absence of law, as emphasized by Peirce.

Instead, Peirce interpreted chance or chaos as a Firstness of primary potential qualities, endowed with the tendency to form habits and regular behavioral patterns through Secondness, which in Thirdness we comprehend as laws. In Peirce's synechistic philosophy, chaos precedes cosmos, as chance precedes order. But chance is not assumed to be the absence of the concept of law, chance is considered to be a first. Chaos – or Firstness – is also spontaneous feelings and potential basic qualities (qualia). Peirce accepts Darwinian evolution as one form of evolution, but posits two other forms as well: fortuitous variation and creative love (Peirce 1992, 352–71). He calls them Tychasm, Anacasm, and Agapasm. Thus Peirce delivers the missing element to both von Uexküll's philosophy of science and Lorenzian ethology, providing a post-mechanistic and a postmodern explanation. Let me explain further.

In modern cybernetics and systems theory we now speak of the self-organizing universe (Jantsch 1980): the tendency of existing complex systems to be self-organized, and of living systems to be autopoietic. To Peirce, the habits of the universe are what we now call laws in physics. They are never absolutely exact as is often assumed in mechanistic physics. Peirce sees laws as emergent phenomena: new laws appear as the Universe evolves. The Universe creates laws – not the other way around. Interestingly, von Uexküll[3] – concurring with Peirce – believes that laws are the plans of nature that are diffused throughout the subjective Umwelt:

> If we contrast nature's plan with the subject's goal, we will not have to discuss the question of instinct, which does not really get anyone anywhere. Does the acorn need an instinct to grow into an oak tree, or does a host of bone-forming cells work instinctively to form a bone? If we deny this and substitute a plan of nature as a regulating factor, then nature's designs will also be recognized as swaying the spinning of a cobweb or the building of a bird's nest, since no subjective goal is involved in either case. Instinct is merely a product of perplexity, a concept which must answer if we gainsay the superindividual plans of nature. These plans are disputed because it is hard to conceive the nature of a plan, since it assuredly is neither matter nor force. Yet it is not so difficult to gain an idea of the plan, if one bears a concrete example in mind ... Without plans, that is, without the sovereign ordinances of nature, there would be no order in nature, only chaos. Every crystal is the product of a plan of nature, and when physicists present Bohr's beautiful atom models, they exemplify the plans of inanimate nature which they seek.
>
> The sovereignty of nature's living plans is expressed most clearly in the study of *Umwelten*. To trace them is one of the most enthralling pursuits.

We shall therefore not let ourselves be turned aside, but will calmly continue on our stroll through the *Umwelten*. (von Uexküll 1957, 42–7)

In Peirce's view, a law is a phenomenon created through the interactions between Firstness, Secondness, and the mediating power of Thirdness in evolution. Law and understanding are thus two sides of the same coin. The pre-linguistic reality that exists before and outside any linguistic understanding cannot be reduced to the mere 'material' or 'mathematical.' Peirce's objective was not to reduce complexity down to something it is not. His categories are only conceptions of complexity. Firstness is all those qualities we perceive as blue, hardness, sweetness, forms, etc. but they are only potentials. They must manifest themselves in 'thing-ness' or difference in order to become manifest as forces, constraints, and objects, and to be known they must be interpreted by a living system that can perceive them as signs of regularity, thereby creating an interpretant inside itself.

Maturana and Varela discuss that the autopoietic character of living systems makes it possible for them to make structural couplings, and that they can establish Eigenvalues of cognition, as von Foerster terms them – systems of recursive processing that stabilize in the mind and make us (re)cognize things. I believe this is what Peirce called the Interpretant – the sign in our mind that makes us see and recognize something as an object. This is an attempt at modeling what von Uexküll describes from 'the inside' of the living system's world when he insists that objects can only be understood in relation to a subject's Umwelt.

The immediate object and the interpretant in Peirce's semiotics are signs. To my way of understanding, this is what makes his theory a second-order theory. There is an important difference between Peirce's object and the vulgar realistic concept of 'thing,' which is the same as that in the theories of von Uexküll, Maturana and Varela, and the ethological theory of the object as a cybernetic perceptual-motor construct. Only some objects refer to things, but all objects refer to 'something.'

In scientific culture, we usually consider physical, chemical, and biological things to be more objectively real, and the social to be a construction. The reality of a social institution, such as marriage, a court, or an auction, depends on our actions. In scientific discourse, natural objects do not depend on humans' perceptual and behavioral construction; on the contrary, science believes that we are constructed by natural objects or 'real things', or have constructed 'ourselves' by organizing real 'things', such as atoms or molecules. There is a tendency in the natural and technical sciences to behave as if the physical aspect of reality was 'more real' than the phenomenological, psychological, or sociological ones, and to consider emotion and semantics as subjective interpretations of an objective reality.

Peirce's consideration of the relationship between humans and nature presupposes that the analogies between human thought and the 'thought' habits of nature are valid. These analogies are based on the commonalities of the forces that make things happen. Natural processes are temporal and irreversible. The evolutionary forces that make things happen in natural processes have – as mentioned above – been classified into three evolutionary categories: Tychasm, Anacasm, and Agapasm. These coexist and exert compulsions of various intensities. This level always implies slight variations. In an evolutionary world, individuals are typical but not identical. To summarize, in natural evolution there are three coexisting principles that together result in the formation of stable habits.

In any kind of materialistic atomistic or field/plenum theory, reality is built from matter–energy patterns. But Peirce's plenum theory is not merely materialistic. His vacuum field – the thycastic, agapistic, and synechistic Firstness – contains random emotions and qualities with a tendency to form habits, and this seems to be the case both 'inside and outside nature.' The concept of thing/object is only Secondness in Peirce's theory. Therefore, humans must be partially creating objects for themselves through the process of semiosis, not out of nothing, but rather out of Firstness through Secondness and Thirdness, which is not only 'out there' but also 'inside us.' Through *the triadic leap of semiosis*, as I call it, our reality comes into being as signs. This is a semiotic reformulation of Bateson's pattern that connects. We appear in, and/or perhaps are caught in, a world of signs. The thing in itself is not only 'outside' in nature, but also inside ourselves, if I understand Peirce correctly. In this conception he provides the most fruitful conceptual and philosophical basis for understanding those biophenomenological processes which von Uexküll highlights as the basic building blocks of our reality, thus allowing us to create a Peircean biosemiotics to reinterpret von Uexküll's foundational work.

The real, then, according to Peirce, is that which information and reasoning would eventually result in, viewed from the perspective of human history. This pertains to the study of human cognition, as the human body consists of matter and thus also consists of the laws that govern matter. But Peirce does not consider nature a collection of things that interact according to absolute, reversible, and mechanical principles; his view of nature is based on a continuous and hylozoistic view of matter. This means that there is an inner living, emotional, mind-like quality in matter. I believe that von Uexküll would accept this alternative to the mechanistic foundation as a better foundation than the Platonic vision he himself proposed, given the recognition of evolutionary theory today.

Most researchers today contend that signs can only be interpreted within a community of observers, significators, and communicators. Signs require a semiotic web of biological and cultural actions in order to acquire their meanings. Language consists of reciprocal structural couplings among members of the semiotic web or the socio-cultural communicative autopoiesis, as Luhmann would agree. We are constantly creating and recreating meaning and ourselves within this reality, which is only revealed to us through signs. The Object in semiosis is only the immediate object, not the final dynamic object.

We construct for ourselves a 'signification sphere' within which we live, and which we modify only if it is perturbed in a way that interests or threatens us. In a certain way we are monads, as Leibniz suggested in his monadology; each of us is enclosed in a separate self-organized world. This is accepted both by von Uexküll and by autopoiesis theory with its theory of the Multiverse and cognitive domains. Each of us consists of several closed systems, such as the biological autopoiesis, the psychological organizational closure, and the social-communicative organizational closure (Luhmann 1990), which interpenetrate one another.

Most of us are not reflectively or consciously aware of our deepest biological needs or innermost thoughts and emotions. We do not even fully control the words that come out of our mouths. Luhmann's concept of the social-communicative system as an organizationally closed system provides a model for understanding why the human conscious subject is not in complete control of language. As Freud demonstrated, many of our impulses come from portions of our psyche – and perhaps also our biology – of which we are not conscious. Furthermore, language is a social (power) game that penetrates us, and, as Bourdieu (2005b) points out, exerts an influence on our way of understanding our role and duties in society with respect to a 'habitus.' One could say that languages' culturally formed concepts infect our psyche like a virus, as earlier mentioned, and through symbiosis create a new living system that steps beyond the animal realm: the linguistically self-conscious, socially and culturally formed human, partially shaped by its linguistic *Umwelt.*

It is only through the workings of the biosocially controlled mind's *Eigenvalue* of perception – the structural coupling – that the Interpretant is constructed as a lawful, stable, and habitual phenomenon of Thirdness. Reality then emerges for us through this triadic semiosis. Qualities manifest themselves through objects such as things and concepts, while individuals act within the hypercomplexity of 'reality.' What we sense is there, but it is only partially real – it is a simplification of the real complexity of which our will, emotions, and consciousness are an integral part.

This provides von Uexküll's theory with a profoundly philosophical basis and establishes the foundation of biosemiotics when tempered by Lorenz's, Tinbergen's, and Reventlow's ethological thinking. Here, signs and the experiences of living systems are the basic components of reality, not objects as independently existing 'things' or entities built from atoms or elementary particles.

The Australian philosopher Freya Mathews, in *The Ecological Self* (1991), develops a modern scientifically based philosophy supporting the signification of living systems as the basic and constructive parts of reality. Next I briefly outline her theory, as it places the original intentions of von Uexküll within a modern ecological framework that is compatible with Peirce's semiotic philosophy.

8.6 Living Systems as the True Individuals of the World

Mathews has researched the connections among science, cosmology, and myth and how these influence our view of our own place 'in the scheme of things' as humans, as culture, and in our relationship with nature. She has developed an alternative cosmology based on the theoretical developments in general relativity theory and geometrodynamic cosmologies of space-time geometry as forming the substance of the world. Her findings are not as rich as Peirce's continuum of Firstness, but they are compatible with it.

In accordance with the development of natural science in the twentieth century, Mathews analyses the plenum theory of general relativity. Here, as with with system theory, everything is interconnected in an organized way. Matter – as in quantum theory – is capable of movement and of creating regular patterns, and substance and process are thus intrinsically interconnected. The geometrodynamics of general relativity are theoretically well developed but not empirically well tested. But it is still a possible world view from a scientific perspective, and the most elaborate theory of a plenum since Aristotle, who saw matter as a continuum and forms as constituting individual things and organisms. In geometrodynamics, substance is not matter but is, rather, the four-dimensional curved space-time from which all forces and forms of matter develop. This curvature generates the force of gravity that Newton could not explain, and the most curved portion of space-time is what we call matter, which is simply another manifestation of the intrinsic energy of the field.

Mathews discusses Spinoza's a priori demands for a basic substance of a cosmology, which to Spinoza would be God. When we try to 'conceive of substance through itself' (as Spinoza demands), the criteria are self-evident: self-realizability, infinitude, and indivisibility. The substance must be able to manifest itself; and it must be all there is – without boundaries – or else it would not be the substance. Along the same lines, it must be that which verifies everything. This clearly leads to the plenum theory, as Mathews suggests. This agrees with Peirce's view of Firstness, Secondness, and Thirdness in combination with Tychism, Synechism, and Agapism and the emptiness he theorizes 'behind' them in the later development of his theory, which we will return to.

The plenum theory is an interesting return to Aristotle's view of substance, but in the modern version evolution is intrinsic to substance. Thus new concepts of form, essence, and natural kinds must be found. As I have analyzed and described it, this is what Peirce was working on with his triadic, pragmatic, and faneoscopic semiotics. As everything in plenum theory is connected, as Matthews points out, we cannot consider things as individuals solely because on the surface they appear separated in time and space by physical boundaries. Something more is needed. Mathews sees the basic concept of a system in systems science and cybernetics as such a principle. Through the works of Beer, Bertalanffy, Bateson, and Ashby, Matthews develops a view of the basic, primary, and real systems in the world as living systems, similar to what von Uexküll did in a less modern and scientific theory. Mathews's analysis concludes that the fundamental systems of individuation are organic systems, because only these exist for themselves, by themselves, and have internal goals and values of existence. Atoms, molecules, and things do not have this world-constitutional property. Only living systems are self-realizing and have self-interest, self-evaluation, and therefore selfhood and value, as Peirce would agree. She calls this 'conatus,' borrowing a concept from Spinoza and further developing it. As I see it, von Uexküll (1986, 244) speaks of subjectivity and *Umwelten* in much in the same spirit, but from his Platonic world view.

> the fact remains that we are surrounded by higher realities that we are incapable of surveying. We must acknowledge ... that that thing which runs from the egg to the hen and extends its purposeful construction through time with no gaps, forming a chain of objects, without itself becoming an object, exists without our being able to recognize it. We are simply surrounded by countless realities that our perceptive abilities cannot reach. They remain imperceptible because they transcend perception. All organisms, plants as well as animals, belong here. Of them, we possess only the image of their momentary appearance. We can make no image for ourselves of their being that reaches in an unbroken chain from the seed to the adult, and of which we know that it harbors a unitary lawfulness. All plants and animal species, which we manipulate as if they were known quantities, are realities transcending perception. Indeed, we ourselves constitute such a reality that we cannot survey, since we can only observe ourselves from moment to moment.

This is a grand theory of living systems connecting past, present, and future, and from their 'Bauplans' creating structures in reality in the form of *Umwelten*, or what I call signification spheres. Life – not matter, energy, or information – becomes the basic reality. These bio-constructivist theories are stepping stones to the development of a cybernetic, systemic, and biosemiotic view of reality – in short, a *cybersemiotics*.

8.7 The Integration of Second-Order Cybernetics, Cognitive Biology (Autopoiesis), and Biosemiotics

Thus it is my view that there are some very interesting commonalities between second-order cybernetics, cognitive biology (autopoiesis), and Sebeok's Peircean bio-semiotics. But there are also some interesting differences, which that lead me to conclude that they need one another. The similarities I see among von Foerster's second-order cybernetics, Maturana and Varela's cognitive biological theory of autopoiesis, and a biosemiotics that Sebeok built both on von Uexküll and on Peircean semiotics, are the following:

1. Second-order cybernetics takes systems science and cybernetics to a new level by including the observer; similarly, biosemiotics takes semiotics to a new level by including all living systems in semiosis.

2. Both take this step through a bioconstructivism – that is, they see every living system constructing its own 'life world.' In biosemiotics this life world is often called *Umwelt* from von Uexküll. I call these 'signification spheres.' Maturana speaks of an organism's 'cognitive domain.' Von Foerster sees a cognitive world constructed of *Eigenvalues* of the nervous system's cognitive processes. *Eigenvalues* are stable systems of recursive processing that stabilize in the mind and make us (re)cognize things, or what Reventlow calls a 'rependium.'

3. In all these systems of thought, the bioconstructive view leads to an idea of 'closure.' This term is used mostly in connection with autopoiesis, but both von Foerster and von Uexküll indicate clearly that the 'signification sphere,' is all there is for an organism.

4. All of these researchers agree that there is no stream of 'information' from the environment going directly into the cognitive system of the organism that can be picked up and thereby offer a more or less 'objective' picture of the 'real environment.'

5. But all acknowledge that 'reality,' or 'the environment,' is to be viewed as some kind of limit that places 'constraints' on the possible ways that an organism can exist as an individual. Von Foerster is most explicit in accepting that the environment must have energy and structure. Von Uexküll also seems to accept some kind of real world outside the many *Umwelten*, since he calls these 'subjective worlds.' Luhmann accepts a universe or a world that is not a system.

6. All agree that life and cognition are two sides of the same coin. Peirce and Sebeok use the terms 'semiosis' and 'signification' for cognition. But broadly speaking, all of them are talking about perception and cognition.

7. Maturana, von Uexküll, and von Foerster all discuss what sorts of experiences there can be behind certain situations, focussing on seeing, in particular. Maturana, for instance, has articles with titles like 'What Is It to See?' and 'What the Frog's Brain Tells the Frog's Mind.' Von Foerster has one entitled 'Through the Eyes of the Others.' But they offer no explicit theory of the origin of an

organism's first-person phenomenological experiences or of the differences between experience and processes in the nervous system.

8. In biosemiotics, von Uexküll's stationary world view is transferred to Peirce's evolutionary world view. Through this operation, the three views share the evolutionary constructivistic – or process – view of the origin of organisms, their cognition, and their ecological 'niches.'

9. None of them considers organisms as deterministic machines. Von Foerster calls them (including humans) non-trivial machines.

10. Von Uexküll clearly has a phenomenological view of the organism, yet neither he nor von Foerster nor Maturana (nor Sebeok) has 'a theory of mind' or how first-person experiences appear in a physical world. Peirce, by contrast, has a profound philosophical theory of the role of 'pure feeling,' qualia, mind, consciousness, and 'evolutionary love' in semiotics.

11. All three views seem more or less explicitly to take life as a basic or constituent aspect of reality, and not as something invented by chance out of a physical deterministic world as Monod (1972) saw so clearly and insightfully was the consequence of biology becoming 'molecular' and thereby using chemistry and physics as foundational platforms. As we shall see, Peircean biosemiotics differ from the rest in that he supports his project explicity with metaphysics.

12. As noted earlier in the book, Varela's second-order and autopoietic cybernetics, with its development of biological cognition (see his 'Calculus for Self-Reference' [1975]) closely approaches Peirce's triadic relational category theory. It was a great accomplishment before his too early death.

Now to what I see as the significant differences between these systems that make the development of a cybersemiotics a necessary project:

1. The concept of 'structural coupling' is unique to autopoiesis. Even so, the structural coupling seems to be a prerequisite for generating cognitive *Eigenvalues* that make cognitive objects possible. Structural couplings are necessary for the 'rependium,' the sudden construction of patterns that attain meaningfulness in the perceptual field. Examples include the 'sign stimuli' in the ethological para-

digm of animal cognition, communication, and behaviour. It is a useful concept for biosemiotics.

2. Maturana and Varela point out that the autopoietic character of living systems is what enables them to make structural couplings. Through these couplings, it is possible to establish von Foerster's *Eigenvalues* of cognition. I suggest that this is what Peirce called the Interpretant – that is, the sign in our mind that makes us see/recognize something as an object – although he does not actually describe this dynamic self-organizing process.

3. Peircean biosemiotics builds on Peirce's unique triadic concept of semiosis, in which the Interpretant is the sign concept in the organism's mind that is its interpretation of what the outer sign vehicle 'stands for' – for instance, a raised fist signifies a 'threat.' A thorough understanding of sign, signification, and semiosis is missing in systems and cybernetics.

4. Peirce's differentiation between the immediate object of semiosis and the dynamical object – that is, the object that is all we can get to know about the object through history – is an evolutionary solution to the problem of the relation between the signification sphere (or 'life world') of the organism and 'the environment' (or 'universe') outside it not present in cybernetics. This view is now part of biosemiotics.

5. Peircean biosemiotics is based on Peirce's theory of mind as a basic part of reality (in Firstness) that exists in the material aspect of reality (in Secondness) as the 'inner aspect of matter' (hylozoism) and that manifests itself as awareness and experience in animals and finally as consciousness in humans. When we combine this with a general systems theory of emergence, self-organization, and closure/autopoiesis, we form an explicit theory of how the inner world of an organism is constituted and, therefore, how first-person views are possible and just as real as matter.

6. Through this foundation for semiosis, a theory of meaning and interpretation including mind – at least as immanent in nature – is possible, and cybernetic views of information as well as autopoietic views on languaging can be combined with pragmatic theories of language in the biosemiotic perspective.

All of this is why I find Sebeok's, Hoffmeyer's, and Emmeche's work on constructing a Peircean biosemiotics so important for second-order cybernetics and for autopoiesis in particular. Biosemiotics makes it possible for us to add a theory of mind, meaning, and signification to our views on cognition. My version is what I call cybersemiotics; others may develop different conceptions.

8.8 Signification Spheres as *Umwelten* of Anticipation

To summarize, Peirce's semiosis can be extended to animals when motivation permits something to stand for something or somebody else in a particular way (the ground of the sign). Wittgenstein (1958) likewise demonstrated that signification is created through language games developed by specific life forms. As animals do not have true language, I have extended Wittgenstein's concept into ethology and biosemiotics by introducing the concept of 'sign games,' which are related to specific motivations and IRMs as these are described by ethology. In a similar vein, Peirce wrote that interpretative sign webs are where interpretations of meanings take place, based on the social habits of sign use in a historical context. Wittgenstein discussed how life forms and language games generate the social meanings of words. Luhmann would furthermore claim, however, that humans reduce the complexity of perturbations in the social-communicative system through meaning. These pragmatic thinkers all conceptualized various aspects of the signification process but never aimed at a comprehensive doctrine as Peirce did.

The semantic capacity of living systems to assign meaning to differences that perturb the system's self-organization seems to be a prerequisite for the phenomena of cognition, communication, language, and consciousness. The ability of a living system to anticipate is connected to its ability to observe and cognate, thereby reducing complexity through signification, by producing a signification sphere.

Life seems to be an anticipatory function (Rosen 1991). As Lorenz argued, it generates expectations through evolution and it generates structural couplings in open genetic programs. The phenomenon of imprinting is a standard example of programmed anticipation. Anticipations are expectations of meaning and order related to the 'signification sphere' that the organism constructs as its individual world. Events that perpetuate the living autopoietic system are 'reduced to meaning' (Luhmann 1990); but through the signification process as Peirce sees it, they are biologically related to the survival and procreation of individual living systems in 'evolutionary love.' When animals try to coordinate their behavioural practices with their various signification spheres, they are participating in 'sign games.'

We should not forget that the scientific thinking of biology – not to mention physics or mathematics – is dependent on our being languaging, self-conscious, perceiving, and knowledge-generating systems/selves. In phenomenological terms, there is another side to our being and knowing besides science. The human condition can never be exhaustively described through science (Merleau-Ponty 2002). Our becoming aware of being in the world is 'before,' 'above,' and 'beyond' science in certain ways. It is also prelinguistic and (in the end) probably beyond the words that are based in our signification sphere's continuous historical drift through space-time and feeling matter.

When von Uexküll's *Umweltlehre* is integrated into a Peircean semiotic framework and further developed through the new knowledge gained by modern biology and cybernetics, it opens the way to a non-reductionist biophenomenology and biosemiotics. In Peirce's semiotics, everything in nature is a potential sign (a Representamen). This is a meeting point with Bateson's cybernetics, according to which everything is potential information, as information is a difference that makes a difference for the self-organizing cybernetic mind function. But actually this only occurs through the creation of meaningful signs. With Peirce, we can say that differences become information when an interpreter sees them as signs.

In humans, these signs are organized into language through social and self-conscious communication; it follows that our universe is largely organized as and through texts (Kirkeby 1997) and sign webs. Peirce's reflexive cybernetic definition of the Interpretant points to culture, history, and the unending search for truth and knowledge.

I think it is a useful biological development of Peirce's idea to suggest that the meanings of signs are created within the semiotic web of society. To integrate Peirce and Wittgenstein, I stress that unlimited semiosis occurs when the Interpretants of signs are generated both through biological evolution and through cultural history, as underscored by Lakoff (1987). Peirce's biological, mental, and social habits are the meanings of the signs and are equivalent to the language games connecting 'life forms' in the theories of Wittgenstein. Wittgenstein did not care much for biology. But seen from ethology, second-order cybernetics, and biosemiotics, the basis for human life forms and language games is sign games in our natural history. These habits are what ethologists call instincts. Instincts can be combined with individual learning in different proportions to conduct a communicative act, such as a bird song, and eventually lead to 'sensitive periods' for the type of learning that occurs during human language acquisition.

The transdisciplinary cybersemiotic approach provides a biopsychosocial framework for an understanding of signification, one capable of supplementing previous ethological models of animal cognition. I contend that perception, cognition, anticipation, signification, and communication are interwoven in autopoietic systems with their own 'signification spheres' that are in mutual historical drift, and that we still understand very little about how meaning is generated during this ecological, evolutionary, and social process. As Lakoff (ibid., xv) has shown, the relations among categorical concepts are not logical; rather they are motivated. They originate in the motivated language games of basic life forms: 'On the experientialist view, reason is made possible by the body – that includes abstract and creative reason, as well as reasoning about concrete things. Human reason is not an instantiation of transcendental reason; it grows out of the nature of the organism and all that contributes to its individual and collective experience: its genetic inheritance, the nature of the environment it lives in, the way it functions in that environment, the nature of its social functioning, and the like.'

Living systems are self-organized cognitive, anticipatory, autopoietic systems. I agree with Spinoza that they have 'conatus,' meaning that the individuality of a life system is valuable because it braces that system's continuing efforts to preserve its own internal organization. I believe that the knowledge that has been developed in ethology and second-order cybernetics has deepened and complemented Lakoff and Johnson's efforts by providing a more profound concept of motivation and a more differentiated view of the experientialist biological framework.

8.9 The Ethological Model of Motivated Cognition Based on a Theory of Feeling

Lorenz (1970–1) discovered that as we move beyond the level of reflexes, there are no clear-cut connections among perception, behaviour, and the structural-processual knowledge of the nervous system. A new level of complexity and causality is reached even though higher animals lack self-conscious awareness as well as linguistic capabilities.

Lorenz' ethological model and von Uexküll's biophenomenological and biosemiotic models all point to the significance of motivation – or tone, in von Uexküll's terminology – in the construction of perceptual and behavioural objects towards which the living system can direct its actions in such a way as to increase its chances for survival. Motivation is crucial for determining the kind of Interpretant established. For learning, some kind of emotional reward seems necessary (Lorenz 1977). Motivation seems to be an intention just below the level of consciousness. One cannot say that von Uexküll has provided a theoretical framework that defines emotions. It is unclear whether his 'tones' have an emotional or conscious element. Innis (1944, 14) makes it very clear how Peirce deals with this problem by combining his metaphysics with his analysis of signification:

> There is, Peirce admits, a sense in which 'introspection' exists: as an interpretation of phenomena that present themselves as external percepts. Percepts, sensory wholes, are our logical data. They involve, as contends of consciousness, three kinds of physical elements – the qualities of feeling, their reactions against my will, and their generalization or associative element. But all that we find out afterward (CP, 8.144). These three kinds of psychical elements correspond to the principal Peircean categorical triad, which makes up the foundation of his metaphysics, and they are all irretrievably in the consciousness of the perceptual object.

It is commonly argued that in evolution emotional capabilities emerged at some moment after amphibians developed, but before reptiles did. The concept of the pure physical causality of animal behaviour has only limited explanatory value. Cybernetic and semiotic types of information and semiotic types of causality provide a highly necessary supplement. We must realize and integrate the emotional element if we are to understand perception, anticipation, and decision making. This is becoming more apparent in modern research into consciousness in higher animals and humans. In a recent paper spelling out the consequences of accepting phenomenal or first person consciousness in the ethological view of animals, Ellis and Newton (1998, 431) wrote:

> It is the organism's emotions that motivate it to act on its environment rather than merely react; the phenomenal aspect of conscious experience requires the organism's emotionally motivated action in relation to the perceived world, particularly in its interest in selecting for attentional focus. If the organism's knowledge of its environment is to involve a '*felt*' dimension, in the sense that there is 'something it feels like' to have a state of consciousness, the conscious processing must first flow from an emo-

tional process within the organism, which pre-exists any particular input, and puts its qualitative stamp on each selected input.

We are suggesting that the 'felt' aspect of experiencing is tied in with the fact that organisms are emotionally motivated to 'look for' elements of the environment that are significant with respect to the organism's motivational purposes; that the organism 'anticipates' experience in terms of motivational categories which preselect for attention; and that the emotions that guide this anticipation and selection process are a major contributor to the conscious feeling of 'what the consciousness of such-and-such an object is like.'

Ellis and Newton go straight to the core of Lorenz's difficulties with the concept of motivation in ethology. They see a clear link between the anticipatory mind of animals and their ability (developed later) to form images in the mind, which biological systems then become aware of, whether these systems are animal or human. Ellis and Newton emphasize strongly the importance of the felt dimension, which Peirce (unlike any other) introduces as the pure feeling in Firstness. In my view, Peirce's framework is necessary if we are to legitimate their theorizing. This phenomenological approach is similar to von Uexküll's original theoretical biology, but with Peirce's three categories and types of evolution added. Innis (1994, 15) writes: 'The time constituted web of semiosis defines the life of consciousness, the meaning of which, as a chain of thought-sign and interpretants is what will be understood subsequently in another thought.'

This acknowledges that the inner world of animals is a causal factor in perception and cognition. Furthermore, it develops Lorenz's work in a fruitful way by connecting ethological and linguistic motivation concepts through the phenomenological world of animals. This theory also dovetails with Peirce's idea that feeling is a basic aspect of the protoplasm, as it was understood in his day (Santaella Braga 1999). Peirce uses this as part of one of his basic categories: Firstness. He provides an extended metaphysics that solves Lorenz's struggle to find a third (biological) way between vitalism and mechanicism. I suggest that this also provides a broader foundation for Lakoff and Johnson's work. In the following quote, Peirce (1992, 42) ties all of this up with his synechistic and evolutionary view: 'At no one instant in my state of mind is there cognition or representation, but in the relation of my states of mind at different instants there is. In short, the Immediate (and therefore in itself unsusceptible of mediation – the Unanalyzable, the Inexplicable, the Unintellectual) runs in a continuous stream through our lives; it is the sum total of consciousness, whose mediation, which is the continuity of it, is brought about by a real effective force behind consciousness.'

This unlimited continous stream of consciousness is the force that gives rise to semiosis at any given moment. Semiosis follows from the temporal nature of consciousness, as it is how the momentary aspect of consciousness is related to each other over time in a kind of self-organization as such, in accordance with Varela's analysis of the self-reflection process in his expansion of Spencer-Brown's calculus. Peirce (CP, 1.306) clarifies the role of feeling (and Firstness) in this process:

> By a feeling, I mean an instance of that kind of consciousness which involves no analysis, comparison, or any process whatsoever, nor consist on whole or in part of any act by which one stretch of consciousness is distinguished from another, which has its own positive quality which consist in nothing else, and which is of itself all that it is, however it may have been brought about; so that if this feeling is present during a lapse of time, it is wholly and equally present at every moment of that time. To reduce this description to a simple definition, I will say that by a feeling I mean an instance of that sort of element of consciousness which is all that is positively, in itself, regardless of anything else.

Thus to Peirce a feeling is a quality of immediate consciousness having its own quality, one that is independent of any other state of mind and that is perfectly simple in itself.[4] This does not contradict Lakoff and Johnson's idea that most mental processes, even in humans, are non-conscious. Ellis and Newton (1998, 434) open a new line in consciousness research when they pick up the problem of motivation and emotion where Lorenz left off. They recognize emotion and purposefulness as real, but they do not deliver a philosophical framework as Peirce does, so they, too, are in need of it:

> Emotions and motivations are characterized by purposive strivings, and there do seem to be *non-conscious* yet *purposive* phenomena in nature, especially in biological organisms. The human organism purposely does what is needed to regulate heartbeat and blood pressure, yet normally is not *conscious* of doing so. Merleau-Ponty defines a 'purposeful organism' as one that changes, replaces, or readjusts the functioning of its own parts as needed to maintain or enhance the functioning of the whole organism. Jacques Monod (1972) and Stuart Kaufmann (1993) have used this defi-

nition as a leading concept in the attempt to show how biological processes tend to maintain their pattern of activity across very multiply-realizable replacements of their components.

This seems harmonious with Lakoff and Johnson's view of the body. These two do not deal in depth with animal cognition or the evolutionary view of the connection between it and the development of human cognition and categorization, but when it comes to bodily metaphors extended through imagery, it is unlikely that this can be modelled in a mechanical way on brain functions. Ellis and Newton (ibid., 435) support my opinion on this:

> Emotions are conscious only to the extent that we form some sort of representation of what they are about and of how they are manifest in our bodies. Usually, this entails imagery of some sort, especially when we consider symbolic utterances as a kind of imagery, as ... both emotion and representation are needed for phenomenal consciousness. Without emotion, we might have unconscious information processing, as in a digital computer or thermostat or thermos bottle; and without the representation, we might have unconscious emotions, as in 'wanting' to fill or empty the outer electron shells of atoms in the various biological systems, so as to restore chemical homeostasis, but not a *conscious* wanting of this outcome. But emotion and representation must be present for phenomenal experiencing to occur.

Ellis and Newton make a solid case for going beyond physicochemical explanations to include the phenomenological (and social) semiotic view as a way of explaining the foundations of cognition and semiosis. This foundation is necessary for understanding how a self-conscious being can master human signs and language. Again, I contend that it is not possible to be consistent here without accepting Peirce's broader foundation, which provides an alternative to mechanism. It is difficult to imagine how a metaphorically driven motivated categorization can be possible without a body–mind driven by emotional motivation: 'In anticipating perceptual objects, we are anticipating the way they may or may not interact with our motivating organismic purposes. There is no attention without motivation to attend, and no motivation without emotional purposes. Furthermore, part of the anticipated outcome in action planning is the hoped-for or feared subsequent emotional state of the organism' (ibid., 438–9).

Humans and animals are always anticipating meaningful contexts connected to their life form. This is also the way humans fit linguistic expressions and categorizations to their perceptions and thoughts, either to perceive something as something, or to communicate knowledge or intentions to another linguistic being. Peirce (CP, 1.377) applies his three basic categories as the basis of his theory of feeling and consciousness and in this way connects them to his metaphysics in a way that none of the other theories we have analysed has done in such a consistent manner: 'First, feeling, the consciousness that can be included with an instant of time, passive consciousness of quality, without recognition or analysis; second, consciousness of an interruption into the field of consciousness, sense of resistance, of an external fact, of another something; third, synthetic consciousness, binding time together, sense of learning, thought.'

I previously suggested using the concept 'signification sphere' for that part of the environment with which a living system is in a semiotic relationship, and therefore able to produce felt perceptions, reactions, and actions above the level of reflexes. I thus combine ethological understandings of instinctive cognition with cybernetic understandings immanent in autopoiesis theory, adding the phenomenological stand of von Uexküll that reappears in the work of Lorenz and that has been further clarified by Ellis and Newton. I combine this with the embodied cognition semantics of Lakoff and Johnson and finally with the semiotic work of Sebeok, Hoffmeyer, Emmeche, and Kull to make von Uexküll's model the foundation of biosemiotics. Nöth has further developed a theory of signification when it is not connected to communication. He calls this ecosemiotics.

8.10 The Ecosemiotics Perspective

In his introduction to the new field of ecosemiotics, Winfried Nöth (2001a, 107) writes about ecosemiotics as an extension of biosemiotics:

> At the interface between semiotics and ecology, ecosemiotics is the study of environmental semiosis, i.e., the study of sign processes, which relate organisms to their natural environment. Ecosemiotics or ecological semiotics is related to several other ecosciences such as eco-ethology, human ecology, philosophical ecology, ecopsychology, ecological history ... In contrast to these disciplines, which study various other aspects of the relationship between humans or animals and their Umwelt, ecosemiotics focuses on how this relationship is mediated by signs?

In the field of semiotics at large, ecosemiotics is situated between the semiotics of culture on the one hand and the semiotics of nature on the other ... The field of ecosemiotics hence overlaps with the fields of bio- or zoosemiotics, but there is a major difference between ecosemiotics and the other domains of the semiotics of nature, which can be accounted for in terms of the distinction between the semiotics of communication and the semiotics of signification ... Not only cultural semiotics, but also bio- and zoosemiotics are hence concerned with processes of communication. Signification, by contrast, which concerns sign processes without a sender, predominates in ecosemiotics, where organisms interact with a natural environment that does not function as the intentional emitter of messages to the interpreting organism.

I agree with Nöth that the semiotics of signification is crucial to the foundation of both bio- and cybersemiotics. I have already shown this in my analysis of ethology and von Uexküll's *Umweltslehre*. Peircean semiotics differs from other semiotic paradigms in that it not only deals with the intentional signs of communication, but also encompasses non-intentional signs, such as symptoms of the body and the patterns of inanimate nature. Peircean semiotics diverges from the traditional dualistic epistemological problem of first-order science by framing its basic concept of *signification* within a triadic semiotic philosophy.

Triadic semiotics is integrated with an evolutionary theory of mind (Agapism) and a theory of continuity between mind and matter (Synechism) where the basic three categories (Firstness, Secondness, and Thirdness) are not only inside the perceiver's mind but also in the surrounding nature. This is connected to the third important ontological belief in Peirce's philosophy – Tychism – which posits chance and chaos as basic characteristics of Firstness. The chaos of Firstness is not the lack of laws, as in mechanicism or rationalism; rather, it is full of potential qualities to be manifested individually in Secondness and, through Agapism, as general habits and knowledge in the dynamic objects and semiosis of Thirdness (Pragmaticism) (Peirce 1992).

Bertalanffy, Luhmann, and Peirce are all clearly influenced by Hegel, notwithstanding their criticisms of him. All three are concerned with the ways in which new hierarchical levels of natural existence can be created by an evolutionary process describable as the regular interaction of a limited number of basic dynamic categories. The genius of Pierce was to find these basic categories in a simplified form within our own perception, thinking, and communication, so that it is clear that these also function in nature, albeit not independently of mind. A deep basic connection between mind and nature is thus established, as has been attempted by the cybernetics pan-information paradigm, where, for instance, Stonier (1997) sees the 'infon' as a type of fundamental 'particle' that drives the organization of nature through evolution. But Stonier lacks Peirce's conception of Firstness, Secondness, and Thirdness, which has semiotic qualities even at the level of evolution, guiding the evolutionary development of natural laws through a weak teleonomic process, and working over space-time magnitudes so immense that they are beyond human comprehension (Deely 1994, 1998, 2001a). This leads us to the threshold problem in semiotics, not least biosemiotics.

9 An Evolutionary View on the Threshold between Semiosis and Informational Exchange

9.1 Introduction

The analysis and conclusions so far have equipped us to deal with the threshold problem in semiotics and information science in the broader context of attempts to develop general scientific theories of information, cognition, and communication. This pertains to questions of physicalism, pan-informationalism, system theory, and pan-semiotics as well as vitalism and various sorts of idealism, all of which attempt to serve as transdisciplinary frameworks. The purpose of these transdisciplinary theories is to help us do two things: (a) frame the problems that are inherent in understanding the interface between humans and machines as well as the linguistic interaction by clarifying the epistemological problems of the difference between how digital machines work and how a living system's cognition of the living and non-living parts of nature works; and (b) understand the biological, psychological, and social bases of communication.

In particular, I wish to discuss the question of threshold in the broader epistemological and ontological context of the metaphysics of knowledge systems, as well as in the context of a philosophy of science emerging from biology, cybernetics, and information science. These discussions have brought the relation and conflict between informational and semiotic approaches into focus. I will return later to the discussion about the semiotic threshold – a discussion that is strongly similar to discussions about whether objective information in nature exists, as claimed by the pan-informational paradigm.

I consider this discussion of thresholds to be situated at the crossroads of the scientific world view, epistemology, and theories of cognition and signification. It is at this point that our conceptions of nature/reality, cognition, and the nature of knowledge meet our understandings of the human mind and the relation of mind to matter. This discussion has been conducted for some time in the context of the informational paradigm. The informational and the Peircean semiotic paradigms are both transdisciplinary, which suggests that solutions to our scientific problems lie in creating a unifying framework for nature, cognition, and mind. Both frameworks see that materialism in whatever form, is an insufficient basis to understand mind, meaning, and communication. Both therefore suggest that the connections among mind, culture, and nature are either informational or semiotic, meaning that informational functionalistic and/or the semiotic significatory processes exist in our mind as well as in nature. Furthermore, both contend that past attempts to understand how we acquire knowledge about nature have not provided satisfactory answers to our questions, be it at a practical or a theoretical level, especially concerning the differences and continuities between inanimate and animate systems, between living and socio-linguistic systems, and among socio-linguistic, mechanical, and cybernetic informational digital systems. At present, I can identify five basic significant models that have attempted to explain all of these, from the basic patterns, laws, and forces of inanimate nature to the phenomena of life and consciousness. I will briefly sketch these five here and discuss them further in this chapter:

1. *Mechanical materialistic or thermodynamic physicalism* refuses to address information and signs in nature, including animals. This model often presumes that the phenomena of human thought via meaningful signs are not connected to consciousness and sometimes not even to intentionality. Such physicalistic understandings are often grounded in the view that these phenomena are illusory (eliminative materialism); it follows that intentionality, free will, and consciousness cannot have any real causal effects on things in the physical/real world, including human bodies (Churchland 2004). Differences in organization levels are observed only among physical, chemical, and biological levels of reality.[1]

2. *Pan-informational metaphysics* posits that information is an objective part of all nature and culture, like matter and energy. In 1929, Szilard suggested a converse relationship between information and entropy by referring to Boltzmann's thermodynamics, also called statistical mechanics. Shannon and Weaver (1969) referred to entropy in their work, mainly because of similarities between the equations that deal

with thermodynamics and those that deal with statistical events – equations that were originally derived to describe the outcomes of games of chance. But it was Norbert Wiener (1961) who declared that information is neither matter nor energy and that thermodynamic entropy is the opposite of the statistical concept of information defined as negentropy. This approach has been supported by Schrödinger in *What Is Life?* (1967), by Ruesch and Bateson (1987), and more recently by Tom Stonier (1997). The result is that information as the opposite of entropy can be understood as the construction of order in the face of disorder (Prigogine and Stengers 1984). Self-organizing, dissipative structures organize energy and information while simultaneously dissipating entropy.

Thus the concepts of energy, order, and information, on the one hand, and entropy, disorder, and loss of information, on the other, became connected in such a way that we perceive information as related to patterned organization and the reduction of uncertainty (Combs and Brier 2001). Information thus becomes the organizational aspect of nature. Stonier (1997) even accepts the 'infon' as a basic constituent of nature.

This approach is often developed within a first-order cybernetics metaphysics, which hypothesizes that the world comes into being as a self-organized system consisting of other self-organized systems. For Wiener, uniting the theory of information with the Bolzmanian interpretation of thermodynamics – and thereby overcoming the Cartesian duality of mind and matter – was a breakthrough, even though he was unable to develop this into a full-fledged metaphysics. Bateson was able to integrate Wiener's work into an ecological and evolutionary theoretical perspective that carried over into anthropology as well.

Many other cyberneticians working with this general model have found inspiration in Bertalanffy's general systems theory. His antidualistic view is based on an organismic evolutionary world view, one that includes a theory of emergence and holism as well as a belief in the continuity through emergent steps between mind and matter. This metaphysical aspect is overlooked by many modern theorists such as Stonier, but not by Jantsch (1980), Laszlo (1995), or Goerner (1993), who have developed a new ecosystem spiritualism or objective idealism as a holistic interpretation of modern science's findings in cosmology and quantum field theory. But how can such a notion of the creation of forms tell us anything interesting about the nature of discourse?

3. *The Luhmanian second-order cybernetics approach* sees nature as a source of countless differences, in which the cybernetic system determines what should make a difference for a system and become information in the organism and in its social communication with society. A cybernetic autopoietic system makes the first distinction by differentiating between the system and its surroundings. Luhmann (1995) never explicates the nature of Firstness before the first distinction, as Peirce does. Luhmann's idea is based on Spencer-Brown, who seems implicitly to work with a mystically objective idealist theory of the Void, or Emptiness, which contains the potentiality of both mind and matter, much as in Peirce (Brent 1998; 208–12). This aspect seems lost in Luhmann's theory. Inspired by Husserl and his theory of intersubjectivity, Luhmann embraces concepts of intentionality and meaning, but he also transforms Husserl's concept to a kind of social-communicative functionalistic framework. Luhmann's paradigm has similarities to the Peircean semiotic view in that it focuses on communication and meaning, but it lacks a triadic theory of the sign vehicle and a developed theory about the contributions of biologically motivated emotional systems to the generation of meaning.

4. *Peircean (bio)semiotics* is distinct from other semiotic paradigms in that it not only deals with intentional signs of communication, but also encompasses non-intentional signs such as symptoms of the body and patterns of inanimate nature. Peircean semiotics breaks with the traditional dualistic epistemological problem of first-order science by framing its basic concept of cognition, *signification through abduction*, within a triadic semiotic philosophy. This in turn is integrated into a theory of continuity between mind and matter (Synechism), in which the three basic categories (Firstness, Secondness, and Thirdness) are not only inside the perceiver's mind, but also in the nature perceived. This is connected to the second important ontological belief in Peirce's philosophy, namely, Tychism, which sees chance and Chaos with a tendency to take habits as basic characteristics of Firstness. This leads to an evolutionary theory of mind (Agapism), wherein mind has a tendency to form habits in nature. Chaos and chance are seen as First, which is not to be explained further (for instance, by regularities). It is the basis of habit forming and evolution. The chaos of Firstness is not seen as the lack of law, as it is in mechanism and rationalism, but rather as something full of potential qualities to be manifested individually in Secondness and as general habits and knowledge in dynamic objects and semiosis in Thirdness (Peirce 1992). Matter and mind are united in the

continuum of Firstness and develop through 'evolutionary law' into Secondness's manifestations of resistance, force, dualistic concreteness, and the impenetrability of objects. Secondness provides what second-order cybernetics views as constraints on perception and cognition occurring in the Thirdness of true triadic sign processes. This is the deep foundation of Peirce's pragmaticism. As a result of the innovative work of Thomas Sebeok, Peirce's semiotics are now interpreted as covering all living signifying systems in biosemiotics.

Biosemiotics studies the signification, communication, and habit formation of living processes. One of the central characteristics of living systems is the highly organized character of their physical and chemical processes, which is based partly on informational and molecular properties. These are interpreted *also* as sign systems. The change in perspective lies in considering life not simply from the perspective of chemistry, but also in terms of signs conveyed. As such, biosemiotics attempts a more unified semiotic perspective on the central phenomena of the living world, from the ribosome to the ecosystem and from the beginnings of life to its ultimate meanings. Thus, it looks at the semiotics of nature, for example, at the grounding of sign processes in the fundamental processes of our universe – processes such as the metaphysics of Darwinism, the emergence of the Interpretant in swarm intelligence, and the semiotics of collective phenomena. Biosemiotics is an attempt to apply the concepts of (mostly) Peircean semiotics to answer questions about the biologic and evolutionary emergence of meaning, intentionality, and a psychic world.

One focus of biosemiotics is the semiotics of cellular communication in the immune system and in the brain. Another is sign functions in physical, biological, and virtual universes – for example, the semiotics of anticipatory systems and of complex systems and artificial life. In which sense is semiosis always a living process, and to what extent are biological processes semiotic? Is it the sign rather than the molecule that is the basic unit for life, as Hoffmeyer argues in several places? Hoffmeyer (1997, 61) also writes that 'The most pronounced feature of organic evolution is not the creation of a multiplicity of amazing morphological structures, but the general expansion of "semiotic freedom," that is to say the increase in richness or "depth" of meaning that can be communicated.'

Semiotic freedom becomes a key concept in the evolution of living systems. The precise role of living systems in establishing true semiosis is unclear in Peirce's theory, yet Peirce views the cytoplasm as a place of Firstness and therefore of chance and feeling, which makes the emergence of an inner world possible in living systems. Peirce did not know much about the specific biological qualities that allow this to happen. He did, however, have the view that chance-spontaneity in nerve cells is 'the outward aspect of that which within itself is feeling' (CP, 7.265; Santaella Braga 1999). The term 'quasi-semiotic objects' (Nöth 2002) recognizes that systems in nature and culture work with differences, often in the form of coding, rather than through either physical causality or meaningful semiosis. Systems of Secondness have established an information level above the energetic and causal level of nature. From a semiotic perspective, this level is part of what classical first-order cybernetics considers its subject area: goal-oriented machines and pattern-forming, self-organized processes in nature that are based on information.

5. *Pan-semiotic metaphysics* argues that all environmental phenomena are ultimately semiotic. The universe is perfused with signs, as Peirce famously stated.

One version of pan-semiotics is constructivistic. Semiosis is every-where, either because everything is semiosis in its nature, or because the only way we can know anything is through semiosis. Pan-semiotic con-structivism encompasses both culture and nature. Reality is constructed by human societies living together in language. It is a radical construc-tivism. Thus it is close to becoming a human-centred metaphysics (a subjective idealism) with no explicit idea of what nature could be in itself – or to put it in another way, what kind of external source there could be for the signs of nature. Signs are all these are.

The other version of pan-semiotics posits that signs are as real as atoms and energy and that the latter are also signs. Signs are the basic constituents of the world. These signs emerge by themselves, as clarified by Merrell in *Signs Grow: Semiosis of Life Processes* (1996). Reading both Merrell and Emmeche's critique of him (2000), it is clear that Merrell views signs as independent living beings that grow by themselves. The pan-semiotic interpretation takes Peirce's teleonomy in causality and a universe perfused with signs to mean that there is Thirdness, and there-fore semiosis, in inanimate nature. Sign processes are thus taken as intrinsic in nature. This interpretation finds support in quotes from Peirce like this: 'Nominalism introduced the notion that consciousness, i.e., percepts, is not the real thing but only signs of the real thing. But … these signs are the very real thing. Reals *are* signs. To try to peel off signs & get down to the real thing is like trying to peel an onion and get down to the onion itself' (Letter to F.C. Russell, 3 July 1905, quoted in Brent 1998, 357).

The difference between the biosemiotic interpretation and a pan-semiotic one is that the former limits the abilities of true semiosis to living systems and thus puts the semiotic threshold between inanimate nature – including machines – and living systems. Biosemiotics considers machine processes and pattern/signal interactions in nature as only quasi-semiotic processes, not truly triadic.

9.2 The Explanatory Quest of the Sciences since Religion Lost Power

As we can see from these short descriptions of the five basic views, the central distinctions to be discussed are the thresholds between living and 'dead' nature, between living and mechanical systems, and between information and meaning. Other important parts of this discussion will concern modern scientific approaches to meaning and the phenomenological part of reality, and the demands being placed on science to deliver true explanations of an independent reality. These demands have increased ever since our religious and mythical frameworks were challenged by the world view of the classical mechanical sciences, the rationality and historical thinking of the Enlightenment, Darwinian evolution, the psychology of modernity, and, finally, the linguistic turn. Let me start, then, with a brief discussion of the history and philosophy of science.

Galileo challenged religion as the upholder of a meaningful world through experiments as well as through theories of an earthly science; these he combined with Copernicus' view of the heavens – in a view that confronted the world view of the Catholic Church. Classical mechanical physical science, with its concept of universal mechanical natural laws, was crucial to breaking the monopoly of the Church's world view. The world view of the Catholic Church was one of the foundations of culturally produced meaningfulness for individuals: it told people, for example, where they originated, where they could go, and what their lives meant.

When the philosophers of the Enlightenment, and later Marx and Engels, challenged the view of the social order as 'heavenly sent,' this further disturbed the belief that everything in our social order had been created 'as it should be once and for all.' Darwin questioned the belief that humans originated from a higher and meaningful place endowed with a meaningful destiny and that the human soul descended into the body from the 'divine above.' Freud destroyed the notion that humans were perfectly conscious and rational beings in control of their selves and drives. Nietzsche and other philosophers finally declared God 'dead,' and this left a nihilistic vacuum without universal meaning or values: we would have to create order and meaning ourselves.

Since then, humans have increasingly looked to science for new explanations about themselves. This has led to what Prigogine and Stengers call 'world formula thinking,' the belief that final explanations can only be found through science, especially through algorithmic approaches such as those utilized in artificial intelligence, in 'the algorithms of the book of life' in genes, and in grand unification theories of physics such as superstring theory.

Descartes's dualism attempted to save the human soul from the mechanistic grip of science, but his own followers' experiments with brain lesions in doves, the development of neuroscience and theories of 'conditioning' in behaviourial science made the human mind and behaviour part of the scientific field.

Cybernetics, information theory and science, and theories of AI have produced functionalistic approaches to understanding cognition and communication. These approaches have now been combined in the transdisciplinary programs of the information processing paradigm of the cognitive sciences. Such programs promote a paradigm of cognition that treats the first-person aspects of cognition as a software program based on algorithms in the brain's neurological hardware (functionalism). At the same time, quantum mechanical field theories have become increasingly interesting as possible tools for explaining the ongoing characteristics of consciousness (Penrose 1995).

Through science we learned to be sceptical about systems that explain too much, such as religious, mythical–magical, and ideological–political systems of belief and power. Nevertheless, by the end of the twentieth century, modern science had made various attempts to combine evolutionary, historical, and developmental theories of the environment, living bodies, individual conscience, and socio-cultural linguistic meanings and values into one overarching scientific narrative, one that completely ignored postmodern warnings that grand narratives were deceptive.

Grand evolutionary theories (GETs) attempt to combine Big Bang cosmology about the self-organization of energy into matter with evolutionary theories of life. Using physics and chemistry, modern science has attempted to explain life by simulating it with computers, and by manipulating genes and other chemicals. The final proof of such a theory would be the artificial construction of life by independently synthesizing macromolecules and combining them into the organelles and membranes of a cell.

In the sciences we are expected to explain matter as a specific form or organization of energy. Energy is then expected to provide a foundation for explaining life as a unique organization of matter. The grand evolutionary story attempts to explain everything by beginning with the transformation of energy from a quantum vacuum into matter, time, and space. Through self-organization, life emerges, followed by central nervous systems, social organization, semiosis, communication, language, culture, and consciousness.

Modern Big Bang cosmology when combined with unified field and superstring theory offers a materialistic story about the reality we inhabit, which we call the universe. It also tells a story about the evolution from radiation to subatomic particles, about how atoms emerged from the fusion processes of stars and supernova explosions and in turn created the basic elements that are the parts for molecules, and eventually the macromolecules that are the essential components of living systems. This is then supplemented with theories of objective information that perceive energy as organizing itself into patterns and systems of matter within the expanding universe, and later into living systems, cognitive systems, and linguistic and conscious systems in culture. The crown of this paradigm is Dawkins' theory of the selfish gene and of culture as a collection of selfish memes (Dawkins 1999). Growing up in a culture, a child's mind is infected with the memes and world view of that culture, which program its mind with a particular paradigm of meanings and causalities (See also Blackmore 1999 for a development of this theory). But I doubt:

1. that such a grand story is scientifically possible,
2. that it is the true nature of science to construct this type of explanation, and
3. that we will ever be able, with shared language, to provide generally accepted, universal explanations that combine into one discussion the four basic constituents of human existence: energy/matter, life, language, and conscious inner life.

But I do contend that the foundation for understanding the sciences, social sciences, arts, humanities, and practical sciences, as well as phi-

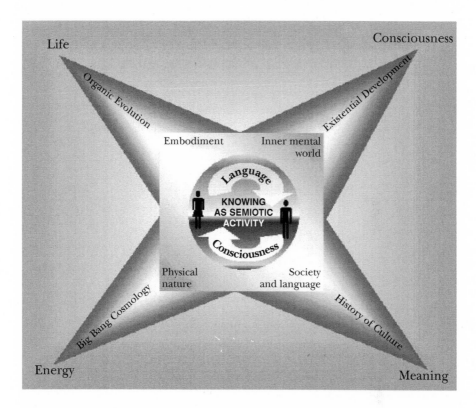

9.1.   *The semiotic star.* A diagram of how the communicative social system of embodied minds' four main areas of knowledge arises. Physical nature is usually explained as originating in energy and matter, living systems as emerging from the development of life processes (for instance, the first cell). Social culture is explained as founded on the development of meaning in language and practical habits. Finally, our inner mental world is explained as deriving from the development of our individual life world and consciousness.

losophy and other systematic searches for meaningful, justified, and true public knowledge, must begin with the prerequisite that human beings are:

1. embodied and biologically situated – our body is the principal system for the manifestation of life and cognition;
2. conscious and intentionally situated – consciousness is the source of

an inner life of cognition, volition, feeling, and perceptual qualities (qualia);

3. meaning-situated in cultural practice – that is, through language in a social and cultural activity with a network of other living, linguistic, conscious systems; and

4. environmentally situated – in a nature or a universe that is partly independent of our perception and being.

Humans are thus embodied, feeling, and knowing cultural beings in language. See the semiotic star in Figure 9.1. We therefore live in four different worlds, as Merleau-Ponty (2002) argues:

1. Our bodyhood and our sharing of bodyhood with other living species.

2. Our inner world of emotions and thoughts, which manifest themselves as mind and consciousness.

3. The physicochemical environment of the natural world.

4. The cultural world of language, meaning, and power.

Each of these four worlds demands its own type of narrative. Physicists and chemists tend to view the universe as consisting of matter and energy, and Wienerian cybernetic interpretations add meaningless objective information. The attempt to explain the universe, life, consciousness, language, and culture on the basis of energy, matter, and information is one powerful angle we have analysed in this book.

Biologists tend to perceive the biosphere as consisting of all living systems, perhaps even one living system as in the Gaia theory. Some even consider the entire universe living because it produces living systems. It is a self-organizing universe (Jantsch 1980)! This view is compatible with Bertalanffy's general systems theory and an organicistic philosophy.

The social and cultural sciences tend to see the world as constructed from social, human, and linguistic interpretations, or they are dualist in terms of nature–culture dualist ontology, which accepts that nature is as science describes it and that only culture is constructed by humans. Still, most researchers from the social sciences consider science to be deeply influenced by values, power, and paradigms.

Those who address the phenomenological aspects of our being tend to be antiscientific and antirealistic, often view the world as a product of human minds, and consciousness as only a part of linguistic systems.

Like Peirce, I see the semiotic mind and social corporation at the

heart of all four worlds. One of the strengths of Peirce's semiotic philosophy is that qualia and mind – as semiosis – are installed in the metaphysics from the beginning. They cannot be explained as such because
they can only be deduced as necessary prerequisites for the production
of that knowledge we wish to discuss!

My main difficulty with the standard materialistic scientific evolutionary paradigm is that I cannot see how physics – as an external science
based on the present definitions of matter, energy, and deterministic
law – can furnish us independently with a complete understanding of
our inner lives and the emergence of consciousness. If one works from
an evolutionary view, one that combines the Big Bang theory, self-organizing thermodynamics, chemistry, and Darwinism, and proceeds with a
materialistic theory of the development of humans and the history of
language and culture, it is a severe challenge to explain consciousness
as this inner quality of perception, feeling, volition, and cognition that
we all experience. I do not see how quantum physics, the theory of relativity, or non-equilibrium thermodynamics or a pan-informational
information science building on information and neg-entropy can help
us solve this problem, although all of these may help in explain physical
aspects of consciousness.

The standard view now combines evolutionary theory with a materialist ontology based on energy (as in quantum physics, the general theory
of relativity, and thermodynamics) to explain life as a chemical-organi-
zational phenomenon. When it is realized that this is not enough, the aid
of some kind of objectivistic information concept is often sought. But
most biologists refuse to admit that their use of the information concepts
in connection with DNA and genes means anything significantly new
with any ontological consequences as the biosemioticians want them to
see (Emmeche 1999). This is probably because this adds new fundamental concepts, entities, and ideas of organization to the paradigm that
are foreign to biology's basic metaphysical conceptions. What I am doing
here is to uncover the hidden metaphysical assumptions in order to
discuss them openly. Other researchers, most often mathematicians and
physicists, are willing to take the last ontological step, realizing that in
doing so they are calling on science – if it wants to include information
science – to see the universe as digitalized and therefore basically as a big
computer. Chaitin (2005) is one example of a high-profile mathematician promoting this view. But I ask: Where in this view will qualia, emotions, meaning, and will emerge? There is no satisfactory theory of life
and the inner world of first-person experiences.

The semiotic epistemological turn illustrated in Figure 9.1 escapes
the explanatory burden of reductionist mainstream science that

attempts to explain both life and consciousness from the same basic assumptions about energy and mathematical mechanistic laws. The cybersemiotic view sees scientific explanations as emerging from our present state of socio-linguistically based conscious semiosis in self-organized autopoietic systems, and as moving towards a better understanding of the prerequisites of language and the self-conscious being. A reduction made in any of the four directions must remain consistent with the point of departure in the centre.

Science explains the world and our place in it only to a limited degree. Our existential questions go beyond that. Knowledge – defined as the combination of qualia, objects, and Interpretants in semiosis – is one of the greatest mysteries of the world. Being in the world, in languaging, in bodyhood, and in a meaningful social context, we always start *in medias res*. We are bound to make metaphysical presumptions based on our present understanding – an understanding whose limitations will only be realized later. But Peirce's semiotics is a good non-reductionist framework to start from because it takes the semiotic mind as its point of departure (see the centre of the semiotic star in 9.1).

Somehow if we want to form connections between science and the phenomenological aspects of reality and the experiences of meaning, we must enlarge the conceptual framework within which we conduct science. Our quest is to explain and understand all four aspects of our reality; our explanations from any one of the corners will be only one aspect of this broader explanation. I suggest that the scientific endeavour and other explanatory systems start in the middle and extrapolate out to the four corners. To explain everything from any one corner would be reductionist, leading to the same reductionist totalitarism as physicalism, scientism, and the pan-energetic, pan-informational paradigms. Peirce's insistence on Secondness as an independent existence that eventually reveals itself as the dynamic object for the final Interpretant insures against all kinds of overly radical constructivisms of the sort that lose their grip on reality and become either subjective or collective idealisms.

One way to deal with this paradoxical problem would be to make less ambitious demands on science to explain the grand scheme of things; Peirce demonstrates this in his deep integration of science and philosophy within semiosis. Science offers adequate understandings of certain processes, often allowing for precise predictions in specific circumstances. But science does not offer universal explanations for the construction of reality, energy, information, life, meaning, mind, or consciousness. Nor does it provide a full explanation of the world or our place in it.

Semiotics begins with the process of knowledge: how signification occurs within living systems, making perception and cognition possible. Peirce's semiotics unites our explanatory schemes of deduction and induction through abduction within the process of semiosis. Peirce suggests that we consider triadic semiosis as the fundamental process of reality. Consciousness is built from semiotic processes. Biosemiotics acknowledges that semiosis is an essential part of all living systems and should encompass the study of sign games of all living systems. But again, the problem of total explanation arises: Can we move to a pan-semiotic view without wanting to explain too much? I believe we cannot, unless we qualify this move in relation to the knowledge enumerated in modern natural science and also the objective versions of information science.

I have argued that it is fruitful to accept this and to work with five different levels of interaction in nature, without assuming any evolutionary causal links between them that would indicate that one level is presumed to give rise to the other, or presuming any simple linear causality:

1. A non-manifest level with hypercomplex or chaotic interactions. The concept of the vacuum in quantum field theory is one attempt by science to describe this state, albeit without a synechistic frame.
2. An energy level with energy-based causal interaction by natural forces.
3. An informational level with signal and/or pattern fitting (formal) causality.
4. A semiotic level with sign game causality within and among living systems based on motivated subconscious purpose (intentionality) and meaning.
5. A linguistic level with language game causality based on self-conscious purpose and meaning among conscious social systems.

Let me offer a metaphor as guidance on how to understand this. In the deterministic chaotic fractal function known as Feigenbaum's tree (its inventor's name was Feigenbaum), we have a mathematical function that after regular development goes into chaos, then becomes regular, then goes into chaos again. If one 'reads' from left to right, it looks like a tree with branches and foliage; the right side is the ground on which the tree is standing. See Figure 9.2.

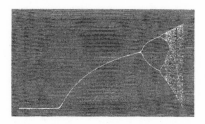

9.2. An example of a computed graph of the Feigenbaum tree. Read from left to right for development in time and complexity.

The evolution of this fractal and chaotic function creates a sandwich with layers of order and chaos, which are connected in a (hyper)complex way that we cannot yet explain or understand mathematically. The layers are just there no matter how much we enhance the figure in order to reveal the atomic details. See Figure 9.3.

We know they started at one end, but we do not know what connects one layer of order with the other, as with phase shifts and symmetry breakings. They emerge as order out of chaos (which is the title of Prigogine and Stengers book). But in this function there is an orderly start, which we know. In reality we are cut off from that part, which in the figure is what falls before the marked number 1.4012. We see only the dynamic patterns of chaos and order intrinsically connected over time in some sort of evolution. Perhaps this is how the world emerges from a hypercomplexity chaos – that is, beyond any precise scientific, philosophical, and religious description in any kind of language – except that it has this tendency to form habits and make patterns and dynamic regularities.

9.3 Critique of Current Approaches

Descriptions of these levels do exist in different areas of modern science, but they have never been brought together into one theoretical or paradigmatic framework. Mainstream eliminative mechanistic science attempts to accomplish this, but it has an insufficient philosophical background. More precisely, past and present efforts at unification have all confronted problems and inconsistencies.

Throughout their book, Prigogine and Stengers point out that although classical mechanistic physics could mathematically describe certain connections, forces, and regularities in nature, and describe –

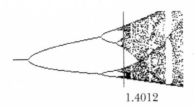

1.4012

9.3.   A further development of Feigenbaum's tree and an indication of Feigenbaum's number for the transition of the function into chaos.

with the help of quantum mechanics – the stability of matter, it is very
difficult to think of evolution from within a mechanistic worldview with
its rigid deterministic universal laws and Newtonian reversible time.

This is resolved by the thermodynamic atomistic view, which is based
on a vision of true chance and complexity, self-organizing dissipative
structures, and irreversible time. But it is still difficult to understand
how information and cognition can arise and organize itself from pure
physical matter and energy.

In the pan-informational paradigm, information as an organizing
power – in connection with, or as an aspect of energy – is present from
the beginning. This makes self-organization and the emergence of cognition more understandable, especially when it is framed by a general
systems theory with an organismic and therefore emergent evolutionary
world view. But it is difficult to understand how living systems can
emerge as individual beings, how they can treat information differently
from mechanical cybernetic systems, and, finally, what the special qualities are of the semiotic creativity of self-conscious, linguistic, embodied
beings. One of Bateson's limitations is that he never, in the foundation
of his theory, really escaped this first-order cybernetic informational
view of the world (see Bateson and Bateson, 2005).

In second-order cybernetics and autopoiesis theory, the idea of
closure at biological, psychological, and social communicative levels, as
explained by the concept of autopoiesis (self-organizing, self-maintaining,
and self-producing abilities), makes it easier to understand the special
self-preserving capacity as well as the individualistic point of view. This
conception – especially as elucidated by Maturana and Varela and by
von Foerster – has some similarities with von Uexküll's *Umweltslehre*. It is
a type of bioconstructivism – for Uexküll in a Platonic world, for the rest
in an evolutionary world view. Von Uexküll is a self-declared vitalist who
sees living systems as species and who stretches the *Umwelt-Bauplan*

through time eternal. He is, in short, an anti-Darwinist. But Lorenz used elements of von Uexküll's theory to found ethology; he fit those elements into a neo-Darwinian paradigm and then struggled to integrate feeling and signification, based on qualia and meaning, into his description. Basically, he failed after all this to establish such a theory. With Mathews, I have suggested that we view living systems as the true building blocks of signification spheres, as making signs of a new quality in the world, in which physics deals only with universal features of matter in ensembles.

It is clear that I have chosen to see the theories analyzed as necessary theoretic developments that have arisen because of the resistance of reality to prior theories that failed to explain adequately the evolution of complex and dynamic forms: life, cognition, and consciousness.

In Peircean semiotic philosophy, these levels can be bound together by Synechism, Tychism, and Agapism, combined with an evolutionary view of the interactions among Firstness, Secondness, and Thirdness. The view that Firstness is a blend of qualities of mind and matter containing qualia and living feeling and having a tendency to form habits is crucial if we are to understand the self-organizing capabilities of nature and how what seems to be 'dead' matter can, through evolutionary self-organization, become autopoietic and alive with cognitive/semiotic and feeling abilities. When we reinterpret von Uexküll on this basis, we arrive at a biosemiotics that is more suited to encompas those phenomenological aspects of life and cognition, which are currently conceptualized as signification. Still, partly missing are aspects of the development of embodiment and meaning in language that von Uexküll did not consider. Concepts of the closure, self-organization, and differentiation of biological, psychological, and social systems developed much further in second-order cybernetics and autopoiesis theory.

The shortcomings analysed above partly explain why I am sceptical about totalitarian and reductionist explanatory paradigms such as mechanicism, pan-informational and pan-semiotic paradigms without thresholds, and radical forms of constructivism that fail to account for any non-linguistic reality.

Ever since Umberto Eco (1979) formulated the problem of the 'semiotic threshold,' semiotics – especially Peircean semiotics – has been penetrating further into the realm of biology. The efforts of Thomas Sebeok (1976, 1989, 2000) – who was also editor of *Semiotica* and *The Semiotic Web*, which published thematic issues on biosemiotics – led to the development of a biosemiotics encompassing all living systems, including plants and micro-organisms, as sign users. As Emmeche (1992, 78) writes:

> Biosemiotics proper deals with sign processes in nature in all dimensions, including (1) the emergence of semiosis in nature, which may coincide with or anticipate the emergence of living cells; (2) the natural history of signs; (3) the 'horizontal' aspects of semiosis in the ontogeny of organisms, in plant and animal communication, and in inner sign functions in the immune and nervous systems; and (4) the semiotics of cognition and language ... Biosemiotics can be seen as a contribution to a general theory of evolution, involving a synthesis of different disciplines. It is a branch of general semiotics, but the existence of signs in its subject matter is not necessarily presupposed, insofar as the origin of semiosis in the universe is one of the riddles to be solved.

This semiotics has even been used to describe endosemiotics – that is, the semiosis between and within body cells (von Uexküll et al. 1993).

The essential question for the current debate over the possibility of a transdisciplinary information/signification science is whether a biosemiotic Peircean framework that includes and reformulates von Uexküll's theoretical biology can comprise uninterpreted 'natural objects,' autocatalytic and dissipative structures, and other spontaneous generations of order and patterns in nature as signs. These objects were previously described in physicochemical terms. Now some adherents of the pan-informational paradigm, such as Stonier, are trying to explain them in purely informational terms.

From a Peircean perspective, these phenomena are *protosemiotic*, or quasi-semiotic, compared to the semiosis of living systems, because they are only displays of Secondness, as I will say, following Nöth (2002). This view may lead us to a moderate form of semiotics that is compatible with modern scientific achievements, in which the signs of living systems are accepted as the first full-blown or genuine triadic signs. This is a discussion not about whether *any natural thing can become a sign* when placed in a meaningful context by a living system, but rather about the objects and their processes per se. Peirce (CP, 5.473) distinguishes clearly between what a thermometer as a physical thing does and how it works when interpreted by a doctor: 'The acceleration of the pulse is probably a *symptom* of fever, and the rise of the mercury in an ordinary thermometer ... is an *index* of an increase of atmospheric temperature, which, nevertheless, acts upon it in a purely brute and dyadic way. In these cases, however, a mental representation of the index is produced, which mental representation is called the *immediate object* of the sign; and this object does triadically produce the intended, or proper, effect of the sign strictly by means of another mental sign.'

A similar question is this: What do machines, such as computers, process when no humans are interpreting them? Are these signs or merely signals? We know that we codify these signals so that they carry meaning for us in our context; therefore they are signs to us, and forwarding the meaning of those signs through a pragmatic view is what these signals do. But does this have to occur in a living context, in which meaning has already been introduced through the existence of the embodied mind? Regarding the semioticity of a calculating machine, Nöth (2002, 8) explains how Peirce coined the term 'quasi-semiosis' to deal with this problem: 'The term quasi-sign suggests an answer to the question whether there can be semiosis in a machine of the kind which Peirce knew. A quasi-sign is only in certain respects like a sign, but it does not fulfill all criteria of semiosis. While some criteria of semiosis may be present in machines, others are missing. The concept of quasi-sign thus suggests degrees of semioticity. Quasi-semiosis does not only begin with calculating machines. It can be found in processes in which much simpler instruments are involved.'

Peirce did not accept the strict dualist separation of mind and matter. His concept of mind was extremely broad and did not include consciousness or intentionality as vital elements, only goal-directedness. Following Nöth (ibid., 9), *the use of the term quasi-semiosis to designate 'degenerated' semiosis near the shift between Secondness in machines and Thirdness in biosemiotic sign games* stems primarily from the lack of a triadic object relation:

> Evidence of the quasi-semiotic nature of data processing comes from the dyadic nature of the signs involved. The view that sign processing in computers is based on dyadic relationships is implicit in a widely held theory which states that computers can only process *signals* ... i.e., mechanical stimuli followed by automatic reactions. Winograd & Flores (1987), e.g., refer to signal processing when they write: 'One could describe the operations of a digital computer merely as a sequence of electrical impulses traveling through a complex net of electronic elements, without considering these impulses as symbols for anything' ... What is missing for these signs to develop from dyadic to triadic signs is an object relationship. The dyadic relations are merely dyadic relations of signification, but there is no denotation, no 'window to the world' which allows to relate the sign to an object

of experience ... the messages produced by a computer in the interface of humans and machines are either messages conveyed by a human sender and mediated by the computer or they are quasi-signs resulting from an automatic and deterministic extension of human semiosis.

This brings us back to cybernetics, especially that of Bateson. Here, information is a difference that makes a difference for a cybernetically defined 'mind.' This mind works primarily on differences with feedback loops based on energy. The energy is not important for the coding process per se, but the critique of the cybernetic concept of information and meaning has emphasized that this type of system, based on information theory, is functionalistic and not capable of encompassing meaning within a biological (not to mention human) perspective. The discrepancies between these two transdisciplinary paradigms of information and signification stem from the fact that their theories of messages originate at opposite ends of the continuum that extends from between science and the humanities. Luhmann attempts to solve this by applying a version of Bateson's information concept and combining it with his new sociocommunicative version of Husserl's intersubjective framework. But he never got around to making his own complete and consistent philosophical framework to support his attempt to combine phenomenology with second-order cybernetics, autopoiesis, and functionalist sociology.

If we hope to move beyond simply accepting that these two incompatible paradigms exist, we must abandon universalist views. In the spirit of Niels Bohr's complementarity theory, we must step back and abandon some of our ambitions to get 'to the bottom of things,' including laws and causality, through scientific approaches.

We must broaden our conceptual frameworks by – among other things – integrating the observer and doer into them. Let us therefore look more deeply into the framework that Peirce constructed in his last period of work.

9.4 The Peircean Theory of Mind

Although to some, pan-semiotics seems compatible with Peirce's triadic philosophy, in which the three categories and their internal dynamics are basic, cybersemiotics suggests a more moderate version, one that encompasses physics and information science. In Peirce's philosophy, the categories work according to the 'law of mind' and there is an inner aspect of Firstness (pure feeling) in matter. But one must be aware of Peirce's special conception of mind and consciousness. Peirce (CP, 7.364) writes:

> Far less has any notion of mind been established and generally acknowledged which can compare for an instant in distinctness to the dynamical conception of matter. Almost all the psychologists still tell us that mind is consciousness. But ... unconscious mind exists. What is meant by consciousness is really in itself nothing but feeling ... There may be, and probably is, something of the general nature of feeling almost everywhere, yet feeling in any ascertainable degree is a mere property of protoplasm, perhaps only of nerve matter. Now it so happens that biological organisms and especially a nervous system are favorably conditioned for exhibiting the phenomena of mind also; and therefore it is not surprising that mind and feeling should be confounded ... that feeling is nothing but the inward aspect of things, while mind on the contrary is essentially an external phenomenon.

Thus, the essence of consciousness is feeling, and an important aspect of Firstness is pure feeling. From a Peircean framework, with its Synechism, one has to admit that the universe is permeated with the pure feeling of Firstness, but that is not the same thing as human awareness (though it is the origin of it); consciousness is nothing but feeling. Peirce (CP, 7.365) writes:

> What the psychologists study is mind, not consciousness exclusively ... Consciousness is a very simple thing ... not ... self-consciousness ... Consciousness is nothing but Feeling, in general, – not feeling in the German sense, but more generally, the immediate element of experience generalized to its utmost. Mind, on the contrary is a very difficult thing to analyze. I am not speaking of Soul, the metaphysical substratum of Mind (if it has any), but of Mind phenomenally understood. To get such a conception of Mind, or mental phenomena, as the science of Dynamics affords of Matter, or material events, is a business which can only be accomplished by resolute scientific investigation.

Peirce is not speaking of human self-consciousness, but of the essence of consciousness as the immediate element of experience in its most generalized form, a phenomenon that develops in nature to emerge in new and more structured forms in living beings, nervous systems, and language-based culture. Thus pure feeling as the most generalized ability to experience is a basic potentiality of the world. It is its basic ability to make distinctions, including Spencer-Brown's and Luhmann's first distinction between system and environment. Peirce's philosophy adds the missing element to systems and cybernetics. It also dovetails with the notions of generalized thought developed in Bateson's philosophy and Luhmann's socio-communicative system. Peirce (CP, 4.551) writes about this concept of thought, understood as a function of mind and semiosis:

> Thought is not necessarily connected with a brain. It appears in the work of bees, of crystals, and throughout the purely physical world; and one can no more deny that it is really there, than that the colors, the shapes, etc., of objects are really there. Not only is thought in the organic world, but it develops there. But as there cannot be a General without Instances embodying it, so there cannot be thought without Signs. We must here give 'Sign' a very wide sense, no doubt, but not too wide a sense to come within our definition.

Thus habit forming in evolution is following the law of mind. The regularities and systems created are all a kind of thinking in the universe. This thinking is not cold logic, however, but semiosis experienced in the field of pure feeling or generalized experience.

Here Peirce is broadening the semiosis concept to include chemical pattern-creating processes as nature's thinking. I would prefer to call these proto- or quasi-semiotic processes, to avoid a too broad sense of the concept leading to pan-semiotic metaphysics. Nevertheless, Peirce's metaphysics operates with the 'inside' of material nature. He writes that: 'Wherever chance-spontaneity is found, there in the same proportion feeling exists. In fact, chance is but the outward aspect of that which within itself is feeling' (CP, 6.265).

Chance, spontaneity, and feeling are connected to Firstness, which constitutes the basic and vague link between all things. However, from a biosemiotic point of view, Firstness does not develop into genuine signs before being organized into living cells. One can see the habits or laws of nature as signs in themselves for the universe, but as a feeling and experiencing 'subject' the universe would be so abstract that it would be far beyond ordinary human rational comprehension of subjects and signs. It would be a matter of extremely abstract signs that do not make sense to ordinary human understanding, which may be why we operate with concepts such as laws, constants, and regularities.

The basic philosophical problem is – as mentioned before – whether in a Peircean framework we can have Thirdness without sign quality. If we want to make the universe in itself an interpreter, the answer is no. But from a biological perspective, those things we call signs and semiosis are working within quite different space and time frames. Peirce wrote that 'the universe is perfused with signs,' that he looks at matter 'as effete mind,' and that his synechistic doctrine connects mind with matter and sees mind as continuity and semiosis (Santaella Braga 2001, 59). Furthermore, he sees 'the one original law to be the recognized law of mind, the law of association, of which the laws of matter are regarded as mere special results' (CP, 6.277). Peirce (CP, 6.268) writes the following, which can be seen as essential to his contribution to a theory of mind:

> Hence, it would be a mistake to conceive of the psychical and the physical aspects of matter as two aspects absolutely distinct. Viewing a thing from the outside, considering its relation of action and reaction with other things, it appears as matter. Viewing it from the inside, looking at its immediate character as feeling, it appears as consciousness ... Remember that mechanical laws are nothing but acquired habits, like all the regularities of mind, including the tendency to take habits, itself ... This action of habit is nothing but generalization, and generalization is nothing but spreading of feelings.

Thus the habits and regularities of and in the universe are the result of the spread of pure feelings.

I do not want to conceptualize the idea of natural laws in any transcendental way. Apart from the law of mind, Peirce sees such laws as immanent. In modern scientific language, one would say that they emerge out of the symmetry breaking that is generated by the cooling of the universe, in much the same way as is suggested in Nielsen's (1989, 1991) random dynamics theory. Nielsen's thinking in physics is also foundational thycistic. In the following quote, Peirce (CP, 6.202) sums up his view on Tychism, which also sheds light on his view of the independent existence of Firstness and Secondness:

> Permit me further to say that I object to having my metaphysical system as a whole called Tychism. For although Tychism does enter into it, it only enters as subsidiary to that which is really, as I regard it, the characteristic of my doctrine, namely, that I chiefly insist upon continuity, or Thirdness,

and, in order to secure to Thirdness its really commanding function, I find it indispensable fully [to] recognize that it is a third, and that Firstness, or chance, and Secondness, or Brute reaction, are other elements, without the independence of which Thirdness would not have anything upon which to operate.

Put another way, Firstness (or chance) and Secondness (or brute reaction) are other elements, without the independence of which Thirdness would have nothing upon which to operate. Clearly Peirce is telling us that Firstness and Secondness must exist independently in order for his metaphysics to work. But it is true that semiosis grows out of the further evolution of these protosemiotic dual relationships. This conclusion is in line with the analysis of Nöth (2001a, b).

The cybersemiotic view on the relation between information and semiosis is that information is a difference or a distinction *that can be determined as* making a difference for a living system. (This is twisting Bateson a little in order to fit him into a semiotic framework.) Information, therefore, belongs to Secondness and must be considered protosemiotic. When we enter Thirdness, the possibility of an Interpretant appears, as Peirce emphasizes and as Varela shows in his calculus of self-reference. But certain conditions are necessary in order for a system to create an Interpretant within our space and time frame. One of these is the closure and self-organization of autopoiesis in a living system so as to be able to create an Interpretant within our space and time frame. But we probably need to add more criteria. Hoffmeyer (1998) describes four additional steps he considers necessary for the creation of living systems:

1. The establishment of an inside–outside asymmetry (closed surface).
2. A proto-communication over those surfaces (a community of surfaces).
3. A digital redescription in the form of DNA to carry on the form of the organism in procreation (Hoffmeyer and Emmeche [1991] call this *code-duality*).
4. The formation of an interface (inside–outside loops), which is essential for the creation of Interpretants.

Machines lack autopoiesis, reproduction, code duality, and an inner organization of membranes (Hoffmeyer 1998), and thus also lack both individual- and species-based motivation and intentionality, and it follows, the ability to establish a genuine Interpretant.

I find Hoffmeyer's four additional steps compatible with an interpretation of Peirce's theory, to see the living system – most of all humans – as the way in which the universe is becoming aware of itself. This is another way of understanding Spencer-Brown's idea of the universe making the first distinction between system and environment in order to be able to see itself. One needs a body and a nervous system in order to become (self)-conscious! As Peirce (CP, 6.489) writes: 'Since God, in His essential character of Ens necessarium, is a disembodied spirit, and since there is strong reason to hold that what we call consciousness is either merely the general sensation of the brain or some part of it, or at all events some visceral or bodily sensation, God probably has no consciousness.'

This astonishing piece of theology can serve as an answer to Spencer-Brown's question of why the world goes through the pain of dividing itself in order to see or experience itself. One is reminded of Schopenhauer's will.' In Peirce's philosophy, however, it is a will to knowledge; Peirce also holds a very generalized concept of mind.

Mind and, therefore, semiosis in Peirce's understanding are connected with purpose and final causation and do not require self-consciousness in order to function. Rather, they are a means to develop self-consciousness. Therefore, final causation and semiosis are functioning in nature as intrinsic parts of evolution. Peirce (CP, 7.336) writes: 'The psychologists say that consciousness is the essential attribute of mind; and that purpose is only a special modification. I hold that purpose, or rather, final causation, of which purpose is the conscious modification, is the essential subject of psychologists' own studies; and that consciousness is a special, and not a universal, accompaniment of mind.'

In this way purpose and therefore also phenomenological 'intentionality,' are introduced – however weakly – from the most basic level of nature, thus paving the way for a natural theory of meaning to supplement the cultural, existential, and spiritual ones. Purpose, therefore, plays as substantial a role in his metaphysics, but as Secondness.

How could such a general purpose which Peirce introduces be formulated in a way useful for science? At the level of organic and cognitive evolution, Hoffmeyer has suggested adding a new level of meaning to the reductionistic Darwinian 'survival of the fittest,' a term (actually coined by Herbert Spencer) that has served economy and management theory so well for so many years, but that now seems to have reached the limits of its usefulness: 'The most pronounced feature of organic evolution is not the creation of a multiplicity of amazing morphological structures, but the general expansion of "semiotic freedom," that is to say the increase in richness or "depth" of meaning that can be communicated' (Hoffmeyer 1997, 61).

Hoffmeyer is attending here to a crucial point, because this is where the possibility of meaning enters the biosemiotic framework. The play of signs in the freedom of consciousness – which is perhaps close to Peirce's 'musement' (in 'A Neglected Argument for God') – becomes an attractor in cosmogony and evolution! Neither survival nor maximal dissipation of entropy is enough to explain the growth of systems with inner worlds of qualia. Peirce (CP, 6.302) writes something about this idea of the spontaneity of mind in his famous *Monist* article 'Evolutionary Love', in which he discusses the Lamarckian aspect of evolution that we shall go into below:

> Remembering that all matter is really mind, remembering, too, the continuity of mind, let us ask what aspect Lamarckian evolution takes on within the domain of consciousness ... the deeper workings of the spirit take place in their own slow way, without our connivance ... Besides this inward process, there is the operation of the environment, which goes to break up habits destined to be broken up and so to render the mind lively. Everybody knows that the long continuance of a routine of habit makes us lethargic, while a succession of surprises wonderfully brightens the ideas ... A portion of mind, abundantly commissured to other portions, works almost mechanically. It sinks to a condition of a railway junction. But a portion of mind almost isolated, a spiritual peninsula, or *cul-de-sac*, is like a railway terminus. Now mental commissures are habits. Where they abound, originality is not needed and is not found; but where they are in defect spontaneity is set free. Thus, the first step in the Lamarckian evolution of mind is the putting of sundry thoughts into situations in which they are free to play.

By connecting this to the problem of emotion and inner reward in ethology – a problem that Lorenz could not solve within his standard materialistic biological framework – and by applying von Uexküll's *Umwelt* concept but in an evolutionary context, biosemiotics regards the sphere of signification, a sphere created by every living system, as the primary living space. What ecologists call the ecological niche in the habitat becomes a meaningful sphere, a signification sphere for the living system. From an ecosemiotic perspective it is a 'semiotic niche,' as Hoffmeyer (1997) calls it. The semiotization of living systems in biosemiotics also goes inwards.

Through *endosemiotics*, the production of meaning is carried inside the organism to the communication between organs, tissue, and cells. In *microsemiotics* meaning is even produced within the cells, albeit without consciousness.

The production of meaning is thus brought into what mechanicism sees as 'dead' nature by the concepts of Firstness and Synechism combined with hylozoism and the development of the universe through the three kinds of evolution:

1. Thycistic (free or random variation, sometimes called fortuitous), such as Darwin's natural selection.
2. Anachastic (dynamic dyadic interactions, a more mechanical necessity). This kind comes closest to Hegel's idea of evolution.
3. Agapastic or 'evolutionary love' (combining the free variation and dyadic interactions through habit formation by the mediating ability of Thirdness). This comes closest to Lamarck's idea of evolution (Brent 1998, 215).

It is in the *Monist* paper entitled 'Evolutionary Love' that he describes this last form of evolution. Peirce (CP, 6.289) adds a very broad and abstract theory of love to his philosophy of evolution and again connects it to his theology.

> Everybody can see that the statement of St. John is the formula of an evolutionary philosophy, which teaches that growth comes only from love, from I will not say self-*sacrifice*, but from the ardent impulse to fulfill another's highest impulse. Suppose, for example, that I have an idea that interests me. It is my creation. It is my creature; for as shown in last July's *Monist* ['Man's Glassy Essence'], it is a little person. I love it; and I will sink myself in perfecting it. It is not by dealing out cold justice to the circle of my ideas that I can make them grow, but by cherishing and tending them as I would the flowers in my garden. The philosophy we draw from John's gospel is that this is the way mind develops; and as for the cosmos, only so far as it yet is mind, and so has life, is it capable of further evolution. Love, recognizing germs of loveliness in the hateful, gradually warms it into life, and makes it lovely. That is the sort of evolution which every careful student of my essay 'The Law of Mind' must see that *synechism* calls for.
>
> Evolution by sporting and evolution by mechanical necessity are con-

ceptions warring against one another. Lamarckian evolution is thus evolution by the force of habit ... Thus, habit plays a double part; it serves to establish the new features, and also to bring them into harmony with the general morphology and function of the animals and plants to which they belong. But if the reader will now kindly give himself the trouble of turning back a page or two, he will see that this account of Lamarckian evolution coincides with the general description of the action of love, to which, I suppose, he yielded his assent.

When pure feeling is in Firstness and will is in Secondness, then love is in Thirdness in its most generalized form. The Platonic inspiration of the *Timaeus* and the *Enneads* of the Neoplatonist Plotinus (2000) is obvious. On the basis of Peirce's philosophy, the emergence of signs and meaning in the living world is to be expected. It is also clear that the world in its vague beginnings was not created with signs, as we understand them in biosemiotics, but only with a tendency to make them through the law of mind. This could be called a vague tendency to final causation that evolved from the tendency to take habits according to the law of mind.

Then how does Peirce understand the relation between efficient cause, or the brute force of Secondness, and the final causation? Peirce (CP, 1.211) writes about final causation:

It is ... a widespread error to think that a 'final cause' is necessarily a purpose. A purpose is merely that form of final cause which is most familiar to our experience. The signification of the phrase 'final cause' must be determined by its use in the statement of Aristotle that all causation divides into two grand branches, the efficient, or forceful; and the ideal, or final. If we are to conserve the truth of that statement, we must understand by final causation that mode of bringing facts about according to which a general description of result is made to come about, quite irrespective of any compulsion for it to come about in this or that particular way; although the means may be adapted to the end.

Thus a final cause in its most abstract form is a tendency to move (things?) in a certain direction. Efficient cause, on the other hand, is brute and mechanical and lacks all goal-directedness. But it is usually guided by final causes. This is the case not only in humans, as in Peirce's example below of hunting with a rifle, but also in the evolution of nature. Peirce (CP, 1.212) writes:

Efficient causation, on the other hand, is a compulsion determined by the particular condition of things, and is a compulsion acting to make that situation begin to change in a perfectly determinate way; and what the general character of the result may be in no way concerns the efficient causation. For example, I shoot at an eagle on the wing; and since my purpose – a special sort of final, or ideal, cause – is to hit the bird, I do not shoot directly at it, but a little ahead of it, making allowance for the change of place by the time the bullet gets to that distance. So far, it is an affair of final causation. But after the bullet leaves the rifle, the affair is turned over to the stupid efficient causation, and should the eagle make a swoop in another direction, the bullet does not swerve in the least, efficient causation having no regards whatsoever for results, but simply obeying orders blindly.

The cybersemiotic interpretation is that efficient causation can exist on its own as Secondness. However, such causation is often found embedded in the formal causations of pattern fitting and signals described in information science and later, clearly, in the living world embedded in final causation, which becomes conscious purpose in human society. Information seen as both protosemiosis (in evolution) and quasi-semiosis (when embedded in machine computational processes) falls between the two. It is connected to formal causation and works through signals and dualities of patterns; it is not yet a fully triadic semiosis, but it is still above the brute force of efficient causation.

The cybernetic thinking of self-organization and system closure has, in my opinion, made an important contribution to our understanding of living systems. Von Uexküll used basic cybernetics in his *Funktionskreis* to lay the foundation for both biosemiotics and biocybernetics (second-order cybernetics and autopoiesis theory). But a combination of Peircean semiotics and modern cybernetics is necessary if we are to develop a theory broad enough to include what is now called biosemiotics, and to encompass the core epistemological problem of the semiotic threshold. Biosemioticians tend to neglect the important contribution of second-order cybernetics and autopoietic theory to their theoretical framework; cyberneticians, whose work goes deep into the area of human social communication, tend to ignore the semiotic component (Ort and Peter 1999). In order to combine the contributions of these two camps, we require a broader foundation. This is why I refer to my work as Cybersemiotics. In order to do so I must show how semiosis and the three categories can fit into emergence theories of evolution.

9.5 Uniting System Science and Semiotics in a Theory of Evolution and Emergence

The cybersemiotic approach I present here unites cybernetic, systemic, informational, and semiotic approaches towards self-organization, intentionality, selection of differences, and constructivism, thus avoiding solipsism and idealism. I accomplish this by focusing on the role of bodyhood in the construction of meaning, using the viable elements of the five views described above, and combining informational, cybernetic, and Peircean views in a non-totalitarian and non-universalist way.

Modern systems thinking views Nature as containing multilevel, multi-dimensional hierarchies of interrelated clusters, which together form a heterogeneous general hierarchy of processual structures: a 'heterarchy.'

Levels emerge through emergent processes when new holons appear through higher-level organization. These principles can be placed in a Peircean perspective, in which potentialities (Firstness) are processes manifested through constraints and forces (Secondness) as regularities and patterns (Thirdness). This process continues in a recursive manner from level to level. The new emergent level then acts as a potential for the development of the next level.

Levels can form and dissolve when their dynamical parameters are near critical points, such as when nucleons form and dissolve in a 'quark soup.' Stabilization requires the system to move farther from the critical point into organizing patterns, such as energy wells.

In hierarchies there is a filtering of lower-level effects rising from the bottom at each new emergent level. But there is also a binding from the top, and the exclusion of alternative possibilities, once one path of emergence has stabilized (downward causation).

Across levels, various forms of causation (efficient: based on energy transfer; formal: based on pattern recognition, signals, and information; and final and thus semiotic) are more or less explicit (manifest). This leads to more or less explicit manifestations of information and semiotic meaning at the various levels of the world of energy and matter. The basic forms of causation can be seen at all levels. Material causation is grounded in quantum vacuum, zero-energy fields. For each level the next-lowest level acts as its material basis.

Emergent process laws are peculiar to each level; they emerge as new habits, Peirce would say. This allows components to function together; it also stabilizes levels in pattern formation and structure that can be described with an objective information concept. This yields the dynamical integration that individuates each level. In special cases in which this integration involves active organizational processes, we have autonomy, which through autocatalytic closure creates agency. It seems that total closure, as in autopoiesis, is important to the creation of living systems.

Meaning is generated through the entire heterarchy, especially through the relations of individual systems to a broader natural or social context. Thus, meaning is generated both at the individual level of living humans and in social systems.

Meaning is most manifest in the living systems that fulfil Hoffmeyer's conditions. But starting from dissipative systems, one can define a heterarchy of preliving self-organized systems as based on degrees of clos-ure, asymmetry between inside and outside, protocomunication over membranes, digital representation, and formation of interfaces.

The autonomous systems are related to various notions of meaningful functionality, which in turn are connected to various types of causality: efficient, formal, and final. The most full-blown version of meaning involves finality in a self-conscious social-linguistic mind

Further differentiations are possible by distinguishing between social, representational meaning and personal, subjective, existential meaningfulness. Doing so, however, requires a theory of consciousness that is yet to be developed, one to which the biosemiotic theory and world view will contribute heavily. Peirce, in *Chance, Love, and Logic* (1923; hereafter Brent 1998) writes about this:

> A general idea is a certain modification of consciousness, which accompanies any regularity or general relation between chance actions.
>
> The consciousness of a general idea has a certain 'unity of the ego' in it, which is identical when it passes from one mind to another. It is, therefore, quite analogous to a person; and indeed, a person is only a particular kind of general idea ... a person is nothing but a symbol involving a general idea ... every general idea has the unified living feeling of a person.

From this reflection springs Peirce's famous theory of the person as a sign, primarily a symbol in the greater scheme of mind and general ideas. To understand this one has to remember the philosophical framework from which the concepts derive their meaning. Peirce is a panentheist. The divine or the suprasensible – as Brent (ibid.) calls it – is represented in the sensible. This is an aspect of the metaphysical framework, which most scientific-oriented system science and cybernetics avoids, in the tradition of avoiding explicit metaphysics beyond science. But the price paid is that they lack theories of meaning, person/subject and first-person experience, and of qualia. To Peirce, a person is a specific semiotic way of organizing consciousness (general experience and feeling).

It is important to note that Peirce does not talk of religion as faith or as a sociological phenomenon and institution: 'Religion per se seems to me a barbaric superstition,' he wrote in a letter to William James (Brent 1998, 261). This reveals that he had thought critically about both Christianity and Buddhism.

Brent (ibid.) notes that Peirce had a mystical experience on 24 April 1892 in St Thomas Episcopal Church in New York City. Brent found a letter Peirce wrote about this only after he published the first edition of his biography; having found it, he made considerable changes to his second edition. In one of his famous *Monist* articles, 'The Law of Mind' (July 1892, 533–59) Peirce made some important remarks to explain his new conception of classical transcendentalism and mysticism:

> I have begun by showing that *tychism* must give birth to an evolutionary cosmology, in which all the regularites of nature and mind are regarded as products of growth, and to a Schelling-fashioned idealism which holds matter to be mere specialized and partially deadened mind ... I was born and reared in the neighborhood of Concord, I mean in Cambridge, – at the time when Emerson, Hedge, and their friends were disseminating the ideas they had caught from Schelling, and Schelling from Plotinus, from Boehm(e), or from God knows what minds stricken with the monstrous mysticism of the East. But the atmosphere of Cambridge held many an antiseptic against Concord transcendentalism; and I am not conscious of having contracted any of that virus. Nevertheless, it is probable that some cultured Bacilli, some benignant form of the disease was implanted in my soul, unawares, and that now, after long incubation, it comes to the surface, modified by mathematical conceptions and by training in physical investigations. (see CP, 6.102–63)

Thus his vision has a different conceptualisation (a benign form). Peirce developed his special understanding that science and religion are mutually dependent and in mutual fruitful evolutionary interaction into what Raposa (1989, 7–13) calls his 'scientific Theism':

He clung to 'the essence of religion,' to its 'deep mystery,' but not to any particular expression or articulation of it. While also adhering 'so far as possible to the church.' At the same time, his perspective was informed by and adapted to his ideals as a scientist. Thus he sought to develop and to advocate for persons of faith a distinctive vision and set of attitudes, rooted in his double optimism that 'God's truth' is one and that it is indeed accessible to a community of open and inquiring minds.

Peirce (CP, 6.433) explained this 'religion of science' as follows:

'Such a state of mind may properly called a religion of science ... It is a religion, so true to itself, that it becomes animated by the scientific spirit, confident that all the conquests of science will be triumphs of its own, and accepting all the results of science as scientific men themselves accept them, as steps toward the truth, which may for a time appear to be in conflict with other truths, but which in such cases merely await adjustments which time is sure to effect.

We know that truth for Peirce is what the unlimited community of inquiries will discover to be the case in the long run. A good idea is one that will eventually get itself thought and then keep living and thereby exerting a gentle influence in exchange with others interested in exploring the same kinds of insights (Raposa 1989, 154).

Thus for Peirce true science and true religion – if they are to be consistent with their own claims of devoted search for and surrender to truth and meaning – must work side by side, exchanging arguments and developing each other towards that singularity in which truth and meaning, through the universe's dialogue and argument with itself, converge at a single point. Peirce (CP, 5.119) writes:

The Universe as an argument is necessarily a great work of art, a great poem – for every fine argument is a poem and a symphony – just as every true poem is a sound argument. But let us compare it rather with a painting – with an impressionistic seashore piece – then every Quality in a Premiss is one of the elementary colored particles of the Painting; them are all meant to go together to make up the intended Quality that belongs to the whole as whole. The total effect is beyond our ken: but we can appreciate in some measure the resultant Quality of parts of the whole.

I remind the reader of Hesse's conceptions in *Magister Ladi*, which is also a blend of insights from East and West, and from science, as well as from art, philosophy, and religion, and which has been one of the inspirations of this book. The quote also underlines my earlier point, that the natural laws may be seen as signs for the universe, but for humans they are not comprehensible as such. We have to define the sign concept from our perspective, which we can then try to enlarge, by developing a biosemiotics, to encompass all living systems.

To sum up, then, the relation between science and Christianity in the West has been somewhat hostile ever since the trials of Bruno and Galileo during the Renaissance and the Enlightenment. But so has the relation between the Church and the mystics ever since Meister Eckhart was excommunicated after his death in the Middle Ages. Peirce's philosophy can be interpreted as an integration of mysticism and science. In Peirce's philosophy, mind is feeling on the inside, and on the outside spontaneity, chance, and chaos with a tendency to take habits. This is the law of mind, with love (as Agape) being the sole reason for his three types of evolution. Peirce sees the processes and habits of the universe as thoughts, and he writes that mind manifests itself best in protoplasm and the nervous system. In some of his manuscripts, Peirce further writes of an emptiness beyond the three worlds of reality (his categories), an emptiness that is the source from which the categories spring. As already mentioned, he also emphasizes that God cannot be conscious in the way humans are, because there is no content in His 'mind.' It seems that since there is a transcendental nothingness behind and before the categories, Peirce had a mystical view of reality with a transcendental Godhead. This strikes one very much as perennial philosophy metaphysics (Stace 1960, Suzuki 2002). Thus Peirce seems to be a panentheist! In fact he is fairly close to Suzuki, as Peirce also combines inspiration from Buddhism and Christianity. Hartshorne (1984, 3) mentions Peirce as the creator of the term 'Buddhist-Christian.' Inada and Jacobson (1984, xii) write:

> The deepest American encounter with Buddhism, however, makes its appearance with Peirce, who related his convictions more specifically to Buddhism than anyone had previously done. For Peirce, as for Buddhism in all its forms ... there is no determinate actuality nor autonomous being or entity at the center of things, the world is ruled neither by the relentless sway of omnipotent matter nor by blind chance.

The world that exists is a result of the *non-existence* of any independent substance, any ultimate, unanalyzable entity. What is universal and concrete is the self-surpassing process and unbroken wholeness of a world in whose microscopic 'point instants' the instantaneous tug and compassion are generated in all who have not turned away.

There is much truth in this description except that Peirce does not stay within the immanent as much. Buddhism demands but also includes the idea of a transcendent emptiness. That, at any rate, is my interpretation of the quotes that follow.

But what has Peirce got to say about that place where meaning and truth merge in the individual's mind? Raposa (1989, 120) writes:

> This point is a 'degenerate Third,' as Peirce explained in another context 'the representation of nothing but itself and to nothing but itself' (CP 5.71). It is therefore the 'precise analogue of pure self-consciousness,' to be regarded as a 'mere feeling that has a dark instinct of being a germ of thought.' Now this is exactly the way that Peirce in his cosmological essays described the universal mind in its primordial state. But *this* point cannot represent that mind because, while it is *self-sufficient*, 'it is not *all-sufficient*, that is, is not a complete representation but only a point upon a continuous map' (CP, 5.71).[2]

Peirce even operates with a superorder, which is not consciousness as we understand it but rather a pure mind without the contents we are used to. In trying to suggest what pragmaticism is and how it can be applied to the highest metaphysical principles, Peirce (CP, 6.490) writes:

> A disembodied spirit, or pure mind, has its being out of time, since all that it is destined to think is fully in its being at any and every previous time. But in endless time it is destined to think all that it is capable of thinking. Order is simply thought embodied in arrangement; and thought embodied in any other way appears objectively as a character that is a generalization of order, and that, in the lack of any word for it, we may call for the nounce, 'Super-order.' It is something like uniformity. Pure mind, as creative of thought, must, so far as it is manifested in time, appear as having a character related to the habit-taking capacity, just as super-order is related to uniformity ... perfect cosmology must ... show that the whole history of the three universes, as it has been and is to be, would follow from a premiss which would not suppose them to exist at all ... But that premiss

must represent a state of things in which the three universes were completely nil. Consequently, whether in time or not, the three universes must actually be absolutely necessary results of a state of utter nothingness. We cannot ourselves conceive of such a state of nility; but we can easily conceive that there should be a mind that could conceive it, since, after all, no contradiction can be involved in mere non-existence.

Here Peirce touches on the necessity for a transcendental superorder behind the evolutionary processes of the three basic categories. This is incompatible with the usual understanding of Plato's transcendental ideas, because with Peirce, Firstness is extremely vague and requires Secondness in order to be manifested. The paradox is that such an order cannot be formulated in any human language. David Bohm (1983) discusses the idea of 'wholeness and the implicate order,' which is the title of his famous book, in which he works with the idea of an immanent order in nature. In an interview he talked about the 'super-implicate order' (Weber 1972), which seems very similar to Peirce's 'super-order.'

Like the Buddhists, Peirce sees this order as no-thing. The Buddhists talk about emptiness. Peirce writes that the three worlds, Firstness (qualia and potentialities), Secondness (resistance, will, and brute force), and Thirdness (mediation and habit taking), must evolve from emptiness in an evolutionary metaphysics. Brent (1998, 212) discusses how this is consistent with Peirce's semiotic[3] realism: 'For Peirce, semiotics should be understood ... as the working out of how the real is both immanent and transcendent and how the infinite speaker may be said to practice semiosis ... in the creation of our universe.'

This paradox is essential to a great deal of mysticism. There is a transcendental reality beyond time and space that cannot be spoken of but is still somehow the source of everything. It is a knowledge we do not have, and which we know we do not have and will never have, because it is beyond words, time, and differences existing in the unspeakable, which is now the hypercomplex and irreversible flow of reality. (Peirce (CP, 6.490) writes:

> In that state of absolute nility, in or out of time, that is, before or after the evolution of time, there must then have been a tohu bohu of which nothing whatever affirmative or negative was true universally. There must have been, therefore, a little of everything conceivable. There must have been here and there a little undifferentiated tendency to take super-habits.

But such a state must tend to increase itself. For a tendency to act in any way, combined with a tendency to take habits, must increase the tendency to act in that way. But there are some habits that carried beyond a certain point eliminate their subjects from the universe ... Thus a tendency to lose mass will end in a total loss of mass. A tendency to lose energy will end in removing its subject from perceptible existence.

All of this is far from what is typically referred to as American pragmatism in mainstream philosophy. The triadic categorical foundation of Peirce's theory is one of the reasons why Peirce renamed his theory 'pragmaticism'; his purpose was to distinguish it from James's and Dewey's pragmatism.

Thus logic and the concept of having properties demand a universal transcendental superorder foundation. The big question is then, how does evolution start from there? Plato writes in *Timaeus* that the 'One' overflows by love to create something that can contain at least some love in an imperfect way, as it is not jealous. Plotinus (2000) developed that theory further. In the *Vedas*, desire makes Brahman create the world through his Shakti (female force of creation). Brahman is in itself the unmovable foundation. Peirce's solution is close to Advaita Vedanta but formulated within his own metaphysics and, therefore, much closer to a view and a wording acceptable from the scientific perspective of, for instance, quantum field theory.

In many ways Peirce's formulation is very close to the definition of modern physics encountered in the vacuum field that underpins the grand unification theory of physics (Hawking 1989). There it is claimed that the vacuum field can, within Planck's time, have outbursts of energy far greater than the whole universe, but that nothing comes into existence before some kind of stabilization makes the virtual manifest. According to quantum physics, Planck time and Planck length are the smallest possible units we can measure. All kinds of *virtual particles* leap out of the vacuum field in pairs of matter and antimatter within the Planck space time framework. But only when they are separated – which is what happens at the event horizon of a black hole – does one of them become materialized in an existence, however short, within space-time geometry. Hawking discovered that this is why radiation emanates from black holes (Hawking's radiation). But as mentioned earlier, mainstream physics has so far stayed away from the feeling and qualia aspects of Peirce's Firstness, although many quantum physicists seem to have mystical world views. According to Peirce, we move over into Firstness as soon as the tendency to take habits has some potential qualitative differences within which to work. These could be understood as the virtual particles. Whenever stable forms of particles establish themselves, we have both Secondness (resistance, force) and Thirdness (regularity and therefore stability). In quantum field physics this would be when the virtual particles have enough energy to manifest themselves as quantum phenomena. Peirce's view is formulated as the tendency to take habits and von Foerster's to have stable *Eigenvalues* – a wording more acceptable from the scientific perspective of, for instance, quantum field theory. This description is very close to the way the origin of the universe is described in quantum field theories today, except that having embraced mechanistic metaphysics, the nuclear physicist and cosmologist would not accept mind qualities as part of their metaphysical foundation. But this convenient mechanism is one of the main reasons why we in the sciences have such great difficulties providing a reasonable scenario for the emergence of life, cognition, and consciousness. As I have previously suggested, it works well as a framework for some parts of physics, but not as an overall metaphysics for the natural and social science and the humanities. But Niels Bohr was close to establishing a semiotics of quantum physics with his theory of complementarity.

Having merged the results of modern science with Peircean metaphysics, and having developed Peirce's semiotics into a biosemiotics, the cybersemiotic framework suggests that the scientific world view should be united with Peirce's framework. This could be done through a combined ontology and epistemology, conceptualized as five levels of existence and knowing:

1. A primary chaotic level of continuity, quality, pure feeling, and potentiality, with the tendency to form habits (Firstness). This would include (as one aspect only) what physics calls the unified quantum vacuum field.
2. A 'causal' level of matter, energy, and causality by natural forces (Secondness and its 'brute force'). From the Peircian hylozoic view, matter has an inner aspect of pure feeling with a tendency to take habits. This is not accepted in present science but is necessary from an evolutionary perspective to explain how first-person experience can arise in living systems in the course of evolution.
3. An informational cybernetic system level of quasi-semiotic signals that encompass the goal-oriented mechanical systems described by first-order classical cybernetics. From a cybersemiotic view, concepts

of information as signals of differences make sense only when interpreted as proto- or quasi-signs.

4. The genuine semiotic level belonging to all living systems (biosemiotics). So far, this is the only level capable of true triadic semiosis – that is, of producing signification spheres in sign games understandable from a human perspective.

5. The level of conscious social language systems (language games, arguments). So far, this level is occupied only by humans.

Sign making is thus *immanent* in nature, but manifest only in full triadic semiosis within living systems. The informational level is seen as intermedial between the physical world of energy, matter, and forces and the semiotic world. Cybersemiotics has so far sided with biosemiotics in not accepting a full-fledged pan-semiotics; it does, however, present a compromise through an evolutionary model.

Peirce accomplishes this in his triadic model of semiosis by making the Interpretant part of his theory, along with the concepts of immediate and dynamic objects. Similar developments have occurred in second-order cybernetics and autopoiesis theory, in which Maturana and Varela's theory of autopoiesis does not utilize the word 'information' when cognition is understood from the observing autopoietic system. Nothing is transferred from the environment to the living system that can be designated as meaningful information. Maturana and Varela do admit, though, that when one observes from the outside, it appears that the system has obtained information. In other words, information is created within the autopoietic system when it receives a disturbance that it is prepared for as a species, through the creation of a structural coupling. Ethologists would argue that the species had an instinctual perception, and that sign stimuli elicited an innate release mechanism (IRM) that caused a preprogrammed instinctive behaviour. From a cybersemiotic perspective, one can view autopoiesis as a precondition for differences in the environment to become meaningful signs through the process of semiosis in addition to the four additional steps of Hoffmeyer.

When information theory attempts to encompass the areas of meaning and semantics, it surpasses and destroys the semiotic threshold by blurring the difference between informational and semiotic processes, and thus between living systems and those which manipulate mechanical signals (or quasi-semiotic systems). This produces all sorts of simplistic theories about intelligences that are unable to account for the cognitive processes unique to embodied living systems, not to mention those unique to conscious socio-linguistic systems.

Sign making is the threshold between cybernetics and semiotics. To create a difference that makes a difference is to establish a sign for it (an Interpretant) in an embodied mind. Before this, it is only second-order cybernetic signals – or quasi-semiotic, according to Peirce. *The whole subject area of cybernetic information theory is therefore quasi-semiotic.* Beneath this is the physicochemical level, which is generally best described in terms of energy, matter, and causality by natural forces (Secondness) but in the long term does have Thirdness processes that develop 'natural law' through symmetry breaking and habit formation in evolution. In the next chapter I will develop a model to illustrate the consequences of this view of cognition and communication.

10 The Cybersemiotic Model of Information, Signification, Cognition, and Communication

10.1 The Cybersemiotic View of Cognition and Communication

Cybersemiotics is a development of biosemiotics achieved by combining the latter with, among other things, Niklas Luhmann's work. Below I will go into this in more detail with a model that describes the levels of signification and communication among humans and animals and that summarizes the theoretical concepts developed so far.

Luhmann generalized the autopoietic concept of Maturana and Varela (1980) to include psychological thinking systems and social-communicative systems. He views the psyche as a silent inner system, a closed system of perception, emotions, thinking, and volitions. A special social-communicative system must be created in order for communication to occur. Communication is an organizationally closed system; 'only communication communicates,' is Luhmann's way of stating this functionalistic sociology (Luhmann 1992). Social systems are communicative systems with human bodies and minds as surroundings (see Figure 10.1 for a recapitulation of Luhmann's model for human social communication). This is step one in the cybersemiotic model of cognition and communication.[1]

One way to understand our inner mental world is as a result of our bodily interactions with the environment through the construction of a felt signification sphere. This creates an individual 'point of view' as the centre of cognition, interest, and interpretation. Self-value and self-interest in preserving the individual's and species' self-organizing structure is basic to living systems' ability to signify. But this individual signification sphere is perturbed by species-specific social interactions such as mating, the rearing of young, competition for hunting territory, hierarchy in a group, co-operation in food gathering, and hunting. These

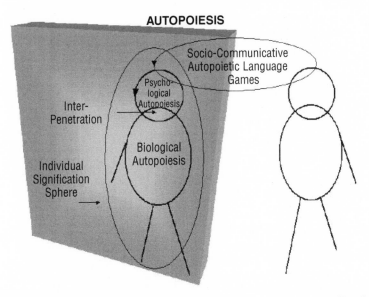

10.1. Luhmann's triple autopoietic model. Three organizationally closed systems work separately to make communication possible; they are here represented symbolically: the body stands for the biological, the head for the psychological, and the space between the two persons for the socio-communicative autopoietic system. In reality, it is difficult to separate these systems in a clear way. 'Signification sphere' is the biosemiotic term for von Uexküll's *Umwelt* and Maturana's 'cognitive domain,' reinterpreted here within a Peircean biosemiotics.

social activities generate sign games and eventually, through the evolution of humans, language games.

The construction of meaningful and informative messages has as a prerequisite autopoiesis, signification, and motivation/intentionality. Only within this triad do selections of information, utterance, and understanding become possible.

Biosemiotics and metaphor theory have argued extensively for the importance of embodiment in semiosis. I have demonstrated the connection between the biosemiotic (ethologically based) concept of motivation and the motivational concept of embodied cognitive semantics. Ethology and embodied metaphor theory have both discovered that the conception of a sign as standing for something for somebody in a particular way is controlled by releasing mechanisms that connect motivation, perception, and behaviour/action in one systemic process, as von Uexküll described in his *Funktionskreis* and which Heinz von Foerster refers to as perceptual *Eigenvalues*. The actual IRM (innate release mechanism) is chosen instinctually through the urges arising from a specific motivation. This is based on biological expectations and vital needs, such as for food and mating. The linguistic motivations that Lakoff and Johnson claim control the ICMs (idealized conceptual models) are very often connected to biological motivations. This is obvious in the example where a woman classifies a man as a bachelor, and therefore as a potential mating partner. It is our biopsychological embodiment that ties these relationships together.

Furthermore, I have shown that a phenomenological–emotional concept is necessary if we are to understand the production of meaning. I want to emphasize that this is consistent with Peirce's placing of feeling as an attribute of Firstness. In his evolutionary theory, feeling becomes a nearly non-manifest inner reality, as it also does in matter.

Knowledge systems thus unfold from our bio-psycho-socio-linguistic conscious being. Their function is to orient us in the world and help us act together in the most productive ways, but they do not explain us to ourselves. Peirce's view that we cannot split the concepts of mind and matter is very sound and a profound basis from which to begin. I do not see any good reason why the inner world of cognition, emotions, and volition should not be accepted as just as real as both the physical world and the cultural world of signs and meaning. To both the spiritualist and the materialist, embodied life – even single-celled life – is a basic component of reality. We are thinking in – perhaps even with – the body. The psyche and its inner world arise within and among biological systems or bodies. Employing Peirce, one may claim that there will always be some type of psyche in every kind of biological autopoietic and dual-code system. Nevertheless, a partly autonomous inner world of emotions, perceptions, and volitions only seems to arise in multicellular chordates with a central nervous system. Lorenz (1977) argues that such a system, one that contains emotions and experiences of pleasure, is necessary for animals to have appetitive behaviours that motivate them to search for objects or situations that elicit their instinctual behaviours and release the motivational urges built up behind them. This is qualitatively different from how reflexes function on a signal, which is at a protosemiotic informational level. Signs function on instincts at a genuinely semiotic level.

Luhmann's theory that the human social-communicative being consists of three levels of autopoiesis can be applied in cybersemiotics to distinguish among the following:

1. The languaging of biological systems, which is the coordination of behaviours between individuals of a species at a reflexive signal level (following Maturana).

2. The motivation-driven sign games of psychological systems.

3. The language games level of the self-conscious linguistic human in a social-communicative system.

A semiotic understanding has thus been added to Luhmann's conception, and his theory has been placed within Peircean triadic metaphysics. I will develop this further below.

10.2 Pheno-, Thought-, Endo-, and Intrasemiotics

It is obvious that what we call language games arise in social contexts in which we use our minds to coordinate our wilful actions and urges with fellow members of our society. Some of these language games concern our conceptions of nature as filtered through our common culture and language. But underneath that, we also have emotional and instinctual *psychological sign games*. For humans these function as unconscious paralinguistic signs, such as facial expressions, hand gestures, and body positions that originate in the evolution of species-specific signification processes in living systems.

Simultaneously, internal communication occurs between mind and body. This differs from what Kull (1998) calls *psychosomatics*, as it is not a direct interaction with culture, but rather only with the psyche. Nor is it merely *endosemiosis*. The terms endosemiosis and exosemiosis were both coined by Sebeok (1976, 3). Endosemiosis denotes the semiosis that occurs within organisms, and *exosemiosis is the sign process that occurs between organisms*. Endosemiosis has become a common term in semiotic discourse (see von Uexküll et al. 1993) to indicate a semiotic interaction at a purely biological level among cells, tissues, and organs. Nöth (2001) introduced the term *ecosemiotics* to designate the signification process of non-intentional signs from the environment or other living beings – a process that creates meanings for another organism, for instance, one that is hunting. The sign signifying that an organism is suitable prey is not intentionally emitted by the organism being preyed upon; it is therefore ecosemiotic rather than exosemiotic.

I call the interaction between the psyche and the linguistic system *thought semiotics*. This is where our culture, through (mostly) linguistic

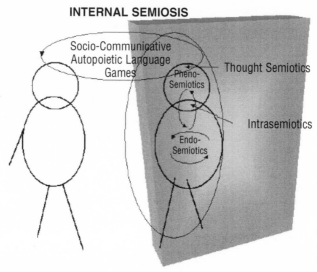

10.2. Shows in a symbolic way the relationships among phenosemiotics, endosemiotics, thought semiotics, and intrasemiotics.

concepts, offers possible classifications of our inner feelings, perceptions, and volitions. In their non-conceptual or prelinguistic forms, these inner states are not recognized by conceptual consciousness (our life world), which I call *phenosemiotic processes* (*phenosemiosis*). These are the silent thinking processes Luhmann speaks of – processes that do not communicate. They are the prelinguistic processes that arose before science split the world into subject and object (as Merleau-Ponty 2002 writes about), and they are the main focus of the phenomenology used by Luhmann in certain aspects of his theory.

As the interactions between the psyche and the body are internal, but not purely biological as in endosemiotics, I call the semiotic aspect of the interpenetration between biological and psychological autopoiesis *intrasemiotics* (Figure 10.2). These terms remind us that we are dealing with different kinds of semiotics, not absolute qualitatively different systems. We need to study more specifically how semiosis is created in each instance.

Today we realize that there are semiotic interactions among hormonal systems, transmitters in the brain, and the immune system, and that these interactions are important for establishing a second-order autopoietic system within a multicellular organism. Such an organism is comprised of cells that are themselves autopoietic systems, and these

EXOSEMIOTICS

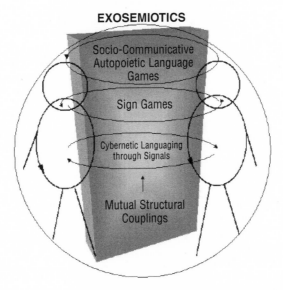

10.3.   The three levels of communication systems described in cybersemiotics.

are organized at a new level into an autopoietic system. But we do not clearly understand the relations between this system and our lived inner world of feelings, volitions, and intentions. It seems that certain kinds of attention on bodily functions, such as imaging, can create physiological effects within this combined system. This is partly carried by various substances that have sign effects on organs and specific cell types in the body (endosemiotics). We also know that hormonal levels influence sexual and maternal responses; that fear releases chemicals which alter the state and reaction time of specific bodily functions; and so on. This is a significant part of the embodiment of our mind, but intrasemiotics seems to function as metapatterns of endosemiotic processes. For example, our state of mind determines our body posture through the tightness of our muscles. There is a subtle interplay between our perceptions, thoughts, and feelings and our bodily state working, among other things, through the reticular activation system. There is much we do not yet know about the interactions among these systems.

The nervous system, the hormonal system, and the immune system seem to be incorporated into one large, self-organized sign web. The autopoietic description of living cybernetic systems with closure does not really leave space for sign production per se, and semiotics itself does not reflect very much about the role of embodiment in creating signification. The cybersemiotic solution to this problem is that signs are produced when the systems interpenetrate in different ways. The three closed systems produce different kinds of semiosis and signification through different types of interpenetration, as well as a level of structural couplings and cybernetic 'languaging,' as Maturana and Varela (1980) call it (see Figure 10.2).

Autopoiesis theory emphasizes that two interpenetrating systems are closed black boxes to each other. But Maturana points out that interpenetration develops over time towards becoming a coordination of coordination of behaviour that he calls languaging. By that point, cybersemiotics says, reciprocal structural coupling has developed between the two systems whereby signs can be produced and exchanged. Maturana's concept of *languaging* seems to involve the biopsychological connection between two individuals in a social species. But that is not the sign and/or language game as such; it is the cognitive coupling that is the necessary coordination for communication to develop as a signification system with its own organizational closure. I would therefore suggest that we distinguish between languaging and *sign games* at the level between reflexes and instinctual movements, as already mentioned (see Figure 10.3).

The perception eliciting reflexes is independent of motivation, whereas the perception of sign stimuli is motivation-dependent, which leads into instinctual sign games. Ethologists would point out here how certain instinctual movements become ritualized and acquire a release value for instinctive behaviour as 'sign stimuli.' During his last period, Lorenz (1977) realized that emotions must be connected to the performances of instinctual movements in order to create the motivational urges of appetitive behaviour; on this basis, we now have criteria to distinguish between the two levels. We can see how the connection between signs and internal or phenomenological understanding is constructed. Lakoff (1987) and Lakoff and Johnson (1998) have shown how metaphorical processes can explain this basic mechanism of bodily meaning as encompassing both socially and culturally produced signs.

Based on ethology and biosemiotics, I contend that our cognition manifests itself as embodied semiosis, motivated by our biological social interest, which is a powerful creator of structure and meaning in our signification sphere. Most animal behaviour – like much of our linguistic categorizations and use of metaphors – is considered to be unconscious. Still, ethologists have come to realize that motivation is not a physiological concept and that emotional experiences are linked to perception and behaviours on an instinctive basis.

Sign games develop into language games through evolution and through the life experiences of the human infant. As we are born and grow into human social communication, the psyche is perfused with language. As our mind is infected with language, we become linguistic cyborgs – or what we call humans. On this view we are born as animals with the capacity to construct interpenetration between psychic and social-communicative systems, thus creating internal Interpretants that are meaningful to us.

Meaning is embodied in biosemiotics, cognitive semantics, autopoiesis theory, and ethology. I suggest that we think of embodiment as broader than the structure of the nervous system, or even the integration of neurotransmitters, hormones, and the immune systems, through reactions to common sign substances that they secrete. As Kirkeby (1997) suggests, we should examine the body-mind or the 'body-thought' as a complex phenomenological dynamical system that includes the construction of the environment (signification sphere) and the other body-mind systems that make it possible for signification to arise.

Realizing that a signification sphere pertains not only to the environment, but also to the perception of members of other species, to cultural and protocultural behaviour, and to perceptions of one's own mind and bodyhood, I use 'eco' as a prefix for the signification sphere when it pertains to non-intentional nature and culture that is external to the species in question. In inanimate nature, in other species, and in cultural processes, we can observe differences that signify meanings to us that were never intended by the object.

10.3 The Cybersemiotic Model of Biosemiotics

I will now present a rather complicated model for differentiating between levels of semiosis and signalling/information – one that pertains to some of the questions already raised about the bases and thresholds of semiosis within biosemiosis, but does so without resorting to a pan-semiotic perspective.

Figure 10.4 outlines the cybersemiotic concepts developed so far. On the left are the described cybernetic–autopoietic–functionalistic processes. In the centre are the communicative aspects, or the exosemiotics, between two organisms. On the right are represented the internal semioses of the organism. Finally, on the far right are the organism's perceptual connections to the environment that create its signification sphere. With Nöth (2001), I call this signification aspect ecosemiotics.

CYBERSEMIOTICS

AUTOPOIESIS   EXOSEMIOTICS   INTERNAL SEMIOSIS   ECOSEMIOTICS

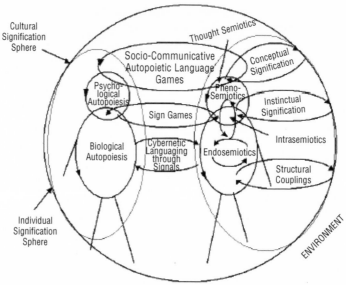

10.4. The cybersemiotic model classifies types of semiosis and protosemiotic processes. The localization of the processes in this diagram is unrelated to actual physical locations; for example, the head is also a part of biological autopoiesis and the location of endosemiotic processes, but symbolically I have used the trunk of the body to stand for the biological autopoiesis and the head for the psychological. To simplify this model, I have placed all the cybernetic–autopoietic concepts on the left and all the semiotic ones on the right, although all concepts concern both individuals in the cybersemiotic conception. Each person is placed within a signification sphere. When these spheres are combined through socio-communicative autopoietic language games in a society, a common signification sphere of culture is created. One part of ecosemiotic signification is based on the linguistic processes of conceptualizations and classifications. Underneath language games is the biological level of instinctually based sign games, and under that is the cybernetic languaging game of the coordination of coordination of behaviour (of two black boxes). Thus, ecosemiotics also has a level of biopsychological, or emphatic, signification, as well as a level of structural couplings that the organism, or rather the species, has developed through evolution. Thus Cartesian dualism has in this conception been replaced by different kinds of semiotic webs interacting with one another inside, outside, and among nature, bodies, and minds. The complexity of the model underscores how complicated an underpinning is necessary for the manifestation of the wonder of human language communication.

Ecosemiotics focuses on those aspects of language which relate to how living systems represent nature within signification spheres, including language games in culture creating its semiotic niche, as Hoffmeyer calls it. Cybersemiotics suggests that the basis of these ecolanguage games is the ecosign games of animals, combined with a signification sphere created through evolution. Furthermore, these ecolanguage games are based on an intricate interplay between the living system and its environment, which establishes what Maturana and Varela call 'structural couplings' and creates what Uexküll calls *Umwelt*. The signification sphere is a workable model of nature for living systems that, as species, have existed and evolved through millions of years. This is also true for the human species, indicating that our language has a deep inner connection to the ecology of our culture. Any existing culture is a collective way of ensuring that a social system will survive ecologically. As such, the cybersemiotic theory of mind, perception, and cognition is realistic but not materialistic or mechanistic. It builds on the inner semiotic connections among living beings, nature, culture, and consciousness carried by the three Peircean categories in a synechistic and thychistic ontology within an agapistic theory of evolution.

Based on the concept relations shown in Figure 10.4, we can see that the linguistic motivation mentioned earlier must be placed within thought semiotics, in which internal, non-linguistic, phenosemiotic processes of mind encounter concepts of language and imbue them with inner meanings. This is unlike animal motivation, which stems from the intrasemiotic area, where endosemiotic processes of the body's cells meet phenosemiotic processes of mind and awareness. Body, mind, and language are encompassed by a shared framework that conceptualizes their interactions at the same process level while integrating concepts of meaning and qualia.

The cybersemiotic model provides a new conceptual framework within which these different levels of motivation can be represented and distinguished in ways not possible within frameworks of biology, psychology, and society/culture. A transdisciplinary framework can be constructed that supersedes some of the limitations of earlier divisions among disciplines by viewing meaning in an evolutionary light, as always embodied, and by seeing the body as semiotically organized. This allows us to hope that the cybersemiotic development of biosemiotics will contribute to an inter- and transdisciplinary semiotic theory of mind, cognition, communication, and consciousness.

10.4 Peirce and Luhmann from a Cybersemiotic Perspective

I will now further explain the details of this model and give an example of its use in ethology. The human inner world represents bodily interactions with the environment and constructs a signification sphere through bodyhood. Intentionality, self-value, and self-interest in preserving the individual's and species' self-organizing structure is fundamental to the ability of living systems to signify through interactions such as mating, the rearing of young, competition for hunting territory, group hierarchy, and cooperation in hunting and gathering food. These activities first generate sign games, and later – at least in humans – language games. Autopoiesis, signification, and motivation/intentionality are prerequisites for the construction of meaningful and informative messages. Only within this triad are selections of information, utterance, and meaning possible. My theory is that *sign and language games arise from the interpenetration of the autopoietic systems.* I believe that Luhmann failed to develop a concept of meaning that relates deeply to the flesh, blood, and life conditions of biological systems or to the existential conditions of human consciousness. Here biosemiotics, as part of pragmatic language philosophy, has something to offer.

Viewed from such a framework, Luhmann's three autopoietic systems (1990) are all necessary in order to create meaning from a message; also, they require the sign concept to explain their interactions. One way to escape the impasse of Luhmann's functionalism, in which the roles of body and mind in the production and meaning of social communication are inadequately theorized, is to view the interpenetration of the three organizationally closed systems semiotically. Signs acquire meaning when systems *interpenetrate,* and signification happens when structural couplings are formed. 'Interpenetration' is Luhmann's term for the interplay between biological autopoiesis, psychic closure, and the social-communicative system (that is closed at the social level) when they use each other as environments and form mutual structural couplings.

The subject that Luhmann either cannot include or does not want or need in his theory, but which I think is necessary – partly because I experience its existence, partly because I find it necessary for the interpretation of whole systems, and partly because a democratic society is based on the emancipation and responsibility of individuals – can then with Peirce be established as the overall sign (here a symbol) of the semiotic webs that connect the living, psychological and linguistic self-conscious being we call human. Pierce writes (CP, 5.470) that 'every thought is a sign.'

Meaning can therefore be seen as generated through the interpenetration of these systems. For example, language is part of the social-communicative system but does not acquire meaning before it interpenetrates the psychic system, thereby indicating differences in emotions, volitions, and perceptions, thus 'putting words' into our silent inner beings. But our cognitive, emotional, and volitional qualities would have only weak connections to reality if they were not connected to biological autopoiesis and the survival of living systems' organizations and interactions with the environment's differences in order to develop signification spheres. Biosemiotics and metaphor theory have argued extensively for the importance of embodiment in semiosis. I have tried here to demonstrate the connections between the ethologically based biosemiotic concept of embodied motivation and the motivational concept of embodied cognitive semantics.

Furthermore, I have elucidated how a phenomenological–emotional concept is necessary for understanding the production of meaning, emphasizing that this is consistent with Peirce's placement of 'feeling' as an attribute of Firstness. In his evolutionary theory, feeling becomes an immanent, inner reality of matter.

Cognitive phenomena can be explained either with functionalist–cybernetic or with meaning-based semiotic approaches, but neither provides a complete explanation. Peirce emphasizes continuity between human thinking and machines. Pure logic is mechanical thinking that follows predetermined rules. This is an aspect of nature that humans have in common with machines. Pierce (CP, 2.59) writes: 'All that I insist upon is, that, in like manner, a man may be regarded as a machine which turns out, let us say, a written sentence expressing a conclusion, the man-machine having been fed with a written statement of fact, as premise. Since this performance is no more than a machine might go through, it has no essential relation to the circumstance that the machine happens to work by geared wheels, while a man happens to work by an ill-understood arrangement of brain-cells.'

The creative work lies in constructing the logical systems per se. But it does not follow that logical reasoning is a foundational aspect of reality more profound than mind, life, or consciousness. For Peirce, semiosis is the most profound aspect: the prerequisite for science, philosophy, and even knowledge as such. Knowledge systems unfold from our bio-psycho-social-linguistic conscious being. Their primary function is to orient us in the world and help us act together in the most efficient way, as both pragmatism and pragmaticism would say. Peirce is the father of both.

Prigogine and Stengers's (1984) view of complexity is compatible with Peirce's view of chaos and chance. But Peirce believes that we cannot justify dividing the concepts of mind and matter, and in this is probably more correct than Prigogine and Stengers. I do not see why the inner world of cognition, emotions, and volition – including our cultural world of signs and meaning (such as Popper's 'world 3' of objective knowledge) – should not be accepted as just as real as the physical world. Living systems think in – perhaps even with – the body, and is with the body that we realize when we are wrong. In fact, Peirce establishes the human self as the instance where we register error in our first childhood experiences.[2] Peirce (CP, 5.233) writes: 'A child hears that the stove is hot. but it is not, he says, and, indeed, that centered body is not touching it, and only what that touches is hot or cold. But he touches it, and finds the testimony confirmed in a striking way. Thus, he becomes aware of ignorance, and it is necessary to suppose a self in which this ignorance can inhere. So testimony gives the first dawning of self-consciousness.' Peirce (ibid., 5.236) continues: 'At the age at which we know children to be self-conscious, we know that they have been made aware of ignorance and error, and we know them to possess at that age powers of understanding sufficient to make them to infer from ignorance and error their own existence.' This insight is fundamental to his fallibilistic and pragmatic philosophy of knowledge, science, and truth. He himself sums it up (ibid., 5.234–5) this way: 'In short, error appears, and it can be explained only by supposing a self which is fallible. Ignorance and error are all that distinguish our private selves from the absolute *ego* of pure apperception.' Inasmuch as Peirce did not believe in introspection and an intuitive self-consciousness, he instead sees the self established as the result of inference (see ibid., 5.237). All thought is sign (ibid., 5.253). Thus the self is an embodied symbol.

Cybersemiotics works at clarifying the metaphysical background of both cybernetics and semiotics. This makes it possible to place cybernetics and semiotics in relation to each other, especially in regard to their versions of second-order cybernetics, autopoiesis theory, and biosemiotics. Cybersemiotics has further accepted the concepts of motivation and embodiment as important parts of the concept of biosemiotic communication. Embodiment and motivation are important commonalities between the sign games of animals and the language games of humans, and this integrates biosemiotics with the cognitive–semantic embodied metaphor theory of Lakoff and Johnson, as well as with Wittgenstein's language philosophy. Peirce (ibid., 5.253) writes: 'From the proposition that every thought is a sign, it follows that every thought must address itself to some other, must determine some other, since that is the essence of a sign ... in the immediate present there is no thought ... all which is reflected upon has passed ... To day, therefore, that thought cannot happen in an instant, but requires time, is but another way of saying that every thought must be interpreted in another, or that all thought is in signs.'

The cybersemiotic view is partly based on Luhmann's (1995) conception that a message consists of three aspects: (1) Information, (2) Utterance, and (3) Meaning. But Luhmann did not develop the semiotic process of signification in order to understand the production of meaning through signification. His theory of the human social-communicative being as consisting of three levels of autopoiesis has been applied by cybersemiotics to distinguish among (1) the languaging of biological systems, which is Maturana's and cybernetics' black box dancing, which from the outside looks like the exchange of information by signals, (2) the sign games of biopsychological systems, and finally (3) the language games (Wittgenstein) of self-conscious linguistic humans through the generalized media of social-communicative systems. A semiotic understanding has thus been integrated into Luhmann's conception, framing his theory within Peircean triadic metaphysics.

'Language games' arise in social contexts in which individual minds coordinate their actions with fellow members of their culture. Some of these language games concern our conceptions of nature, as filtered through a common culture and language. But underneath that lies an emotional and instinctual biological sign game of what have become paralinguistic signs that originated in the evolution of the signification processes of living systems. Sebeok's experiments with 'clever' and 'talking' animals (Sebeok 2000) demonstrate a clear boundary between sign games and actual language.

Autopoiesis theory underscores the fact that two interpenetrating systems are closed black boxes to each other. But Maturana suggests that interpenetration develops over time, generating a coordination of coordination of behaviour that he calls 'languaging.' When reciprocal structural coupling has formed between two systems, signs can be produced and exchanged. Maturana's concept of languaging is the biological connection between two individuals in a social species, not the sign or language games as such; the cognitive coupling is the necessary environment for the development of communication as a signification system with its own organizational closure. I therefore suggest that we distinguish between language games, sign games, and the level of reflexes and information called *languaging*, which is basically working at a chemical and physiological level. The perception that elicits reflexes is independent of motivation, whereas the perception of sign stimuli is *dependent* on motivation, which according to Lorenz leads to instinctual sign games. Ethologists would highlight here how particular instinctual movements become ritualized and acquire a signal release value for instinctive behaviour as 'sign stimuli.' In his later work, Lorenz (1977) hypothesized that emotions are connected to the forming and urging of instinctual movements; in this way, connections in the form of Interpretants are built between signs and internal or phenomenological understandings. Lakoff (1987) and Lakoff and Johnson (1999) demonstrate how this basic mechanism of bodily meaning can be explained by metaphorical processes that encompass socially and culturally produced signs.

Based on ethology and biosemiotics, I suggest that human cognition manifests itself as embodied semiosis, motivated by biological social interests, which are powerful creators of structure and meaning in signification spheres. In his famous book *Animal Behaviour* (1970), ethologist and comparative psychologist Robert Hinde came to realize that motivation is not a physiological concept and can therefore not be used within the standard biological vocabulary, which has no place for an inner world of first-person experiences, which can have causal influence on what bodies and their organs do. In humans, sign games develop into language games. As we are born and grow in the context of human social communication, our psyches are perfused with signs. As mentioned earlier, we are born as animals with the capacity to construct this interpenetration between the psychic and social-communicative systems in order to create internal Interpretants that are meaningful to us, based on the mutual structural couplings of languaging established through evolution. For Peirce (CP, 5.264) it is vital that we, in opposition to Cartesianism, understand the following:

1. We have no power of introspection, but all knowledge of the internal world is derived by hypothetical reasoning from our knowledge of external facts.
2. We have no power of intuition, but every cognition is determined logically by previous cognitions.
3. We have no power of thinking without signs.
4. We have no conception of the absolutely incognizable.

These four so-called incapacities are vital for Peirce's semiotic and evolutionary understanding of the development of semiosis in living systems; inasmuch as all signs are connected this, is also the semiotic development of the world.

In this way, I suggest a tentative model of how advanced, second-order cybernetics and systems theory can be united to complement pragmatic semiotics, cognitive semantics, and language game theory. By integrating Luhmann's three organizationally closed systems with semiotic and cognitive semantics, I break through the limitations of his thought to theorize the relationship between ethology and cognitive embodied semantics within a biosemiotic framework.

The work of Lakoff and Johnson (Lakoff 1987; Lakoff and Johnson 1999) bridges biological and cultural levels of cognition and communication. First though, we must extend their concept of embodiment beyond up-down, in-out, front-back, container-and-path schemes with the ethological knowledge of motivations and further embrace the signification spheres of living systems. The cybernetic view of embodiment should be further developed by connecting it to the biological research paradigms of Lorenz (1970–1), Tinbergen's (1973) ethology, the modern work in cognitive ethology, von Uexküll's presemiotic phenomenological biology, and Maturana and Varela's autopoiesis theory. Connecting to the evolutionary epistemology developed from ethology, Peirce (CP, 6.10) writes that the reason we can know anything of the world is that we are developed in it thus: 'Our minds having been formed under the influence of phenomena governed by the laws of mechanics, certain conceptions entering into those laws become implanted in our minds, so that we readily guess at what the laws are.'

Lakoff and Johnson might benefit from accepting Peirce's semiotics as a basic research framework for understanding signification in both animal and human systems, even though Lakoff has expressed reservations about the utility of this approach. We become self-conscious humans in and through language as Peirce also argued; before that we are only prelinguistic (phenosemiotic) animals with the potential to become human. Social webs of languaging among members of the same species and sign games of emotional awareness are prerequisites for the rise of human self-conscious linguistic beings. Human beings are linguistic cyborgs, in that we are natural beings programmed by culture through language and therefore very much cultural products. *There are no wild humans.*

We are biopsychological beings infected with language, which irreversibly alters our nervous systems and awareness. As Terrance Deacon emphasizes in *The Symbolic Species* (1997), the social-communicative being's living existence within the structural coupling of language games and generalized media (although these are terms Deacon himself does not use) provided so great an advantage in early humanoid evolution that language and linguistic activities became an important selection pressure, favouring structures better suited to support linguistic processes. As the brain and skull grew larger, children were born at an increasingly immature stage so they would be more susceptible to cultural linguistic programming. The instinctual system became more open to programming via personal experience. The advantage of learning processes is that they pertain to present environmental and social situations, and not simply to past situations that were instrumental to gene selection.

This system of adaptation in the early part of an individual's lifetime, combined with the mental tools of conceptual communication and internal thinking, was so advantageous for the survival and proliferation of the human species that we developed into linguistically and culturally programmed cyborgs. It is important to bear in mind the observations of both Heidegger and Wittgenstein. We are more than linguistic beings who think, learn, communicate, and coordinate through language; language also thinks *with* us, and behind our backs. Insofar as we speak language, *we are also spoken by language*, which makes it difficult for us to think 'behind' language. We must begin our search for knowledge by realizing that the human mind is semiotic. It is built on – or from – semiotic processes even at the animal stage. Peirce (CP, 5.289) writes:

> no present, actual thought (which is a new feeling) has any meaning, all thought is without meaning ... At no one instance in my state of mind, is there cognition or representation, but in the relation of my states of mind at a different instance there is. In short, the immediate (and therefore in

itself unsusceptible of mediation – the unanalyzable, the inexplicable, the unintellectual) runs in a continuous stream through our lives, it is the sum total of consciousness, whose mediation, which is the continuity of it, is brought about by a real effective force behind consciousness.

Cybersemiotics employs the epistemological stance of internal realism as developed by Putnam, as applied by Lakoff (1987; and see above), and as compatible with the conceptions of Prigogine, Luhmann, and Peirce. We observe the universe from our world – or rather, from our signification spheres. We can examine the semiotic relation in and between our bodies, our inner awareness, our language, our society, and the surroundings of the natural environment to attempt systematically to determine the necessary prerequisites for our world to function the way it does. There is no single way to accomplish this. As both Peirce and Popper recognize, such examination must be carried out through bold hypothesis (abduction), logical thinking to determine internal consistency and concise consequences (deduction), and testing for both the empirical (induction) and theoretical coherence of what we presently believe to be solid knowledge. Peirce (CP, 5.383) writes:

> Whenever we think we have present to consciousness some feeling, image, conception, or other representation, which serve as a sign. But it follows from our own existence (which is proved by the occurrence of ignorance and error) that everything which is present to us is a piecemeal manifestation of ourselves. This does not present its being a phenomenon of something without us, just as a rainbow is at once a manifestation both of the sun and the rain. When we think then, we ourselves, as we are at that moment, appear as a sign.

The self as a sign – as a symbol, in fact – is thus what grows out of these experiences to the extent that our hypothesis about a situation proves to hold. This will determine whether it is possible to understand our present situation, and whether this understanding can guide our common pursuit of prosperity and happiness until new, unexpected consequences and aspects of reality appear that urge us to develop our models further or even fundamentally revise them. Cybersemiotics can serve as such a model for the perception of ourselves, our society, and our environment, at least until a better theory is developed.

A short example, drawn as a model in Figure 10.5, will illustrate how

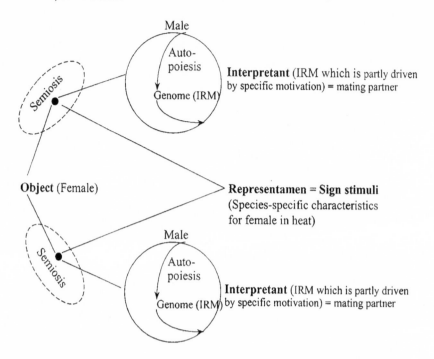

10.5.   Two autopoietic systems (males) of the same species (gene pool) see the same sign in an object, creating the Interpretant of a female of the same species. This occurs through the partially inherited structural coupling that ethology calls the 'innate response mechanism' (IRM), which is tuned to anticipate certain differences as significant for survival and proliferation, that is, as sign stimuli. The entire model is within one life form (naturalizing Wittgenstein's concept), mating, which again generates the mating sign game or ground (Peirce). For simplicity, I have excluded here the female's point of view as a species-specific autopoietic system.

a biosemiotic and autopoietic understanding of ethological processes functions. Inspired by Reventlow's work, we can imagine two male sticklebacks observing a female stickleback. How do they determine that this is a proper mate for their species? More theoretically formulated: How do they establish the right Interpretant for the sign stimuli that the female manifests? The interpretation of the digital code in their genome is transformed into an analogue by which cells create a second-order autopoietic system interested in preserving its individuality and the species-specific core carried in its genetic structure; this creates an embodied emotional signification sphere. In the historical drift of evolution, structural couplings are generated as innate release response mechanisms, which create Interpretants when the correct motivation is present. One could also mention that in ducks the ability to recognize an appropriate mating partner is determined by early imprinting on the mother. If the duckling is given a mother from another species of duck, it will attempt to mate with this species when it matures, often failing because the IRMs and sign stimuli between it and its potential mate are slightly different.

When the male sticklebacks recognize the moving object as a female, they also recognize one another as competing males (a new Interpretant), which leads to other types of species-specific behaviours, intermingled with learned behaviours.

Autopoiesis, motivation, and semiosis are all necessary for cognition to establish itself as Interpretants with a behavioural outcome, as can be seen in Figure 10.5. Motivation consists of unconscious intentions in animals, and their behaviour generates self-value and self-preservation at both species and individual levels. Living systems always act to protect their own organization (as suggested by autopoiesis theory) and to proliferate their own kind.

I contend that in considering this experimental and theoretical development in cognitive biology, we must include motivation, attention, and emotion if we are to generate a realistic picture of what actually occurs in the cognitive and semiotic world of biocultural linguistic systems, such as those of humans.

We must not forget that the nervous system is itself an organizationally closed system within the autopoietic system of the organism. Furthermore, the nervous system is activated by attention and stimulation from the body – for instance, through the reticular activation system (RAS) – and guided by motivation and intention. This is related to the embodiment of feelings as emotions. All of this underlies any attempt to communicate with other members of the species, and plays a role in the categories we create, the way we recognize things as being a part of a category, and the metaphorical extensions we draw to link basic-level material categories to more abstract relations through processes of iconicity. Although motivation establishes itself differently at the level of sign play in animals from the way it does at the level of language games in humans, it draws on the same species-specific drives of the autopoietic system: embodiment. But the sign and the self cannot be reduced to its embodiment as Santaella Braga (2001, based on Colapietro 1989) points out in her paper on the self.

An important conclusion in Lakoff (1987) is that biology is decisive for formulating concepts and categorizations. He criticizes linguistics for lacking a general theory of motivation based on embodiment that would explain how we meaningfully extend metaphors from the concrete to the abstract, and how we categorize concepts. He hypothesizes that cognitive models are embodied, or based on an abstraction of bodily experiences, so that many concepts, contents, and other properties are motivated by bodily or social experience in ways beyond the usual linguistic idea of motivation. Here, cognitive models provide a non-arbitrary link between cognition and experience. This means that human language is based on human concepts motivated by human experience; it is simply easier to learn something that is motivated, than to learn something arbitrary or logically arranged. One of Lakoff's conclusions, therefore, is that motivation is central to human cognition, especially in categorization. Lakoff suggests that humans' motivated categorization is based on idealized cognitive models (ICMs) that are the result of accumulated embodied social experiences and that give rise to certain anticipations. This dovetails with ethological thinking about concepts such as sign stimuli and imprinting; unfortunately, its physiological and energy-oriented models for motivation, cognition, and communication are insufficiently developed to encompass areas ranging from animal instinctive communication to human linguistic behaviour. Further development is required that focuses on signification and communication. Lakoff develops only a simplistic model of bodily kinetic-image schemata as the source of metaphor and metonymy. His theory could be developed further by drawing on combined ethological and, for instance, psychoanalytical knowledge of the connections between motivational states and the cognition of phenomena as meaningful signs.

Figure 10.5 offers a graphic representation of this integration of ethological, autopoietic, and semiotic interpretations of the cognition of living systems. As mentioned earlier, ethology calls partly inherited structural couplings 'innate release mechanisms.' Of course, this applies only to autopoietic systems with a genome. This organization of the nervous system permits it to anticipate certain stimulus patterns, connected to fixed behavioural patterns, as signs when specific motivational states are present such as hunger, defense of territory, and caring for young. Only through established structural couplings can signs acquire meaning.

The biological sign game thus makes a frame for the human cultural language game, in which cultural capital as well as ICMs of social power and economics play just as important a role in, for example, the concept of 'bachelor.' There are important links among the ethological approaches, semiotics used in biology (biosemiotics), second-order cybernetics, cognitive semantics, and pragmatic linguistics. The key to the understanding of understanding and communication is that both animals and humans live within self-organized signification spheres, which they project not only around themselves, but also deep inside their systems. The organization of signs, and the meanings those signs acquire through the habits of the mind and body, follow the principles of second-order cybernetics in that they produce their own *Eigenvalues* of sign and meaning and thereby their own signification spheres and internal mental organizations in autopoietic systems. Cybersemiotics thus connects ethological knowledge with second-order cybernetics and cognitive semantics, providing new insights into combined biological and cultural experiences in the processes of signification and communication. Peirce's development of triadic philosophy makes this possible.

Language is about nature, culture, and our inner world of emotions, volitions, and rationality. Ecosemiotics focuses on that part of cognition which concerns how living systems represent nature in signification spheres, eventually resulting in language games. The signification sphere is a workable model of nature for living systems that, as species, existed and evolved over millions of years. It is also applicable to the human species, indicating that our languages have deep inner connections to the ecologies of our cultures. An existing culture is, among other things, a collective way for ensuring the survival of a social system. In other words, cultures have signification spheres or semiotic niches that determine their ecosemiosis, and vice versa. These spheres are largely created through the life forms and language games of that culture, be they animistic in a hunting and gathering society, or materialistic–energetic and informational in a post-industrial society such as ours. With this analysis, we can then distinguish three levels of ecosignification spheres, as well as the ecocognitive domain:

1. The individual/personal ecosignification sphere of each individual or person as a symbol.
2. The cultural ecosignification sphere, which is based on a system of signification spheres organized through a long historical process.
3. The biologically developed species-specific ecosignification sphere. The prehuman animal species has developed through evolution.

These three levels depend on one another. Even though they do not necessarily fit neatly into one another, they are all essential parts of our ecosemiotics.

Now let us try to use this theory on Library and Information Science as an example of its usefulness.

11 LIS and Cybersemiotics

11.1 Indexing and Idealized Cognitive Models

The other area of practice and research we have chosen to illustrate the problems that cybersemiotics attempts to solve is information and document retrieval. Returning to our previous analysis and discussions of information seeking, now armed with the integration through cybersemiotics of the various ways of determining signification and meaning, we can offer a new understanding of the meaning and use of Idealized Cognition Models (ICMs). I earlier defined the ICM concept as a contextual one and argued that meaning springs from given social uses. However, it is important to distinguish how user-oriented ICM, the context/discourse of a document, and the ground of the domain all relate to one another.

I regard ICM as a subject-carried concept: a contextual understanding of the world embodied and defined by a user through an intersubjective understanding of the user's surroundings. ICM is a social and cultural concept that is intersubjective and individually acquired by a single user. ICM is thus a superordinate contextual concept that structures the way we understand the world. In comparison, context and discourse refer to documents in a knowledge domain in which the content of a single document defines a discourse. This understanding of discourse is analogous with discourse analysis in the literal sense, where context resides in the content of the documents (Johansen and Larsen 1994).

The context/discourse concept is thus at the level of the document. The common context that anchors a series of documents with common ideas referred to as a knowledge domain can also be designated as 'ground.' The ground is a domain-defined concept. We can distinguish three types of contexts; there is, however, interaction and interplay among them. ICM determines how we perceive and understand a knowledge domain, whereas the ground characterizes the meaning of the knowledge domain. Similarly, ICM determines how we understand the content of a document, whereas the discourse of the document defines its meaning.

The ICM of the user is expressed through the user's application of concepts, which in turn are determined by the ground of the knowledge domain. It must be emphasized that the user, who here is posited to be a researcher within a knowledge area, is a social actor within the knowledge domain. The historical and evolutionary character of the knowledge domain suggests guidelines for good research, and thus guidelines for a particular use of language.

On the basis of our previous discussion, we can see that the user's ICM must be in accordance with the ground of the domain. This is necessary if we are to talk about a specialized knowledge domain at a scientific level.

This is also why I contend that the meaning of descriptors must first signify the special discourse of the document – the terminology of the document – whereas decoding the descriptor depends on the user's ICM (ground) and understanding of the domain. This places heavy demands on the documents' indexer, who must therefore be a domain expert.

The relationship between the context/discourse of the document and the domain ground, or its self-understanding, is interesting from this perspective. When researchers act within a domain, they are under its influence. The conceptual understanding within the domain influences the conceptual understanding of the researchers, and vice versa. The relationship between researchers and their domains is one of mutual exchanges of meaning. However, it is difficult for a single researcher to influence the domain, because the domain is developed over a long period of time and because research within it is subject to certain methods and traditions – paradigms – that maintain the research within a certain domain understanding or ground. Thus we can speak of metaphorical displacement between a single researcher and the domain, because documents acquire contextual meanings from the domain ground; the document thus becomes a sign of the domain, and part of its self-understanding is expressed within the domain. For instance, any article in *Journal of Documentation* becomes a sign of the domain from which *Journal of Documentation* emanates.

It is difficult to transfer basic-level concepts directly from everyday perceptions of the world to an understanding of scientific and specialized knowledge domains, such as LIS's specialized terminology, because obvious descriptors in a scientific vocabulary do not consist of all the characteristics of basic-level concepts described by Lakoff and Rosch.

Instead, we have labelled the basic level of technical language in a knowledge domain the *significance level* (Thellefsen, Brier, and Thellefsen 2001). The significance level and the basic level are similar in many ways. Both communicate the maximum amount of information to a user in a given situation and have the greatest information value. The significance level is where the three semiotic webs (author, indexer, and user) are most equal. The significance effect is an expression of the ability of concepts to communicate the maximum amount of information to the user at a certain level.

11.2 The Need for an Alternative Metatheory to the Information Processing Paradigm in the LIS Context

A science must have a metatheory of the subject area over which it claims cognitive authority. Without a metatheory, LIS will not be able to discuss with other sciences what 'true' LIS is, or what is unique about the work of librarians and documentalists such that LIS deserves to be recognized by other fields as a science with cognitive authority. Few computer scientists recognize that DR (document retrieval) is as complex as the many other areas for which computer science has tried to create automated expert systems. Keith van Rijsbergen (1996, 1–10) proposed a 'logic of uncertainty' that seems to have affected fields outside of LIS.

I applaud van Rijsbergen and others' efforts to resolve the difficulties of computer document mediation by creating new kinds of logic, but I would still argue that the core relationship for mediating documents is semantic and therefore semiotic, and that semantic relationships are not built primarily on logic, but rather on motivated relations that influence the intentionality of conscious awareness. These are established through the evolution of living systems (ethology) and through the history of life forms and language games in societies. They are created as structural couplings of significance within a semiotic web, and they are established through the relationships of the living system to nature and other bodies within social systems.

The computer has seduced us into framing our questions within its algorithms. It seems that we have forgotten to develop and maintain a theoretical framework for our subject area that allows us to see beyond the horizon of the computer and to make demands on those researchers developing computer systems. If we do not provide a metatheoretical description of LIS, it will become difficult for others, such as computer scientists and software developers, to understand that they have entered a new territory with different rules. We must provide a strong theoretical understanding of the difference between physical and intellectual access. The growth of the Internet makes this knowledge more important every day.

What is new in the cybersemiotic approach is the development of a theoretical framework for LIS from recognized theories of cybernetics, systems, semiotics, communication, science, and linguistics – a framework that is bridging the gaps separating technical, scientific, social scientific, and humanistic approaches to the design and development of DR systems in LIS. This transdisciplinary framework will make possible communications among the various approaches and theories of these processes, without reducing everything to mere information processing (as was done in *Information Science – Theory and Practice*; Vickery and Vickery 1989). Figure 11.1 shows the information processing paradigm suggested by Vickery and Vickery as the theoretical basis for LIS.

Vickery and Vickery define information science as the study of the communication of information in society. But their concept of information seems to be based on the statistical Shannon–Wiener concept of information and its mechanistic concept of a sender, a channel, and a receiver. This is combined with the cognitive science idea of information and information processing as a phenomenon unifying human, artificial, and natural systems. Vickery and Vickery contend that their concept of information encompasses all types of communication and causal connections and that information is as fundamental to reality as matter and energy (1989, 43).

Vickery and Vickery see nature as full of information. This is similar to the classical cybernetic perspective, in which information is understood as neg-entropy. According to this world view, natural objective information must have existed in the expanding universe before living beings and human minds. Information is more fundamental than either observers or interpreters. Accepting information as an objective, universal, law-determined thing that humans and machines absorb from nature, change, and multiply by thinking and by bringing it into

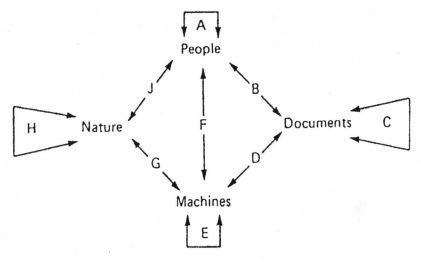

11.1.   Vickery and Vickery's (1989, 28) model of the information processing paradigm, where information is a very basic entity that can be freely exchanged among nature, machines, documents, and people. Clearly, it is unable to describe the higher functions of living, social, conscious systems.

society through language, suggests that it must be possible to establish a unifying science of information. This development – along with the development of the computer, computer science, and the cognitive sciences – has, as mentioned earlier, promoted the idea of a unified information science for humans and living, physical, and artificial systems: the information processing paradigm (IPP). The major challenge here is that, as analyzed and argued, there is no path leading from this rationalistic and physicalistic concept of information to a theory of signification and semantics.

One of the most important theoretical moves within LIS, coined by Belkin and Ingwersen as 'the cognitive viewpoint,' involved changing the concept of information from Vickery and Vickery's objectivistic–mechanistic view, in which the observer plays no vital role, to a more semiotic and process-oriented view, in which the observer is foundational. Belkin and Ingwersen posit that it is not information but rather *signs* that are objectively exchanged between living communicators, or between documents and users. Signs are potential information. They depend on the interpretation of the receiver. There is no information without an interpreter. This theory is in accordance with the practice in LIS of beginning a search for semantic relationships among concepts used in documents and then indexing in the human social realm of discourse communities and knowledge domains – through semiotics, therefore, rather than in an objective universal classification schema.

I have found that the functionalistic models that prevail in the information processing paradigm (IPP) of cognitive science, consistently encounter difficulties dealing with semantics; furthermore, they cannot encompass the complexity of the interdisciplinary subject area of LIS and the various types of expertise developed within it. So I have examined those theories which aim to understand the special quality of knowing, surviving, and communicating among living social systems. We must achieve a firmer grasp on the social-pragmatic connotations of words and concepts in order to fit them into the semantics of semiotic nets as a basis for thesaurus building. This will require us to distinguish and characterize different domains, levels, and language games in an organization – for instance, by mapping the ways that different user groups utilize concepts. These analyses will benefit not only from the methods already employed by LIS, but also from those employed in discourse and conversation analysis, cognitive semantics, speech act theory, and semiotics.

11.3 Indexing and Significance Effect

Is it possible for descriptors to contain both the documental context and the domain ground? I have made it clear how the document is a sign of the domain and how it is anchored in the ground of the domain. There is a semantic/semiotic exchange of meaning between the domain and the document. This semantic exchange makes it possible to index while maintaining a contextual understanding of the descriptor. The significance-level concepts of the domain (Thellefsen, Brier, and Thellefsen) are an expression of self-understanding within the domain, and by indexing with the identified concepts at the significance level, it is possible to signal the ground of the domain in the descriptors. On this basis, there is good reason to believe that the sign function of the concepts at the significance level has the greatest information value and strength of reference to the interpreter. That is why indexing with significance-level concepts specific to a defined user group submits the most information to that group. Cognitive semantics and pragmatic semiotics are excellent tools for analysing the ground of a knowledge domain and are regarded as the best way to index documents within a knowledge domain.

There is a semantic/semiotic relation between document and domain; it follows that the context of the documents appears in the descriptors as a metaphorical displacement that maintains their meanings through the ground of the domain. Indexing theory is capable of maintaining the context of the documents in the indexing, provided that it is possible to identify the significance-level concepts of the domain.

The words Rosch uses as examples of basic-level concepts are all everyday words – oak, chair, table, lamp – not words that are part of a scientific domain. Is it possible, within a knowledge domain, to identify basic-level terms at a scientific level?

If we posit that basic-level concepts are signs, we must anticipate that these signs can alter their (information) nature according to the knowledge level of a single user, so that the basic-level theory will also apply to specialized knowledge domains.

As sign types, the words oak, fugue, and autopoiesis are similar. As nouns (Rhemes), they all refer to a certain idea at a basic level. However, it is decisive that the sign's user is able to understand and thus conceptualize the sign. Thus signs, which are analogous to basic-levelness, seem to work as a conceptualizing function at all levels of cognition. This argues solidly for the possibility of understanding terms within specialized knowledge domains as signs of conceptualization at the significance level.

To accept a social pragmatic theory is to acknowledge that semantics springs from a socio-linguistic context, not from referential truth conditions. One must adapt the system – or at least the mediation of it through human or machine intermediaries – both to the domain of knowledge and to how the organization actually uses that domain based on its interests and language games.

Motivation stems from the type of medium, but the actual language game chosen within the medium determines a large part of the motivation for the relationships among concepts. If there is no proper feedback among producers, indexers, and users, the system will not produce information – it will not fulfil our expectations. We all participate in several language games simultaneously, but professionally we must deliberately select and maintain one at a time whenever possible.

As information is only potential when there is no Interpretant, the only information in our systems is relevant retrieved documents. This further supports much of Bates's (1989) work on the sense-making approach.

As mentioned earlier, the pragmatic approach generally means that in order to describe how our systems are used, it is important to conduct a philosophy of science analysis of the domain/subject area/work tasks and paradigms in science – as well as a knowledge-sociological analysis of communication patterns such as the discourse analysis of written text. These must be adjusted to our context, the work task, and the budget allocated the research. These methods should be supplemented by questionnaires, association tests, and registration of retrieval methods. The expenses of this research are a challenge. The willingness to pay for basic research is connected to the users' awareness of the importance of insights into the socio-pragmatic linguistic framework to the perform-ance of the designed systems. We are moving past the phase of unre-flective fascination with electronic information systems and into a more realistic evaluation of how they can help us mediate communications among humans via documents. All these points are equally valid for any information system designer and programmer dealing with a system like electronic journals where doctors, nurses, and administrators all produce, search for, and have access to documents.

This knowledge also tells us that the enormous scientific and techni-cal bibliographic data bases, in which many millions of documents have been categorized into Boolean systems by trained documentalists, have limited utility to non-professional users. In these specialized informa-tion systems, the users are the documentalists themselves, and trained researchers from part of the domain search in bases that have not been made generally accessible through the Internet. New digital libraries based on the same outdated principles and word-to-word matches are constantly being established. Based on the present theory, a biblio-graphic system such as BIOSIS will only function well within a commu-nity of biologists. This means that both the producers and the users must be biologists – and so must be the indexers. Even then there will be difficulties, because the producers and the users of the bibliographic database will also be researchers. This is a life form that follows a lan-guage game different from that of indexers. But if indexers maintain contact with both users and producers, solicit their feedback, attend their conferences, and investigate their ways of utilizing literature and scientific concepts, the system will holistically produce information.

Document-mediating systems should not be understood as mere information keepers and deliverers. They are information *producers*, once we include interactions with users as part of the system! This is also an important point in Gadamer's hermeneutic philosophy.

In the enormous domain-specific systems, we have to accept a centrally organized knowledge system. We can simplify through menu-driven systems only at the cost of speed and precision. We can help users understand what kind of system they are working with by providing a thesaurus to consult and work from directly and by investing money and time to teach and train them. We can remind them to consider specific vital details by asking them to answer questions as part of an obligatory procedure. All of this is now being done in new types of interfaces. Blair (1990) suggests that users be offered the opportunity to view extracts of paper samples that specific index terms will access and that other users have accessed using similar searches. Any technique that helps users understand the language game they are participating in, how it is structured, and how words work within it is useful when combined with opportunities to navigate, explore, and learn the system through trial and error.

In such cases we cannot bring the system to the user, so we must bring the user to the system. This will not happen if we simply install a natural language processing interface that pretends to the users that this system will do most of the thinking for them. We should make it clear that these systems only help users who do not have the time or ability for other types of search processes, because users will have practically no control over the processes by which papers are accessed. This might nevertheless be useful if these users want only a few documents on a subject of interest. The same can be said for the automatic indexing of full-text documents (Blair 1990), unless it is in a sharply delineated and rigidly formalized subject area. Automated procedures give users little insight into what occurs within a system. Users have very little opportunity to control the language game they are participating in. And this does not even begin to broach the issues that arise when index terms from one language game are used to seek documents in another.

When we contemplate designing a new document-mediating system from the bottom up, the suggestion is to specialize document-mediating systems for specific knowledge domains, knowledge levels, and points of interest, and to consider the size of the system. This means constructing bases entirely from the needs and conceptual worlds of users. We must supplement current methods with the pragmatic analysis of discourse communities with various knowledge domains, both scientific and non-scientific.

Most current bibliographic databases contain documents produced by different paradigms, specialties, and subject areas, all of which have different language games even when they share a vocabulary. I only need mention how data engineers, cognitive psychologists, and information scientists use the concept of information, or how Newtonian physics and Einstein's general relativity use the concept of space. Ideally each subject area with interest in the documents of a database should have these documents indexed according to its own language game in order to make precise searches possible. As is already acknowledged in BIOSIS, for example, chemists, physicians, and biologists each have specific terms for chemicals, illnesses, and classifications of plants and animals that are respected by the BIOSIS indexing procedure. But under current indexes, as a biologist I must use chemical notation when searching for a chemical, and chemists must use the correct biological name for a plant in order to find articles about a chemical substance it produces. This takes considerable effort. What is not addressed are those words common to all three subject areas that have different meanings in each knowledge domain because they are part of different language games.

Bøgh Andersen (1990) offers a semiotic framework for a computer semiotics as well as some applicable methods in a non-LIS context. One can imagine that interest groups from different domains will eventually develop their own systems for indexing documents, so that they can choose their own points of entry into these systems. In addition, there will be various means developed to visualize systems and their language games – aimed at searchers who lack domain knowledge or technical search knowledge – combined with many possibilities for navigation. Semantic network approaches and specific ontologies are now under development in many areas – still, these are not language games.

To summarize, our major challenge in LIS now is how to map semantic fields of concepts and their signifying contexts into our systems in ways that move beyond the logical and statistical approaches that until now seemed the only realistic strategies, given available technology. As Blair (1990) has suggested, one of the major problems of subject searching is that indexers and searchers do not participate in the same language games. Their work and social environments are different, and therefore their uses of words will be different.

I hope this book will inspire other LIS researchers to take a new approach to the problems they work with, and I encourage feedback.

12 Summing Up Cybersemiotics: The Five-Level Cybersemiotic Framework for the Foundation of Information, Cognition, and Communication

12.1 Introduction

The result of preceding analysis of cognitive science, information science, the information processing paradigm, the cybernetic information paradigm including Bateson, second order cybernetics, ethology, and library and information science document retrieval problems is this: it does not seem possible to establish a foundation for a transdisciplinary information science without relating it to theories of cognition, communication, mind, and meaning that span the humanities and social sciences on one hand, and the classical sciences and a theory of evolution on the other.

As Prigogine and Stengers (1984) have argued, one cannot build a thorough evolutionary theory, one that extends from the physical and chemical levels up to the level of living organisms, on a mechanistic basis. Classical physics is not a sufficient foundation; some kind of complexity theory that accepts chance as real must also be included. This view is supported by Peirce (1892a, b). But beyond this, an organicistic theory with emergence and downward causation seems necessary also.

We have rather good explanations for how the physiological processes influence mental experiences, but we have no idea whatsoever of how mental decisions based on free will can have any causal influence on our physiology. Thus we need to be able to integrate first-person experience into a theory of information, meaning, and nature if we hope to capture the process of understanding and interpretation in human communication and in animal cognition and communication. This means that we require internal consistency in our evolutionary theory all the way from inanimate matter to human first-person social language-borne conscious life. Such consistency requires a broader metaphysical framework than physicalism combined with some sort of objective informationalism. Matter, energy, and information alone are not sufficient to explain how inner life – the ability to experience in general – can arise. Organicism – both in dialectical materialism and in general system science – evokes the concept of emergence in order to explain how new qualities come into existence when a new complex system manifests abilities that were not present in the parts before they were combined. To make that a reasonable conclusion, we need to add an alternative metaphysical framework to any kind of physicalism combined with informationalism. I see Peirce's triadic philosophy and its pragmatic semiosis as satisfying the requirements of such a framework with its tychism, synechism, agapism, and pure feeling in Firstness. I am reluctant to make our internal mental experiences less real than matter – which is what much mainstream thinking does – and to deny them causal effects on our behaviour. At the same time, such a framework must be able to respect the nature of the various subject areas, from matter to living systems, cognitive as well as conscious systems, and their specific types of knowledge. This is an aspect that systems theory has worked with for quite a long time in terms of the various ontological levels and types of emergence, as Emmeche and colleagues (2003) have pointed out. It may provide a good framework if placed on the right foundation, but it is still a problematic area in system science. Ervin Laszlo (1995, 1996, 2004) is one respected researcher who has worked intensively with the problem of mind and spirit in a general evolutionary theoretical framework that can also include quantum mechanics; Schwarz (1997) is another. So far, a full-blown theory of signification, semiotics, and consciousness has not come out of it. Luhmann is the only one who works with a theory of meaning inspired by Husserl's phenomenology. On the one hand, he has adapted Husserl's philosophy, on the other, he has not managed fully to integrate Husserl's basic framework with system science, Bateson's information theory, and second-order cybernetics and autopoiesis theory. I do believe, however, that much of this work has the potential to strengthen Peirce's philosophy.

Thus, I do not believe that a functionalistic information processing paradigm based in an objective statistical information concept, in itself, can provide a sufficient frame that encompasses the phenomenological aspects of meaning and mind. I know that many researchers working with the processes of emergence hope to be able to explain how new qualities, such as life and mind, arise out of matter. In my view, however, emergence is merely a descriptive concept for these qualitative shifts – phase shifts, to some – it is not a causal explanation. For example, as far as we know, a brain is necessary to have consciousness but we cannot show that the brain creates consciousness and that consciousness is therefore solely a product of the brain. Even theories of emergence based on dissipative structures such as Kaufman's (1995), that are synergetic with Maturana and Varela's (1980) on autopoiesis and further developed to triple autopoiesis by Luhmann[1] cannot lead us into theories of first-person experience and meaning on a physicalistic basis. This is why Luhmann tries to integrate Husserl's phenomenology.

Thus we need a new, broader, and deeper foundation. We cannot simply add information theory on top of the old mechanistic foundation, or use a physicalistic foundation improved by complexity theory or random dynamics (Nielsen 1989), as none of these theories includes a theory of the emergence of life, meaning, and language. We need some kind of reflective metaphysical frame extending beyond Platonic mathematical determinism. Such determinism lacks a profound theory of how matter, life, and meaning relate to one another. Peirce places his theory somewhere between Plato and Aristotle but adds an overall evolutionary theory that starts from vague beginnings.

Let me support my claim concerning the importance of combining information theory with a theory of first-person experience, with a quote from the ongoing discussions in *Journal of Consciousness Studies*. Here Velmans (2002, 3) discusses, in a way I find very convincing, the problem that science lacks a theory of mental causation at the physiological levels:

In everyday life we take it for granted that we have conscious control of some of our actions and that the part of us that exercises control is the conscious mind. Psychosomatic medicine also assumes that the conscious mind can affect body states, and this is supported by evidence that the use of imagery, hypnosis, biofeedback and other 'mental interventions' can be therapeutic in a variety of medical conditions. However, there is no accepted theory of mind/body interaction and this has had a detrimental effect on the acceptance of mental causation in science, philosophy and in many areas of clinical practice. Biomedical accounts typically translate the effects of mind into the effects of brain functioning, for example, explain-

ing mind/body interactions in terms of the interconnections and reciprocal control of cortical, neuroendocrine, autonomic and immune systems.
While such accounts are instructive, they are implicitly reductionist, and
beg the question of how conscious experiences could have bodily effects.
On the other hand, non-reductionist accounts have to cope with three
problems: (1) The physical world appears causally closed, which would
seem to leave no room for conscious intervention. (2) One is not conscious
of one's own brain/body processing, so how could there be conscious
control of such processing? (3) Conscious experiences appear to come too
late to causally affect the processes to which they most obviously relate.

As to problem (1), it is thus clear that FIS constitutes an attempt to
develop a theory in which the physical universe as classically understood
is enlarged theoretically by adding the concept of information, which
helps to explain how matter organizes itself into life in what becomes
the evolution of the universe, and how communication is possible. This
is a great step forward; however, the theory of information does not
really include a theory of the 'inner aspects of mind and emotion' and
their causal effects on the body at the animal level, not to mention at
the level of the human consciousness. If one believes that our conscious
understanding of messages is relevant to a transdisciplinary theory of
communication, then a systems and cybernetics based theory such as
that of autopoiesis, even in Luhmann's version, needs a theory of signification (Luhmann 1999), as Ort and Peter (1999) argue in their analysis. As to problem (2) in the quote above, we do know from biofeedback
and yoga that we can become aware of our own bodily processes and
control them. Even rats can learn to control their bladders to some
degree through biofeedback.

But we are not able scientifically to present a model of how this is possible, or even conceptualize the most important forces and mechanisms. If the human mind did not 'fall from the sky' then it developed
through evolution. Yet, to this day, 'mind' is completely outside the
explanatory powers of physics, chemistry, and biology as they are understood in mainstream science; furthermore, theories based on quantum
theory are highly controversial and far reaching (Chalmers 1996).
Biosemiotics is a means to explain some of the inner organizational
processes in the body as endosemiotic. This leads us to (3), referring to
those well-known experiments, which show that decisions to act seem to
be made at a level below consciousness, a few seconds before we
become aware of them. Consciousness seems to be only the tip of the

iceberg. But even if this means that we do not have a completely independent free will that initiates things, we still have a 'free won't,' which can say no to some of the spontaneous impulses of our body-mind, and which does not rule out the possibility that logical thinking can initiate decisions to move the body.

12.2 The Problem of Meaning

Thus my main dissatisfaction with most of the theoretical offers within the foundation of information science (FIS) is that it is not possible to have a theory of information, cognition, and communication without a concept of meaning. Classical logic, and the way it is used in analytical philosophy, with its content-free symbols drawing their content from a truth table, is not a sufficient framework for understanding cognition and communication.

Meaning is related mostly to life, mind, language, culture and consciousness and usually is not considered relevant to the chemical and physical realm. Following this, we must admit that it is not simply a question of reductionism versus holism or general system theory, but more of a 'two-cultures' problem, with theoretical explanations based on science and technology on the one side, and the humanities and qualitative social sciences, including philosophy, on the other.

Classical science still seems to harbour the general aim of explaining biology chemically, and chemistry physically. But in chemistry we already clearly see formal causation and information processes.[2] Chemical processes and structures can describe and explain crucial aspects of the physiological structure as well as the processes of the nervous system that are necessary for first-person experiences, but chemistry cannot describe the experiences as such. Furthermore many biologists would argue that even the function of an organ cannot be described sufficiently without referring to its biological purpose, which brings us to final causation. As a science, biology as some qualitative differences from physics and chemistry.

It is my hope that the cybersemiotic theory of meaning and mind can integrate classical scientific thinking and the functionalistic thinking of systems and cybernetics with the evolutionary framework and finally with the phenomenological analysis of mind as found in Merleau-Ponty (1958). This is a great challenge but one that is necessary to overcome for the sake of our culture. Peirce has made most of this framework available.

In one of our exchanges at the FIS internet conference 2002–3, in our e-mail discussion of bio- and cybersemiotics, Jerry Chandler very succinctly stated the fundamental challenges:

> The issue of (bio)semiotics opens another avenue that was scarcely explored here. Currently, two primary sets of symbols are used in the natural sciences. One set of symbols consists of traditional logical and mathematical symbols and represent abstractions. Chemical symbols consist of representations of unique forms of matter and are used for the partially abstract natural sciences. Chemical symbols form a basis for the synthesis of matter and are used in molecular biology to communicate the structures of biomolecules and to describe biological signaling processes, internally within the organism, among organisms and between the organism and its ecoment. If (bio)semiotics is to become established as a source of description of biological and biomedical information, how will it establish logical consistency with either of the two existing symbol sets? Would a (bio) semiotic symbol set bridge the relations between chemical symbols and mathematical symbols? What within the current values and philosophies of the scientific communities, would motivate the creation and acceptance of a third symbol set for (bio) semiotics? Among the four terms (semiotics, information, communication, and meaning), the issue of the meanings of a symbol set may be the most difficult. Indeed, the specific meaning assigned to a specific symbol is often intertwined with preexisting conceptualizations of emergence, history, philosophy, culture and related structural processes.

I believe that the biosemiotics that Sebeok (1976, 1989) developed on a Peircian theoretical basis can be applied as a framework for integrating the various ontological levels of description. Within such a framework we further need to develop a theory of possible interactions among those levels and types of causality which we operate with in everyday language and medical and psychotherapeutic practices. Although I do not support his attempt at a solution, Velmans (2002, 4) states part of the problem very clearly in his paper:

> Within conventional medicine, physical → physical causation is taken for granted. Consequently, the proper treatment for physical disorders is assumed to be some form of physical intervention. Psychiatry takes the efficacy of physical → mental causation for granted, along with the assump-

tion that the proper treatment for psychological disorders may involve psychoactive drugs, neurosurgery and so on. Many forms of psychotherapy take mental → mental causation for granted, and assume that psychological disorders can be alleviated by means of 'talking cures,' guided imagery, hypnosis and other forms of mental intervention. Psychosomatic medicine assumes that mental → physical causation can be effective ('psychogenesis'). Consequently, under some circumstances, a physical disorder (for example, hysterical paralysis) may require a mental (psychotherapeutic) intervention. Given the extensive evidence for *all* these causal interactions ... how are we to make sense of them?

How can we offer a kind of scientific explanation of the causal interaction? To accomplish this, we must do more than include physics, chemistry, and biology with their functional explanations into our definition of science; we need to embrace a Peircian biosemiotic interpretation of biology. Cybersemiotics combines this with a theory of levels, information, semiotics, and language interactions. This means that we do not dismiss the results obtained so far, but rather that we relativise their implicit frameworks and integrate the science into a new framework while adding semiotics.

Cybersemiotics suggests that we leave the concept of information to a mathematical information theory without a concept of living meaning, and instead place the informational interactions at a level between the physical and biological levels of reality, which is mostly described by the chemical and physiological sciences. But these levels will be understood within a framework of Peircian biosemiotics that introduces a theory of pure feeling, the law of mind and meaning, into its basic ontology.

All interactions can be understood within a semiotic framework. However, as previously discussed, it is not useful to call all relations semiotic; some are better called protosemiotic (Nöth 2001b) – for instance, the informational relation. Thus the development of a hierarchy of different kinds of causality seems necessary, as Peirce saw. Inspired by Aristotle, but within his own evolutionary pragmaticist framework, he distinguished between the following:

- *Efficient causality*, mainly related to the physical level's exchange of force and energy between masses (part of Peirce's Secondness).
- *Formal causality*, from a modern scientific view, mainly related to informational and signal exchange through pattern fitting. It has no

intentionality, as in chemistry and that part of physiology which does not use the purpose of the living systems as part of their explanation. It is well described in cybernetics. From a Peircean point of view, this is protosemiotic interaction.

- *Final causality*, in which the goal influences the result. At the semiotic level, it is through more or less unconscious motivation and drive (teleonomy); at the linguistic level, it is conscious intention.

I thus see information as a kind of formal cause that works through pattern fitting. Since there is no manifest individual mind involved, I will not call this process pattern recognition, as is so often done in computer science and AI, for this would imply some kind of intention as well as a conscious comparison to an image of a pattern in consciousness.

Even among animals, meaning is communicated through sign games based on at least some weak form of intentionality which, as final, causes free will at the level of linguistic self-consciousness. One might talk of existential goal-directed causes. Let me quote from the conclusion of the most elaborate work to date on Peirce's semiotic account of causation (Hulswit 2002, 215): 'Peirce proposed to strictly distinguish the concept of *cause* from the concept of *force*. While he reserved the forms for the whole of human experience and of nature, he restricted the latter to the context of the formal laws of physics. Whereas 'cause' concerns irreversible processes, 'force' pertains to reversible processes. 'Cause' deals with concrete reality, 'force' only with abstraction.'

In this way, the efficient cause based on 'force' of classical physics, which was later inspired by thermodynamics on 'energy transfer,' is removed from a foundational position within a general theory of causality. A position it can have only in a physicalist, mechanistic world view. Hulswit (2002, 215) continues: 'Peirce held the view that (i) cause-effect relationships are irreversible, (ii) causes only partially determine their effects, (iii) cause-effect relationships are mediated by 'laws' (final causes), and (iv) causes precede their effects in time ... each act of *causation* involves an efficient component, a final component, and a chance component. While each event is brought about by a previous event (the efficient cause), it is also part of a continuous sequence that is marked by a definite tendency (final cause), and involves an aspect of irreducible novelty objectives (chance).'

Especially the last part dovetails nicely with Prigogine's work irreversibility and the reality of chance, and therefore a foundational hypercomplexity view.

12.3 Mind and Reality

The quantum vacuum fields are our closest candidates to a foundational reality, and they are only described in physicalist terms. Consciousness researchers are aware of this problem (Chalmers 1996) and try to deal with by changing to Platonic sorts of ontological frameworks (Penrose 1995). Many researchers are trying to build theories of consciousness on quantum field theory. I think they will fail – and that we will all fail – if we do not address the ontological and epistemological foundations of mind and meaning. I do not believe that life and mind can be adequately described by mechanistic models and communicative interactions based on energy-based efficient causality. I do not think that Platonic dualistic frameworks that lack an intrinsic evolutionary theory, and evolutionary information science frameworks, will do the trick either. Therefore I think we must look for a theory that allows evolution and mind to be parts of foundational reality. This is why I am working with a Peircian-based biosemiotics, combined with a systems and cybernetic perspective with ontological levels, and a concept of emergence. To this end Peirce redefined the relation between form, cause, and event. Hulswit (2002, 216) writes:

> Peirce made clear that causation must involve a transmission of forms. However, unlike Aristotle's formal causes, Peircean forms are *relational structures* rather than something embodied in a substance. They are general rules which have the logical structure of a material implication: if *p* then *q*. Thus, the fundamental difference between Peircean forms and Aristotelian formal causes is that, while Aristotelian formal causes were thought to explain the stability of the world by explaining the structure of *things*, Peircean forms were meant to explain the stability of the world by explaining the *dynamic relations between elements*.

We see here why Deely calls Peirce the first of the postmoderns as he basically has a process philosophy and he is also often compared with Whitehead. But the difference is that for Peirce *causation involves a transmission of forms* (ibid., 216–17) and that involves a semiotic process, which mediates between cause and effect. Effects may function as signs pointing to their causes, and certain events ('causes') may function as signs of future effects. In both cases the Interpretant is the mediator in the transmission of forms ... the transmission of forms from causes to effects is a semiotic process, and it is because semiosis involves real continuity that there is a continuous transmission from causes to effects ... Peircean events do not happen in time, but they are the condition of time (whatever that may be).

Hulswit makes the transition from a physicalist to a semiotic world clear. From an evolutionary point of view it must be acknowledged that mind has emerged from nature. This requires a metaphysics that allows for this to happen. It seems obvious that a mechanistic view, one which claims that basic reality is simple, mathematical, and deterministic, is contradictory to an evolutionary theory of mind. Complexity theory is one step along the path towards a better explanation, and information science takes things one step farther when combined with theories of self-organization and closure. But still we somehow need to allow for mind and qualia to be part of that basic reality.

This is what Peirce does. He makes them immanent in Firstness, thus making it possible for them to emerge and manifest themselves increasingly through the course of evolution, self-organization, and autopoiesis. In Peirce's triadic philosophy, in which the three categories work according to the 'law of mind,' there is an inner aspect of Firstness (pure feeling) in matter. This is, thus, immanent in all things, but it does not develop into genuine signs until it is organized into living cells. Thus the world is bound together, not rather by an ideal prefixed pattern as in Aristotle, but by a continuum (plenum) of events of pure feelings and spontaneity, organized by the tendency of the law of mind to take habits. I share with Peirce a belief in the fundamental spontaneity of nature as the basis of existence. Hulswit (ibid., 215) discusses the Peircean concept of event and process:

> Peirce held the view that causation is a production event as a part of a teleologically determined sequence (process). The main difference between processes and events is that processes share three characteristics which events lack: *complexity*, *teleology* and *coherence* ... it belongs to the nature of an event, not only *that* it creates a new event (Secondness), but also that it creates a new event of *a certain type* (Thirdness) ... (i) each event assimilates the past event from a definite perspective, (ii) the past event is related to the present event as an official cause, and (iii) this relationship is mediated by the final cause, which is the perspective ... each perspective reflects a conditionally necessary relationship, which has the structure of a material implication.

Thus according to Hulswit (ibid., 216), a Peircean process is 'a continuous sequence of events that derives its unity or internal order (distinguishing it from other processes) from a final cause, which directs the sequence to some state which may itself evolve.' This basic spontaneity can also be seen as the prerequisite for the possibility of free will in humans, which scientists who base their thinking on a classical determinism would have to deny.

12.4 The Role of Information

In my view, information – as we use the concept in the sciences – is protosemiotic and tied to the level of formal causation. But that which is usually called 'information processes' on the level of cells I acknowledge as sign processes or sign games. Language games are seen only among humans and are connected to socio-linguistic self-consciousness. The 'physical universe' can be considered closed only if it encompasses mind and its evolution. Thus mind is a part of the natural sciences, but on a new philosophical foundation. Thus human communication has at least these three levels: the informational, the semiotic, and the socio-linguistic.

Not everything is information or signs, because if all objects are signs and all signs are objects then I do not see how the difference between Representamen and Object can be upheld. If it could be, the triadic sign connecting representamen (primary sign) with the Object and the Interpretant in semiotics would collapse. There must be a dynamical object 'out there' that is not a sign, which a sign through semiosis and the evolution in the semiotic web moves towards; otherwise the truth concept will disappear. This is how I understand Peirce. We cannot reject the objective resistance of forces and will (that is, Peirce's Secondness) and the regularity and stability arising from the natural laws and regularities in nature (Peirce's Thirdness).

My problem is that if we cannot have Secondness and Thirdness in nature without them being signs, then all there is in the world is signs and there can be no objects to refer to. Laws of nature in themselves simply *are*. They are not signs for us. But their descriptions are. You can choose to see them as signs for the universe or Cosmos. If you do, you have to work with very different levels of semiosis, depending on who is creating the interpreter. To me, this is an acceptable approach, but it seems more useful to work first from the perspective of human social and living systems.

I would prefer an interpretation in which the living systems are the universe's way of becoming aware of itself. Because here Firstness, through the law of mind and its tendency to take habits, not only unites with Secondness and Thirdness, but also organizes itself in autopoietic closure and thereby creates individuals with an interest in preserving their own organization. This seems to dovetail with Hulswit's (ibid., 217) analysis of causation as a production event: '... causes and effects are abstractly separated aspects of an ongoing process in which *causes are said to precede their effects* ... the explanation of natural process requires reference to final causes, which are general principles. These can be causation only if there are boundaries set forth by general principles ... *the status of cause and effects* is that they are both objective and perspectival. Since they are aspects abstractly derived from the concrete reality, but also by the abstraction power of our thought, they are *facts* rather than *events*.'[3]

From a Peircian framework one must admit that the universe is permeated with abstract pure Firstness, which is not the same as human awareness, though it is the origin of that awareness. We may all be one in the Firstness of the pure feeling of mind at the deepest level of existence, as the mystics – including the Buddhists – suggest, but the world is still there too with its partially ordered processes of events.[4]

To this, one must add or integrate the concept of abduction, the third of the inference methods beyond deduction and induction, as it is crucial to our understanding of how semiosis functions in signification and interpretation beyond classical logic.

12.5 Abduction as a Meaningful Rationality

Abduction is crucial to Peirce's theory of semiotics and logic. Abduction is not driven solely by classical logical inferential power or determinism. Like most inferences in daily life, abduction is always carried out on a basis of too little knowledge. But it is the main function in perception and thinking that makes sense of things as forms or causal processes through the creation of a sign relation. Thus abduction has an important function in creating meaning. I can see here a relation to Husserl's intentionality concept and Heidegger's *Sorge* concept, both of which have to do with how the mind relates to and interprets phenomena.

But on the basis of our present information-based cognitive theories of intelligence, information, and cognition, we cannot grasp this abduction function of perception and cognition. We know it bears on context and how this context is seen by the observer (motivation and intentionality) through the interest with which he or she enters it. Biological, psychological, and social relations and their history and relations to the habits of nature and society are important, and therefore are factors shaping the process of perception, as Gadamer (1975) describe it in his hermeneutics. The semiotic and linguistic levels of communication all influence the process. But in the end that process is still based on a combination of biological determination – the conservation of the organization of the living partly based on genes and other forms of heredity, in addition to the unique way it constructs its 'signification sphere' (*Umwelt*) – and the free will of the individual.

The symbols of classical logic are supposed to be meaningless in themselves. Content and meaning arise from what you apply them to. Conversely, Peirce sees logic as evolving from signification and therefore as always being in a meaningful context. I consider this one of the great strengths of his theory. Logic does not become an inhuman, meaningless, static ground pattern in human intelligence – which seems to be the preferred modern scientific interpretation of the Greek Logos, which itself is based on the idea of an ultimate order of nature and mind as seen in both Plato and Aristotle. This view seems to have been inherited in much information science as well. Instead, Peirce sees logic as part of a dynamical process of the evolution of living intelligence. According to Peirce it has a vague beginning from the transcendent into the first layer of immanence in Firstness. From there it develops into manifestation through the law of mind and evolutionary love, becoming Secondness as matter, force, will, and information. Then, through Thirdness, it starts to create that semiotic process network (sign action) that is the dynamic pattern upholding causality and developing especially the living systems (biosemiosis) as well as the mental and the social systems, which then develop into a new level of hyper-complexity (Qvortrup 2003), which can again only be (partly) reduced through interpretation by meaning (Luhmann). The present book is an attempt at such an interpretation.

12.6 Summary

I have developed an informational theory that accepts several 'levels of existence.' When talking about nature, I think we should distinguish the following from one another:

1. An entangled form of causality on the quantum level. This is the most abstract expression of mind, which Peirce calls Firstness, con-

taining qualia as well as 'pure feeling.' From this level, the 'virtual particles' of quantum field theory jump in and out of manifest existence. Also from here, the mystical 'entanglement' functions – what some physicists call 'ghostlike causal connection' – appears beyond the time and space limits of general relativity and the Planck scale.

2. A Secondness dual level, which in its physical-energetic aspect produces efficient causality (described in physics as exchange of energy), and its mind aspect produces will.

3. An informational-signal organizational causality in dissipative structures, in cybernetic machines, and at the chemical level. There is a protosemiotic level influenced by both Secondness and Thirdness, producing, at the mental level, differences that may come to make a difference.

4. A semiotic level of final causality and understanding in and among all living systems.

5. Finally, a linguistic–communicative causality in human conscious and social systems. Final causation as conscious and meaningful purpose through sign interpretation among embodied conscious linguistic individuals involved in social-communicative systems making purposeful actions. Man becomes a sign to himself or, rather, a symbol in self-conscious processes!

The scientific subject areas and their findings are thus conserved. The place of information theory as a new level, one at which we can understand the organization processes of complicated dynamic systems, is also conserved and now viewed as protosemiotic. It is placed within the broader cybersemiotic framework, which combines Peirce's triadic semiotics with systemic and cybernetic views, including autopoiesis and second-order cybernetics and emergent evolution.

The level of quantum vacuum fields and Firstness is not considered physically dead, as it usually is in physicalistic physics. Cybersemiotics conceives them as a part of Firstness, which also holds qualia and pure feeling. Although physicists may be troubled by this new metaphysical understanding of this level of reality, they cannot claim that physics has a complete understanding of it and that there is no room for new interpretations. On the contrary, this is one of the most mysterious levels of reality we have encountered; and its implications have been discussed since the 1930s and were central in the disputes between Bohr and Einstein.[5] The view I have developed seems compatible with Hameroff's (1998) attempts to develop a theory of consciousness that incorporates modern physics.

The second level of efficient causation is clearly what Peirce describes as Secondness. This realm is ontologically dominated by physics as classical kinematics and thermodynamics. But for Peirce it is also the willpower of mind.

The third level of information is where the formal causation manifests itself clearly and where the regularities and Thirdness become crucial for interactions through stable patterns. This level is ontologically dominated by the chemical sciences, including molecular biology and physiological explanations of brain function. This difference in ontological character may be one of the keys to understanding the differences between physics and chemistry. It is a matter not only of complexity but also of organization and type of predominant causality.

At the fourth level, where life has organized itself, the actual semiotic interactions emerge. First life develops internally in multicellular organisms as 'endosemiosis' and among organisms as exosemiosis through 'sign games.' Thus, the understanding of this level – based on biosemiotics – points out that the informational concept may be useful at the chemical level of analysing life, but it is not sufficient to capture the communicative, dynamic organizational closure of living systems. This is one of the reasons why Maturana and Varela avoid using the information concept in their explanations of the dynamics of life and cognition. But they do not use a semiotic concept either.

Finally, at the fifth level, with syntactic language games, human self-consciousness emerges and with it rationality, logical thinking, and creative inferences (intelligence). Intelligence is closely connected to abduction and conscious finality. Abduction is crucial to signification. It is the capacity to see something as a sign for something else, which is the deep wonder of consciousness and human intentionality and linguistic interpretation and understanding. This 'something else' must be a habit of nature. Some kind of regularity or stability in nature that the mind can recognize as somewhat lawful is necessary for it to be a fairly stable Eigenvalue in the mind (an interpretant).

This is an inclusive heterarchy, in that the natural habits – which we call laws – are the broadest and most universal ordering principles. Basically, these habits create order. For instance, gravity is the force that causes the primordial matter, which was a little unevenly dispersed in the early universe, to move into different attractor places and begin to form stars. In these stars all the basic elements were made through fusion. The heaviest ones were finally created in the supernova explosions and spread all over the galaxy, making planet formation possible and generating the possibility for the chemical self-organization, which is the basis of life. But at the level of chemistry, pattern fitting and key-lock principles in three dimensions become more crucial for the interactions that create molecules and for molecules to create the macromolecules that are the material basis for life (molecular biology). These interactions become informational. A realm with more freedom from laws is created, with the laws as a basis. A new type of creativity is allowed to emerge, especially in dissipative structures with an energy and information flow through them and in the creation of new molecules combining the fairly few stable basic elements in all possible combinations. When these structures obtain an autocatalytic stable process, besides developing membranes they become autopoietic systems, beginning through cybernetic feedback to preserve themselves. When they make a digital representation of themselves in an interchange with the analogue one and start reproducing themselves, they transcend the pre-semiotic stage and through code duality become full-blown living semiotic beings engaged in sign games. A new realm of semiotic freedom, one in which living beings can start navigating through meaning, has been created on the basis of the informational realm making possible the manifestation of motivations, intentionality, and emotions. A kind of species interest or subjectivity has been created, and from there individual subjectivity develops through the emergence of an inner life of experience which creates a symbol of itself with which it can converse (Peirce's inner dialogue). As communication diversifies and becomes more and more important, it develops until actual language emerges at the same time as culture and self-consciousness. A new level of semiotic freedom is obtained through the combination of life forms and language games. Self-consciousness, understanding, empathy, pain, free will, and the search for meaning emerge through the conscious abductive actions of human beings and cultures. We begin manipulating the laws to our advantage through technology. If we do this well we will gain more semiotic freedom and a deeper understanding of ourselves and the universe. If not, we may well destroy both ourselves and most multicellular life systems on the planet.

Notes

Introduction

1 Hermann Hesse, a Swiss-German novelist, wrote *Steppenwolf, Siddhartha, Demian,* and *Narcissus and Goldmund.* He won the Nobel Prize for Literature for his final novel and masterpiece, *Magister Ludi,* also known as the *Glass Bead Game,* published in German in 1943. The book is an intricate *Bildungsroman* about humanity's eternal quest for enlightenment. Hesse delineates the problem of the synthesis of the intellectual–contemplative and the participatory–active life through the figure of a supremely gifted intellectual. He learns to master the summit of cultural intellectual purity in the form of the Glass Bead Game. The game combines all the insights, noble thoughts, and works of art that humanity has produced in its creative eras. Subsequent periods of scholarly study have reduced the insights to concepts and converted them into intellectual property that can be played like an organ with manuals and pedals that range over the entire intellectual cosmos. Theoretically, this instrument of the Glass Bead Game is capable of reproducing the entire intellectual content of the universe. In the introduction, Hesse writes:

> The Glass Bead Game is thus a mode of playing with the total contents and values of our culture; it plays with them as, say, in the great age of the arts a painter might have played with the colors on his palette. All the insights, noble thoughts, and works of art that the human race has produced in its creative eras, all that subsequent periods of scholarly study have reduced to concepts and converted into intellectual values the Glass Bead Game player plays like the organist on an organ. And this organ has attained an almost unimaginable perfection; its manuals and pedals range over the entire intellectual cosmos; its stops are almost

beyond number. Theoretically this instrument is capable of reproducing in the Game the entire intellectual content of the universe.

But unfortunately it is only possible in a purely theoretical game, which is completely separated from the impurity of actual lives in social practice. This book represents the pinnacle of Hesse's lifelong investigation of man's breaking out of the established modes of civilization to find his essential spirit through self-realization. Hesse writes:

> This same eternal idea, which for us has been embodied in the Glass Bead Game, has underlain every movement of Mind toward the ideal goal of a universitatis litterarum, every Platonic academy, every league of an intellectual elite, every rapprochement between the exact and the more liberal disciplines, every effort toward reconciliation between science and art or science and religion.

The Game Hesse describes in his novel is played with ideas. The ideas themselves can be musical, mathematical, verbal, or visual. The game draws its profound beauty from the clash of those ideas. Hesse writes:

> Every transition from major to minor in a sonata, every transformation of a myth or a religious cult, every classical or artistic formulation was, I realized in that flashing moment, if seen with a truly meditative mind, nothing but a direct route into the interior of the cosmic mystery, where in the alternation between inhaling and exhaling, between heaven and earth, between Yin and Yang, holiness is forever being created.
>
> The ideas played are linked to one another, in much the same way in which melodies are presented in a musical form such as a fugue.

In another metaphor, Hesse compares the Games to games of chess, but in this logical-strategic game, meaning has somehow to been added to every move. These ideas are then represented in a 'hieroglyphic language,' which is capable both of expressing their structure (as an equation may express the structural commonality of a diverse range of phenomena in physics, or symbolic logic the structure of an argument), and of being presented in its own concise and beautiful calligraphy. Hesse invented for the Glass Bead Game the principles of a new language, a language of symbols and formulas, in which mathematics and music played an equal

part, so that it became possible to combine astronomical and musical formulas, to reduce mathematics and music to a common denominator, as it
were.

Each country's commission produces an archive of the game. This is a
register of all hitherto examined and accepted symbols and decipher-
ments, whose number long ago by far exceeded the number of the
ancient Chinese ideographs.

Hesse thinks of uniting the natural, technical, and social sciences with
the humanities, and of uniting these in turn with the performative arts
and then, finally, seeking to combine Western intellectualism with Eastern
mysticism; an ambition close to Peirce's. Hesse attempts to fathom the
place of intellectualism in history, but he also realizes the danger that lies
in this project, in that the Academy of the Glass Bead Games sets itself
apart from society. He explores the symbiosis of the intellectual and spiritual world with the practical social world. His Magister Ludi feels the call
to be a bridge between the two, seeing the dangers of each feeling separate from the other and not part of a working Whole.

Hesse sees the weakness of his imaginary intellectual society: its creative
sterility. At the end of the novel, Joseph Knecht (the Magister Ludi) ends
his life by drowning. In Jungian symbolism, water represents the subconscious. It is the female side of the psyche and the wellspring of creativity,
which cannot safely be ignored.

Magister Ludi is a manifesto for the reintegration of intellectual life with
the 'real' world, of intellectual and mystic enlightenment with practice,
and as such an acceptance by both poles that each needs the other for civilization to work. We are in serious need of a broader global view of knowledge and enlightenment in individuals as well as in society.

2 As this is a summary there will be a minimum of references. If you read a
stand-alone version of the summary, there will be no reference list.

3 I am using the term 'phenomenological,' whenever it is not connected to
specific philosophers such as Husserl and Heidegger, to signify research
on the *experience* of things, happenings, thinking, and meaning.

4 I here refer to the spontaneity of the quantum fields and the human
mind.

5 Here I agree with phenomenology as Merleau-Ponty (2002) understood
it.

6 In PI §23 he writes: 'Here the term "language-game" is meant to bring
into prominence the fact that the speaking of of *language* is a part of an
activity, or a form of life.

Review the multiplicity of language-games in the following examples, and in others:

Giving orders, and obeying them –
Describing the appearance of an object, or giving its measurements –
Constructing an object from a description (a drawing) –
Reporting an event –
Speculating about an event –
Forming and testing an hypothesis –'

7 Physicalism believes that mental properties are identical to or at least somehow realized, determined, or constituted by physical properties. Even if we experience ourselves as autonomous agents with beliefs and desires that act the way they do because they have those beliefs and desires, we are a part of the physical world and obey the physical laws in the same 'mechanistic' way as any other physical system, and are therefore in the end a kind of 'automata' (Walter et al. 2003, preface). Physicalism includes various forms of 'non-reductive' physicalisms. There is no special mental causation.

8 I have taken this short description from the home page of the *Journal of Critical Realism*: 'Critical realist philosophy and social theory elaborate a general conceptual schema or meta-theory, via the immanent critique of other traditions and its own previous phases and the transcendental analysis of scientific and other human practices, for emancipatory science, i.e. science that makes genuine discoveries and can therefore help to promote human flourishing. It combines and reconciles epistemic relativism (all knowledge is socially produced, or transitive, and fallible) with judgmental rationalism (there are rational criteria for preferring one judgment or theory to another, genuine knowledge of the causally and/or existentially intransitive objects of science is possible) and ontological depth (the world is intransitive or irreducible to epistemology, transfactual or open, and stratified and emergent, hence differentiated and changing).

'On such a view of the world, there is more to what is than what are known, more to laws of nature than regular succession, more to society than human agents and more to human agents than effects of society; and objective explanations need not be practically neutral.

'Itself plural, open, and developing, critical realism is compatible with, and promotes, a wide range of emancipatory research programs (which incorporate additional premises), and explicitly espouses methodological pluralism; every science is a science only insofar as it deploys a methodology appropriate to the specificities of its object. Critical realism is accordingly also plural in its political affinities within a broad emancipatory remit. Emancipation refers to the historical process of freedom whereby people remove constraints on the fulfillment of their needs and seek to create the positive social conditions for the full flourishing of their potential as a species. The theory of explanatory critiques and the dialectics of freedom (which are substantive as well as formal) suggest broadly how a unity of theory and political practice might be effected by movements for change, with realist science and social science playing an important role; while the recent work of a leading critical realist philosopher, Roy Bhaskar, elaborates a theory 'within the bounds of secularism, consistent with all faiths and no faith,' of the spiritual presuppositions of emancipatory projects.' http://www.journalofcriticalrealism.org/index.php?sitesig =JCR&page= JCR 050 About JCR. Accessed 2 April 2005. Baskar 1975 and 1989 are foundational works.

9 On the death of Professor Luhmann, *Cybernetics and Human Knowing* in the fall of 1999 produced a theme issue on Luhmann's approach to semiotics, with his paper 'Sign as Form' as the central discussion paper.

Chapter 1

1 Cognitive science is thus a transdisciplinary paradigm that encompasses cognitive psychology as only one part of the research paradigm.

2 As with phenomenology, I here use the broadest possible conception of hermeneutics. I approach it as a general systematic study of interpretations of text (cultures as text).

3 'Signification sphere' is my concept for the new Peircean biosemiotic interpretation of Jakob von Uexküll's idea of *Umwelt*. More about this later in the book.

4 Which we will unfold more as the book's argument develops. My approach is to explain the many theories, philosophies, and concepts as I go along, without drowning the reader – a sort of 'need to know' strategy. I am aware that my selection of what is necessary to know will not satisfy all readers, who will at times have to use dictionaries or the like. But I think this is the most viable way.

5 An Eigenvalue is the value that a recursive process will eventually reach. For example, the eigenvalue of $\sqrt{2}$ is 1.

6 Like Blair (1990), I find it useful to distinguish between information retrieval (a piece of information with a specific address) and document retrieval (complex semiotic systems with many semantic access points).

Some would prefer to name the first 'data retrieval' and the other 'information retrieval.'

7 Actually, only the part of a computer program that is designed to communicate with humans. The rest is just commands for the machine.

8 This was a major subject of discussion at the 1996 SIGIR Conference in Copenhagen.

9 Though I agree with Prigogine and Stengers (1984) and Hayles (1999) that there are deep incompatibilities between a mechanistic and a probabilistic complexity view, among other things based on the views on irreversibility of time and the limits to scientific knowledge.

10 Through Lakoff's analysis, in the next, more general epistemological chapter, we will go further into the roots of, what he calls, 'objectivism.'

11 It is only reluctantly that I will use the concept 'symbol' at all in relation to these concepts because they do not, as they are defined, draw their meaning from the context of the historical-cultural time-dependent and inexhaustibly dynamic complexity of human social interaction.

12 In Fodor (2001) this perspective is modified considerably, especially with regard to its universality.

13 On this subject, both Popper and Kuhn hold that there is no direct semantic or logical-syntactic connection between observation and knowledge. One can measure how many bits the senses 'take in,' but the world is not constructed out of objective bits that then, so to speak, are channelled into the mind through the senses. This is one of the realizations that gave the impetus to second-order cybernetics, which we will return to shortly.

14 Oral communication at FIS96.

15 I am using 'meaningful information' to avoid confusion with Shannon and Weaver's mathematical information concepts.

16 I am here using the hermeneutic concept of horizon instead of cognitive science's concept of semantic network. Ingwersen has accepted horizon as compatible with the paradigm of the cognitive perspective.

17 Maturana, 'Autopoiesis,' in Milan Zeleney, ed., *Autopoiesis: A Theory of Living Organization* (New York: North Holland, 1981), 21.

18 We are dependent on the energy from the sun to get rid of our heat and entropy production through the expanding cold universe. The atoms we are made of are constructed in the fusion processes in the stars, and the very heavy ones in the explosions of supernovas.

Chapter 2

1 Aristotle worked with five virtues of thought: *technê, epistêmê, phronêsis, sophia,* and *nous.* Of these, *epistêmê* is closest to the modern idea of science.

2 That is at least one way to narrate what happened.

3 This figure springs from groundwork done by the Danish physicist Peder Voetmann Christiansen (Roskilde University), which he communicated in a public lecture to a Mind Ship Seminar in Copenhagen in 1996. He was further inspired by some semioticians who knew of Greimas's square – which Winfried Nöth later identified for me. It is further developed here with his consent and approval of the result. This is one of the many inspirations I have received during nearly twenty years of interdisciplinary exchange with this remarkable semiotically and interdisciplinary thinking physicist, who has been a major inspiration to many Danish biosemioticians.

Chapter 3

1 Douglas Adam sees this point very clearly in his book *The Ultimate Hitchhiker's Guide* (113–20). The ultimate computer, 'Deep Thought,' having been built, is asked to answer the question about the meaning of 'Life, the Universe and everything.' 'Deep Thought' takes seven-and-a-half million years to calculate the answer to 'Life, the Universe and everything.' And the answer is '42'! Very profound. 42. Think about it!

2 By the Galilean tradition, I mean the attempt within a realistic world view to uncover universal mathematical (natural) laws as the causal agents behind the behaviour of things.

3 A detailed analysis of Lorenz and Tinbergen's work is found in Brier 1980, a prize essay in psychology for which I won Copenhagen University's Gold Medal. But it is unfortunately still only in Danish. I have not wanted to add a hundred pages or more to the present book to bring in the detailed documentation for this analysis, which I have also lectured on at the Konrad Lorenz Institute for Evolution and Cognitive Research.

4 This section has been discussed with and approved by Reventlow, who was my supervisor for three years.

5 I presented my original analysis of this topic in 1980, developed it in two other Danish papers (1985, 1986), published the first analysis in English in 1992, commented most directly on Reventlow's work in 1993, and developed the semiotic theory in 1995. I further touched on the subject the following year.

Chapter 4

1 Personal communication with Kauffman on this question during a conference at the Niels Bohr Institute, Copenhagen, in 1995.

2 To go deeper into Spencer-Brown's philosophy, one has to read *Only Two Can Play This Game*, which he wrote in 1971 under the pseudonym James Keys. It was published by Cat Books and distributed by G. Spencer-Brown & Co., Cambridge, and by Julian Press, New York (1972).

3 Based on personal discussions with Lucia Santaella Braga, John Deely, Jesper Hoffmeyer, Claus Emmeche, Frederick Stjernfelt, Jørgen Dines Johansen, Winfried Nöth, etc.

Chapter 5

1 I am aware that Sommerhoff writes this in relation to his own theory, but I think his words have general value. I do not have the space here to deal with Sommerhoff's theory, so I have deleted references to it.

2 I think this is because he is not – like Maturana, Varela, and myself – primarily a biologist by training; rather, his thinking has developed from a foundation of mathematics, physics, and basic considerations about the nature of computing and cognition.

3 I will return to the similarities between von Foerster's view of the difference and the nature of the cognitive and the material world, and the dualistic views of Galileo and Descartes.

4 In spite of several discussions with Maturana about this subject, I can only interpret this as a pure epistemological statement.

5 There are now results which indicate that the immune system is also a closed system, a third non-trivial machine, one that is dynamically connected to the other two.

6 Ludwig Wittgenstein was von Foerster's uncle.

7 For Maturana, objects arise only in language, so for living systems that do not operate in language there are no objects (1988). Biosemiotics views animals as using signs, so we still think that animals have semiotic objects in their signification sphere, although they are not as refined as linguistically based objects.

8 Mingers (1995) reports the debate in second-order cybernetics as to whether one can extrapolate the autopoietic viewpoint to communication systems, as Luhmann does in his generalization of a systems autopoietic theory. I tend to side with him and Varela: psychological and socio-communicative systems are only organizationally closed and not truly autopoietic. But this does not affect the validity of his theory.

Chapter 6

1 This work was done in collaboration with Thorkild and Martin Thellefsen and was reported in a paper to *Semiotica* with Thorkild Tellefsen as the main author. The formulations here represent further development of that work.
2 This semiotic analysis of index terms was originally done with Torkild Thillefson and Martin Thillefson and has been further developed here.

Chapter 7

1 For instance, see Gilbert Ryle's analysis (1990, 170–1) and interpretations of Husserl's phenomenology and theory of intuitions of essence.
2 Although Mark Johnson is not a cowriter of this book, the analyses are consistent with their first book, *Metaphors We Live By* (Lakoff and Johnson 1999).

Chapter 8

1 Aristotle's idea of form and order is not so different from the concept of law as construction plans in von Uexküll's (1986, 224) biology: '(7) The construction plan stands over the inner world and the environment, dominating everything. Only research on the construction plan can, in my estimation, give a healthy and certain basis for biology. It also brings anatomy and physiology together again in a productive mutuality ... If the organization of the construction plan is placed at the focus of research for every species, then each newly discovered fact finds its natural place, and only thus does it gain sense and significance.'
2 This analysis is based on Lorenz's collected works (Lorenz 1970–1), and quotation page numbers refer to this work, although I refer to individual dates of publication of the articles in the collection.
3 I do not think that when Uexküll talks about instinct, he is referring to the modern ethological concept developed by Lorenz and Tinbergen.
4 I owe these quotes and the analysis to the superb work done by Innis (1994, 27), whose analysis and synthesis are going in much the same direction as mine. However, Innis uses Polanyi, Bühler, and Dewey to supplement Peirce, whereas I am working more with the animal foundations of signification and consciousness to develop a biosemiotics and then using the results to integrate information theory with a theory of information technology and AI.

Chapter 9

1   This is of course a highly simplified description, as there are ongoing discussions on what physicalism means and to what degree it can describe
mental phenomena. See for instance Walter and Heckmann (2003). But I
am highly sceptical about this paradigm. The explanations do not make
sense to me, or they make sense only when I see them as extreme attempts
to hold on to a specific world view, without which a certain view of science
and reason could not be kept.

2   This is a classical discussion of pure mysticism or what Leibniz and Huxley
both called 'The Perennial Philosophy.' Peirce was aware of the similarities
between the deepest Christian and Buddhist teachings, as is Suzuki
(2002), who in his famous book on Christian and Buddhist mysticism compares Meister Eckhart's mysticism with Buddhism and finds strong similarities. Meister Eckhart (c. 1260–1327/8) was one of the great Christian
mystics. Actually, Peirce thought that Buddhism in some ways was more
profound than Christianity and its true inspiration; see Brent (1998, 261,
314). We shall not here enter this complicated discussion of what enlightenment could mean for the mystics from the psychological, theological,
and philosophical perspective. But see Stace (1960).

3   Peirce's theory of signs asserts that all modes of thinking depend on the
use of signs. Every thought and act of reasoning is interpretation of signs.
Semiosis is a process of establishing connections among signs, their
objects, and their Interpretants through a mediating function. Semiotics
studies the conditions that are necessary in order for representations of
objects to function as signs. Thus the logic of semiotic is the theory of the
conditions that determine the truth of signs. Peirce conceptualizes this as
a normative science. This is because it is a theory of the kind of reasoning
that should be employed in order to discover truth. Thus it is normative
for the search for truth.

Peirce then divides philosophy into three areas of study:

1. phenomenology (the study of phenomena as objects of perception),
2. normative science (the study of the proper relations of phenomena), and
3. metaphysics (the study of the nature of ultimate reality).

Peirce argues for the division by stating that phenomenology is the study
of phenomena in their 'Firstness,' normative science is the study of phenomena in their 'Secondness,' and metaphysics is the study of phenomena
in their 'Thirdness' (CP, 5.122–4). He then divides normative science into:

1. aesthetics (understood as the science of ideals),
2. ethics (understood as the science of right and wrong conduct), and
3. logic (as the more classical idea of science of the laws of thought).

He then divides logic into:

1. critical logic, seen as the study of the relations of signs to their objects,
2. speculative grammar understood as the study of the 'meaning' of signs, and
3. speculative rhetoric or methodeutic as the study of the relation of signs to their Interpretants.

All of this is an important deviation from the logocentrism that classical science inherited from the Greeks and developed through logical positivism and later analytical philosophy, because the understanding is now based on the evolution of signs and on a theory of meaning that goes beyond truth tables.

Chapter 10

1 Thus in the graphic model the autopoietic system of socio-communication should be seen as having both the biological and the psychological autopoiesis as its environment, not only the psyche.
2 I am grateful to Lucia Santaella Braga for letting me read a draft of her inspiring paper 'Peirce's and Bakhtin's Anti-Cartesian Concept of the Self' prior to publication.

Chapter 12

1 I think Luhmann was aware of this, so he added Spencer-Brown and Husserl to his foundation. But he never really worked out his metaphysical framework to make it consistent. Rather, he used it as a specific research strategy in sociology.
2 See for instance Kauffman's (1995) work on autocatalytic closure.
3 I wish to thank Menno Hulswit for sending me his remarkable book that represents an important milestone in the modern interpretation of Peirce.
4 Brent (1998) points out how the theory of having transcendence and immanence at the same time is a crucial point in most mysticism. I might add that Plato and his follower Plotinus are good examples.

Brent writes on page 212: 'I believe that, for Peirce, semeiotics should be understood, after his mystical experience, as the working out of how the real is both immanent and transcendent and of how the infinite speaker may be said to practice semiosis, the action of signs, in creating our universe.'

5 Einstein, Podolsky, Rosen paradox, Bell inequalities, Aspects experiments, and so on.

References

Abraham, R. 1993. *Chaos, Gaya, Eros: A Chaos Pioneer Uncovers the Three Great Streams of History*. San Francisco: Harper.

Andkjær, O., and S. Køppe. 1986. *Freud's Psykoanalyse*. Copenhagen: Gyldendalske boghandel. English version: Anscombe, New York: Macmillan.

Appel, H.-O. 1981. *Charles Sanders Peirce: From Pragmatism to Pragmaticism*. Amherst: University of Massachusetts Press.

Aristotle. 1976. *The Nicomachean Ethics*. Harmondsworth: Penguin.

Aristotle. 1995. *Den Nikomacheiske Etik*. Copenhagen: Det Lille Forlag.

Åkerstrøm, N. 2003. *Discursive analytical strategies: Understanding Foucault, Kosselleck, Laclau, Luhmann*. Bristol: Policy Press.

Barrow, J.D. 1998. *Impossibility: The Limits of Science and the Science of Limits*. New York: Oxford University Press.

Baskar, R. 1989. *Reclaiming Reality: A Critical Introduction to Contemporary Philosophy*. London: Verso.

– 1997. *A Realist Theory of Science*. London: Verso Classics. (Orig. pub. 1977.)

Bateson, G. 1973. *Steps to an Ecology of Mind*. Chicago: University of Chicago Press.

– 1980. *Mind and Nature: A Necessary Unit*. New York: Bantam.

Bateson, G., and M.C. Bateson. 2005. *Angels Fear: Towards an Epistemology of the Sacred*. Crosshill, NJ: Hampton Press.

Beer, C.G. 1982. 'The Study of Vertebrate Communication – Its Cognitive Implications.' In *Animal Mind – Human Mind: Report of the Dahlem Workshop on Animal Mind – Human Mind Berlin 1981*, ed. D.R. Griffin, 251–67. Berlin: Springer.

Belkin, N. 1978. 'Concepts of Information for Information Science.' *Journal of Documentation* 34:55–85.

Berkeley, G. 2000. *Principperne for den menneskelige erkendelse*. Copenhagen: Det lille forlag. Translation of 'A Treatise Concerning the Principle of Human

Knowledge,' in A.A. Luce and T.E. Jessop. 1949. *The Works of George Berkeley, Bishop of Cloyne.* London: Nelson.

Bertalanffy, L. von. 1976. *General System Theory: Foundations, Development, Applications.* New York: Braziller. (Orig. pub. 1968.)

Bird, A. 1998. *Philosophy of Science.* London: UCL Press.

Bittermann, M.E. 1965. 'The Evolution of Intelligence. *Scientific American* (January).

Blackmore, S. 1999. *The Meme Machine* Oxford: Oxford University Press.

Blair, D.C. 1990. *Language and Representation in Information Retrieval.* Amsterdam: Elsevier.

Bøgh Andersen, P. 1990. *A Theory of Computer Semiotics: Semiotic Approaches to Construction and Assessment of Computer Systems.* Cambridge: Cambridge University Press.

Bohm, D. 1983. *Wholeness and the Implicate order.* New York: Routledge and Kegan Paul.

Bohm, D.J., and R. Weber. 1983. 'Of Matter and Meaning: The Super-Implicate Order.' *ReVISION* 6 (1): 34–44.

Bohr, N. 1954. 'Kundskabens Enhed.' In *Atomfysik og menneskelig erkendelse,* 83–99. Copenhagen: J.H. Schultz Forlag, 1957.

Bourdieu, P. 2005a. *Viden om Videm og Refleksivitet.* Copenhagen: Hans Reitrels Forlag. (*Science de la science et réflexivité,* 2001.)

– 2005b. *Udkastil en praksisteori.* Copenhagen: Hans Reitrels Forlag. (*Esquisse d'une théorie de la pratique – precede du trois etudes d'ethnologie kabyle,* 2000.)

Brent, J. 1998. *Charles Sanders Peirce: A Life.* Revised and enlarged edition. Bloomington: Indiana University Press.

Brier, S. 1980. 'Der ønskes analyseret (evt. v.h.a. egne undersøgelser), om hierarki-og sandsynlighedsbetragtninger i beskrivelsen af adfærd kan anvendes i – og udbygge – een eller flere motivationspsykologiske teorier eller modeller.' (University Prize Essay in psychology about the fruitfulness of hierarchy – and probability – deliberations in constructing models of motivation from behavioural analysis. Awarded with the Gold Medal in psychology of Copenhagen University).

– 1994. *Information er Sølv.* Aalborg: Biblioteksarbejde.

– 2005. *Informationsvidenskabsteori.* Copenhagen: Forlaget Samfundslitteratur. Revised edition, 2006.

– 2006. 'Biosemiotics.' *Encyclopedia of Language and Linguistics.* Amsterdam: Elsevier.

Brockmann, J. 1995. *The Third Culture.* New York: Simon and Schuster.

Buckland, M. 1991. *Information and Information Systems.* New York and London: Greenwood.

Carrington, B.M. 1990. 'Expert Systems: Power to the Experts.' *Database* (April).

Casanova, M.B. 1990. 'Information: The Major Element of Change.' In *Information Quality: Definitions and Dimensions*. Proceedings of a NORDINFO seminar, Royal School of Librarianship, ed. I. Wormell, 42–53. London: Taylor Graham.

Cassirer, E. 1944. *An Essay on Man: An Introduction to a Philosophy of Human Culture*. New Haven, CT: Yale University Press.

Chaitin, G. 2005. *Meta Math: The Quest for Omega*. New York: Pantheon.

Chalmers, D.J. 1996. *The Conscious Mind: In Search of a Fundamental Theory*. New York and Oxford: Oxford University Press.

Chomsky, N. 1994. *Critical Assessments*. Ed. Carlos P. Otero. New York: Routledge.

Christiansen, P.V. 1970. *Information, entropi og udvikling*. Kompendium. Copenhagen: H.C. Ørsteds institut, Copenhagen University.

– 1984. 'Informationens elendighed' (The misery of information). Synopsis to a workshop on the information society, IMFUFA. Roskilde, Denmark: Roskilde University Centre.

– 1989. 'Tidens tre tegn.' *Weekend-avisen* (13 October): 22.

– 1995. 'Habit Formation and the Thirdness of Signs.' Presented at the semiotic symposium, 'The Emergence of Codes and Intentions as a Basis of Sign Processes.' Hollufgaard, Odense, 26–29 October. IMFUFA text no. 307. Roskilde, Denmark: Roskilde University.

Churchland, P. 2004. 'Eliminative Materialism and the Propositional Attitudes.' In *Philosophy of Mind: A Guide and Anthology*, ed. J. Heil, 382–400. Oxford: Oxford University Press.

Colapietro, V. 1989. *Peirce's Approach to the Self: A Semiotic Perspective on Human Subjectivity*. Albany: State University of New York Press.

Combs, A., and S. Brier. 2001. 'Signs, Information, and Consciousness.' *SYSTEMS – Journal of Transdisciplinary Systems Science* (Wroclaw, Poland) 5 (1/2): 15–24.

Danesi, M., ed. 2001. *The Invention of Global Semiotics: A Collection of Essays on the Life and Work of Thomas A. Sebeok*. Ottawa, ON: Legas, 2001.

Darwin, C. 1859. *The Origin of Species*. New York: Random House.

– 1899. *The Expression of Emotion in Man and Animals*. New York: Appleton (www.charles=darwin.classic=literature.co.uk).

Davidson, D. 1984. *Inquiries into Truth and Interpretation*. Oxford: Oxford University Press.

Dawkins, R. 1987. *The Blind Watchmaker*. Harlow, Essex: Longman Scientific and Technical.

– 1999. *The Selfish Gene.* Oxford: Oxford University Press. (Orig. pub. 1984.)

De May, M. 1980. 'The Relevance of the Cognitive Viewpoint for Information Science.' In *Theory and Application in Information Research.* Proceedings of the Second International Research Forum on Information Science, Royal School of Librarianship, Copenhagen, 3–6 August 1977, ed. O. Harbo and L. Kajberg, 48–62. London: Mansell.

Deacon, T.W. 1997. *The Symbolic Species: The Co-Evolution of Language and the Brain.* New York: Norton.

Deely, J. 1990. *Basics of Semiotics.* Bloomington; Indiana University Press. (4th ed., 2005. Tartu: Tartu University Press.)

– 1994. 'How is the Universe Perfused with Signs?' In *Semiotics,* ed. C.W. Spinks and J. Deely. New York: Peter Lang.

– 1998. 'Physiosemiosis and Semiotics.' In *Semiotics,* ed. C.W. Spinks and J. Deely. New York: Peter Lang.

– 2001a. 'Physiosemiosis in the Semiotic Spiral: A Play of Musement.' *Sign System Studies* 29 (1): 27–48.

– 2001b. *Four Ages of Understanding: The First Postmodern Survey of Philosophy from Ancient Times to the Turn of the Twenty-First Century.* Toronto: University of Toronto Press.

Dennett, D.C. 1979. 'Conditions of Personhood.' In *Brainstorms: Philosophical Essays on Mind and Psychology.* Montgomery, VT: Bradford Books.

– 1983. 'Intensional Systems in Cognitive Ethology: The "Panglossion Paradigm" Defended.' *The Behavioral and Brain Sciences* 6 (3).

Dewey, J. 1991. *How We Think: A Restatement of the Relation of Reflective Thinking to the Educative Process.* Loughton, Essex: Prometheus. (Org. pub. 1910.)

Dreyfus, H.L., and S.E. Dreyfuss. 1986. *Mind over Machine: The Power of Human Intuition and Expertise in the Era of the Computer.* New York: Free Press.

– 1995. 'Making a Mind vs Modeling the Brain: AI back to a Branchpoint.' *Informatica* 19 (4): 425–41.

Dubois, D. 1994. 'Identity and Autonomy of Psychology in Cognitive Sciences: Some Remarks from Language Processing and Knowledge Representation.' *World Futures: The Journal of General Evolution* 42 (12): 73.

Eco, U. 1979. *A Theory of Semiotics.* Bloomington: Indiana University Press.

Eigen, M., et al. 1981. 'The Origin of Genetic Information.' *Scientific American* (April): 78–94.

Ellis, R.D., and N. Newton. 1998. 'Three Paradoxes of Phenomenal Consciousness: Bridging the Explanatory Gap.' *Journal of Consciousness Studies* 5 (4): 419–42.

Emmeche, C. 1992. 'Modelling Life: A Note on the Semiotics of Emergence and Computation in Artificial and Natural Living Systems.' In *Biosemiotics:*

The Semiotic Web 1991, ed. T.A. Sebeok and J. Umiker-Sebeok, 77–99. Berlin: Mouton de Gruyter.

– 1998. 'Defining Life as a Semiotic Phenomenon.' *Cybernetics & Human Knowing* 5 (1): 33–42.

– 1999. 'The Sarkar Challenge to Biosemiotics: Is There Any Information in a Cell?' *Semiotica* 127 (1/4): 273–93.

– 2000. 'Transdisciplinarity, Theory-Zapping and the Growth of Knowledge.' *Semiotica* 131 (3/4): 217–28.

Emmeche, C., S. Køppe, and F. Stjernfelt. 'Explaining Emergence: Towards an Ontology of Levels.' In *Systems Thinking*. Vol. 1, *General System Theory, Cybernetics and Complexity*, ed. G. Midgley. Thousand Oaks, CA: Sage.

Flyvbjerg, B. 1991. *Rationalitet og Magt*. Bind 1, *Det konkretes videnskab*. Copenhagen: Akademisk Forlag.

Fodor, J.A. 1987. *Psychosemantics: The Problems of Meaning*. Cambridge, MA: MIT Press.

– 2001. *The Mind Does Not Work That Way: The Scope and Limits of Computational Psychology*. Cambridge, MA: MIT Press.

Foerster, H. von. 1970. 'Thoughts and Notes on Cognition.' In *Cognition: A Multiple View*. ed. P.L. Garvin, 25–48. New York: Spartan.

– 1979. 'The Cybernetics of Cybernetics.' In *Communication and Control in Society*, ed. K. Krippendorff, 5–8. New York: Gordon and Breach.

– 1980. 'Epistemology of Communication.' In *The Myth of Information: Technology and Postindustrial Culture*, ed. K. Woodward. London: Routledge and Kegan Paul.

– 1981. 'On Cybernetics of Cybernetics and Social Theory.' In *Self-Organizing Systems: An Interdisciplinary Approach*, ed. G. Roth and H. Schwegler, 102–5. Frankfurt: Campus.

– 1984. *Observing Systems*. Seaside, CA: Intersystems Publications.

– 1986. 'From Stimulus to Symbol.' In *Event Cognition: an Ecological Perspective*, ed. V. McCabe and G.J. Balzano, 79–91. Hillsdale, NJ: Lawrence Erlbaum.

– 1988. 'On Constructing a Reality.' In *Adolescent Psychiatry*. Vol. 15, *Developmental and Clinical Studies*, ed. S.C. Feinstein, A.H. Esman, J.G. Looney, and G.H. Orvin, 77–95. Chicago: University of Chicago Press.

– 1989. 'The Need of Perception for the Perception of Needs.' *Leonardo* 22 (2): 223–6.

– 1991. 'Through the Eyes of the Other.' In *Research and Reflexivity*, ed. F. Steier, 63–75. London: Sage.

– 1992a. 'Cybernetics.' In *Encyclopedia of Artificial Intelligence*, ed. S. Shapiro, 309–12. New York: Wiley.

- 1992b. 'Ethics and Second-Order Cybernetics.' *Cybernetics & Human Knowing* 1 (1): 9–19.
- 1993a. 'Für Niklas Luhmann: Kommunikation ist das Eigenverhalten in einem rekursiv operierenden, zweifach geschlossenen System.' *Teoria Sociologica* 1 (2): 61–85.
- 1993b. 'On Seeing.' In *Adolescent Psychiatry.* Vol. 19, *Developmental and Clinical Studies*, ed. S.C. Feinstein and R.C. Marohn, 102–3. Chicago: University of Chicago Press.

Franck, D. 1999. 'Auswirkung der Uexküllschen Umweltlehre auf die moderne Verhaltensbiologie.' *Folia Bavaeriana* 7:81–91. Institute of Zoology and Botany, Karl Ernst von Baer Museum, Estonian Academy of Sciences, Estonian Naturalistic Society.

Gadamer, H.-G. 1975. *Truth and Method.* New York: Seabury Press.

Gardin, J.-C. 1973. 'Document Analysis and Linguistic Theory.' *Journal of Documentation* 29 (2): 137–68.

Gardner, H. 1985. *The Mind's New Science: A History of the Cognitive Revolution.* New York: Basic Books.

Gibbons, M., C. Limoges, H. Nowotny, S. Schwartzman, P. Scott, and M. Trow. 1994. *The New Production of Knowledge. The Dynamics of Science and Research in Contemporary Societies.* London: Sage.

Gibson, J.J. 1966. *The Senses Considered as Perceptual System.* Boston: Houghton Mifflin.

Gilbert, S.F., and S. Sarkar. 2000. 'Embracing Complexity: Organicism for the 21st Century.' *Developing Dynamics* 219:1–9.

Glasersfeld, E. von. 1991. 'Distinguishing the Observer: An Attempt at Interpreting Maturana.' *Methodologia* 5 (8): 57–68.

- 1992. 'Why I Consider Myself a Cybernetician.' *Cybernetics & Human Knowing* 1 (1).

Goerner, S.J. 1993. *Chaos and the Evolving Ecological Universe. World Future General Evolution Studies*, Vol. 7. Luxembourg: Gordon and Breach.

Gustavsson, B. 2001. *Vidensfilosofi.* Århus, Denmark: Klim.

Habermas, J. 1974. *Vitenskab som ideology.* Oslo: Gyldendal Norsk Forlag.

- 1987. Excursus on Luhmann's Appropriation of the Philosophy of the Subject Through System Theory.' In *The Philosophical Discourse of Modernity: Twelve Lectures*, 368–85. Cambridge, MA: MIT Press.

Hartshorne, C. 1984. 'Towards a Buddhist-Christian Religion.' In *Buddhism and American Thinkers*, ed. K.K. Inada and N.P. Jacobson. Albany: State University of New York Press.

Hawking, S.W. 1989. *A Brief History of Time.* 10th Anniversary Edition. New York: Bantam.

Hayles, N.K. 1999. *How We Became Posthuman: Virtual Bodies in Cybernetics, Literature, and informatics.* Chicago: University of Chicago Press.

Heidegger, M. 1973. *Being and Time.* Trans. J. Macquarrie and E. Robinson. London: Basil Blackwell.

Hesse, H. 2002. *Magister Ludi.* London: Picador. (Orig. pub. 1943.)

Hinde, R. 1970. *Animal Behaviour: A Synthesis of Ethology and Comparative Behaviour.* Tokyo: McGraw-Hill.

Hintikke, J. 1998. 'What is Abduction? The Fundamental Problem of Contemporary Epistemology.' *Transaction of the Charles S. Peirce Society* 34 (3): 503–34.

Hjørland, B. 1997. *Information Seeking and Subject Representation: An Activity-Theoretical Approach to Information Science.* New York: Greenwood.

Hjørland, B., and H. Albrechtsen. 1995. 'Toward a New Horizon in Information Science: Domain Analysis.' *Journal of the American Society for Information Science* 46 (6): 400–25.

Hoffmeyer, J. 1984. *Naturen i hovedet: om biologisk videnskab.* Charlottenlund, Denmark: Rosinante.

– 1992a. 'Some Semiotic Aspects of the Psycho-Physical Relation: The Endo-Exosemiotic Boundary.' In *Biosemiotics: The Semiotic Web,* ed. T.A. Sebeok and J. Umiker-Sebeok, 101–23. Berlin: Mouton de Gruyter.

– 1992b. 'Semiotic Aspects of Biology: Biosemiotic.' In *Semiotics: A Handbook on the Sign-Theoretic Foundations of Nature and Culture,* ed. R. Posner, K. Robins, and T.A. Sebeok. Berlin: Walter de Gruyter.

– 1995. 'The Swarming Cyberspace of the Body.' *Cybernetics & Human Knowing* 3 (1): 16–15.

– 1997. *Signs of Meaning in the Universe.* Bloomington: Indiana University Press.

– 1998. 'Surfaces inside Surfaces.' *Cybernetics & Human Knowing* 5 (1): 33–42.

– 2002. 'The Central Dogma: A Joke That Became Real.' *Semiotica* 138 (1/4): 1–13.

– Hoffmeyer, J., and C. Emmeche. 1991. 'Code-Duality and the Semiotics of Nature.' In *On Scientific Modeling,* ed. M. Anderson and F. Merrell, 117–66. New York: Mouton de Gruyter.

Hofstadter, D.R. 1983. 'Artificial Intelligence: Subcognition as Computation.' In *The Study of Information,* ed. F. Machlup and U. Mansfield, 263–85. New York: Wiley.

Hulswit, M. 2002. *From Cause to Causation: A Peircean Perspective.* Dordrecht: Kluwer.

Huntington, S. 1993. 'The Clash of Civilizations.' *Foreign Affairs* 72 (3): 22–49.

Husserl, E. 1977. *Cartesian Meditations.* Dordrecht: Kluwer. (Orig. pub. 1929.)

– 1997. *Fænomonologiens idé.* Copenhagen: Hans Reitzels Forlag. (*Die Idee der Phenomenologie.*)

– 1999. *Cartesianske Meditationer.* Copenhagen: Hans Reitzels Forlag.

Inada, K.K., and N. Jacobson. 1984. *Buddhism and American Thinkers.* Albany: State University of New York Press.

Ingwersen, P. 1992. *Information Retrieval Interaction.* London: Taylor Graham.

– 1995. 'Information and Information Science.' In *Encyclopedia of Library and Information Science,* 137–73. New York: Marcel Dekker.

– 1996. 'Cognitive Perspectives of Information Retrieval Interaction: Elements of a Cognitive IR Theory.' *Journal of Documentation* 52 (1): 3–50.

Innis, R.E. 1994. *Consciousness and the Play of Signs.* Bloomington: Indiana University Press.

Jantsch, E. 1980. *The Self-Organizing Universe.* New York: Pergamon.

Johansen, J.D., and S.E. Larsen. 1994. *Tegn i brug.* Copenhagen: Forlaget Amanda. (English: S.E. Larsen and J.D. Johansen. 2002. *Signs in Use: An Introduction to Semiotics.* London: Routledge.)

Jaynes, J. 1969. 'The Historical Origins of 'Ethology' and 'Comparative Psychology.'' *Animal Behavior* 17:602–6.

Kant, E. 1990. *Critique of Pure Reason.* Buffalo, NY: Prometheus. (Orig. pub. 1781.)

Kauffman, S. 1995. *At Home in the Universe.* Oxford: Oxford University Press.

Keller, K.D. 1999. 'Sociotechnics and the Structuring of Meaning: Beyond the Idea of Autopoietic Social Systems.' *Cybernetics & Human Knowing* 6 (2): 76–96.

Kierkegaard, S. 1964. *Samlede værker.* Bind 15, *Sygdommen til døden.* Copenhagen: Gyldendal. (Orig. pub. 1848.)

Kirkeby, O.F. 1994. *Begivenhed og kropstanke: en fænomenologisk-hermeneutisk analyse.* Åarhus, Denmark: Forlaget Modtryk.

– 1997. 'Event and Body-Mind. An Outline of a Post-Postmodern Approach to Phenomenology.' *Cybernetics & Human Knowing* 4 (2/3): 3–34.

Krippendorff, K., ed. 1979. *Communication and Control in Society,* New York: Gordon and Breach.

– 1991. 'Stepping Stones Towards a Constructivist Epistemology for Mass-Communication.' Lecture prepared for presentation to the annual meeting of the Deutsche Gesellschaft für Publizistik und Kommunikationswissenschaft, Bamberg, 8–10 May.

– 1993. 'Major Metaphors of Communication and Some Constructivist Reflections on Their Use.' *Cybernetics & Human Knowing* 2 (1): 3–26.

Krois, J.M. 2004. 'Ernst Cassirer's Philosophy of Biology.' *Sign System Studies* 32 (1/2): 277–95.

Kuhn, T. 1970. *The Structure of Scientific Revolutions.* 2nd ed. Chicago: University of Chicago Press.

Kull, K. 1998. 'Semiotic Ecology: Different Natures in the Semiosphere.' *Sign System Studies* 26:344–64.

– 1999. 'Biosemiotics in the Twentieth Century: A View from Biology.' *Semiotica* 127 (1/4): 385–414.

– 2001. 'The Proxemics of Ecosystems, and Three Types of Attitudes toward the Community of Other Species: An Attempt at Ecosemiotic Analysis.' Proceedings of the Nordic-Baltic Summer Institute for Semiotic and Structural Studies, Imatra, Finland, 12–21 June, 70–7.

Lakoff, G. 1987. *Women, Fire and Dangerous Things: What Categories Reveal about the Mind.* Chicago: University of Chicago Press.

Lakoff, G., and M. Johnson. 1980. *Metaphors We Live By.* Chicago: University of Chicago Press.

– 1999. *Philosophy in the Flesh: The Embodied Mind and its Challenge to Western Thought.* New York: Basic Books.

Laszlo, E. 1995. *The Interconnected Universe: Conceptual Foundations of Transdisciplinary Unified Theory.* Singapore: World Scientific.

– 1996. *The Whispering Pond: A Personal Guide to the Emerging Vision of Science.* Rockport, MA: Element Books.

– 2004. *Science and the Akashic Field: An Integral Theory of Everything.* New York: Inner Traditions International.

Latour, B. 1993. *We Have Never Been Modern.* New York: Harvester Wheatsheaf.

– 1999. *Pandora's Hope: Essays on the Reality of Science Studies.* Cambridge, MA: Harvard University Press.

Leff, H.S., and A.F. Rex, eds. 1990. *Maxwell's Demon: Entropy, Information, Computing.* Bristol: Adam Hilger.

Lewin, K. 1935. *A Dynamic Theory of Personality: Selected Papers.* New York: McGraw-Hill.

Leydesdorff, L. 2005a. 'Anticipatory Systems and the Processing of Meaning: A Simulation Study Inspired by Luhmann's Theory of Social Systems.' *Journal of Artificial Societies and Social Simulation* 8 (2). http://jasss.soc.surrey.ac.uk/8/2/7.html.

– 2005b. 'The Biological Metaphor of a Second-Order Observer and the Sociological Discourse.' *Kybernetes* (forthcoming).

– 2007. 'Luhmann's Communication-Theoretical Specification of the 'Genoma' of Husserl's Phenomenology.' In *Public Space, Power and Communication*, ed. E.B. Pires (forthcoming).

Liebenau, J., and J. Backhouse. 1990. *Understanding Information: An Introduction*, London: Macmillan.

Lindsay, P., and D.A. Norman. 1977. *Human Information Processing: An Introduction to Psychology.* 2nd ed. New York: Academic Press.

Lindström, J. 1974. *Dialog och förstaaelse.* Göteborg, Sweden: Avdelingen för Vetenskapsteori.

Lorenz, K. 1935. 'Der Kumpan in der Umwelt des Vogels.' *Journal für Ornithologie* 83:137–213, 289–413.

– 1950. 'The Comparative Method in Studying Innate Behavior Patterns.' *Symposia of the Society for Experimental Biology* 4:221–68.

– 1966. *On Aggression.* London: Methuen.

– 1970–1. *Studies in Animal and Human Behaviour.* Vols. I and II. Cambridge, MA: Harvard University Press.

– 1973. *Die Rückseite des Spiegels: Versuch einer Naturgeschichte menschlichen Erkennens.* Munich: Piper.

– 1977. *Behind the Mirror: A Search for a Natural History of Human Knowledge.* London: Methuen.

Luhmann, N. 1985. 'Complexity and Meaning.' In *The Science and Praxis of Complexity*, ed. I. Prigogine et al. Tokyo: United Nations University.

– 1989. *Ecological Communication.* Cambridge: Polity Press.

– 1990. *Essays on Self-Reference.* New York: Colombia University Press.

– 1992. 'What is Communication?' *Communication Theory* 2 (3): 251–8.

– 1993. 'Zeichen als Form.' In *Probleme der Form*, ed. D. Baecker, 45–69. Frankfurt: Suhrkamp.

– 1995. *Social Systems.* Stanford, CA: Stanford University Press.

– 1999. 'Sign as Form.' In 'Luhmann: Cybernetics, Systems and Semiotics,' special issue, *Cybernetics & Human Knowing* 6 (3): 21–37.

Luntley, M. 1995. *Reason, Truth and the Self: The Postmodern Reconditioned.* London: Routledge.

Machlup, F. 1983. 'Semantic Quirks in Studies of Information.' in *The Study of Information: Interdisciplinary Messages*, ed. F. Machlup and U. Mansfield, 641–71. New York: Wiley.

Madsen, K.B. 1974. *Modern Theories of Motivation: A Comparative Metascientific Study.* Copenhagen: Munksgaard.

– 1978. 'Motivationsbegrebets udvikling i psykologien.' *Pædagogik* 2.

Mathews, F. 1991. *The Ecological Self.* London: Routledge.

Maturana, H.R 1981. 'Autopoiesis.' In *Autopoiesis: A Theory of Living Organization*, ed. M. Zeleney. New York: North Holland.

– 1983. 'What Is It to See?' *Archivos de Biologia y Medicina Experimentales* 16:255–69.

– 1988a. 'Ontology of Observing: The Biological Foundation of Self Consciousness and the Physical Domain of Existence.' In *Conference Workbook for 'Texts in Cybernetic Theory.' An In-Depth Exploration of the Thought of Humberto R. Maturana, William T. Powers, Ernst von Glasersfeld*, ed. R.E. Donaldson, 4–52.

Proceedings of the American Society for Cybernetics, Felton, California, 18–23 October.

– 1988b. 'Reality: The Search for Objectivity, or the Quest for a Compelling Argument.' *Irish Journal of Psychology* 9 (1): 25–82.

– 1990. Personal Communication at the Conference of the American Society for Cybernetics, Oslo.

– 2000. 'The Nature of the Laws of Nature.' *Yearbook Edition of Systems Research and Behavioral Science* 17 (5): 459–68.

Maturana, H.R., and F. Varela. 1980. *Autopoiesis and Cognition: The Realization of the Living*. London: Reidel.

– 1986. Tree *of knowledge: Biological Roots of Human Understanding*. London: Shambhala.

Meister, J.C. 1995. 'Consensus ex Machina. Consensus qua Machina!' *Literary and Linguistic Computing* 10 (4).

Merrell, F. 1996. *Signs Grow: Semiosis of Life Processes*. Toronto: University of Toronto Press.

Merleau-Ponty, M. 2002. *Phenomenology of Perception*. Trans. C. Smith. London: Routledge and Kegan Paul.

Miller, G.A., E. Galanter, and K.H. Pribram.1960. *Plans and the Structure of Behavior*. New York: Holt, Rinehart and Winston.

Mingers, J. 1995. *Self-Producing Systems: implications and Applications of Autopoiesis*. New York: Plenum.

Mittelstrass, J. 1974. *Die Möglichkeit von Wissenschaft*. Frankfurt: Suhrkamp.

Monod, J. 1972. *Chance and Necessity: An Essay on the Natural Philosophy of Modern Biology*. New York: Vintage.

Morin, E. 1992. *Method: Towards a Study of Humankind*. Vol. 1, *The Nature of Nature*. New York: Peter Lang.

Næss, A. 1973. 'The Shallow and the Deep, Long-Range Ecology Movement.' *Inquiry* 16.

Nagel, T. 1986. *The View from Nowhere*. New York: Oxford University Press.

Nielsen, H.B. 1989. *Random Dynamics and Relations Between the Number of Fermion Generations and the Fine Structure Constants*. Niels Bohr Institute NBI-HE-89–01, January 1989. Published in *Acta Physica Polonica* B20:427.

– 1991. *Random Dynamics, Three Generations and Skewness*. Niels Bohr Institute NBI-HE-91–04. Contribution to the 3rd Summer Meeting on Quantum Mechanics of Fundamental Systems, Santiago, Chile, 9–12 January 1990. In *Santiago 1990, Proceedings, Quantum Mechanics of Fundamental Systems 3*, 179–208.

Nielsen, H.B., and S.E. Rugh. 1992. *Chaos in the Fundamental Forces?* Niels Bohr

Institute NBI-HE-92–85. Presented at International symposium on Quantum Physics and the Universe. Tokyo, 19–22 August 1992.

Nöth, W. 1995. *Handbook of Semiotics.* Bloomington: Indiana University Press.

– 2001a. 'Introduction to Ecosemiosis.' In *Ecosemiotics: Studies in Environmental Semiosis, Semiotics of the Biocybernetic Bodies, Human/Too Human/Post Human,* ed. E. Tarasti, 107–23. ISI Congress papers, Nordic Baltic Summer Institute for Semiotic and Structural Studies, Part IV, Imatra, Finland, 12–21 June 2001.

– 2001b. 'Protosemiosics and Physicosemiosis.' *Sign System Studies* 29 (1): 13–26.

– 2002. 'Semiotic Machines.' *Cybernetics & Human Knowing* 9 (1).

Nowotny, H., P. Scott, and M. Gibbons. 2001. *Re-thinking Science.* Cambridge: Polity Press.

Ort, N., and Peter, M. 1999). 'Niklas Luhmann: "Sign as Form" – A Comment.' *Cybernetics & Human Knowing* 6 (3): 39–46.

Østergård, S. 1997. 'Matematik og semiotic.' In *Anvendt semiotik,* ed K.G. Jørgensen. Copenhagen: Samlerens Bogklub.

Peirce, C.S. 1891. 'The Architecture of Theories.' *The Monist* 1 (2): 161–76.

– 1892a. 'The Doctrine of Necessity Examined,' *The Monist* 2 (3): 321–37.

– 1892b. 'The Law of Mind.' *The Monist* 2 (4): 553.

– 1892c. 'Man's Glassy Essence.' *The Monist* 3 (1): 1.

– 1893. 'Evolutionary Love.' *The Monist* 3 (2): 176.

– 1891–3. *Mursten og mørtel til en metafysik: fem artikler fra tidsskriftet 'The Monist.'* Introduktion og oversættelse Peter Voetmann Christiansen. Roskilde, Denmark: Roskilde University, 1988.

– 1931–58. *Collected Papers, Vols. I–VIII.* Ed. C. Hartshorne and P. Weiss. Cambridge MA: Harvard University Press.

– 1955. *Philosophical Writings of Peirce: Selected and Edited with an Introduction by Justus Buchler.* New York: Dover.

– 1958. *Selected Writings: Values in a Universe of Chance.* Ed. P.P. Wiener. New York: Dover.

– 1992. *The Essential Peirce: Selected Philosophical Writings,* vol. 1 (1867–1893). Ed. N. Houser and C. Kloesel. Bloomington: Indiana University Press.

– 1994. *The Collected Papers of Charles Sanders Peirce.* Electronic edition reproducing vols. I–VI, ed. C. Hartshorne and P. Weiss. Cambridge: Harvard University Press, 1931–1935), and vols. VII–VIII, ed. A.W. Burks (same publisher, 1958). Charlottesville: Intelex Corporation.

– 1994. *Semiotik og pragmatisme.* Ed. A.M. Dinesen and F. Stjernfeldt. Gyldendal, Denmark: Moderne Tænkere.

– (n.d.). *Peirce MS.* Quoted at http://www.door.net/arisbe/arisbe.htm.

Penrose, R. 1995. *Shadows of the Mind: A Search for the Missing Science of Consciousness.* London: Oxford University Press.

Petersen, A.F. 1972. *Personlighed og tænkning: en teoretisk biologisk analyse.* (Psykologisk Skriftserie 2). Copenhagen: Psykologisk Laboratorium, Københavns Universitet.

Petito, J., F. Varela, and J.-M. Roy. 1999. *Naturalizing Phenomenology: The Issues in Contemporary Phenomenology and Cognitive Science.* Stanford, CA: Stanford University Press.

Plato. (n.d.). *Timaeus.* http://www.ac-nice.fr/philo/textes/plato-works/25–timaeus.htm.

Plotinus. 2000. *Det ene: Udvalgte Eneader.* Frederiksberg: Det Lille Forlag.

Polanyi, M. 1973. *Personal Knowledge: Towards a Post-Critical Philosophy.* London: Routledge and Kegan Paul.

Polkinghorne, J.C. 1996. 'Heavy Meta.' *Scientific American* 2755:121–3.

Popper, K. 1960. *The Logic of Scientific Discovery.* London: Hutchinson.

– 1972. *Objective Knowledge: An Evolutionary Approach,* Oxford: Clarendon.

Prigogine, I. 1980. *From Being to Becoming.* San Francisco, CA: W.H. Freeman.

– 1996. *The End of Certainty. Time, Chaos, and the New Laws of Nature.* New York: Free Press.

Prigogine, I., and I. Stengers, I. 1984. *Order out of Chaos: Man's New Dialogue with Nature.* New York: Bantam.

Putnam, H. 1981. *Reason, Truth and History.* Cambridge: Cambridge University Press.

– 1992. *Representation and Reality.* Cambridge, MA: MIT Press.

Qvortrup, L. 1993. 'The Controversy over the Concept of Information: An Overview and a Selected Bibliography.' *Cybernetics & Human Knowing* 1 (4): 3–26.

– 2003. *The Hypercomplex Society,* New York: Peter Lang.

– 2004. *Det vidende samfund – mysteriet om viden, læring og dannelse.* Copenhagen: Unge Pædagoger.

Raposa, M. 1989. *Peirce's Philosophy of Religion.* Peirce Studies no. 5. Bloomington: Indiana University Press.

Reventlow, I. 1954. *Tendenser indenfor den nyeste; dyrepsykologi, der kan have betydning for personlighedsforskningen.* Masters dissertation, University of Copenhagen.

– 1959. 'The Influence of Benactyzine on Learning in Cats.' *Acta Pharmacologica et Toxicologica* (16): 136–43.

– 1961. 'Ethopsychopharmacological Research in Denmark.' *Bulletin de L'association Internationale de Psychologie Applique* 10:118–25.

– 1970. 'Studier af komplicerede psykobiologiske fænomener.' Doctoral thesis, University of Copenhagen.

- 1972. 'Symbols and Sign Stimuli.' *Danish Medical Bulletin* (19):325–00.
- 1973. 'Konfliktforschung im Tierexperiment.' In *Bericht über den 27. Kongress der Deutschen Gesellschaft für Psychologie in Kiel 1970*, ed. G. Reinert. Göttingen: Hogrefe.
- 1977. 'Om dyrepsykologien i dansk psykologi og om dens betydning for begrebsdannelsen i psykologien.' In *Dansk Filosofi og Psykologi*. Bind 2, ed. S.R. Nordenbo and A.F. Petersen, 127–37. Copenhagen: Filosofisk Institut, Københavns Universitet.
- 1980. 'Etologi.' In *Psykologisk Leksikon*, ed. K.B. Madsen. Copenhagen: Gyldendal.

Rorty, R. 1982. *Consequences of Pragmatism*. Minneapolis: University of Minnesota Press.

Rosen, R. 1986. 'On Information and Complexity.' In *Complexity, Language, and Life: Mathematical Approaches*, ed. J.L. Casti and A. Karlqvist, 174–96. London: Springer.

- 1991. *Life Itself: A comprehensive Inquiry into the Nature, Origin and Fabrication of Life*. New York: Columbia University Press.

Rowley, J. 1993. 'The Controlled versus Natural Indexing Languages Debate Revisited: A Perspective on Information Retrieval Practice and Research.' *Journal of Information Science* 20 (2).

Ruesch, J., and G. Bateson. 1987. *Communication: The Social Matrix of Psychiatry*. New York: Norton. (Orig. pub. 1967.)

Ryle, G. 1990. *The Concept of Mind*. London: Penguin.

Salthe, S.N. 1993. *Development and Evolution: Complexity and Change in Biology*. Cambridge, MA: MIT Press.

Santaella Braga, L. 1999. 'Peirce and Biology.' In 'Biosemiotica,' special issue, *Semiotica* 127 (1/4): 5–21.

- 2001. 'Matter as Effect Mind: Peirce's Synechistic Ideas on the Semiotic Threshold.' *Sign Systems Studies* 29 (1): 49–62.

Schiller, C.H., ed. 1957. *Instinctive Behavior. The Development of a Modern Concept*. New York: International Universities Press.

Schopenhauer, A. 2006. *Verden som vilje og forestilling*. Copenhagen: Cljyldendals bogklubber. (*Die Welt als Wille und Vorstellung*.)

Schrödinger, E. 1967. *What is Life? The Physical Aspect of the Living Cell and Mind and Matter*. Cambridge: Cambridge University Press.

Schwartz, D.G. 1981. 'Spencer-Brown's Laws of Form and Varela's Calculi for Self-Reference.' *International Journal of General Systems* 6:239–55.

Schwarz, E. 1997. 'About the Possible Convergence between Science and Spirituality.' *Cybernetics & Human Knowing* 4 (4): 26–42.

Searle, J. 1989. *Minds, Brains and Science*. London: Penguin.

Sebeok, T. 1972. *Perspectives on Zoösemiotics.* Toronto: University of Toronto Press.

– 1976. *Contributions to the Doctrine of Signs.* Bloomington: Indiana University Press.

– 1989. *The Sign and Its Masters. Sources in Semiotics VIII.* New York: University Press of America.

– 2000. *Life Signs – Essays in Semiotics – I.* Toronto: Legas.

Shannon, C.E., and W. Weaver. 1969. *The Mathematical Theory of Communication.* Urbana: University of Illinois Press.

Shear, J. 1997. *Explaining Consciousness: The Hard Problem.* Cambridge, MA: MIT Press.

Short, T.L. 1982. 'Life Among the Legisigns.' *Transaction of the Charles Peirce Society* 18 (4): 285–309.

Smart, J.J.C. 1963. *Philosophy and Scientific Realism.* London: Routledge.

Snow, C.P. 1993. *The Two Cultures.* Cambridge: Cambridge University Press.

Sommerhoff, G. 1991. *Logic of the Living Brain.* Department of Anatomy and Embryology, University College, London. Also 1974. London: Wiley.

Spencer-Brown, G. 1972. *Laws of Form.* 2nd ed. New York: Julien Press.

– 1993–4. 'Self-Reference, Distinctions and Time.' *Teoria Sociologica* 2–3 (1): 47–53.

Spinoza, B. de. 1996. *Etik.* Copenhagen: Rosinante.

Stace, W.T. 1960. *Mysticism and Philosophy.* London: Macmillan.

Stonier, T. 1990. *Information and the Internal Structure of the Universe: An Exploration into Information Physics.* London: Springer.

– 1992. *Beyond Information: The Natural History of Intelligence.* London: Springer.

– 1997. *Information and Meaning: An Evolutionary Perspective.* Berlin: Springer.

Suzuki, D.T. 2002. *Mysticism: Christian and Buddhist.* London: Routledge.

Szilard, L.1929. 'Über die Entropieverminderung in einem thermody-namichen System bei Eingriffen intelligenter Wesen.' *Zeitschrift für Physik* 53:840–56. (English trans. in Leff and Rex 1990.)

Thellefsen, T.L., S. Brier, and M.L. Thellefsen. 2003. 'Problems concerning the Process of Subject Analysis and the Practice of Indexing: A Peircean Semiotic and Semantic Approach toward User-Oriented Need in Document Searching.' *Semiotica* 144 (1/4): 177–218.

Thorpe, V.H. 1979. *The Origin and Rise of Ethology: The Science of the Natural Behaviour of Animals.* London: Heinemann.

Thyssen, O. 2006. 'Epistemology as Communication Theory: A Critique of Niklas Luhmann's Theory of the Vanishing World.' *Cybernetics & Human Knowing* 13 (2): 7–24.

Tinbergen, N. 1968. 'On War and Peace in Animals and Man: An Ethological Approach to the Biology of Aggression.' *Science* 160:1411–18.

– 1973. 'Ethology.' In *The Animal in Its World*, ed. N. Tinbergen, 136–96. London: Allan and Unwin.

Uexküll, J. von 1957. 'A Stroll through the Worlds of Animals and Men. A Picture Book of Invisible Worlds.' In *Instinctive Behavior. The Development of a Modern Concept*, ed. C.H. Schiller, 5–80. New York: International Universities Press. (Orig. pub. 1934.)

– 1982 [1973]. 'The Theory of Meaning.' In 'Jakob von Uexküll's "The Theory of Meaning,"' ed. T. von Uexküll, special issue, *Semiotica* 42 (1982).

– 1986. 'Environment (Umwelt) and Inner World of Animals.' In *Foundations of Comparative Ethology*, ed. G.M. Burghardt. New York: Van Nostrand Reinhold.

Uexküll, T. von, W. Geigges, and J.M. Herrmann. 1993: 'Endosemiosis.' *Semiotica* 96 (1/2): 5–51.

Van Rijsbergen, C.J. 1996. 'Information, Logic and Uncertainty in Information Science.' In *Information Science: Integration in Perspective*, 1–10. Proceedings of COLIS 2, Second International Conference on Conceptions of Library and Information Science, Royal School of Librarianship, 13–16 October, Copenhagen.

Varela, F.J. 1975. 'A Calculus for Self-Reference.' *International Journal for General Systems* 2:5–24.

– 1984. 'The Ages of Heinz von Foerster.' In *Observing Systems*, ed. H. von Foerster (The Systems Inquiry Series). Seaside, CA: Intersystems Publications.

Varela, F.J., E. Thompson, and E. Rosch. 1992. *The Embodied Mind*. Cambridge, MA: MIT Press.

Velmans, M. 2002. 'How Could Conscious Experience Affect Brains?' *Journal of Consciousness Studies* 9 (11): 3–29.

Vickery, A., and B. Vickery. 1987. *Information Science – Theory and Practice*. London: Bowker-Saur.

Walter, S., and H. Heckmann. 2003. *Physicalism and Mental Causation: The Metaphysics of Mind and Action*. London: Imprint Academic.

Warner, J. 1990. 'Semiotics, Information Science and Computers.' *Journal of Documentation* 46 (1): 16–32.

– 1994. *From Writing to Computers*. London: Routledge.

Weaver, W. 1963. 'Introductory Note on the General Setting of the Analytical Communication Studies.' In *The Mathematical Theory of Communication*, ed. C. Shannon and W. Weaver, 3–8. Urbana: University of Illinois Press.

Weber, R. 1972. 'The Implicate Order and the Super-Implicate Order.' In *Dialogues with Scientists and Sages: The Search for Unity*. New York: Routledge and Kegan Paul.

Wiener, N. 1961. *Cybernetics or Control and Communication in the Animal and the Machine.* Cambridge: MIT Press.

– 1988. *The Human Use of Human Beings: Cybernetics and Society.* Oxford: Da Capo Press.

Wilson, E.O. 1999. *Consilience: The Unity of Knowledge.* New York: Vintage.

Wimmer, M. 1995. 'Evolutionary Roots of Emotions.' *Evolution and Cognition* 1 (1): 38–50.

Winograd, T., and F. Flores. 1986. *Understanding Computers and Cognition.* Norwood, NJ: Intellect Books and Ablex.

Wittgenstein, L. 1958. *Philosophical Investigations.* Trans. G.E.M. Anscombe. New York: Macmillan.

Witt-Hansen, J. 1980. *Filosofi: Videnskabernes historie; i det 20. århundrede.* Copenhagen: Gyldendal.

Wormell, I., ed. 1990. *Information Quality: Definitions and Dimensions.* Proceedings of a NORDINFO seminar, Royal School of Librarianship. London: Taylor Graham.

Index